MW01506102

A MOLINIST-ANABAPTIST
SYSTEMATIC THEOLOGY

Kirk R. Macgregor

University Press of America,® Inc.
Lanham · Boulder · New York · Toronto · Plymouth, UK

To my parents,
Ian and Melanie,
for all their love and support

Contents

Preface

Two pressing needs confront the church in the twenty–first century: the yearning for a potent philosophical theology that furnishes logically consistent and biblically sound answers to the most highly charged metaphysical dilemmas; and the indispensability of a New Testament–based ecclesiology which calls all believers in Jesus to lives of discipleship and holiness in their dealings both inside and outside the church. Concerning the first, humans are essentially rational beings (*homo sapiens*), in virtue of their creation in the *imago Dei*, and possess an innate drive for intellectual satisfaction that increases in proportion to the importance of the questions being raised. Since God is, by definition, the ultimate concern of humanity, the vitality of the mind and its intellectual fulfillment is paramount to Christian theology. Contra the post–Enlightenment distinction between the "heart" and the "head," both the Hebrew Bible and New Testament conceive of the "heart" (לֵבָב and καρδία) as the center of one's being (not as the seat of the emotions, thought to reside in the liver or bowels!), which always includes the mind and sometimes refers exclusively to the mind. The Church of God theologian R. R. Byrum points out, moreover, that right thinking produces right emotions, not vice versa: "[Humanity] has not only an emotional nature, but also an intellectual nature. God is the author of both. . . . In fact, one's emotions are largely controlled by one's thinking."[1] Not surprisingly, since our actions spring from the interrelated set of intellectual underpinnings we have laid as the foundational structure for our daily lives, Scripture repeatedly emphasizes that bad thinking, especially bad doctrine, leads inevitably to bad morality. This fact has been illustrated time and again in the often public failings of "Christian leaders," whose suspicious theology long preceded their

---

1. R. R. Byrum, *Christian Theology: A Systematic Statement of Christian Doctrine for the Use of Theological Students*, rev. ed. (Anderson, Ind.: Warner Press, 1982), 5–6.

falling prey to sin, and poignantly sharpens Paul's explicitly stated motivation for maturity in thinking:

Become mature, attaining to the whole measure of the fullness of Christ. Then we will no longer be infants, tossed back and forth by the waves and carried around by every wind of false doctrine, *leading to the scheming of deception with craftiness* (Eph. 4:13b–15, emphasis mine).

Here Paul bluntly asserts that false doctrine triggers the crafty scheming of deception, a cause–and–effect relationship which can only be averted by intellectual growth in the matters of God. In addition to comprising the first step for restoring the church's ethical integrity, theological excellence is pivotal to the evangelistic enterprise, whose success directly depends upon the strength of Christian apologetics.

By apologetics I mean simply the literal meaning of the New Testament term ἀπολογία, namely, the intellectual and rational defense of the Christian faith in all the broad and diverse forms such defense may take. Thus apologetics, as properly understood, encompasses not only arguments and evidences, but also the way that one lives (indisputably the most important apologetic for which disciples are responsible) and the *testimonium internum Spiritum Sanctum*, or the properly basic witness of the Holy Spirit to each individual that the Kingdom message of Jesus is true. Let those engaged in apologetics never forget that Scripture refers to the Holy Spirit as the παράκλητος (Defender, Counselor, Helper, and Comforter), a concept whose semantic range necessarily includes "the provider of evidence." As Jesus himself delineated the Spirit's role, "But when the παράκλητος comes, whom I will send to you from the Father, the Spirit of truth who goes out from the Father, he will testify (equally well translated as 'bear witness'; μαρτυρήσει) about me" (Jn. 15:26). Our biblical definition of apologetics therefore repudiates the caricature of "intellect not emotion" and the phenomenon of masquerading hollow and logically fallacious appeals to Christianity as intellectually valid argumentation, which duplicity has rightly earned the monicker of "sacred dishonesty" betraying the bleeding heart of a "fundamentalist." [2] Rather, biblical apologetics look to Jesus, Peter, Paul,

---

2. Paul Tillich, *Systematic Theology*, 3 vols. (Chicago: University of Chicago Press, 1967), 1:36. Attempting to restore the true meaning of apologetics, Tillich rightly exposes and condemns false claimants to the name: "The term 'apologetic,' which had such a high standing in the early church, has fallen into disrepute because of the methods employed in the abortive attempts to defend Christianity against attacks from modern humanism, naturalism, and historism. An especially weak and disgusting form of apologetics used the *argumentum ex*

and first through third century Christian theologians as models, all of whom viewed the life of the mind as a compulsory part of discipleship. Peter famously commanded believers to sanctify Christ as Lord in their hearts by "always being prepared to give a defense (ἀπολογίαν) to everyone who asks you the reason for the hope you have, yet with gentleness and respect" (1 Pet. 3:15–16a). The Elder John identified Jesus as the incarnate λογός (Jn. 1:1–18; 1 Jn. 1:1), appealing to its late antique understanding among Gentiles and Jews (via Plato and Philo) as "the divine mind, reason, or logic which functions as the supreme ordering principle governing the universe." So for the Elder John, Jesus was literally logic itself, a recognition amplified by the latter's insistence on loving God with all the mind (seen by comparing Mk. 12:30 with Deut. 6:5) and his employment of every logical method of proof (deductive in direct and indirect modes, inductive, etc.) in proclaiming the Gospel. Expressing his divinely ordained purpose as Apostle to the Gentiles, Paul remarked, "I am put here for the defense (ἀπολογίαν) of the gospel" (Php. 1:16b), which the Book of Acts reveals he faithfully discharged: "As his custom was, Paul went into the synagogue, and on three consecutive Sabbath days he reasoned with them from the Scriptures, explaining and proving that the Christ had to suffer and rise from the dead" (Acts 17:3; *cf.* 9:22; 17:22–34; 19:8–10). In order to effectively advance the Kingdom of God, therefore, mastery of the academic disciplines, personal "denial of oneself, taking up one's cross daily, and following" Jesus (Lk. 9:23), and trust in the Holy Spirit to use our efforts as the backdrop for his testimony to Jesus and offer of prevenient grace stand as *sine qua non* components to the obligatory task of apologetics.

Concerning the second need, hypocrisy and corruption plagues the church today from within, and Western Christian involvement in society at large has damaged the church's reputation from without. These travesties lead outsiders to wrongly associate the miscreants' way of life with the effects that Christian faith produces in one's life. Hence many non–Christians demur, "If following Jesus will turn me into a hypocritical and self–righteous person like those other Christians I know, then I don't want any part of it." In view of this monstrous blasphemy perpetuated among bearers of Christ's name, we must be reminded that Jesus denounced its propagators in the strongest possible language, dubbing them "children of hell" (Mt. 23:15) and consigning them to the greatest punishment on the Day of Judgment (Mk. 12:40). What outsiders fail to realize, having never personally

---

ignorantia; that is, it tried to discover gaps in our scientific and historical knowledge in order to find a place for God and his actions within an otherwise completely calculable and 'immanent' world" (1:6).

experienced the transforming power of Jesus, is that such "false brethren" (Gal. 2:4) have never been regenerated, thus leading outsiders to compare themselves not with the elect, who have been transformed by Jesus' revolutionary power, but with the reprobate, who are at best in the same spiritual condition as, and at worst far more depraved than, they are. But when non–Christians measure their lives against authentic disciples of Jesus, a dramatic—indeed, ontological—difference cannot help but manifest itself, a fact both Scripturally guaranteed and historically verified. Paul predicts the inevitable outcome of comparison between an unbeliever and members of the church of God: "The unbeliever will be convicted by all that he is a sinner and will be judged by the example of all, and the secrets of his heart will be laid bare to him . . .exclaiming, 'God is really among you'" (1 Cor. 14:24–25). In the sixteenth century, the evangelical Anabaptists impressed their enemies, including their persecutors, by the sanctity and consistency of their Christian witness, which they maintained even in the face of certain death. Thus Wolfgang Capito, a chief pastor of the Reformed Church at Strasbourg and unsympathetic witness, acknowledged in 1527:

> I frankly confess that in most [Anabaptists] there is in evidence piety and consecration and indeed a zeal which is beyond any suspicion of insincerity. For what earthly advantage could they hope to win by enduring exile, torture, and unspeakable punishment of the flesh. I testify before God that I cannot say that on account of the lack of wisdom they are somewhat indifferent toward earthly things, but rather from divine motives.[3]

Writing in 1582, the Roman Catholic theologian and positively hostile witness Franz Agricola provides independent verification of the Anabaptists' spiritual fruit borne out of fidelity to the ethics pronounced by Jesus:

> As concerns their outward public life they are irreproachable. No lying, deception, swearing, strife, harsh language, no intemperate eating and drinking, no outward personal display, is found among them, but humility, patience, uprightness, neatness, honesty, temperance, straightforwardness in such measure that one would suppose that they had the Holy Spirit of God.[4]

---

3. C. A. Cornelius, *Geschichte des Münsterschen Aufruhrs* (Leipzig, 1860), 2:52.

4. Franz Agricola, *Against the Terrible Errors of the Anabaptists*, in *Die Wiedertäufer im Herzogtum Jülich* , ed. Karl Rembert (Berlin, 1899), 564.

What made the pre–Constantinian church and the Anabaptists so successful where other Christian groups have failed? The answer is binary and remarkably straightforward: on the one hand, they obeyed the pattern of church discipline established by Jesus in Matthew 18:15–20 and executed by Paul in 1 Corinthians 5:1–13; on the other hand, they understood what the historical Jesus meant by "the Kingdom of God" and successfully distanced this meaning from any anachronistic renderings of their contemporaries.

It may be safely said that no biblical text is at once so clear and at the same time so flagrantly disobeyed by Christ's followers both historically and presently as Matthew 18:15–20. Here Jesus outlines the threefold method of church discipline, which if practiced would serve as the second step for restoring ecclesiastical integrity by eliminating all hypocrisy and flagrant sin among those who claim Christian allegiance which remains after the aforementioned commitment to academic excellence in theology has uprooted false doctrinal motivations for such vices. In other words, once churchgoers are educated in a right way of thinking, abiding sin will no longer be a matter of their sincerely believing it to be acceptable in the sight of God or "not knowing any better," but it will be wholly spawned by the σάρξ, or sinful inclination to carry out the desires of one's own soul rather than, and in spite of knowing full well, the desires of the Holy Spirit. But once gradual moral suasion is exercised by the believing community individually, then if necessary multiply, and if necessary collectively, then the miscreant will be forced to either repent of sin, for which they will be eternally grateful, or exposed among true followers of Christ as a false disciple (Mt. 22:12–13). However, the Jesuanic directive is so often intentionally neglected as a reactionary movement against the way many communities have misapplied it. While Christ's directive only applied to sin—namely, thoughts and practices which directly violate at least one objective moral standard rooted in the very nature of God, such that God could no longer be God if he regarded it as potentially morally neutral or beneficial—churches have often "rebuked" or doled out punishment to members for phenomena which are not sin themselves but concerning which some (especially senior) members of the group disapprove due either to personal preference or fear that the phenomena will lead to sin.

To put it quite frankly, individuals thus practicing discipline are either "playing God" by raising their own opinions to the level of objective moral values, thereby usurping God's authority as Sovereign Ruler of his creation, or engaging in nothing less than a distrust in the power of the Holy Spirit to regenerate those who have entered into personal commitment to Jesus. In the latter case, instead of believing that the Holy Spirit has regenerated all that enter into spiritual marriage with Christ—namely, transformed into new creations by shifting their fundamental inclination from the desires of the σάρξ to the desires of God—in which case true disciples are free to engage or disengage in acts about which Scripture makes no moral claim, we cast dispersions on the Spirit's power by treating disciples as if they were still "natural / carnal people" (ψυκικοί / σαρκικοί ἄνθρωποι) and predicting their future actions based on the behavior of "natural people." Ironically, both of these crimes were among those that Jesus accused the Jewish re-ligio–political authorities of committing. Skeptical of the power of God to redemptively transform his followers and so deeming their natures to be the same as unregenerate persons, the religious elites imposed artificial rules lacking biblical sanction to prevent faithful Jews from not only breaking the 623 *mitzvoth*, but from coming anywhere close to breaking them, a practice which seems plausible if enforcing these rules on worldly people. This prac-tice, which the *Pirke Avot* calls "building a fence around Torah,"[5] was first flouted and then condemned by Jesus on several occasions (Mk. 7:1–19; Mt. 12:1–8; 23:1–4, 23–24; Lk. 11:39–52). In short, this historical lesson teaches that only misdeeds measuring up to the highest ontological standards can be disciplined: unless something can be proven (notice I did not say "made probable" or any such thing) as sin from Scripture, believers are sinning themselves if they invoke discipline against others for performing them. On the contrary, we will see that if the church simply submitted in obedience to Jesus' model of church discipline, then we would truly reflect the kind of "set–apart" or "called out of exile community" (the literal meaning of ἐκκλησία) that Jesus intended.

Against the backdrop of American nationalistic imperialism posing as divinely ordained, an encouraging trend has begun among evangelical schol-ars to rediscover and reimplement Jesus' Kingdom program. As Gregory A. Boyd perceptively delineates this dominical philosophy of life:

> The kingdom of God is not a Christian version of the kingdom of the world. It is, rather, a holy alternative to all versions of the kingdom of the world, and everything hangs on kingdom people appreciating this uniqueness and preserving this holiness. . . . As we allow Christ's char-acter to be formed in us—as we think and act like Jesus—others come under the loving influence of the kingdom and eventually their own hearts are won over to the King of Kings. The reign of God is thus es-tablished in their hearts, and the kingdom of God expands. . . . [T]he primary thing God is up to [is] . . . gathering together a group of people

---

5. *Mishnah*, Pirke Avot 1:1.

who individually and corporately manifest the reality of the reign of God on the earth.[6]

In the terminology of early modern historiography, the Kingdom of God is "radical" or bottom–up instead of "magisterial" or top–down. Rather than using "the domination system" or the power of the government to forcefully impose allegiance to the Kingdom and its particular moral imperatives— precisely, in its historical context, the temptation which Jesus faced of "worshiping the Satan" (Lk. 4:5–8)—disciples of Jesus must exclusively use the powers of ἀγαπή, or the love of God flowing through them and toward others, and of non–violent resistance to social injustice, in advancing the Kingdom of God. If any other power than these are employed under the guise of "carrying out God's work," then by definition the Kingdom of God is not being advanced.

Synthesizing the scholasticism of Aquinas with the biblical mysticism of Bernard of Clairvaux, this volume conceives of theology broadly as the science of knowing and loving God through the twin avenues of divine revelation and human reason, or a marriage of sacred history and philosophy which is greater than the sum of its parts. Thus Thomas Aquinas rightly identified theology as the "queen of the sciences" which "is taught by God, teaches of God, and leads to God."[7] When genuinely engaged, the theological enterprise naturally causes the theoretical aspect of doctrinal formulation to lead into the applied aspect of transforming the spiritual and social lives of Christians so that they can faithfully serve as salt and light to the world. In all ways, then, the church will fulfill its divinely anointed mission of being "the pillar and foundation of the truth" (1 Tim. 3:15). It is in contribution to the accomplishment of this eternal goal that I submit this construction.

Kirk R. MacGregor
Cedar Falls, Iowa
April 2007

---

6. Gregory A. Boyd, *The Myth of a Christian Nation: How the Quest for Political Power is Destroying the Church* (Grand Rapids, Mich.: Zondervan, 2005), 30.

7. Aquinas, *Summa Theologica*, 1.1.7.

Chapter 1

Prolegomena

History and Theological Distinctives of Molinism and Anabaptism

Unity is the hallmark of all biblical diversity, as exemplified by the Pauline analogy of the one body of Christ with many differently and specially gifted members (1 Cor. 12:12–27). With rhetorical verve Paul emphasizes,[1] quite possibly recalling the dominical oral tradition now undergirding the Johannine high priestly prayer (see Jn. 17:11, 20–23), that the need for unity is inextricably bound with the Church's vocation to constitute a reflection of, and participation in, the essential oneness of the divine multiperson-

---

1. Scholarly opinion on the authorship of Ephesians is divided between Proto–Pauline and Deutero–Pauline. If composed by Paul, the epistle comprises a genuine "Prison Epistle" drawn up during his house arrest at Rome between 60–62 C.E.; if written by one of Paul's disciples, its origins lie in Ephesus *c.* 90 C.E. with a *terminus ante quem* of 95 C.E., when Clement of Rome cited the letter throughout his *First Epistle to the Corinthians*. In my judgment the evidence is finely balanced, with the scale tipping slightly in favor of Pauline authorship; for excellent presentations of the respective arguments pro and con see Donald Guthrie, *New Testament Introduction*, 4th rev. ed. (Leicester: Apollos, 1990), 496–528 and Raymond E. Brown, *An Introduction to the New Testament* (New York: Doubleday, 1997), 610–15, 627–30. In either case, my point is in no way compromised; even if the epistle is Deutero–Pauline, Paul's disciple remains faithful to the historical memory of his teacher's emphasis on ecclesiastical unity abundantly evidenced in the Proto–Pauline corpus.

ality which would, by the end of the second century,[2] be known as Trinitarian: "Make every effort to keep the *unity* of the Spirit through the bond of peace. There is *one* body and *one Spirit*—just as you were called to *one* hope when you were called—*one* Lord, *one* faith, *one* baptism, *one* God and Father of all, who is over all and through all and in all" (Eph. 4:3–6; emphasis mine). Thus Paul exhorts mixed communities of native–born Jewish and Gentile converts to the Way to form one new Israel, or people of God, characterized by reconciliation of ancient discord:

> For Jesus himself is our peace, who has made the two one and has destroyed the barrier, the dividing wall of hostility . . . his purpose was to create in himself one new humanity out of the two, thus making peace, and in this one body to reconcile both of them to God through the cross, by which he put to death their hostility (Eph. 2:14–16).

This mission of reconciling individuals to God and to one another through Christ lies at the heart of biblical evangelism—namely, liberation from the kingdom of the αἰών ("age" or "world," *i.e.* the godless philosophical system of domination and oppression constituting the world's *modus operandi* that manifests itself in the "works of the flesh" of Gal. 5:19–21) and initiation into the kingdom of God,[3] which is first and foremost the philosophy of life where the Trinitarian God is King over all realms of life and existence rather than simply over the religious realm.

Although the Church experienced relative unity for the first ten centuries of its existence, such unity was eventually displaced by a tradition of division, whose seeds were sown in the eleventh century, germinated beneath the ecclesiastical surface during the High and Late Middle Ages, and sprung up feverishly in the sixteenth century. Yet simultaneously with the

---

2. Textual use of "Trinity" (Τριάδος) as a linguistic handle for the New Testament affirmation of three Persons in one God (Mt. 28:19) is first made *c.* 180 by Theophilus of Antioch, *To Autolycus*, 2.15 and echoed *c.* 200 by Clement of Alexandria, *Stromata*, 5.14. However, Marcus Dods points out that Theophilus' employment of "Trinity" is incidental and assumes prior understanding on the part of his audience, thereby showing that the term was already widespread in patristic oral tradition by 180 (*Ante–Nicene Fathers*, eds. Alexander Roberts and James Donaldson, rep. ed. [Peabody, Mass.: Hendrickson, 1994], 2:101).

3. As rightly argued by William J. Abraham, *The Logic of Evangelism* (Grand Rapids, Mich.: Eerdmans, 1989), 92–115, whose explication of the evangelistic task is masterful and ought to be given thorough consideration by anyone professionally devoted to expanding God's Kingdom.

life cycle of these tares ran the positive development, analogous to wheat seeds (Mt. 13:24–30), of increasing transformation to the image and mind of Christ. Disagreements between the Greek East and the Latin West concerning matters of both doctrine and praxis, including the theological admissibility of the *filioque* clause in the Niceno–Constantinopolitan Creed, iconoclasm, clerical celibacy, language, and culture, coalesced at the Schism of 1054, in which Michael Cerularius, patriarch of Constantinople, and a team of papal legates led by Cardinal Humbert mutually excommunicated one another.[4] Hence the Eastern Orthodox Church and Roman Church went their separate ways, impelling the latter over the next four centuries to, *pace* the historical Jesus, wield the power endemic to the αἰών in extinguishing movements perceived as further threats to unity, encompassing the reforming efforts of Vaudès (*c.* 1150–1217),[5] John Wycliffe (1329–84), Jan Hus (1373–1415), and Savonarola (1452–98) as well as ostensibly heretical groups such as the Cathari and the Eschatological Joachimites. With the Northern Renaissance advent of biblical humanism and the 1456 invention of the printing press, however, dissent could no longer be so quelled, and the Magisterial (*i.e.* Protestant), Radical, and English Reformations reaped an ambivalent inheritance. On the one hand, these traditions of religious reform called attention to significant departures from scriptural beliefs and behaviors in the late medieval Western Church as well as legitimate exegetical, coupled with symbiotically related theological, disputes between Catholic, Lutheran, Reformed, Anabaptist, and Anglican communities of believers,[6] all of whom exhibited authentic commitment to the Lordship of Christ. Like the Matthean harvest of wheat, such diversity appears, in my assessment,

---

4. Earle E. Cairns, *Christianity Through the Centuries*, 3rd rev. ed. (Grand Rapids, Mich.: Zondervan, 1996), 196–98.

5. Contrary to the somewhat widespread Protestant misappropriation of Waldensianism as a forerunner of sixteenth–century reforming traditions, Gabriel Audisio, in *The Waldensian Dissent: Persecution and Survival, c. 1170–c. 1570*, trans. Claire Davison (Cambridge: Cambridge University Press, 1999), 1–24, 161–88, persuasively demonstrates that the medieval movement exhibits severe dissimilarity from later Protestantism but formally renounced its separate ancestral identity when the extant community embraced the theology formulated by Strasbourg reformer Martin Bucer and Basel reformer Johann Oecolampadius at the 1532 Synod of Chanforan.

6. Undisputedly the leading controversy in the Reformation surrounded the meaning of justification, with the character and celebration of the Eucharist ranking a close second; see James D. Tracy, *Europe's Reformations* (Lanham, Md.: Rowman & Littlefield, 1999), 3–119, for a comprehensive survey of the host of issues at stake.

both biblically consonant and evangelistically advantageous, akin to the complementarity of the four Gospel portraits of Jesus and the assortment of theological distinctives which contributed to the richness of the Jewish Way. But this judgment is true if, and only if, theological disagreement is kept in perspective as merely secondary and thus consistently subordinated to the *sine qua non* of Calvary–quality love plus unified fellowship and service as fellow sisters and brothers in Christ. Illustrating the acceptability of diversity in belief among Christian brethren on matters lacking clear or conclusive scriptural adjudication is Paul. Concerning the *mitzvoth* pertaining to food, Sabbath, and other *adiaphora*[7] the Apostle writes:

> Welcome those who are weak in conviction without passing judgment on disputable matters. Some believe in eating everything, but the weak eat only vegetables. Those who eat everything must not look down on those who do not, and those who do not eat everything must not condemn those who do, for God has accepted them. Who are you to pass judgment on the servants of someone else? Before their own master they stand or fall. And they will stand, for the Lord is able to make them stand. Some consider one day more sacred than another; others consider every day to be alike. Let all be fully convinced in their own minds. Those who observe the day, observe it in honor of the Lord. Likewise, those who eat, eat in honor of the Lord, for they give thanks to God; while those who abstain, abstain in honor of the Lord and give thanks to God. . . . Why, then, do you judge your brother or sister, or why do you look down on your brother or sister. . . . Therefore, let us stop passing judgment on one another (Rom. 14:1–6, 10a, 13a).

Like a quilt whose beauty emanates from its panoply of uniquely colored and designed patches, the multifaceted spectrum of human responses to the winds of the Spirit in scripture and tradition contributes greatly to the breadth and vibrancy of Christianity while bearing eloquent testimony to its Christ–enabled power in successfully mediating Ultimate Reality to individuals of every culture and background.

On the other hand, the tares of strife against which Paul forewarned received nourishment from a combination of two factors. First, the Nominalist concept of what might be denominated an "all–or–nothing" theological approach, incipient in the treatises of William of Ockham (1288–1348) but reaching maturity in his successor Gabriel Biel (1425–95), maintained that

---

7. The term "adiaphora" means "indifferent matters"; thus an item is *adiaphora* if it can be regarded as nonessential to a religion but rather is a matter of personal preference.

all dogmatic systems naturally possess irreducibly complex structures, such that each element in a given system is *de facto* logically dependent upon every other element in the system even when it appears *prima facie* to be logically independent from its counterparts. Due to the acceptance of this presupposition by all factions in the Reformation, thinkers from each confession held that denial of any point in their respective systems spelled the effective denial of these systems in their entirety. Consequently, the systems formulated by second–generation and later Magisterial, Radical, and English Reformers presented barriers to unity, as the various confessions believed they could not find agreement without abandoning their whole systems. Second, the perceived necessity for church–government amalgamation across early modern city–states, substantiated in the minds of Christian thinkers in all branches except Anabaptism by the unbroken tradition of integration between the "two arms of God's rule" commencing with the decree of Emperor Theodosius I (381) to make Christianity the state religion of the Roman Empire, prevented individual believers in particular and their confessions in general from placing their differences aside without severe political repercussions. Hence the tares of strife gave rise to a plethora of religious wars, including the Schmalkaldic Wars in Germany led by Catholic Holy Roman Emperor Charles V against the Protestant princes (1546–52), no less than eight fierce wars and massacres in France between Catholics and Huguenots (1562–98), and the infamous Thirty Years' War (1618–48) pitting Catholics, Lutherans, and Reformed Christians on the Continent against one another.

The first theologian who attempted to create a unified diversity of Christian branches, in obedience to the spirit of the New Testament and the Patristic era encapsulated in the maxim "unity in essentials, liberty in nonessentials, grace in all things,"[8] was the Helmstedt reformer Georg Calixt (1586–1686). Denying the Nominalist presupposition that all systematic elements are inextricably intertwined, Calixt made a watershed division of Christian

---

8. Although typically ascribed to Augustine, or, less commonly, Chrysostom, neither of these thinkers use the phrase but respectively paraphrase it (*On Baptism, Against the Donatists*, 6.6–7; *Homilies on the Epistle to the Romans*, 15) from its coiner, Tertullian (*De baptismo*, 6.1), who notably grounded such unity via diversity in his fully developed Trinitarian doctrine of one *substantia* containing three *personae*. In 1627 Lutheran irenicist Peter Meiderlin, a supporter of Calixt's endeavors, gave the expression its modern form, "In essentials, unity; in non–essentials, liberty; in all things, charity" (*Paraenesis votiva pro Pace Ecclesiae ad Theologos Augustanae Confessionis*, 4).

doctrine into three categories: antecedents, constitutents, and consequents.[9] Calixt defined antecedents as the corpus of natural theology, or all religious matters which humanity, without the aid of special revelation, can know by general revelation within nature, reason, and conscience, such as the existence of God and the immortality of the soul. Most important to Calixt's trichotomy were constituents, defined as the corpus of catechetical theology, namely, the set of fundamental doctrines of the Christian faith which one must believe in order to be saved. Appealing to the *consensus quinquesaecularis* (*i.e.* the first five centuries of Christian history), Calixt insisted that the salvific message of Scripture coupled with strictly logical deductions from Scriptural premises (*i.e.* the doctrines of the Trinity and Christology), encapsulated by the symbols of the first four Ecumenical Councils, collectively constitute the sole prior norm needing no outside source of authentication. Finally, Calixt defined consequents as inferences from the constituents which typically comprise the bulk of a theological system and give each system its confessional distinctiveness. Arguably over 250 years ahead of his time, Calixt championed the notion that Roman Catholics, Lutherans, and the Reformed should acknowledge the genuine Christianity of one another and abandon all internecine conflict, resolving in Pauline fashion to respectfully disagree on the consequents. Perceiving the existence of a *communio interna* (virtual union) between the three great Western confessions, Calixt asserted that this union needed only to be recognized; nevertheless, Calixt cautioned that such *communio actualis* (outward union) would be impossible as long as these churches were wrongly charging each other with fundamental errors.[10] Due to the firmly entrenched animus against theological compromise, Calixt's call for unity not only went unheeded in his own day but elicited virtually unanimous opposition from Lutherans, Reformed, and Catholics alike.

In the last half–century, Christian scholars in biblical studies and church history have stood at the forefront of a remarkable shift in theological climate, generating the conditions identified by Calixt as necessary for restoring ecclesiastical unity without undermining confessional individuality. Called by Pope John XXIII in 1962 and continued by successor Pope Paul VI from 1963–65, the Second Vatican Council displayed a new tolerance and openness toward non–Catholic believers, recognizing their genuine Christian pedigree and viewing them as "separated brethren." This led Patriarch Athenagoras I of Constantinople to meet with Paul VI in hopes of im-

---

9. J. L. Neve, *A History of Christian Thought*, 2 vols. (Philadelphia: Muhlenberg Press, 1946), 2:4.

10. Ibid., 2:7.

proving Orthodox relations with Rome. Their conference resulted in the *Catholic–Orthodox Joint Declaration* read concomitantly at Vatican II and a special ceremony in Istanbul on 7 December 1965, lifting the mutual excommunication between the two Christian branches. Stemming from their shared goal of counteracting secularism in the modern world, Evangelicals and Catholics have experienced a growing cooperation and convergence in recent years, thereby prompting both communities to explore areas of spiritual commonality. Such a joint venture gave birth in 1992 to the Evangelicals and Catholics Together movement, chartered by a historic fivefold declaration in 1994 characterized by the bridging of major theological divides formerly regarded as impassible. Establishing a measure of concord over the central dispute of the Reformation, Section I declares, "We affirm together that we are justified by grace through faith because of Christ."[11] In Calixtine fashion, the section proceeds to formally recognize the New Testament standard (Mk. 3:34–35; Jn. 1:12–13; 1 Jn. 5:1–2) as the sole determinant of spiritual familial authenticity: "All who accept Christ as Lord and Savior are brothers and sisters in Christ."[12] While making no attempt to overlook or minimize "the deep and long standing differences between evangelicals and Catholics," of which ten are explicitly stated, Sections II and III admirably chart their course along Pauline waters by insisting, "Not all differences are authentic disagreements, nor need all disagreements divide," and observing the indispensability of interconfessional oneness for effectual evangelism: "Unity and love among Christians is an integral part of our missionary witness to the Lord whom we serve. . . . As evangelicals and Catholics, we pray that our unity in the love of Christ will become even more evident as a sign to the world of God's reconciling power."[13] On account of the recognition that evangelicalism and Catholicism both constitute valid paths of discipleship for following one and the same Jesus, Sections IV and V condemn "sheep–stealing" by revealing its true colors as a disingenuous and counterproductive redistricting of evangelism out of the valid realm of winning people for Christ and into the parochial realm of pressuring members of God's Kingdom to switch allegiances from one community to another over Calixtine consequents (*i.e.* secondary issues not pertaining to salvation). Drawing an incisive distinction between evangelism and proselytism, the Declaration asserts that "in view of the large number of non–Christians in the world and the enormous challenge of our common evangelistic task, it is

---

11. "Evangelicals and Catholics Together: The Christian Mission in the Third Millennium," *First Things* 43 (May 1994): 16.
12. Ibid., 17.
13. Ibid., 18.

neither theologically legitimate nor a prudent use of resources for one Christian community to proselytize among the active adherents of another Christian community."[14] While advocating individual freedom of conscience to transfer confessional allegiances over consequents, the Declaration condemns "the practice of recruiting people from another community for purposes of denominational or institutional aggrandizement."[15] In 1999 the sentiments of the Evangelicals and Catholics Together Movement were echoed on a larger denominational scale with the composition of the *Joint Statement on Justification* by the Lutheran World Federation and the Roman Catholic Church.[16] Heralding a monumental reversal, this document brought reconciliation between the very two groups whose opposition over the topic under consideration yielded the single most tragic division in Church history.[17]

As a direct result of fresh linguistic discoveries in New Testament scholarship, Lutheran and Catholic scholars came to realize that their two apparently contradictory positions—each of which respectively drew the anathema of the other at the Council of Trent (1545–63) and in the Lutheran

---

14. Ibid., 20.

15. Ibid., 21.

16. Appropriately the document was signed in Augsburg, Germany on 31 October 1999, the anniversary of Luther's dissemination of the *95 Theses* in 1517.

17. Although the misunderstanding which directly caused the Reformation has been resolved in this text, it should be emphasized that Lutherans and Catholics still disagree on the theological issues—namely, divergent conceptions of original sin and hence divergent conceptions of soteriology—which incited the misunderstanding. On the one hand, Lutherans hold to a late–Augustinian doctrine of original sin, according to which our primal ancestors, on behalf of the entire human race, destroyed the mental faculty by which humanity could freely choose to respond to the grace of God and be saved. Thus, for them as for Augustine following the Pelagian controversy, salvation is monergistic, or accomplished entirely by the work of God without any human effort, including the human exercise of free choice to believe in Christ. On the other hand, the Catholic doctrine of original sin follows Bernard of Clairvaux in asserting that, while humanity surrendered its freedom from sin and freedom from misery in the Fall, humanity did not lose its freedom from necessity or libertarian free will, since such a loss would constitute a logical impossibility if humanity is to remain in the *imago Dei*, as Genesis 9:6 and James 3:9 testifies. Hence Catholics subscribe to a synergistic model of salvation, where God offers prevenient grace (the *initium fidei*) to every person he creates, which the individual then has the free choice to accept or reject; if accepted, the process of cooperating with logically prior divine grace continues throughout the believer's life.

Confessions (1530–77)[18]—were actually saying the same thing in different words. The two terms whose enhanced understanding resolved the seeming incongruity were πίστις (faith) and σωτήριον (salvation). Heralded by the disciplinary advent of biblical archaeology in the late nineteenth century and the tens of thousands of nonbiblical Koinē Greek manuscripts from the first century C.E. which it unearthed, full knowledge of Koinē semantic domains eclipsed the partial knowledge upon which Catholic and Magisterial Reformers alike had to rely.[19] The evidence disclosed that neither πίστις nor σωτήριον are univocal but can both be used in broad and narrow senses. Applied to the context of the Way, πίστις refers broadly to acceptance of God and his offer of salvation in Christ, as seen in Paul's epistles to the Romans and Galatians. By contrast, the narrow use of πίστις alludes simply to intellectual belief, which is employed elsewhere by Paul (1 Cor. 13:2, 13) and most famously in the denials by James that such πίστις alone saves (Jas. 2:14–26). Furthermore, σωτήριον in the broad sense encompasses the entire process of being made holy, spanning from regeneration to glorification (*cf.* Rom. 8:30), which requires faith as well as a continuing cooperation with divine grace manifested in good works. But conceived narrowly, σωτήριον denotes being accepted by God and forgiven of sin. Coupling the broad sense of πίστις with the narrow sense of σωτήριον, the *Joint Statement on Justification* proclaims unanimity between Catholics and Protestants that humans gain σωτήριον through πίστις alone.[20] The *Statement* also calls attention to interconfessional agreement that neither broad nor narrow σωτήριον can be accessed through πίστις, defined narrowly.[21] This consensus view of justification is summarized by Catholic philosopher Peter

---

18. The strongest possible denunciation, an anathema stipulates that if an individual holds to the accursed belief willingly and persistently up to the moment of death, then that individual will be eternally condemned. The first use of this reproach in Christian literature comes from Paul: "But if any human or even an angel from heaven preaches to you a different gospel than the gospel we proclaimed to you, let that one be ἀνάθεμα. As we have said once, so let me say again: If anyone preaches to you a different gospel than the gospel you received, let that one be ἀνάθεμα" (Gal. 1:8–9). For a detailed synopsis of the divergent Lutheran and Catholic conceptions of justification during the initial codifying stage of Reformation theology see Reinhold Seeberg, *Text-book of the History of Doctrine*, 4 vols., trans. Charles E. Kay (Grand Rapids, Mich.: Baker, 1956), 2:337–433.

19. John McRay, *Archaeology and the New Testament* (Grand Rapids, Mich.: Baker, 1991), 354–55.

20. *Joint Declaration on the Doctrine of Justification*, 3:14–18.

21. Ibid., 4.7:37–39.

Kreeft: "a. we are neither justified (forgiven) nor sanctified (made holy) by intellectual faith alone (belief); b. we *are* justified by will–faith, or heart–faith alone; c. but this faith will necessarily produce good works; d. and we are not sanctified by faith alone, in either sense, but only by faith plus good works."[22] Thus while salvation is by faith alone, the quality of faith which saves is one that naturally manifests itself in good works, in the same way that the sun naturally shines. At this point Roman Catholics remarkably now concur with the portrait of Christian freedom painted by Luther:

> Believers are a new creature, a new tree. Therefore all those modes of speech, which are customary in the law, do not belong here, such as, "A believer is bound to do good works," in the same way that it is not proper to say, "The sun is bound to shine," since it does this of itself, unbidden, as it is made for this. So a good tree of itself brings forth good fruits; three and seven are ten already, they are not first bound to be ten. To say of a sun that it ought to shine, or of a believer that he must do good, is ridiculous.[23]

Historically the foregoing endeavors suggest that, for the first time after the Reformation, the major branches of Christianity are making a concerted effort to apply a hermeneutic of charity to the positions of their alleged opponents, thus aiming to genuinely understand and even strengthen these positions, rather than applying the converse hermeneutic of suspicion, aiming only at refutation and normally coupled with *ad hominem* and straw–person argumentation, which dominated virtually all sixteenth–century interconfessional dialogues. Without denying or attempting to downplay the secondary matters which give each confession its own particular emphasis and distinctiveness, therefore, the contemporary ecumenical advances among groups committed to essential Christian doctrine[24] are increasingly drawing the

---

22. Peter J. Kreeft, *Catholic Christianity* (San Francisco: Ignatius, 2001), 25–26.

23. Martin Luther, *Works* (Halle, 1883), 22:717.

24. This is not at all to sanction, however, abandonments of essential Christian doctrine, usually in the form of redefining historic terminology in comportment with the modernist critique of religion, under the guise of ecumenicity. Often scholars adhering to this critique will employ a kind of theological double–talk in drawing up doctrinal statements worded in such a way as to persuade laity that traditional beliefs are simply being perpetuated while unsuspectedly making ideological room for post–Enlightenment thought within the official standards of their denominations. In such statements every selection or omission

Church together into one common spectrum of biblically acceptable beliefs and practices featuring a panoramic diversity of brilliant colors and subtle shades. However, it needs to be emphasized that such unification will only be completed when these groups rescind affirmation of their own particular consequents as prerequisite to Eucharistic reception and allow all believers in constituent Christian doctrine to receive the Lord's Supper at each other's gatherings, thus enabling common Eucharistic fellowship among all the redeemed. In this way, the meal that Jesus instituted to unite his diverse followers as one body with many differently gifted members (1 Cor. 10:14-17; 11:17-34; 12:12-31) will no longer be sinfully exploited to divide the flock but will return to its original purpose. This multifaceted conception of the Christian faith objectively considered (in Thomistic nomenclature, *fides quae creditur*)[25] emerges as quite advantageous in performing the biblical role of the διδάσκαλος (scholar–teacher),[26] especially when considering

---

of terminology carries a score of logical implications which are known only to others with formal theological training.

25. See Richard A. Muller, *Dictionary of Latin and Greek Theological Terms* (Grand Rapids, Mich.: Baker, 1985), 117, for a fine distinction between this species of *fides* and its complement, *fides qua creditur*. In *Summa Theologica* 2.2.4.1 Aquinas argues, rightly in my judgment, that Hebrews 11:1 defines authentic faith as a synthesis of these two species through its mutually balancing clauses, where the act of faith as "the ὑπόστασις (conviction, confidence; not "substance" as in KJV) of things hoped for" illustrates the subjective nature of New Testament faith as personal commitment and trust in Jesus (*fides qua creditur*), and where the object of faith as "the ἔλεγχος (proof, evidence) of things not seen" (*fides quae creditur*) carries the monumentally important consequence that faith is not opposed to evidence but actually entails the existence of objective proof for the truth of its claims as a conceptually necessary component. Sadly the latter point has been lost on modern expositors, who ironically find themselves arguing against the plain meaning of the Greek (since they supposedly "know" but have unwittingly presupposed the Kierkegaardian assumption, virtually ubiquitous in the West since the late nineteenth century, that faith precludes proof) in translating this verse. For a typical exegesis of this passage, in which the *prima facie* interpretation of the text is begrudgingly presented but then eliminated as conceptually absurd, see Paul Ellingworth, *The Epistle to the Hebrews: A Commentary on the Greek Text* (Grand Rapids, Mich.: Eerdmans, 1993), 558–59.

26. That the διδάσκαλος is, according to the New Testament, the Church office (one of four permanent offices, along with the pastor, elder, and deacon; see Eph. 4 and 1 Tim. 3) requiring scholarly knowledge of the Word of God and carrying the responsibility of discovering profound theological verities was cor-

issues of philosophical and practical theology. Unlike biblical theology, in which doctrines are (or, at least, should be) formulated exclusively from the application of deductive logic to Scriptural premises, its philosophical and practical subdisciplinary cousins attempt to craft possible solutions to dilemmas raised by the perennial interaction between the Scriptural witness and the changing intellectual and social climates that followers of Jesus endeavor to redemptively transform.[27] Since, by the nature of the case, Scrip-

---

rectly observed by John Calvin: *"Teachers,* with whom the Church never can dispense . . . preside not over discipline, or the administration of the sacraments, or admonitions, or exhortations, but the interpretation of Scripture only, in order that pure and sound doctrine may be maintained among believers" (*Institutes of the Christian Religion,* trans. Henry Beveridge [Grand Rapids, Mich.: Eerdmans, 1989], 4.3.4).

27. Clearly my conception of biblical theology in particular and of the theological enterprise in general depends for its validity upon the propositional truth of didactic (but not poetic, anthropomorphic, parabolic, apocalyptic, and other types of figurative) statements in Scripture, including those pertaining to God. Hence I am following in the tradition of the *via positiva,* which holds that God is incomprehensible and not, as maintained by the opposing *via negativa,* ineffable. Contrary to appearance, the theological attribute of incomprehensibility does not mean that humans are unable to know any literal truths about God, but rather that, although didactic statements about God in Scripture are propositionally true, the finite nature of the human spirit renders it incapable at any point of fully apprehending the infinite set of propositional truths about God. Hence the redeemed will always face the exhilarating prospect, in both time and eternity, of continuing to learn increasingly more objective truths about God, never being able to exhaust the limitless set of such truths. However, the concept of ineffability alleges that God is beyond all rational thought, thereby precluding the possibility of conveying in words or concepts anything objective about God, such that all pertinent didactic statements, while literally false, are metaphors pointing beyond themselves to suprarational realities which participate in the realities that they symbolize or, in other words, the best human approximation for verities lying beyond the laws of logic. While I take divine ineffability to be self-contradictory, it possesses a therapeutic appeal stemming from its ability to comfort and guide individuals through states of crisis in which God and his ways seem completely unknowable, termed by sixteenth–century Spanish Carmelite John of the Cross as "the dark night of the soul" (*The Dark Night,* 8.1). It seems that the correct balance between these competing perspectives was struck by the leading fourteenth–century theologian Catherine of Siena, whose double-sided mysticism affirmed the ultimate veracity of the *via positiva* while accentuating the fact that the *via negativa* often psychologically seems true because of

ture itself does not provide adequate information to decisively answer such questions, the logical necessity inherent to biblical theology is unattainable in philosophical and practical theology, which instead deal in probabilities and can at best offer high levels of confidence. In such cases, one is obviously more likely to devise the correct, or a nearly correct, explanation drawing eclectically upon a range of biblically tenable models than from working within the confines of a single and confessionally predetermined model. Moreover, a multifaceted Christian theological canopy safeguards the freedom of thought heralded by Paul as the adoptionary birthright of all whom Jesus has chosen for service in his Kingdom (Gal. 5:1).

It is in the character of this encouraging trend toward a Christianity exemplified by its multidimensional unity that the present systematic theology will follow. To avoid confusion about the content of this work, however, let us distinguish at the outset between two implied antecedents to the adjective "systematic," namely, with respect to scope or to method. My project is systematic only according to its method, in that it is grounded in the timeless truths of Scripture and meticulously attempts to furnish complete answers to heretofore unsolved quandaries arising at the intersection of biblical studies and other disciplines by meticulously appealing to and then integrating data from all realms of knowledge, including philosophy, history, and the sciences, within the presuppositional boundaries of essential Christian doctrine. For this reason, my understanding of systematic theology is broad and coterminous with apologetic theology, as defined by Paul Tillich: "Apologetic theology is 'answering theology.' It answers the questions implied in the 'situation' in the power of the eternal message and with the means provided by the situation whose questions it answers."[28] Nevertheless, my project makes neither presumption nor attempt to be systematic in its scope, as I am uninterested in "reinventing wheels" by repeating sound and preexisting doctrinal expositions or solutions to philosophical dilemmas, for which the

---

the human epistemic distance from God (*The Dialogue*, trans. Algar Thorold [Grand Rapids, Mich.: Christian Classics Ethereal Library, 2000], 70–82).

28. Tillich, *Systematic Theology*, 1:6. Gordon Lewis and Bruce Demarest have coined the phrase "integrative theology" in reference to the broad theological methodology which I adopt; see their *Integrative Theology*, 3 vols. (Grand Rapids, Mich.: Zondervan, 1994). By contrast, an equally large number of thinkers, none more eminent than Wayne Grudem (*Systematic Theology* [Grand Rapids, Mich.: Zondervan, 1994], 21), use "systematic theology" in the narrow sense of what I have described as "biblical theology," *i.e.* collecting and understanding all the relevant Scriptural texts on various topics and then employing deductive logic to clearly summarize the emergent canonical doctrines.

interested reader already possesses a host of outstanding resources.[29] Rather, I endeavor to analyze only those issues which have not received adequate treatment in current philosophical or theological discussion and which pose direct and pressing challenges to the coherence of the biblical worldview or to the vitality of Christian discipleship in contemporary society. To this end, I will principally, but not exclusively, draw from the wellsprings of the two traditions in Church history which I respectively consider to be superlative on matters of theory and application but have never previously been conjoined: Roman Catholicism and Anabaptism. Within the Catholic tradition is found a philosophical brilliance unequaled among other Christian confessions; similarly, the Anabaptist tradition has since its sixteenth–century inception far surpassed its contemporaries in spiritual formation, envisioned as the development of committed followers of Jesus who rightly understand their Lord's all–inclusive conception of the Kingdom of God and strive to live as faithful citizens therein.

The Historical Background Sparking the Roman Catholic Contribution

The theology of divine omniscience known as Molinism takes its name from Luis de Molina (1535–1600), a Spanish Jesuit and Catholic Reformer who ranks, in my assessment, as perhaps the greatest philosophical theologian in Church history. Earning his doctor of theology degree from the University of Évora in 1571, Molina proceeded to occupy his career with resolving the dispute which he rightly perceived as underlying the Reformation dispute over justification and which, even after the Council of Trent, still divided his nascent Society of Jesus from the Dominicans and other like–minded religious orders. This dispute concerned the perennial theological question of how best to reconcile the doctrine of human freedom with the interrelated doctrines of divine grace, foreknowledge, predestination, and providence. Opposing himself to what he considered the central error of the Magisterial Reformation, namely, the denial of genuine human freedom in virtue of God's sovereignty and omniscience, Molina framed an explanatory

---

29. For two overviews of biblical doctrine encyclopedic in their scope and unswervingly faithful to the testimony of Scripture see Grudem, *Systematic Theology*, and Charles R. Swindoll and Roy B. Zuck, gen. eds., *Understanding Christian Theology* (Nashville: Nelson, 2003). A comparable masterwork in the field of philosophy of religion is J. P. Moreland and William Lane Craig, *Philosophical Foundations for a Christian Worldview* (Downers Grove, Ill.: Inter-Varsity Press, 2003).

order among the various logical moments of omniscience, the power and ingenuity of which revolves around the schematic placement and content of the second moment. Denominating this moment as *scientia media* (middle knowledge) since it fell between the first and the concluding third moment, Molina insisted that it provided the key to avoiding the Protestant error of obliterating human free choice without relinquishing divine sovereignty in the process.[30] Via his proposed resolution of this ancient tension, Molina boldly professed the ability to consistently affirm both divine sovereignty and human freedom in his 1588 *Liberi Arbitrii cum Gratiae Donis, Divina Praescientia, Providentia, Praedestinatione et Reprobatione Concordia* (The Compatibility of Free Choice with the Gifts of Grace, Divine Foreknowledge, Providence, Predestination, and Reprobation).

To best understand Molina's theology of divine omniscience, we must place it in its early modern theological context against the particular backdrop of the views of human freedom held by Luther, Calvin, and his Dominican co–religionists to which Molina was reacting. On this score we should acknowledge the accuracy of Molina's reading of his theological opponents, remarkable in a day where similar instances of fair representation ran far and few between. Indeed Luther and Calvin denied humans the ability to choose otherwise in the circumstances in which they find themselves, at least in their dealings with God, and followed the late–Augustine in reducing creaturely freedom to mere spontaneity of choice and voluntariness of will. Luther's aversion to human free choice was predicated on what he understood as the incompatibility of such freedom with divine omnipotence and prescience. Anticipating the arguments of modern theological fatalists, Luther maintained that the infallible certainty of God's foreknowledge coupled with God's ability to bring about whatever he desires entails that everything God foreknows and wills happens necessarily. In his famous 1525 treatise *On the Bondage of the Will* Luther reasoned:

> God knows nothing contingently, but . . . he foresees and purposes and does all things by his immutable, eternal, and infallible will. . . . If he foreknows as he wills, then his will is eternal and unchanging (because it belongs to his nature), and if he wills as he foreknows, then his knowledge is eternal and unchanging (because it belongs to his nature). From this it follows irrefutably that everything we do, everything that happens, even if it seems to us to happen mutably and contingently, happens in fact nonetheless necessarily and immutably, if you have regard to the will of God. For the will of God is effectual and cannot be

---

30. Luis de Molina, *On Divine Foreknowledge*, trans. Alfred J. Freddoso (Ithaca, N.Y.: Cornell University Press, 1988), 4.52.9.

hindered . . . moreover it is wise, so that it cannot be deceived. Now if his will is not hindered, nothing can prevent the work itself from being done, in the place, time, manner, and measure that he himself both foresees and wills.[31]

Thus Luther summarizes: "God's foreknowledge and omnipotence are diametrically opposed to our free choice."[32] Grasping the ramifications of his position with respect to the divine–human relationship, Luther does not refrain from declaring that Judas betrayed Jesus necessarily, as the only human freedom permitted by this relationship is that the will chooses voluntarily and without external coercion, albeit whatever the will chooses it chooses necessarily.[33] But failing to comprehend his position's implications for horizontal relationships, Luther exempted natural choices in earthly affairs from this necessity, inconsistently alleging that humans should be regarded as free in things below but bound in things above.[34] Conversely, Calvin did not allege the preclusion of creaturely contingency by divine prescience, but rather contended that human free choice is ruled out by the universal and total providence of God. Pressing late–Augustinian monergism to an extreme which its originator was unwilling to yield, Calvin declares that nothing can happen unless God has decreed and willed it:

> [W]hat is called providence describes God, not as idly beholding from heaven the transactions which happen in the world, but as holding the helm of the universe, and regulating all events. Thus it belongs no less to his hands than to his eyes. When Abraham said to his son, "God will provide," he intended not only to assert his prescience of a future event, but to leave the care of an unknown thing to the will of him who frequently puts an end to circumstances of perplexity and confusion.

---

31. Martin Luther, *The Bondage of the Will*, in *Luther and Erasmus: Free Will and Salvation*, eds. E. Gordon Rupp and A. N. Marlow (Philadelphia: Westminster, 1969), 118–19.

32. Ibid., 243.

33. Ibid., 246–49.

34. Ibid., 170. Expressing incredulity at Luther's position, William Lane Craig rightly observes, "But as other proponents of theological fatalism have clearly seen, since God's foreknowledge embraces all future contingents, the argument, if sound, would apply equally to human choices concerning worldly affairs as well as to choices concerning divine affairs. Everything that happens does so necessarily" ("Middle Knowledge: A Calvinist–Arminian Rapprochement?", in *The Grace of God, The Will of Man*, ed. Clark H. Pinnock [Grand Rapids, Mich.: Zondervan, 1989], 143).

Whence it follows that providence consists in action; for it is ignorant trifling to talk of mere prescience. . . . . [W]e make God the Arbiter and Governor of all things, who, in his own wisdom, has, from the remotest eternity, decreed what he would do, and now, by his own power, executes what he has decreed. Whence we assert, that not only the heaven and the earth, and inanimate creatures, but also the deliberations and volitions of men, are so governed by his providence, as to be directed to the end appointed to it. What then? you will say; does nothing happen fortuitously or contingently? I answer . . . that *fortune* and *chance* are words of the heathen, with the signification of which the minds of the pious ought not to be occupied. For if all success be the benediction of God, and calamity and adversity his malediction, there is no room left in human affairs for fortune or chance. . . . And though [Augustine] elsewhere decides, that all things are conducted partly by the free will of man, partly by the providence of God, yet he just after shows that men are subject to it and governed by it, assuming as a principle that nothing could be more absurd, than for any thing to happen independently of the ordination of God; because it would happen at random. By this reasoning he excludes also any contingence dependent on the human will.[35]

Clearly for Calvin, then, sovereignty is equated with complete control, such that God cannot be sovereign save for his strong actualization of every event in the physical and spiritual realms.[36] Although reached from a different perspective, Calvin's view of human freedom is in the end the same as Luther's—spontaneity without external coercion—although divine sovereignty or prescience respectively exclude the genuine possibility of the will choosing in any circumstances other than it does in fact choose.

Whether manifesting itself through divine foreknowledge or divine sovereignty, the logical impossibility of libertarian free will and consequent

---

35. Calvin, *Institutes*, 1.16.8.

36. Here the distinction between strong and weak actualization is instructive. An agent *A* strongly actualizes a state of affairs *x* if and only if *A* causally determines *x*'s obtaining. By contrast, *A* weakly actualizes *x* if and only if *A* strongly actualizes that another agent *A** is in a situation *C*, where it is true that if *A** were in *C*, then *A** would freely choose to strongly actualize *x*. Hence in Calvin's model of divine sovereignty, it is not enough for God to somehow cause (*i.e.* either to strongly or weakly actualize) all events, but God must specifically cause all events via strong actualization. For a thorough discussion of these modes of actualization see Alvin Plantinga, *The Nature of Necessity* (Oxford: Oxford University Press, 1974), 172–73.

relegation of humanity to compatibilist freedom[37] ultimately stem for both Luther and Calvin not from the theandric vehicles through which they are dispensed but rather from their shared presuppositional forestructure of divine omnisicience first proposed by Thomas Aquinas, a fact of which both Reformers were unaware, and which foundation was mediated to them as a staple of the Catholic theological curriculum.[38] Not surprisingly, the Thomistic logical blueprint of omniscience was vigorously defended by Dominicans following the Council of Trent. On each logical side of God's decree to create the set of circumstances now comprising the actual world, Aquinas placed one moment within God's timeless act of knowledge. Logically prior to the divine creative decree, Aquinas claimed that God apprehended his *scientia simplicis intelligentiae* (knowledge of uncompounded or unqualified intelligence), by which God perfectly knows himself as well as all logical *possibilia*. Such exhaustive knowledge furnishes God with a range of options, from which he chooses to actualize a logically consistent set in his creative decree. Logically posterior to the divine creative decree, Aquinas held that God perceives his *scientia visionis* (visionary knowledge), by which he knows all past, present, and future tense truths in the world he has freely created.[39] Aquinas emphasized that his logical sequence of moments in no way implies any temporal priority or succession in God's omniscience, as an omniscient being cannot know more or less at one point in time than at another but must possess complete knowledge at every point in time. How-

---

37. Elsewhere I have delineated these two conceptions of human freedom as follows: "Since the late medieval period, scholastic theologians have differentiated between two competing views of free will: libertarian and compatibilist. Libertarian free will entails the freedom to choose between opposites in both the physical and spiritual realms, regardless of whether or not a person has been regenerated. Thus, a libertarian concerning free will would maintain that fallen humanity can freely choose whether or not to respond to God's saving grace. Compatibilist free will, by contrast, is the freedom to choose between the options compatible with one's nature. Thus, unregenerate humans, while possessing the freedom to choose between opposites in the physical realm, lack the ability to choose between spiritual good and evil due to original sin. Just as a bad tree can bear bad fruit or no fruit at all, unregenerate humanity can either perform spiritual wickedness by actively rebelling against God or do nothing spiritual at all by displaying passivity toward God" (Kirk R. MacGregor, *A Central European Synthesis of Radical and Magisterial Reform: The Sacramental Theology of Balthasar Hubmaier* [Lanham, Md.: University Press of America, 2006], 15).

38. Seeberg, *History of Doctrine*, 185.

39. Aquinas, *Summa contra Gentiles*, 1.66.4; *Summa Theologica*, 1.1.14.8.

ever, Aquinas equally insisted that his progression is no figment of the imagination, but exists in the same mode as the progression between various premises in a syllogism. Just as the antecedent premises are explanatorily prior to the conclusion, such that the conclusion follows as a result of the conditions posited by the antecedent premises, so the *scientia simplicis intelligentiae* furnishes the necessary ground for the divine creative decree, which in turn jointly furnish the necessary ground for *scientia visionis*. Absent from Aquinas' ordering of divine cognitive events was God's knowledge of all counterfactual truths, an attribute which the *doctor angelicus* resolutely affirmed,[40] because he believed that its apprehension was a motion parallel to and simultaneous with the divine apprehension of *scientia visionis*. In other words, Aquinas proposed that God, as part of his divine creative decree, freely assigned truth–values to all counterfactual statements.[41] Thus both divine knowledge of all tensed facts (*i.e. scientia visionis*) and divine knowledge of all counterfactuals follow immediately from God's combined awareness of his creative decree and of his almighty power to bring it about. Nevertheless Aquinas, failing to see the implications of making counterfactual knowledge a direct result of the divine volition, made the unsubstantiated assertion that his schema in no way undermined genuine human freedom, which nomenclature carried the *prima facie* connotation of libertarianism.[42] But Luther, Calvin, and Molina, in a stunning concord,

---

40. As did all Christian theologians up to the advent of liberal Protestant theology, where Freidrich Schleiermacher became, by his own admission, the first to deny divine possession of counterfactual knowledge, due to his redefinition of the term "God" in a manner that rendered God relevant to and active in a Kantian, and thus causally closed, universe (*Der Christliche Glaube*, 1.2.4).

41. I follow the accepted custom in philosophy of religion, notwithstanding its counterintuitive appearance, of broadly defining the term "counterfactual" to encompass not only statements which are contrary to fact, but also true conditionals in the subjunctive mood; for the history of this terminology see David Lewis, *Counterfactuals* (Cambridge, Mass.: Harvard University Press, 1973), 3, 26–30.

42. Since the contemporary advent of Neo–Thomist Catholic systematics launched by Leo XIII's 1879 promulgation of *Aeterni Patris*, making Aquinas the standard of Catholic orthodoxy, Catholic theologians have understood Aquinas as endorsing libertarian free will (*Catechism of the Catholic Church: Libreria Editrice Vaticana* [Boston: St. Paul Books and Media, 1994], 1705, 1731–34); yet in an ironic but ecumenically promising twist, many recent Protestant scholars, including Arvin Vos (*Aquinas, Calvin, and Contemporary Protestant Thought* [Grand Rapids, Mich.: Eerdmans, 1985], 134) and Norman L. Geisler (*Thomas Aquinas: An Evangelical Appraisal* [Grand Rapids, Mich.: Baker,

alike perceived that Aquinas' dependence of counterfactuals upon God's selection obliterated libertarian freedom, as it is God who determines what every creature would do in every set of circumstances in which they found themselves. Hence the different doctrines with which Luther and Calvin associate libertarian impossibility prove to be two ways of skinning the same proverbial cat amounting to a mere difference in emphasis rather than substance, as these Reformers stress different sides of the symbiosis found in their Thomistic *Vorhabe*[43] to explain God's counterfactual knowledge. On the one side, Luther highlighted the epistemic contribution of the divine creative decree, naturally linking the absurdity of libertarian freedom to the logical moment with which its exposure is simultaneous, namely, the divine prescience of *scientia visionis*. On the other side, Calvin highlighted the omnipotent means prohibiting libertarianism, which omnipotence falls under the umbrella of divine sovereignty.

Molina, as part of his Scholastic inheritance, concurred with his Reformation theological contemporaries as to the basic structure of God's omniscience, but both sharpened the two existing logical moments and postulated the existence of a new logical moment by elevating God's counterfactual knowledge from the consequential realm of the divine creative decree onto the causal realm of God's epistemic structure and then repositioning it as logically prior to the creative decree. Molina began by renaming the *scientia simplicis intelligentiae* and *scientia visionis* to better reflect their roles in the divine cognition, dubbing the former *scientia naturalis* (natural knowledge) and the latter *scientia libera* (free knowledge), while explaining more fully than Aquinas the broad implications of each.[44] At this point it should be emphasized that Molina, consistent with the anthropology of twelfth–century Cistercian monastic reformer Bernard of Clairvaux[45] defined as Roman dogma by the Council of Trent, held a moderate version of original sin, according to which the ontological damage suffered by our primal ancestors, and genetically transmitted to their descendants, did not extend to human

1991], 81), have tried to exempt Aquinas from error on this score by explaining his phraseology as a forceful endorsement of compatibilist free will as the only genuine form of freedom.

43. This linguistic handle was devised by Martin Heidegger, *Being and Time* (New York: Harper & Row, 1962), 122, 153 and expanded by Hans–Georg Gadamer, *Truth and Method*, trans. Garrett Barden and John Cumming (New York: Crossroad, 1986), 235–40 to denote the conceptual scheme or matrix which one brings to a problem and determines what one finds intelligible.

44. Molina, *Foreknowledge*, 4.52.9.

45. For a complete description of Bernard's anthropology see my *Central European Synthesis*, 38–61.

free choice. Thus Molina would have agreed entirely with Bernard's sentiment that libertarian free will "belongs equally to God and to every rational
creature, good or bad. . . . [n]either by sin nor by misery is it lost or de-
creased; nor is it greater in the just person than in the sinner, nor fuller in the
angel than in humanity."[46] Before treating Molina's explications of *scientia
naturalis* and *scientia libera*, therefore, an excursus at this point on the
events of Genesis 3 and various views of its impact upon the human race is
in order.

A Historical–Scriptural Assessment of Libertarian Human Freedom and Original Sin

Without in any way endorsing the totality of Bernard's anthropology,
this systematic theology takes the position that Bernard and Molina faithfully represent the teaching of Scripture when asserting that post–Genesis 3
humans possess libertarian free will, including freedom to choose between
opposites on matters pertaining to salvation or any other spiritual good. This
immediately raises questions surrounding the concept of original sin. The
expression "original sin" was first used by Augustine in the wake of the
Pelagian controversy.[47] Upon arriving at Rome in 400 C.E., the British monk
Pelagius was horrified to see the open immorality prevalent among so–called
Christians,[48] which was the direct result of Theodosius I nineteen years earlier (381) declaring Christianity the state religion of the Roman Empire and
so decreeing everyone who lived within its borders to be Christian.[49] Since
only 25–30% of people in the Roman Empire prior to the edict were Christians with the other 70–75% literally pagans and barbarians,[50] the transformation of Christianity from a voluntary religion (one that people freely

---

46. "Verum libertas a necessitate (freedom from necessity = libertarian free
will) aeque et indifferenter Deo universaeque, tam malae quam bonae, rationali
convenit creaturae. . . . Nec peccato, nec miseria amittitur vel minuitur; nec
maior in iusto est quam in peccatore, nec plenior in angelo quam in homine."
Bernard de Clairvaux, *De gratia et libero arbitrio*, in *Sämtliche Werke
lateinisch/deutsch* I (Innsbruck: Tyrolia–Verlag, 1990), 186.
47. Augustine, *De Gratia Christi, et de Peccato Originali, contra Pelagium*,
2.1–5.
48. Pelagius, *Commentary on St. Paul's Epistle to the Romans*, trans. Theodore de Bruyn (Oxford: Oxford University Press, 1995), 107.
49. Cairns, *Christianity*, 120–21.
50. Jean–Rémy Palanque, *Church in the Christian Roman Empire*, 4 vols.,
trans. Ernest C. Messinger (New York: Macmillan, 1953), 3:27.

choose to join) to a natural religion (one into which people are born) spawned both an immediate decline in morality among those bearing the name of Christ and the long–lasting tragedy of individuals calling and thinking of themselves as Christian without ever having personally committed their lives to Jesus. A morally austere and disciplined person who never experienced any profound struggle to overcome sin, Pelagius exhorted the Romans to live worthy of their Christian calling with an argument logically summarized in two steps. First, Pelagius affirmed that humans possessed libertarian free will, a position universally accepted by Christians from the time of Jesus up to Pelagius' day. Conversely, the application Pelagius drew from this premise was extremely controversial and patently unbiblical. He argued, second, that humans should use their libertarian freedom to be good enough people to earn their own salvation.[51] Since embracing the notion that humans could earn their own salvation would require excising the entire Pauline corpus (and several other documents) from the New Testament, Pelagius was almost unanimously opposed by Christian theologians East and West, none more resolutely than by Augustine, unquestionably the preeminent theologian of the Patristic era.

Unfortunately, as so often happens in the history of thought generally and in the history of religious thought particularly, one extreme position meets the response of an equally extreme opposing position, thus fully swinging the ideological pendulum from one side to the other. Very rarely is prudence taken in shifting the pendulum back to the center, where truth is most likely to be found, by developing an enhanced position that both preserves and rectifies the valid concern wrongfully replied to by the extreme. In this case, such an enhanced position would have first denounced the possibility of Christianity as a natural religion and insisted upon a return to Matthean and Pauline church discipline. Finally, it would respond to Pelagius' argument by denying his inference that libertarian freedom in any way makes it possible for humans to earn their own salvation.[52] This, as implied by the future course of church history, was not the position taken by

---

51. Pelagius, *Romans*, 108–12.

52. As explained in chapter 5, this inference was decisively overturned by Anselm in his *Cur Deus Homo*, 1.20–23, 2.6. Accordingly, it is beyond the power of any person to make compensation for her or his sin by right employment of libertarian freedom. Contextualizing these insights to the issue of contemporary religious pluralism, it seems that Anselm has correctly identified the central problem with non–Christian world religions—regardless of how morally good they make their followers, they are powerless to enable their followers to undo the ontological ramifications of sin (*i.e.* to restore their myriad self–invoked privations of good).

Augustine. Falling prey to the fallacy of hastily granting the validity of the opponent's logic,[53] Augustine concurred with Pelagius that libertarian freedom proved a genuine threat to the Pauline teaching of salvation by grace.[54] As a result, Augustine was not content merely to reject Pelagius' conclusion but insisted on preventing the argument from getting off the ground. Denying both Pelagian premises, therefore, Augustine asserted that post–Genesis 3 humans lacked libertarian free will and so could not use this ability to earn salvation.[55] But such a negative argument naturally required an affirmative counterpart, seen in Augustine's consequent anthropology of radical depravity. According to the late–Augustine, our primal ancestors possessed libertarian free will or "free choice," defined as the mental faculty whereby its holder could freely choose to respond to the grace of God.[56] Moreover, Adam and Eve were created immortal, meaning not that they were impervious to death but that they had the capacity for bodily immortality. However, Augustine proposed an innovative interpretation of Genesis 3, henceforth styled "the Fall," according to which the primal couple, in the supreme act of self–violation, paradoxically committed a sort of "spiritual suicide" by freely employing their mental faculty whereby they could freely respond to God to destroy that very faculty.[57] As federal heads or chief representatives acting

---

53. A fallacy committed on a grand scale by many American Christians, who have granted the absurd and non–scientific claim by many Kantian-presupposing scientists that the truth of evolutionary biology implies atheism, since the 1859 publication of Darwin's *Origin of Species*. To the contrary, as I will contend in chapter six, the truth of evolutionary biology implies theism, as the probabilities entailed in the natural development of life from a single–celled organism to *Homo sapiens* screams out for the existence of God. Moreover, as Del Ratzsch has persuasively argued, God must have possessed *scientia media* in order to bring about this development; see his "Design, Chance, and Theistic Evolution," in *Mere Creation*, ed. William Dembski (Downers Grove, Ill.: InterVarsity Press, 1998), 289–312.

54. A position that Augustine had not previously held in either of his previous two periods of literary output, the works emanating from which are respectively termed "early–Augustine" and "middle–Augustine," and which heralded the advent of his final period of literary output, designated "late–Augustine."

55. Augustine, *De Gratia et Libero Arbitrio*, 29–30.

56. Augustine, *De Peccatorum Meritis et Remissione*, 2.

57. Ibid., 5–16; but Henri Blocher wisely cautions on exegetical grounds: "Traditionally the churches, commentators, and theologians entitle the third chapter of Genesis 'The Fall'. There is nothing in the text, however, to suggest that metaphor. It could put the reader's thoughts on the wrong track altogether by implying that the event was a sudden, dramatic change of level downwards,

on behalf of the entire human race, Adam and Eve rendered their own individual natures as well as human nature in general as devoid of libertarian free will, a privation which Augustine coined "original sin." The late–Augustine encapsulated the doctrine of original sin with the following three linguistic handles: from the state of *posse non peccare et mori* (ability not to sin and die) our first parents, if they had not sinned, would have passed to the state of *non posse peccare et mori* (the inability to sin and die); but because they chose to irrevocably break the initial covenant with their Creator, they, and derivatively their posterity, entered into the state of *non posse non peccare et mori* (the inability not to sin and die).[58]

By contrast, the combined results of Hebrew Bible, late Second Temple Jewish, and New Testament scholarship since the 1953 launching of the "Third Quest for the Historical Jesus" have disclosed that, historically speaking, neither the author (or authors) of the creation narrative nor ensuing Judaism nor the first–century followers of the Way subscribed to the belief that, due to the events of Genesis 3, humanity lost the mental faculty necessary for freely responding to divine grace.[59] In other words, if grammatico–historical exegesis, or drawing the meaning out of a text most likely intended by the original author and understood by the original audience via objective literary and historical criteria,[60] is performed upon each of the pertinent Scriptural passages rather than theological eisegesis, or reading preconceived doctrine into each text, it quickly becomes apparent that post–Genesis 3 unregenerate humans in fact possess the freedom to choose between opposites on "matters above," which is precisely what the late–Augustinian doctrine of original sin denies. As for Genesis 3, nothing in the text even remotely suggests that humans surrendered the libertarian freedom with which

---

of a metaphysical order" (*In the Beginning: The Opening Chapters of Genesis*, trans. David G. Preston [Downers Grove, Ill.: InterVarsity Press, 1984], 135).

58. Augustine, *De Correptione et Gratia*, 12.

59. Blocher, *Beginning*, 173–91; Jay A. Holstein, *The Jewish Experience*, 3rd ed. (Minneapolis: Burgess, 1990), 85–90; Jacob Neusner, *Judaism* (New York: Penguin, 2003), 136, 183; N. T. Wright, *Paul: In Fresh Perspective* (Minneapolis: Fortress, 2006), 29–37; F. W. Danker, "Romans V.12: Sin Under Law," *New Testament Studies* 14 (April 1968): 424–39.

60. For any interpretation to be correct, it must be consistent with five criteria: the rules of the literary genre; the obvious sense of the literary context; the facts of the historical–cultural background; the normal meaning of the words in such a context; and the proper grammatical relationship between the words. An expanded treatment of these criteria can be found in William W. Klein, Craig L. Blomberg, and Robert L. Hubbard, Jr., *Introduction to Biblical Interpretation* (Dallas: Word, 1993), 155–214.

they were created; prior to the late–Augustine, whose post–Pelagian reading was admittedly motivated by extrabiblical concerns, no expositor Jewish or Christian interpreted this chapter as either explicitly or implicitly teaching the eradication of free choice.[61] Rather than Augustine's Fall, the chapter was construed as recounting via metaphorical and figurative language the breaking of the initial covenant established by God with the first humans. Thus the eighth–century B.C.E. prophet Hosea indicts the ostensibly disobedient Northern Kingdom and the clandestinely rebellious Southern Kingdom, "Like Adam, they have broken the covenant—they were unfaithful to me" (6:7).[62] The later attempts by sixteenth–century Reformers, notably Luther, Zwingli, and Calvin, to find New Testament precedent for seeing in Genesis 3 a late–Augustinian deeper meaning must historically be judged unsuccessful due to their conceptual misunderstanding at best and redefinition at worst of "spiritual death." For in Scripture the concept of an entity's death spells not its extinction but its separation from the immaterial entity without which it lacks meaningful existence.[63] Hence a human's death denotes the separation of the body from its vivifying soul; by the same token, spiritual death, namely the death of a finite spirit or soul, signifies the separation of that finite spirit from the Infinite Spirit, the Trinitarian God, with which that finite spirit requires union if not to succumb to the existential threat of absurdity.[64] So when Paul asserts that unregenerate humanity is spiritually dead or dead "in transgressions and sins" (Eph. 2:1), he means that their spirits are alienated from the Divine Spirit and thereby relegated to lives of pointlessness; this is why Paul interchanges phrases connoting spiritual death with such descriptive phrases as "separate from Christ," "without hope and without God in the world" (2:12), "living in the futility of their thinking" (3:17), and "darkened in their understanding and separated from

---

61. As conclusively demonstrated by Jaroslav Pelikan, *The Emergence of the Catholic Tradition (100–600)*, Vol. 1 of *The Christian Tradition: A History of the Development of Doctrine* (Chicago: University of Chicago Press, 1971), 279–86.

62. A text of which the followers of the Way were thoroughly cognizant, as it constituted the implicit background that Jesus called to mind in his frequently issued challenge to gain understanding of its preceding sentence: "But go and learn what this means: 'I desire mercy, not sacrifice' [Hos. 6:6]; for I have not come to call the righteous, but sinners" (Mt. 9:13; *cf.* 12:7).

63. Colin Brown, ed., *The New International Dictionary of New Testament Theology*, 3 vols. (Grand Rapids, Mich.: Zondervan, 1975), 1:443–46.

64. The point of the book of Ecclesiastes, which poignantly illustrates the futility of life "under the sun," a poetic way of saying "*sans* God," in an attempt to persuade the reader to embrace a purposeful life "under God."

the life of God" (3:18). Although exempting the Magisterial Reformers from mishandling the Scriptures, as they lacked the tools of modern grammatico–historical hermeneutics, the aforementioned reasons render it historically irresponsible for contemporary exegetes, regardless of confessional allegiances, to equate spiritual death with the extinction of the libertarian cognitive faculty, a notion utterly foreign to the thought of Paul.

The *prima facie* interpretation of several Scriptural texts not merely imply but define the presence of libertarian human freedom—namely, the freedom to choose between opposites on matters pertaining to salvation and other forms of spiritual good—in unregenerate humans. Granting in grammatico–historical fashion the sense of literary context as well as the normal connotations of and relationships between terms, it follows that any text where God offers people a choice requires that people have the mental faculty necessary for making that choice.[65] Denying this inference not only makes the text meaningless, but it carries the deleterious theological consequences of either invalidating God's omniscience (for wrongly thinking people could make the impossible choice) or God's veracity (for intentionally deceiving people into thinking they could make a choice which he knew they lacked the ability to make and for inspiring a Scripture which foisted this ruse upon its readers). Since the biblical evidence for libertarian free will is exhaustive, a representative sample of texts covering the breadth of biblical Jewish and early Christian history will be given. The concept of libertarian freedom is plainly seen in the Torah's frequent insistence that all members of national Israel perform divinely dictated spiritual goods and avoid the spiritual evils for which God would displace the natives of Canaan. Thus Moses exhorts the Israelites before entering the Promised Land, most of whom were, according to New Testament theology, unregenerate, concerning their keeping the 623 *mitzvoth*[66] which constituted the terms of the covenant between God and the Jewish nation:

Now what I am commanding you today is not too difficult for you, nor

---

65. Irenaeus, in *Against Heresies*, 4.37.2–3, averred in the face of Gnostic determinism that the prophetic rebukes for spiritual evil and exhortations to spiritual good presupposed human ability to obey, as did the religious teachings of Jesus. Hence both Old and New Testaments substantiated τὸ αὐτεξούσιον (the self–determination) of humanity.

66. My enumeration of *mitzvoth* ("commandments, regulations"; sg. *mitzvah*) assumes that the Decalogue is distinct from the other 613 instructions divinely given to the Jewish people through Moses which span Exodus through Deuteronomy (10 + 613 = 623); however, some scholars view the Decalogue as a summation of these 613 instructions and thus present a total smaller by ten.

is it out of reach. It is not in heaven, so that you have to ask, "Who will ascend to heaven to get it and proclaim it to us so that we may obey it?" Nor is it beyond the sea, so that you have to ask, "Who will cross the sea to get it and proclaim it to us so that we may obey it?" No—the word is very near you, in your mouth and in your heart, so that you may obey it. Behold, I set before you today life and prosperity, and death and destruction. For I command you today to love Yahweh your God, to walk in his ways, and to keep his commands, decrees, and laws; then you will live and increase, and Yahweh your God will bless you in the land you are entering to possess. But if your heart turns away and you are not obedient, and if you are drawn away to worship other gods and serve them, I declare to you this day that you will certainly be destroyed. You will not live long in the land you are crossing the Jordan to enter and possess. This day I call heaven and earth as witnesses against you that I have set before you life and death, blessings and curses. So choose life in order that you may live, you and your descendants (Deut. 30:11–19; *cf.* 11:26–28).[67]

Such freedom between spiritual opposites characterizing libertarian choice is echoed by Joshua in his ultimatum after the Conquest for the spiritually fickle tribes to follow Yahweh rather than the polytheistic deities of the surrounding nations: "Choose for yourselves this day whom you will serve, whether the gods your forefathers served beyond the Jordan, or the gods of the Amorites . . . [or] Yahweh. . . . Throw away the gods your forefathers worshiped beyond the Jordan and in Egypt, and serve Yahweh" (Josh. 24:14–15). Books of the Kethuvim composed during the United Monarchy are similarly replete with commands to choose spiritual good over evil, epitomized by the following Davidic cry: "Whoever of you loves life and desires to see many good days, keep your tongue from evil and your lips from speaking lies. Turn from evil and do good; seek peace and pursue it" (Ps. 34:12–14).

The divine attribute of perfect justice emerges in several contexts indicating that every person will be judged according to their individual responses to God's salvific grace. Since the idea of God's holding people accountable for spiritual choices over which they had no control violates the

---

67. The cogency of our argument is underscored by the fact that the same freedom of spiritual choice was divinely presented to Cain, whom no one would dare posit as regenerate, just before committing the first murder: "Then Yahweh said to Cain . . . 'If you do what is right, will you not be accepted? But if you do not do what is right, sin is crouching at your door. It desires to have you, but you must master it" (Gen. 4:6–7).

very essence of justice, any passage depicting either the divine offer of grace to unregenerate persons (the *initium fidei* in classical theology) or divine judgment for failing to appropriate such grace logically demands that unregenerate individuals possess the faculty whereby grace can be freely embraced. Amidst the Divided Monarchy Isaiah counsels the rebellious children of Israel performing correct sacrificial externals but harboring spiritual depravity within: "If you will and are obedient you will eat the goodness of the land; but if you do not will and if you oppose me, then you will be devoured by the sword, for the mouth of Yahweh has spoken it" (1:19–20). Quite clearly enunciated by God, who cannot lie, is that the willing or notwilling of spiritual good falls under the power of post–Adamic free choice. The same point is implied by Isaiah's prophetic successor, promulgating the divine offer of salvation to the Jewish people at the close of the Babylonian Exile:

> Come, everyone who is thirsty, come to the waters. . . . Listen carefully to me, and eat what is good, and your soul will delight in abundance. Incline your ear and come to me; listen to me, that your soul may live. I will make an everlasting covenant with you, my faithful love promised to David. . . . Seek Yahweh while he may be found; call on him while he is near. Let the wicked forsake her way and the unrighteous person his thoughts. Let all of them turn to Yahweh, and he will have compassion upon each one, and to our God, for he will abundantly pardon (Isa. 55:1–3, 6–7).

The book of Proverbs, probably assembled early in the Second Temple Period,[68] relates edicts of divine judgment unwarranted save for libertarian free will: "Since they hated knowledge and did not choose to fear Yahweh, since they would not accept my advice and spurned my rebuke, they will eat the fruit of their ways" (vv. 29–31). Moreover, the Apocryphal or Deuterocanonical literature demonstrates the pervasiveness of the belief in libertarian free will among the Jewish people during the Intertestamental Period. Holding, in concurrence with our grammatico–historical exegesis, that libertarian freedom follows inescapably from the Hebrew Biblical text, the Intertestamental authors often expressed their conviction through commentary, of which Sirach's remarks on Deuteronomy 30:11–19 are characteristic.

> Do not say, "It was the Lord's doing that I fell away"; for God does not do what he hates. Do not say, "It was God who led me astray"; for he

---

68. Bernhard W. Anderson, *Understanding the Old Testament*, 4th ed. (Upper Saddle River, N.J.: Prentice Hall, 1998), 516–17.

has no need of the sinful. The Lord hates all abominations; such things are not loved by those who fear him. It was he who created humankind in the beginning, and he left them in the power of their own free choice. If you choose, you can keep the commandments, and to act faithfully is a matter of your own choice. He has placed before you fire and water; stretch out your hand for whichever you choose. Before each person are life and death, and whichever one chooses will be given (Sir. 15:11–17).

In the first century B.C.E., the Pharisaic rabbinic academies proceeded further by applying midrash, an interpretive method which surpasses the limits intrinsic to literal exegesis in extrapolating doctrine consistent with but lying beyond authorial intent, upon the pertinent biblical and intertestamental passages to formulate an entirely dualistic theological anthropology. Championed by Rabbi Hillel (*c.* 50 B.C.E.–10 C.E.), this anthropology held that each human possesses two opposite dominating principles toward which she or he can be fundamentally oriented—either the *yetzer tov* (the good tendency) or the *yetzer ra* (the evil tendency)—rendering one's whole life a battleground between these forces upon which the individual must struggle to master the latter with the former.[69] During the time of Jesus the *yetzer* model of humanity was perpetuated through Hillel's grandson Rabbi Gamaliel (8–52 C.E.), under whom the Apostle Paul studied, and which in turn would be utilized by Paul as a springboard for his own reflections upon the ontological impact of humanity's initial alienation from God and the means by which any resulting damage could be overcome. As the greatest dominical interpreter, Paul reshaped the rabbinic categories around the memorizable oral forms of the Jesus tradition, to the enscripturation of which we now turn.[70]

Nowhere are the two categories of texts whose conjunction with divine justice entail libertarian human freedom better exemplified than in the preaching of the historical Jesus. Treating the first category, Jesus' Sermon on the Mount admonished the Jewish crowds to find salvation by embracing his Way of being the people of God rather than embarking, as did many of his hearers, on a path of "holy violence" against the Roman occupying forces which would ultimately lead to damnation.[71]

---

69. H. H. Ben–Sasson, ed., *A History of the Jewish People* (Cambridge, Mass.: Harvard University Press, 1976), 283–84.

70. David Wenham, *Paul: Follower of Jesus or Founder of Christianity?* (Grand Rapids, Mich.: Eerdmans, 1995), 380–410.

71. N. T. Wright, *The Original Jesus: The Life and Vision of a Revolutionary* (Grand Rapids, Mich.: Eerdmans, 1996), 48–55.

Enter through the narrow gate; for wide is the gate and broad is the road that leads to destruction, and many enter through it. But small is the gate and narrow is the road that leads to life, and only a few find it. . . . Therefore everyone who hears these words of mine and acts on them is like a wise man who built his house on the rock. The rain fell, the rivers rose, and the winds blew and slammed against that house; yet it did not fall, because it had its foundation on the rock. But everyone who hears these words of mine and does not act on them is like a foolish man who built his house on sand. The rain fell, the rivers rose, and the winds blew and slammed against that house, and it fell with a tremendous crash (Mt. 7:13–14, 24–27).[72]

Obviously Jesus would have no right to use this manner of speech with a throng of non–disciples if they enjoyed no spiritual freedom at all, as such would be disingenuously singing a proverbial song to the dead. The same consideration applies to the dominical pleadings with the faithless, liberally peppered throughout the Gospel of John, to receive salvation by personally committing their lives to him.

"But I, when I am lifted up from the earth, will draw all humanity to myself." Jesus said this to show the kind of death he was going to die. . . . Then Jesus told the crowd, "For a little while longer the Light is among you. Walk while you have the Light, so that darkness will not overtake you. The person who walks in the dark does not know where he is going. While you have the Light, put your trust in the Light, so that you may become children of Light" (Jn. 12:32–36; *cf.* 1:11–13; 3:14–21; 5:24; 6:66–69; 8:31–38; 14:15–24).

That such offering of *gratia ingrediens* by Jesus enjoys multiple independent attestation across the source critical strata is illustrated by its confirmation in the pre–Gospel sayings document Q: "Come to me, all you who are weary and heavy–laden, and I will give you rest. Take my yoke upon you and learn from me, for I am gentle and humble in heart, and you will find rest for your souls. For my yoke is easy and my burden is light" (*cf.* its recension in Mt. 11:28–30).[73] Treating the second category, Jesus asserts that he will judge all

---

72. The historical criterion of form criticism establishes the authenticity of this passage, as it originally comes from Q 6:47–49, thus falling within the first layer of the Jesus tradition.

73. This text's origin in Q, despite its anomalous Lucan omission, is guaranteed by its starkly non–Matthean and otherwise inexplicable redaction in the Gospel of Thomas 90.

humans on the basis of their response to him: "But I say to you, everyone who confesses me before other people, the Son of Man will also confess that person before the angels of God; but everyone who denies me before other people will be denied before the angels of God" (Lk. 12:8–9). In addition to meeting the criterion of coherence, this passage emanates from Q, and the same sentiment is multiply attested by the independent testimonies of Mark 8:38, John 5:22–27, and the M source (as evinced in Mt. 7:21–23). Here Jesus' promised standard of "judging not according to appearances but according to righteous judgment" (Jn. 7:24) in determining people's eternal destiny necessitates his acknowledgment by the redeemed when they could have freely chosen rejection and his rejection by the condemned when they could have freely chosen acknowledgment.[74] Likewise Jesus' warning to the Jewish ruling elites, "Therefore I said to you that you will die in your sins, for unless you believe that I AM (ἐγώ εἰμι),[75] you will die in your sins" (Jn. 8:24), could be legitimately countered on the day of judgment by appeal to the unimpeachable prophetic maxim (Mt. 5:17–18; Jn. 10:35) that "the descendant will not share the guilt of the father" (Ezek. 18:20) if these religious leaders were born due to Adam's sin without the mental capacity for such faith.

The Pauline Dichotomy Between the Flesh and the Human Spirit

Availing himself of the rabbinic categories, Paul accepted that the *yetzer tov* and *yetzer ra* amounted to the two polarities comprising the Scripturally defined and Jesuanically affirmed libertarian freedom with which humans are endowed necessarily by virtue of the *imago Dei*. While the exegesis of the Genesis creation narrative will be dealt with in chapter six, suffice it to say here that Paul displays no trace of thinking that the events of Genesis 3 caused any change in human nature in and of itself; by contrast, the ontological change introduced into the human situation by Adam and Eve and

---

74. Jesus certifies the latter inference by overtly juxtaposing his desire for the beatitude of the condemned with their free rejection of his proffered salvation: "How often I have longed to gather your children together, as a hen gathers her chicks under her wings, *but you were not willing*" (Mt. 23:37; emphasis mine).

75. Associated by the majority of New Testament scholars with Exodus 3:14, I AM WHO I AM (אֶהְיֶה אֲשֶׁר אֶהְיֶה; Ἐγώ εἰμι LXX), the supreme self-revelation of God in Torah.

then freely shared by their posterity in following their example[76] was one of separation from God, hence bringing alienation from the Holy Spirit, the Trinitarian Person whose theandric role it is to motivate and spur on individuals to follow the impulses of the *yetzer tov*. Under Gamaliel Paul also learned the thought of Philo of Alexandria (20 B.C.E.–50 C.E.), the greatest Jewish philosophical theologian of the first century C.E., who embraced a

---

76. Here we must call attention to a pivotal mistranslation of Romans 5:12 first appearing in the Vulgate which has plagued and still plagues accurate understanding of this verse. Due to their heavy reliance on Augustine, a Vulgate reader whose Greek illiteracy has become legendary, both the Magisterial Reformers and the KJV translators unwittingly read this verse as they had recurrently perceived it in the Augustinian corpus and not as it actually appeared in the original Greek. The Vulgate renders this passage, "[P]ropterea sicut per unum hominem in hunc mundum peccatum intravit er per peccatum mors et ita in omnes homines mors pertransiit *in quo* omnes peccaverunt" (Therefore, just as sin entered the world through one man, and death through sin, and so death spread to all men, *in whom* all sinned; emphasis mine), such that all humans sinned in Adam. Calvin famously proposed three ways in which this concept could be understood. First, it follows from Adam's federal headship over the human race, in the same way that a king would take a fief from a nobleman and all his heirs if the nobleman, upon receiving the fief, acts against the king; the descendants must carry the guilt of their forefather in both cases. Second, Calvin postulated that every human being was consciously present with Adam in seminar form (*i.e.* in his loins) and freely chose along with him to rebel against God, thus justly accruing guilt and surrendering libertarian freedom. Third, Calvin asserted that even if one finds his previous two explanations unconvincing, original sin would comprise a mystery that must be accepted by virtue of its presence in Romans 5:12 (*Institutes*, 2.1.8). The Calvinist bent of the KJV translators is evident in their amplification of the Vulgate error, interpreting the text as stating that all humans have sinned prior to birth by virtue of Adam's sin: "[B]y one man sin entered into the world . . . *for that* all have sinned" (emphasis mine). However, the Greek text actually reads, "Διὰ τοῦτο ὥσπερ δι' ἑνὸς ἀνθρώπου ἡ ἁμαρτία εἰς τὸν κόσμον εἰσῆλθεν καὶ διὰ τῆς ἁμαρτίας ὁ θάνατος, καὶ οὕτως εἰς πάντας ἀνθρώπους ὁ θάνατος διῆλθεν, ἐφ' ᾧ πάντες ἥμαρτον" (Therefore, just as sin entered the world through one man, and death through sin, and in this way death spread to all men, *because* all sinned; emphasis mine), as correctly translated in all modern versions. In other words, death spread to all humans *because* they freely chose to sin by following the example Adam had brought into the world, not that they sinned simply by being descended from Adam.

tripartite understanding of the soul[77] divided thus: reason, the faculty that calculates and decides; memory, the capacity to store encountered data of all sorts; and spirit, the courageous and valiant inclination to live in harmony with Plato's Good, which Philo defined as the moral nature of Yahweh. However, due to humanity's relation to the animal kingdom, Plato, and then Philo, claimed that the human body naturally presents the soul with desire or appetite, in the sense of bare physical and instinctive craving, which the soul is then free to accept, ignore, or reject. Paul embraced the soul's tripartite structure and its relation to the body while renaming and amplifying each component in line with Jewish anthropology. While retaining the language of πνεῦμα (spirit), Paul termed the reason νοῦς (mind) and the desire or appetite σάρξ (flesh, sinful nature). Far more significantly, Paul identified the σάρξ with the *yetzer ra* and the πνεῦμα with the *yetzer tov*, giving rise to his famous dichotomy between the flesh and the spirit, with the mind left to choose which to follow.[78]

In his Epistle to the Romans Paul makes it quite clear that, in his assessment, each person is born into exactly the same situation as were the newly created Adam and Eve—namely, spiritually alive, rooted in, or using the dominical metaphor, connected to, God, the tripersonal ground of being–itself,[79] just as the branches are connected to a vine (Jn. 15:4–8). Thus the

---

77. Which Philo borrowed from Plato (*The Republic*, 4.2) and then successfully harmonized with Jewish sentiments.

78. So Paul J. Achtemeier, Joel B. Green, and Marianne Meye Thompson, *Introducing the New Testament: Its Literature and Theology* (Grand Rapids, Mich.: Eerdmans, 2001), 294–95: "[Paul] uses vocabulary associated with the popularized Platonism that characterized much of the intellectual framework of the Greco–Roman world (*e.g.* the contrast between flesh and spirit in Rom 8:9–13). . . . Yet Paul puts that vocabulary and those attitudes in a framework that is quite different from those of the secular world . . . [namely] Pharisaic thought, and his concern for entering and remaining in a right relationship with God reflects the very core of the Pharisee's approach to both covenant and law."

79. To my mind Tillich is quite right to describe God as the suprapersonal ground of being–itself, but his Kantian *Weltanschauung* of the universe as a closed system coupled with his logical positivism hinders him from drawing the implications, metaphysically necessary if the universe is instead an open system, which has in the past century been scientifically proven by the cosmological discovery of the Big Bang, of what it means to be the suprapersonal ground of being–itself. Then the philosophical outworkings of this description yield a dramatic recovery, remarkable via general revelation alone, of many of the specifically Christian divine attributes. We shall see in chapter five that the only way for God to be suprapersonal, without the term becoming theological double–talk

"default situation" of every human being is a right relationship with God.[80] However, at some point after every person apprehends the moral law written on their hearts (Rom. 2:14–15), they all freely choose to follow the σάρξ by violating that law,[81] even though it were logically possible for each one to live a sinless life.[82] Stemming inescapably from the divine justice, this choice separates each person from God, thus rendering them spiritually dead: while no change in the πνεῦμα has transpired, it is now severed from the Holy Spirit who drastically strengthens its appeal to the νοῦς. At this point Paul's insistence should be noted that the body naturally supplies the attractiveness of the σάρξ but not the πνεῦμα, which is designed to receive its attractiveness (one that completely trumps the attractiveness of the σάρξ) from the Holy Spirit. Hence the mind is faced with the libertarian free, but unequally motivated, choice to follow the flesh or the spirit, where the former enjoys a disproportionately strong appeal to that of the latter. Accordingly a person following the initial choice for σάρξ—of which any such choice is Paul's definition of ἁμαρτία (sin)—is designated as unregenerate. Although logically possible for an unregenerate person to always choose the impulses of the spirit and resist those of the flesh, God knows in his *scientia media* that no one will actually so choose. Instead the unregenerate will carry out the impulses of both the flesh and the spirit, with the number and magnitude of fleshly actions, not surprisingly, abundantly outweighing the number and magnitude of spiritual actions. In fact, the unregenerate's choices in line with the spirit constitute the exceptions that prove the rule of domination by the flesh. Such domination, appropriately characterized as "slavery to sin" or "marriage to condemnation by the law," as well as its cause are precisely encapsulated by Jesus: "Truly I say to you, everyone who sins is a slave to sin" (Jn. 8:34).

---

for "impersonal," is for God to have non–personhood in one sense and person-hood in another, which is precisely what the doctrine of the Trinity teaches: God's one οὐσία (spiritual substance, essence) has non–personhood (it is not a person), while God's three ὑπόστασεις have personhood (each one is a distinct person).

80. Hence Lawrence Boadt, a proponent of the doctrine of original sin, is forced to admit that Scripture "does not so much teach an original sin, i.e., that Adam passed his guilt on to his descendants, as it stresses the common human tendency toward sinful desires, a weakness present from the beginning" (*Reading the Old Testament* [New York: Paulist, 1984], 121).

81. Which counterfactuals of creaturely freedom God first apprehends via his *scientia media* and subsequently decrees to actualize.

82. A logical possibility, as explained in chapter five, certified by the sinlessness of Jesus.

The solution to the existential predicament of the unregenerate is, for Paul, provided by the propitiatory work of Jesus, as validated by his resurrection, and universally accessible through personal commitment to Jesus, either explicitly (*i.e.* with conscious knowledge of the Christ–event) or implicitly (*i.e.* committing one's life to God while "informationally B.C.E." such that, like the Gentile Job or the Jewish patriarchs, one is unaware that the Second Person of the God to whom one has committed oneself is, in fact, Jesus).[83] The motivation behind making this commitment can be equated with the *initium fidei* supplied by the Holy Spirit. When an individual freely chooses to make this commitment, she or he is reconciled with, and thereby reconnected to, God the Trinity, enabling the Holy Spirit to supply the human spirit with the divinely powered impulse for which it was created. This cluster of divine restorative acts is classed by Paul as "regeneration." Obviously, the strength of the resultant impulses of the spirit now far surpass strength of the flesh, leading to a total reversal of the individual's previous behavior patterns. While the regenerate person may still freely choose to comply with the flesh, such sins become the exceptions that prove the new rule of a life dominated by the spirit, where the number and magnitude of spiritual actions abundantly outweigh the number and magnitude of fleshly actions.[84] Since these spiritual actions are ultimately incited by the Holy Spirit, Paul calls their totality "the fruit of the Spirit" (Gal. 5:22). For these reasons, the regenerate's new Spirit–empowered life is "freedom" (Gal. 5:1) and "marriage to Jesus," for whom the law's condemnation has been put to death by Jesus' atoning work on the cross and the previous marriage to that condemnation consequently annulled. As Jesus explained, "So if the Son sets you free, you will be free indeed" (Jn. 8:36). In the following quotation Paul draws together all the threads of this section into a salvific narrative, where the first person represents the collective experience of the redeemed:

Do you not know, sisters and brothers—for I am speaking to people who know the law—that the law has authority over a person only as long as she or he lives? For example, by law a married woman is bound

---

83. John Sanders, ed., *What About Those Who Have Never Heard?* (Downers Grove, Ill.: InterVarsity Press, 1995), 148; D. A. Carson, *The Gagging of God* (Grand Rapids, Mich.: Zondervan, 1996), 298.

84. This is what the Elder John means in his discourse, "No one who lives in Christ keeps on sinning (not the KJV's finite verb "sins," as ἁμαρτάνει is a continuous aspect verb). . . . The one who keeps on sinning is of the devil, because the devil has been sinning from the beginning. . . . No one who is born of God will continue to sin . . . that person cannot go on sinning, because she or he has been born of God" (1 Jn. 3:6, 8–9).

to her husband as long as he is alive, but if her husband dies, she is re-leased from the law of marriage. So then, if she marries another man while her husband is still alive, she is called an adulteress. But if her husband dies, she is released from that law and is not an adulteress, even though she marries another man. So, my sisters and brothers, you also died to the law through the body of Christ, so that you might belong in marriage to another, to him who was raised from the dead, in order that we might bear fruit to God. . . . Once I was alive apart from law; but when the commandment came, sin sprang to life and I died. I found that the very commandment that was intended to bring life actually brought death. . . . Therefore there is now no condemnation for those who are in Christ Jesus, because through Christ Jesus the law of the Spirit of life set me free from the law of sin and death (Rom. 7:1–4, 9–10, 8:1–2).

Let it be emphasized that Paul's statement "Once I was alive apart from law" stands as the death–knell to any suggestion that the Apostle subscribed to the belief in original sin, thus rendering it historically certain that Augustine, not Paul, was the true originator of this doctrine.

However, Augustine's successors from the Third Ecumenical Council of Ephesus (431) to the outbreak of the Black Death (1347) embraced the term "original sin" while redefining its doctrinal content, thereby accepting the name of the thing but not the thing itself.[85] This reconceptualization of "original sin" as a sinful predisposition rather than a sin itself and thus an impediment that can be overcome via the appropriation of *gratia praeveniens* by libertarian human freedom, as we have previously seen, achieved its most sophisticated articulation with Bernard of Clairvaux. It should be noted that such a moderate version of original sin, harmonious with the biblical record, was embraced by both major theological wellsprings undergirding the present constructive theology, namely, Molina and the Anabaptist movement. Thus no revision of Molina or the Anabaptists on this score is necessary. Nevertheless, adhering to the premise that extrabiblical language is only warranted when it illuminates biblical truth or builds philosophically builds upon a foundation of such truth and never when it obfuscates the meaning of Scripture, I submit that the term "original sin" should be dropped as a description of the post–Genesis 3 condition into which humans are born, as the term is typically associated with such notions as that people have

---

85. Justo L. González, *A History of Christian Thought: From Augustine to the Eve of the Reformation*, rev. ed. (Nashville: Abingdon, 1971), 56–63, 243.

sinned simply by virtue of being human,[86] that human nature compels every individual to sin,[87] and that humans are conceived without the mental faculty necessary for responding to *gratia praeveniens*. Since all of these beliefs are invalidated by a grammatico–historical reading of Scripture, the usage of "original sin" as a biblical description should be judged as causing more harm than good. Thus I propose limiting the definition of "original sin" to the content which the late–Augustine originally assigned to it, thus removing this term from the domain of biblical theology and confining it to the realms of historical and confessional theology, where it serves its proper and indispensable purpose and unequivocally carries its *prima significatio*. When professing to do strict exegesis, therefore, contemporary scholar–teachers would do well in returning to the Pauline anthropology, which enjoys ample explanatory power and scope to account for all the biblical data, and resisting the confessional temptation to replace it with a traditional model lacking both of these virtues.

---

86. Assuming that it is an anthropological statement at all, Psalm 51:5 does not serve as a counterexample to this point, as it in this case would simply describe David's conception and birth with what the rabbis would dub a *yetzer ra* and not his free adherence to its promptings. As explained in chapter seven, Paul duplicates this possibly Davidic sentiment in his affirmation that each human is conceived and indeed lives until death with a σῶμα ψυχικὸν or σαρκικόν (soul–ish or fleshly body), *i.e.* a body which naturally empowers the σάρξ and is thus primarily inclined toward fulfilling the selfish desires of the human's own soul (1 Cor. 15:43–49; 3:3). Alternatively, it is equally possible that Psalm 51:5 is a statement concerning the gravity of David's sins of adultery with Bathsheba and murder of Uriah, in which David affirms that the magnitude of these sins is so deep that it outweighs and thus invalidates every bit of purity he ever possessed, going all the way back to his pristine innocence at his conception and birth.

87. This conclusion cannot be validly supported with biblical affirmations that all humans in fact sin (*e.g.* Eccles. 7:20; Rom. 3:23), as it in no way follows from such passages that their humanity forces them to sin. Conversely, a *prima facie* reading of such texts suggests, and the methodological tenet that every part of Scripture must be understood in the context of the entire canon demands, that God foreknows the counterfactual of creaturely freedom that all humans would freely choose to sin even though it would be entirely possible for them to freely refrain from wrongdoing. Further, this conclusion is philosophically necessary, since it is logically impossible for an all–just God to punish people for actions they were compelled to commit.

Molinism as the Pinnacle of *Philosophia Christi*

Due to our historical examination of the biblical–theological context pertaining to the relationship between the essential libertarian character of human nature and the divine gifts of grace necessary for both conversion and Christian discipleship, we are now in a position to reveal the culminating role of Molina in this doctrinal trajectory through an analysis of his tripartite structure of omniscience. In *scientia naturalis*, the first logical moment of Molina's structure, God knows all *possibilia*, including all necessary truths (*e.g.* the laws of logic), all the possible individuals and world orders he might create, as well as everything that every possible individual *could* freely do in any set of circumstances in which that individual found itself. Molina insists that God does not determine his *scientia naturalis* by willing certain *possibilia* to be true, as this first logical moment precedes any decision or decree of the divine will. Rather, God knows his *scientia naturalis*, as Molina's nomenclature suggests, as indispensable to his very nature, such that God could not lack this knowledge and still be God.[88] Skipping ahead to what would comprise Molina's third logical moment, immediately following the divine creative decree is *scientia libera*, where God fully knows the actual world, including his foreknowledge of everything that will happen therein.[89] So called because this knowledge is predicated upon his free decision of which world to create, God has control over which statements are true and false in *scientia libera*. By choosing to create another world, God would have brought it about that statements which are in fact true would be false and statements which are in fact false would be true. For instance, if God had created a world where Augustine never existed, then all the true statements about things he actually did would be false. Moreover, if God had decided not to make any world at all, then he would not even possess *scientia libera*.[90] Therefore, neither the content nor even the existence of *scientia libera* is necessary to God, as God could lack such knowledge and still be God.

Molina made his revolutionary contribution to philosophical theology with the second logical moment in his structure of divine omniscience; des-

---

88. Molina, *Foreknowledge*, 4.50.17.
89. Ibid., 4.52.9.
90. Ibid., 4.53.4.3. Such is correct, Molina points out, only if discussing positive states of affairs; if the assessment is extended to negative states of affairs, we would affirm God's possession of a *scientia libera* comprised entirely of negative propositions.

ignated *scientia media*, this moment stood between God's *scientia naturalis* and his *scientia libera* and logically preceded his divine creative decree. It is in *scientia media* that Molina asserted God apprehends his counterfactual knowledge, including that which every possible individual *would* freely do in every possible set of circumstances.[91] To illustrate the distinction between the first two moments of divine omniscience, God knew in his *scientia naturalis* that Peter, if placed in the courtyard of the Sanhedrin, could freely affirm or deny Christ, but God discerned in his *scientia media* that Peter would freely deny Jesus under those circumstances. That is not because the circumstances compelled him to deny Jesus—indeed, given Molina's utterly indeterministic doctrine of freedom, all sets of circumstances are necessarily freedom–preserving in character—but rather that God knew which way Peter would freely choose.[92] Parting company from the unbroken philosophical tradition beginning with Aquinas, Molina alleged that God's counterfactual knowledge is logically neither simultaneous with nor analogous to his *scientia libera* (or *visionis*) for two interrelated reasons. First, *scientia media* is prior to the divine creative decree or, in fact, any free decree of God's will. It follows from this, secondly, that the content of *scientia media* does not lie within the scope of God's omnipotence, meaning that God cannot control what he knows via *scientia media*, any more than he can control what he knows via *scientia naturalis*.[93]

These two features of *scientia media* are extremely significant. The first implies that God's counterfactual knowledge of what contingent events would take place in every set of circumstances serves as a prerequisite for God's foreknowledge of what will occur in the world he creates. Both God's decision to actualize a world and his consequent knowledge of what will in fact transpire therein presuppose and depend on his knowing what would occur under any given set of circumstances.[94] Appealing again to his Petrine example, Molina illustrated poignantly the difference between his and Aquinas' concepts of omniscience on this score. For Molina God did not first know, as Aquinas maintained, what Peter would do in the Sanhedrin courtyard and then on this basis know what Peter would have done had he been placed in some other set of circumstances. In precisely the opposite vein, Molina reasoned that prior to God's decision to create any set of circumstances, he knew what Peter would do within every possible set of circumstances; then, given his free decision to actualize a certain set of circum-

---

91. Ibid., 4.52.10.
92. Ibid., 4.51.1, 17–19.
93. Ibid., 4.50.15.
94. Ibid., 4.52.31–32.

stances, God knew what Peter would in fact do.[95] Owing to the fact that *scientia media* is independent of God's will and thus beyond the pale of his omnipotence, the second feature entails that in the same way as God's knowledge of logical truths falls outside his control and is simply given, so his knowledge of what would be the free choices of individual essences if instantiated in various circumstances is simply given and beyond his control.[96] Certainly God could easily preclude the free choice of an individual essence by not instantiating that essence at all or by instantiating that essence in different circumstances in which it would freely choose to do something else. Nonetheless, it is logically impossible for God to alter the fact that if an instantiated individual essence were placed in a certain set of circumstances, it would choose to perform a particular action. For instance, God could prevent Peter's denial of Jesus by not instantiating Peter's individual essence while still actualizing many of the same Jesuanic circumstances or else by instantiating Peter's individual essence in an altered set of circumstances in which that essence would not have disowned Jesus. But since omnipotence does not encompass the ability to do that which is logically impossible, God cannot control the fact that if he were to instantiate Peter's individual essence in a specific set of circumstances, then Peter would freely disown Jesus.[97]

Contingent upon what various libertarian individual essences, if instantiated, would do in various circumstances, the content of *scientia media* cannot be divinely controlled, meaning that there exist a countless number of circumstances discerned by God in his *scientia naturalis*—circumstances logically possible in and of themselves without taking libertarian freedom into consideration—which it is impossible for him to create because instantiated individual essences would not freely choose to cooperate. Thus God's *scientia media* serves to reduce the range of circumstances logically possible in and of themselves to those logically possible for him to create given libertarian freedom.[98] To avoid confusion, Molina designated the

95. Ibid., 4.53.3.7–9.
96. Ibid., 4.49.13.
97. Ibid., 4.52.30.
98. Expressing this insight in philosophical terminology, *scientia media* delimits the higher–order infinite range of circumstances possible *in sensu diviso* to a lower–order infinite subset of circumstances possible *in sensu composito*. The *sensus divisus* (divided sense) analyzes each realm of reality in and of itself and takes other realms into account only insofar as they exert logically prior causal restraints upon the realm in question, while the *sensus compositus* (composite sense) examines the full scope of reality by taking all of its realms into account as well as the interplay, regardless of whether or not such interplay

former as "possible circumstances" and the latter as "feasible circumstances."[99] Not only does *scientia media*, Molina proclaimed, allow for human freedom, but it also furnishes God a means of choosing which compossible, or logically compatible, sets of individual essences and circumstances
to instantiate. For by knowing what instantiated libertarian essences would
do under any circumstances, God is able to construct a world providentially
fine–tuned down to the last detail without violating libertarian human freedom. Such a world would contain divinely strongly actualized circumstances
(*e.g.* miracles and other direct supernatural interventions), decisions freely
performed by the individual essences which God chooses to instantiate,
God's responses to such free creaturely decisions, and further circumstances
generated by creaturely actions, divine reactions, or the combination of
both.[100] By employing his counterfactual knowledge, therefore, God can
bring about his ultimate providential purposes through, not against, free
creaturely decisions, since what creatures would freely do under various circumstances is already factored into the equation by God. Following his deliberation regarding his construction of a world, God issues his creative decree.[101] Finally, on the basis of his decree, God knows in his *scientia libera*
every detail about the world he has chosen, including not only the circumstances he will directly cause and the decisions he will make, but also the
free decisions that humans will make and the contingent circumstances that
will result from those decisions.

We may now summarize Molina's doctrine with the following enumeration of the logical moments comprising his proposed structure of divine omniscience:

1. *Scientia naturalis*: God's knowledge of all possible truths.
2. *Scientia media*: God's knowledge of all counterfactual truths.
    Divine creative decree
3. *Scientia libera*: God's knowledge of all actual truths.

Why should we regard Molina's structure of divine omniscience as correct?
Since all sides concur that God apprehended what Molina dubbed *scientia
naturalis* logically prior to the divine creative decree and that God discerned

---

stems from cause and effect relationships or of the logical order in which it occurs, between the various realms. For a thoroughgoing examination of these
concepts see Alfred J. Freddoso, "Accidental Necessity and Logical Determinism," *Journal of Philosophy* 80 (1983): 257–78.

99. Molina, *Foreknowledge*, 4.53.1.14–20.
100. Ibid., 4.53.3.10–18.
101. Ibid., 4.52.13.

what Molina dubbed *scientia libera* logically posterior to his decree, to prove the accuracy of Molina's scheme it only remains to show that God discerned his *scientia media* logically prior to his decree. We shall accomplish this in two steps: by arguing that if God possesses counterfactual knowledge, then he must have apprehended it logically prior to his decree; and by demonstrating from Scripture that God possesses counterfactual knowledge. First, God's decision to endow humanity with libertarian free will, *i.e.* the ability to choose between opposites in any state of affairs *S*, rules out the possibility that God apprehended his counterfactual knowledge logically posterior to the divine creative decree. For asserting that God apprehends his counterfactual knowledge after his creative decree is equivalent to asserting that God determines, or strongly actualizes, all counterfactual truths, including creaturely decisions, through his *fiat*. In that case, God strongly actualizes what each creature would do in every *S*, which contradicts the creature's God–given ability to choose between opposites in *S*. By *reductio ad absurdum*, therefore, God could only discern counterfactual knowledge before issuing his decree.

Second, the Bible is replete with texts whose grammatico–historical exegesis demand that God possesses counterfactual knowledge. An account frequently cited by Molina portrayed David inquiring of Yahweh through an ephod, a divining device containing the *Urim* and *Thummim*, or differently colored stones respectively connoting an affirmative or negative reply, out of which one of these stones would be drawn.[102]

> David knew that Saul was plotting evil against him, so he said to Abiathar the priest, "Bring the ephod here." David said, "O Yahweh, God of Israel, your servant has surely heard that Saul seeks to come to Keilah and destroy the city on my account. Will the citizens of Keilah surrender me into his hand? Will Saul come down, as your servant has heard? O Yahweh, God of Israel, tell your servant." And Yahweh said, "He will come down." Again David asked, "Will the citizens of Keilah surrender me and my men into the hand of Saul?" And Yahweh said, "They will surrender you." So David and his men, about six hundred in number, departed from Keilah, and they went wherever they could go. When Saul was told that David had escaped from Keilah, he did not go there (1 Sam. 23:9–13).

In this text David queries whether Saul would attack Keilah, where David was stationed, and whether the citizens of the city would deliver David over to Saul. Both times the ephod yielded the *Urim* for an affirmative answer,

---

102. Ibid., 4.53.10.

leading David to flee the city, such that the predictions did not in fact come to pass.[103] Due to the divine attribute of infallibility, we cannot construe the given answers as mistakes on God's part, which they would be if the ephod was mediating to David simple foreknowledge. Rather than simple fore-knowledge, therefore, it follows that God was imparting to David counter-factual knowledge, letting David know that if he were to remain at Keilah, then Saul would come to get him, and that if Saul were to come to get David, then the townspeople would hand David over to Saul. Hence the divinely provided answers were correct despite their nonoccurrence, as they revealed what would occur under different circumstances than the circumstances which in fact obtained. Other prophecies also convey counterfactual knowledge rather than categorical declarations of simple foreknowledge, of which Jeremiah 38:17–18 is representative.[104]

> Then Jeremiah said to Zedekiah, "Thus says Yahweh, the Almighty God, the God of Israel: 'If you indeed surrender to the officials of the king of Babylon, then your life will be spared, this city will not be burned down, and you and your house will live. But if you do not surrender to the officials of the king of Babylon, then this city will be given into the hand of the Babylonians, they will burn it down, and you will not escape from their hand.'"

Hence we find that God, as an omniscient being, knew the free creaturely response to whichever course of action Zedekiah freely chose. As evidenced by the Babylonian Exile, Zedekiah refused to submit and was subsequently killed by Nebuchadnezzar; however, God also knew the counterfactual truth that if Zedekiah had instead submitted to Nebuchadnezzar's officials, then Zedekiah and the city of Jerusalem, which was in fact razed to the ground, would have been spared.

Statements of counterfactual knowledge frequently occur on the lips of Jesus as well. Perhaps the most complete and theologically wide–ranging example is Jesus' denunciation of Tyre and Sidon in Q:

> Then Jesus began to denounce the cities where most of his miracles had been performed, because they did not repent. "Woe to you, Chorazin! Woe to you, Bethsaida! For if the miracles that were performed in you

---

103. Merrill C. Tenney, ed., *The Zondervan Pictorial Encyclopedia of the Bible* (Grand Rapids, Mich.: Zondervan, 1978), 5:850–52.

104. William Lane Craig, "The Middle–Knowledge View," in *Divine Fore-knowledge: Four Views*, eds. James K. Beilby and Paul R. Eddy (Downers Grove, Ill.: InterVarsity Press, 2001), 123–24.

had been performed in Tyre and Sidon, they would have repented long ago in sackcloth and ashes. But I say to you, it will be more bearable on the day of judgment for Tyre and Sidon than for you. And you, Capernaum, will you be exalted to the skies? No, you will be brought down to the depths. For if the miracles that were performed in you had been performed in Sodom, it would have remained until this day. But I say to you, it will be more bearable on the day of judgment for Sodom than for you" (*cf.* Mt. 11:21–24; Lk. 10:13–15).

Here Jesus articulated his knowledge that if he had performed his miracles in different spatio–temporal locations than in those he actually performed, then certain groups of individuals who had not in fact repented and were damned would have repented and been saved, a statement significantly touching on divine predestination. Thus God was aware, prior to his creative decree, that he could have created a different world in which some of the same individuals who are reprobate in our world would have been elect and, notwithstanding this fact, chose to create the actual world instead.[105] This remarkable statement not only illustrates Christ's possession of counterfactual knowledge, but it also reveals that the reprobate citizens of Tyre, Sidon, and Sodom possessed the mental faculty necessary to appropriate salvation, a direct refutation of the late–Augustinian (and subsequently Lutheran and Reformed) concept that the lost, lacking such a faculty, would need to receive again this faculty, exegetically identified with the "new heart" or "new spirit" given by God to his children (Ezek. 36:26),[106] for their salvation to be possible.

That Jesus claimed counterfactual knowledge concerning people's salvation is substantiated via multiple independent attestation in John: "If I had not done among them the signs which no one else did, they would not have sin. But now they have seen these miracles, and they have hated me and my Father as well" (15:24). In a fascinating converse to the Q statement, Jesus disclosed that the Jewish religious leaders would have found salvation if he had presented himself as the human political Messiah they were expecting and thus refrained from performing his deity–attesting miracles, but due to his authenticity in self–disclosure as a divine as well as human person, the religious leaders hated both him and his Father, thereby placing themselves

---

105. Molina, *Foreknowledge*, 4.51.1–3, 13–25.

106. Restoration of the libertarian faculty is also equated by late–Augustinian interpreters with the result of God's transforming people's hearts of stone into hearts of flesh (Ezek. 36:26), writing his law on their hearts and putting it into their minds (Jer. 31:33), and giving them a "heart to know him" (Jer. 24:7).

under God's wrath.[107] Paul reiterated the divine possession of counterfactual knowledge in deriving the corollary that a Messianic presentation consistent with the leaders' reading of the Hebrew Bible would have prevented Jesus' execution: "None of the rulers of this age understood it [the divine wisdom of Jesus' messiahship], for if they had, they would not have crucified the Lord of glory" (1 Cor. 2:8).[108] Finally, when interrogated by Pilate, Jesus divulged counterfactual knowledge concerning what his followers would have done if his messianic program had been political in character:[109]

> Pilate asked, "Am I a Jew? Your own people and the chief priests have delivered you over to me. What have you done?" Jesus answered, "My kingdom is not of this world. If my kingdom were of this world, my servants would have been fighting to keep me from being delivered over to the Jewish religious leaders" (Jn. 18:35–36).

For these reasons, it is indisputable that Scripture attributes the possession of counterfactual knowledge to God. Coupled with the premise that if God has counterfactual knowledge, then he must have apprehended it logically prior to his creative decree, it follows deductively that God has *scientia media*, or pre–decree acquisition of counterfactual knowledge.

Having philosophically demarcated and biblically substantiated the Roman Catholic contribution, we shall now turn to a historical overview of the second major theological wellspring undergirding the present construction.

The Contribution of Radical Reform

The Anabaptist movement was one of three major branches comprising the tremendously diverse Radical Reformation, alongside the Spiritualists, led by the Silesian nobleman Caspar Schwenckfeld (1489–1561), and the

---

107. Ben Witherington III, *The Christology of Jesus* (Minneapolis: Fortress, 1990), 267–78.

108. While the idea of miracles generating rejection rather than acceptance of God seems counterintuitive, it is consistent with their multifaceted role in the Hebrew Bible, including their execution of judgment by exposing the shallowness of individuals' commitment to God, *i.e.* their lack of faith. For a handful of the many examples see Exodus 15:19–17:7, Numbers 11, and 1 Kings 18:16–19:18; note well Yahweh's lament in Numbers 14:11, "How long will these people refuse to believe in me, in spite of all the miraculous signs I have performed among them?"

109. N. T. Wright, *Jesus and the Victory of God*, Vol. 2 of *Christian Origins and the Question of God* (Minneapolis: Fortress, 1997), 604–08.

Anti–Trinitarian Rationalists, which gave birth to the modern Unitarian church. Despite the major theological and socio–political disagreements between these branches, the one defining trait characterizing each as "Radical" was a determination to renew the Christian faith by returning to its *radix*, or root, in the New Testament.[110] Hence all three movements regarded the New Testament Way as their ecclesiastical model, an innovation at a time when their Magisterial contemporaries idealized the Patristic Church, perceived as untainted by the hierarchy and layers of tradition accumulating since the papacy of Gregory the Great (*r.* 590–604) which covered up the true Gospel. In effect, while the Magisterial Reformers wanted to shift the Church back in time to the year 590, the Radical Reformers wanted to bring it back to the year 90, just when the final books of the New Testament canon were being composed. This, however, is where agreement between the three branches ends, as the Anabaptists repudiated as heretical both the Spiritualist emphasis on the "inner light," or new and immediate revelation given by the Holy Spirit to the individual believer which trumped the ethical dictates of the Law,[111] and the *raison d'être* of Anti–Trinitarian Rationalism, since Anabaptism, while not recognizing the authority of the ecumenical confessions, concurred with Luther that the doctrine of the Trinity equaled a conclusion reached by applying deductive logic to Scriptural premises and thus belonged to the category of biblical theology.[112] Achieving greatest popularity in territories now making up Switzerland, Germany, the Netherlands, Austria, the Czech Republic, and Alsace, Anabaptism is distinguished among other sixteenth–century movements by its Christocentrism, a stress on new birth and discipleship in the power of the Spirit, the establishment of believers' churches free from state control, and a commitment to pacifism and issues of social justice. Referring to themselves simply as "Christians" or as "sisters and brothers," their opponents derisively labeled them "Anabaptists" (employing the Greek prefix ἀνα–, "again"), meaning "rebaptizers" or "those who baptize again," due to their conviction that the New Testament stipulated personal commitment to Jesus as essential to salvation and a prerequisite to valid baptism.[113] Since infants could not make a conscious decision to follow Christ, the Anabaptists regarded infant baptism as a contradic-

---

110. George Huntston Williams, *The Radical Reformation*, 3rd ed. (Kirksville, Mo.: Sixteenth Century Essays and Studies, 2000), xxviii–xxx, 385–87, 1253.

111. MacGregor, *Central European Synthesis*, 4.

112. William R. Estep, *The Anabaptist Story: An Introduction to Sixteenth–Century Anabaptism*, 3rd rev. ed. (Grand Rapids, Mich.: Eerdmans, 1996), 182.

113. Ibid., 14.

tion in terms and thus a mere "baby washing" which was "no true baptism at all."[114] While believers' baptism was certainly not the defining issue in Anabaptism, such that some sixteenth–century Radical reformers who practiced rebaptism did not belong to the Anabaptist fold,[115] it functioned as a powerful symbol which crystallized the movement's rejection of Christendom, *i.e.* the civil–ecclesiastical amalgam which had prevailed in Europe since the fourth–century legislation of Christianity as the state religion by Theodosius I.

As a bottom–up or grass–roots association with troubling ramifications for the church–state amalgam at the center of the European social order, Anabaptism faced staunch opposition from those whose vested interests it threatened yet found substantial receptiveness among communities and lay groups which had secretly perpetuated radical beliefs that the official Church presumed dead. Hence Anabaptism was neither Catholic nor Protestant, but the extension of an alternative tradition that had persisted throughout the centuries since the reign of Constantine (306–37), which saw the legalization of Christianity and the inauguration of governmental involvement in ecclesiastical affairs.[116] Although resonating with such "old evangelical brotherhoods" as the *Unitas Fratrum*, Waldensians, Lollards, and Bohemian Brethren, Anabaptism assumed its definitive shape in the context of the sixteenth century;[117] hence Anabaptism can be genealogically described as fathered by medieval evangelicalism and mothered by the Magisterial Reformation,

---

114. Conrad Grebel, *Letter to Thomas Müntzer*, in *Spiritual and Anabaptist Writers*, trans. George Huntston Williams and A. M. Mergal (Philadelphia: Westminster, 1957), 80–81; Pilgram Marpeck, "Confession," in *The Writings of Pilgram Marpeck*, trans. William Klassen and Walter Klaassen (Scottdale, Pa.: Herald Press, 1978), 129–30.

115. Such as Balthasar Hubmaier, who dissented from six of the seven articles in the *Schleitheim Confession* (1527), the charter for the Anabaptist movement, and is for this and other reasons better classified as an evangelical reformer and bridge figure between the Radical and Magisterial Reformations than an Anabaptist (for a comprehensive treatment see my *Central European Synthesis*, 9–13, 264–66), and indisputable outsiders to Anabaptism including Schwenckfeld, his followers, and the Anti–Trinitarian Rationalists in Poland, Czechoslovakia, and Lithuania (Williams, *Radical Reformation*, 627, 1011, 1054, 1090, 1094).

116. Walter Klaassen, *Anabaptism: Neither Catholic nor Protestant* (Waterloo: Conrad Press, 1973), 17–18.

117. Guy F. Hershberger, ed., *The Recovery of the Anabaptist Vision* (Scottdale, Pa.: Herald Press, 1957), 36; Thomas M. Lindsay, *A History of the Reformation*, 2 vols., rep.ed. (Whitefish, Mont.: Kessinger, 2003), 2:441.

leading to its official birth at Zurich on 21 January 1525 among the erstwhile disciples of Huldrych Zwingli. Under Zwingli's leadership, the Reformation in Zurich proceeded along clearly defined lines from its inception in 1519. Surmising that clerical exhortation alone could not accomplish the task of reform, Zwingli merged preaching together with teaching, the disputation, and the legal authority of the Zurich City Council.[118] Further, Zwingli's winsome personality and rare combination of scholarly, humanistic, and pastoral talents attracted a following of gifted young intellectuals, whom the reformer was eager to teach Greek language and literature.[119] Perceiving their love of learning and admiration of Erasmus, in 1522 Zwingli introduced his pupils to the Greek New Testament, which quickly impelled them to grow more zealous for religious change than their instructor. The first signs of fallout between Zwingli and his followers materialized at the Second Zurich Disputation, 26–29 October 1523, over the Eucharist: while the latter insisted on the abolition of the Mass and removal of images in favor of a strictly biblical observance of the Lord's Supper, the former deferred to the will of the City Council regarding the sacramental disposition.[120] So after the young humanist Conrad Grebel pleaded for the immediate implementation of the Synoptic model for the Supper, Zwingli motioned to the Council members and retorted, "My lords will decide whatever regulations are to be adopted in the future in regard to the Mass."[121] This response provoked Simon Stumpf, another hitherto Zwingli student, to sharply rebuke his teacher: "Master Ulrich, you do not have the right to place the decision on this matter into the hands of my lords, for the decision has already been made; the Spirit of God decides."[122] Wryly exploiting his dialectical skills, Zwingli countered by drawing the distinction between truth as determined from study of the Scriptures and the implementation of truth by the Council, without which he claimed any endeavors at reformation would be impossible. Finding this dichotomy disingenuous, Stumpf threatened to publicly expose and oppose such veiled

---

118. Samuel Macauley Jackson, *Huldreich Zwingli* (New York: G. P. Putnam's Sons, 1900), 200–05.

119. Harold Bender, *Conrad Grebel* (Goshen, Ind.: Mennonite Historical Society, 1950), 56–57; Estep, *Anabaptist Story*, 12.

120. John Howard Yoder, "The Turning Point in the Zwinglian Reformation," *Mennonite Quarterly Review* 32 (April 1958): 128–140.

121. *Transcript of the Second Zurich Disputation*, in *Huldreich Zwingli Sämtliche Werke*, eds. Emil Egil and Georg Finsler (Leipzig: M. Heinius Nachfolger, 1908), 2:784.

122. "Meyster Ulrich! Ir hand desse nit gwalt, das ir miren herren das urteil in ir hand gebind, sunder das urteil ist schon geben: der geist gottes urteylet." Ibid.

betrayal of the Scriptures: "If my lords adopt and decide on some other course that would be against the decision of God, I will ask Christ for his Spirit, and I will preach and act against it."[123] This hostility between Zwingli and those who had at one time been his most devoted students proved a mere foreshadowing of things to come.

The next year marked the birthpangs of Anabaptism, in which leaders emerged from a group of young radicals who discerned the full implications of their biblicism. Emerging as their spokesperson was Conrad Grebel, under whose guidance the band grew to a few dozen members notably including Felix Manz, Jörg Cajacob (better known as George Blaurock because he always wore a "blue coat" = *blaurock*), Simon Stumpf, Claus Hottinger, Andreas Castelberg, and Hans Oggenfuss.[124] Grebel, Manz, and Stumpf made several attempts to persuade Zwingli and close collaborator Leo Jud to adopt a more biblical program of reform, all of which met with indifference. Unsuccessful in a last–ditch endeavor to win the Zurich Reformers to their position, the radicals started worshiping clandestinely in each other's residences, most popularly in Manz's house on Neustadt Street, and in the homes of sympathetic friends. Meetings featured Bible study, with expositions given by Manz and Hottinger, and reading the works of, and drawing up correspondences with, Luther, Thomas Müntzer, Andreas Carlstadt, and others.[125] Styling themselves the Swiss Brethren, there soon developed a serious question concerning the validity of infant baptism. Wilhelm Reublin, fellowship member and pastor at Wytikon, a neighboring hamlet to Zurich, appears to have been the first among the Brethren to preach against infant baptism. Within the year, three fathers at Zollikon withheld their children from baptism amid the support of ex–priest Johannes Brötli, sparking both official retaliation by the City Council—Reublin was imprisoned in August and driven out of Zurich and its environs upon his release—and the total commitment of the Brethren.[126] Although their disillusionment with the Swiss Reformation began with Zwingli's unwillingness to demand the observation of the Lord's Supper in a simple apostolic pattern by Christmas Day 1523, by the end of 1524 the protest Brethren movement involved far more than just the Mass or even believers' baptism, but the very nature of

---

123. "So dann mine herren etwas erkennen wurdind und urteylen, das wider das urteyl gottes were, so wil ich Christum umb sinen geist bitten, und wil darwider leren und thûn." Ibid.

124. Leonhard von Muralt and Walter Schmid, eds., *Quellen zur Geschichte der Täufer in der Schweiz* (Zürich: S. Hirzel Verlag, 1952), 1:21.

125. Bender, *Grebel*, 103, 107, 109–24.

126. Estep, *Anabaptist Story*, 19.

the Church itself. The Brethren had reached the Scriptural conviction that the Church ought to be composed exclusively of committed believers and thus visible and not, as the Magisterial Reformers asserted, composed of a mixed multitude of saved and lost, thereby giving rise to the perceived pseudo–distinction between the invisible Church, known only to God, and the visible Church made up of both wheat and chaff.[127] Like that of the New Testament, this true Church was to be made up only of those confessing Christ as Lord (and not merely as Savior) and subsequently baptized, instead of everyone born in a given parish. The baptized would observe the Eucharist in a simple manner, denuded of its "medieval trappings," as a pledge of fraternal love in *anamnēsis* of the one unlimited sacrifice of Jesus.[128] Specialists in Reformation studies have found that the totality of these characteristics was not present anywhere else at this time. In answer to the question "What is the source of this new view of the Christian church?" Grebel poignantly replied, "We were listeners to Zwingli's sermons and readers of his writings, but one day we took the Bible itself in hand and were taught better."[129] It should be emphasized here that, despite its future appellation, the issue of infant baptism was not the defining mark of the new movement, as others, including Zwingli, Oecolampadius, Jud, Müntzer, and the Zwickau prophets, had previously expressed doubt concerning the validity of infant baptism,[130] with the latest scholarship demonstrating Balthasar Hubmaier as the first to act on that doubt no later than 1523 and probably as early as 1521.[131] By contrast, the dispute over the nature of the church and ecclesiastical authority, of which the baptismal disagreement was symptomatic, set the Swiss Brethren apart from any other contemporary group.

The public split between Zwingli and his former students occurred with evident finality at the pivotal 17 January 1525 First Zurich Disputation on Baptism; presided over by the City Council, it not surprisingly declared Zwingli the victor and presented the radicals with a rather disagreeable trilemma: to conform, leave Zurich, or face imprisonment. Choosing the latter, about a dozen men quietly yet resolutely trudged through the snow on 21 January 1525 to Manz's house. In what has been called "the most revolu-

---

127. MacGregor, *Central European Synthesis*, 148–49.

128. Grebel, *Letter to Müntzer*, 76–77.

129. Fritz Blanke, *Brothers in Christ*, trans. Joseph Norden Haug (Scottdale, Pa.: Herald Press, 1961), 14.

130. Albert Henry Newman, *A History of Anti–Pedobaptism*, rep. ed. (Eugene, Ore.: Wipf & Stock, 2004), 70.

131. MacGregor, *Central European Synthesis*, 104–08.

tionary act of the Reformation,"[132] Blaurock requested baptism from Grebel, Grebel baptized Blaurock by affusion, and Blaurock proceeded to baptize all the others present. An eyewitness account relates the details surrounding this dramatic event:

And it came to pass when they were meeting that angst came upon them—indeed they were quite struck within their hearts. Afterwards they fell upon their knees to the Most High God of heaven and called upon him as the Knower of Hearts, and they prayed that he would empower them to carry out his divine will and show them his mercy. For flesh and blood and human advisability did not motivate them, since they fully knew what they would have to suffer for it. Following the prayer, George of the House of Jacob stood up and entreated Conrad Grebel for the sake of God to baptize him with the true Christian baptism upon his faith and outward acknowledgment. And when he knelt down with this request and desire, Conrad baptized him, for at that time there was no ordained minister to perform this act. Then the others entreated George in their turn, asking him to baptize them, which he did. And thus, in great fear of God, together they surrendered themselves to the Name of the Lord.[133]

Each of the newly baptized pledged themselves as true disciples of Christ to live separated from the world, teach the gospel, and hold the faith and then, quite provocatively, "ordained one another to the ministry of the Gospel."[134]

---

132. Estep, *Anabaptist Story*, 14.

133. "Vnd es hat ſich begeben/das ſie ſein beÿeinander gweſen bis die angſt angieng vnd auff ſie kam/Ja Inn Iren Hertzen gedrungen wurden/da haben ſie angfangen Ire Knie zu biegen vor dem höchſtenn Gott im himel/vnd In angerüefft als ein Hertzenkundiger/vnd gebeeten das er Inen wolt geben zu thuen ſein götlichen willen/vnd das er Inen Barmhertzigkait wolt beweiſen/Denn fleiſch vnd bluet oder menſchlicher fürwitz hat ſie gar nit getriben/weil ſie wol gewiſſt was ſie darüber warden dulden vnd leiden müeſſen/Nach dem gebeet iſt der Geörg vom hauß Jacob auffgeſtanden/vnd hat vmb Gottes willen gebeeten den Conrad Grebel/das er In wöll tauffen/mit dem recht Chriſtlichen Tauff/auff ſeinen Glauben vnnd erkanndtnus. Vnd da er nidergekniet mit ſolchem Bitt vnd begeren/hat der Conrad In getaufft/weil dazumal ſonſt keinn verordneter dienner ſolcher wreck zu hanndlen war. Wie nun das beſchehen/haben die andern gleicherweis an den Geörgen begert/das er ſie Tauffen ſoll/welches er auff Ir begeren auch alſo thet/Vnd haben ſich alſo in hoher forcht Gottes miteinander an den Namen des Herren ergeben." A. J. F. Zieglschmid, *Die älteste Chronik der Hutterischen Brüder* (New York: Carl Schurz Memorial Foundation, 1943), 47.

134. "ainer den andern zum dienſt des Euangelij beſtätet." Ibid.

As we have seen, these acts were not unpremeditated but the climactic fulfillment of convictions derived from an intense study of the Scriptures and a sequence of disappointing circumstances. Following this night, Anabaptism spread throughout the Continent, though by no means in a linear progression from Zurich; rather, a host of divergent stimuli caused it to spring up in various places, producing regional variations and some harsh internal disagreements.[135] As a result, there developed four distinct strains of Anabaptism: the Swiss Brethren, a direct expansion of the Zurich community; the German Anabaptists, led by Hans Denck (1500–27) and Pilgram Marpeck (1495–1556); the Hutterites, founded by Jakob Hutter (1500–36) and socioeconomically unique for their community of goods; and the Mennonites, shaped by namesake Menno Simons (1496–1561).[136] Notwithstanding such diversity and fluidity, Anabaptism was, with few (yet highly publicized) exceptions,[137] a coherent movement whose members shared the following convictions, all of which contribute immensely to the groundwork of this systematic theology.

---

135. James M. Stayer, Werner O. Packull, and Klaus Deppermann, "From Monogenesis to Polygenesis: The Historical Discussion of Anabaptist Origins," *Mennonite Quarterly Review* 49 (April 1975): 83–121.

136. Hans–Jürgen Goertz, *The Anabaptists* (New York: Routledge, 1996), 6–35.

137. Most notably the Münster debacle, where the chiliastic Jan Matthys and Jan of Leyden, supposing that Münster marked the site of the New Jerusalem, respectively declared themselves to be Enoch and King David as well as the "two witnesses" of Revelation 11:1–13, seized the city as their base of operation, and attempted to inaugurate the Kingdom of God on earth through "holy violence"; for a full account see Cornelius Krahn, *Dutch Anabaptism: Origin, Spread, Life and Thought (1450–1600)* (The Hague: Martinus Nijhoff, 1968), 80–164. Through an unjustified "guilt by association," this atrocity reinforced the position of those who persecuted the Anabaptists and gave the entire movement a bad name. Of Münster Estep offers the astute assessment: "This fiasco, the most serious aberration of sixteenth–century Anabaptism, has long been exaggerated out of all proportion to its true importance. . . . It belongs on the fringe of Anabaptist life, which was completely divorced from the evangelical, biblical heart of the movement. One should interpret Münster in the light of the whole movement and not the movement in the light of Münster" (*Anabaptist Story*, 3–4).

Key Tenets of Anabaptism

The major Anabaptist convictions can be summarized in six categories, first introduced by Stuart Murray: the Bible, salvation, the Church, evangelism, ethics, and suffering.[138] First, Anabaptists insisted, like most of the Magisterial Reformers, on the authority of the Bible as the inerrant and ultimate standard for faith and practice but disagreed strongly with the Magisterial Reformers about its interpretation and application. Anabaptists prioritized the New Testament, and especially the life and teaching of Jesus, over the Old Testament, and complained that the Magisterial Reformers illegitimately appealed to Old Testament passages to dispense with clear New Testament instructions.[139] Christocentrism proved to be the hallmark of Anabaptist hermeneutics, which took Jesus as its starting point and interpreted all else in light of him. Such was a significant departure from Magisterial hermeneutics which, in the judgment of the Anabaptists, began with doctrinal passages and then attempted to superimpose these onto Jesus as exegetical lenses through which his ministry should be understood.[140] Refusing to treat the Bible as a "flat" book, Anabaptists viewed it as a progressive unfolding of God's purposes, with the New Testament furnishing normative guidelines for ethics and ecclesiology. Hence the Anabaptists challenged the Magisterial Reformers' employment of Old Testament models to substantiate teachings on baptism, war, tithing, church polity, and swearing oaths which appeared to run contrary to the dominical example.[141]

Second, the Anabaptists taught that saving faith equaled a personal commitment to Jesus as both Savior and Lord rather than simply intellectual assent to the Gospel message. This showed itself in a difference of emphasis between the Magisterial and Anabaptist reformers: while the former stressed justification by faith and forgiveness of past sins, the latter stressed regeneration and the power to live as disciples.[142] Consequently, while the Magisterial Reformers were afraid that Anabaptists were reverting to salvation by works, Anabaptists charged the Magisterial Reformers with failure to ad-

---

138. Stuart Murray, "Anabaptists," in *The Dictionary of Historical Theology*, gen. ed. Trevor A. Hart (Grand Rapids, Mich.: Eerdmans, 2000), 15–16.

139. Goertz, *Anabaptists*, 135–39.

140. Stuart Murray, *Biblical Interpretation in the Anabaptist Tradition* (Kitchener, Ont.: Pandora Press, 2000), 48.

141. Ibid., 62.

142. Robert Friedmann, *The Theology of Anabaptism* (Scottdale, Pa.: Herald Press, 1973), 87–88.

drcss ethical issues and toleration of non–Christian behavior in their churches.[143] Thus Menno Simons railed against the Magisterial Reformers:

> Shame on you for the easy–going gospel. . . . If you repent not, and are not born of God, and become not one with Christ in Spirit, faith, life, and worship, then is the sentence of your condemnation on your poor souls already finished and prepared. . . . This is the narrow way through which we all must walk and must enter the straight gate, if we would be saved. Neither emperor nor king, duke nor count, knight nor nobleman, doctor nor licentiate, rich or poor, man nor woman, is excepted. Whoever boasts that he is a Christian, the same must walk as Christ walked. If any man have not the Spirit of Christ, he is none of his. Whosoever transgresseth and abideth not in the doctrine of Christ, hath not God.[144]

As this quotation suggests, Anabaptists underscored the Spirit's work in believers and taught that Jesus was to be followed and obeyed as well as trusted. So Dirk Philips (1504–68), Menno Simons' proverbial second–in–command, proclaimed: "Jesus with his doctrine, life, and example is our teacher, leader, and guide. Him we must hear and follow."[145] On this score, then, the Anabaptists were ahead of their time in perceiving what, in the last century, has been shown by New Testament scholarship to be the common understanding of saving faith presupposed by both Paul and James.

Third, Anabaptists formed free churches, or voluntary churches of committed disciples outside the control of the state. Denying that all citizens should naturally be deemed as members of the church, Anabaptists differentiated believers from unbelievers and challenged all forms of coercion in matters of faith, the most damaging of which they identified as infant baptism. This is because infant baptism gave people who had never personally committed themselves to Christ the false sense of security that they already possessed salvation, thus hampering them from making the salvific commitment.[146] Rejecting clericalism and extreme formalism, their gatherings were charismatic and simply ordered, centered around Bible study and not merely permitting but encouraging women to perform all the same ecclesias-

---

143. C. Arnold Snyder, *Anabaptist History and Theology* (Kitchener, Ont.: Pandora Press, 1995), 236–39.

144. Menno Simons, *Foundation of Christian Doctrine*, in *The Complete Writings of Menno Simons*, trans. J. C. Wenger (Scottdale, Pa.: Herald Press, 1956), 225.

145. Dirk Philips, *Enchiridion*, trans. A. B. Kolb and Dietrich Philips (Alymer, Ont.: Pathway, 1966), 422.

146. Friedmann, *Theology*, 130.

tical functions as men.[147] Such an ecclesiology is reflected in the *Congregational Order* of 1527.

[A]ccording to the command of the Lord and the teachings of his apostles, in Christian order, we should observe the new commandment in love one toward another, so that love and unity may be maintained, which all brothers and sisters of the entire congregation should agree to hold to as follows: 1. The brothers and sisters should meet at least three or four times a week, to exercise themselves in the teaching of Christ and his apostles and heartily to exhort one another to remain faithful to the Lord as they have pledged. 2. When the brothers and sisters are together, they shall take up something to read together. The one to whom God has given the best understanding shall explain it, the others should be still and listen, so that there are not two or three carrying on a private conversation, bothering the others.[148]

Anabaptists also practiced church discipline according to the model articulated in Matthew 18:15-20 and supplemented by the Pauline corpus, especially 1 Corinthians 5.[149] Dubbed "the ban," their implementation of this model is outlined in the 1527 *Schleitheim Confession*, the foundational Anabaptist statement of faith embraced by all four of the movement's distinctive strains.

We have been united as follows concerning the ban. The ban shall be employed with all those who have given themselves over to the Lord, to walk after him in his commandments; those who have been baptized into the one body of Christ, and let themselves be called brothers or sisters, and still somehow slip and fall into error and sin, being inadvertently overtaken. The same shall be warned twice privately and the third time be publicly admonished before the entire congregation according to the command of Christ (Mt. 18). But this shall be done according to the ordering of the Spirit of God before the breaking of bread, so that we may all in one spirit and in one love break and eat from one bread and drink from one cup.[150]

---

147. Kenneth R. Davis, "Anabaptism as a Charismatic Movement," *Mennonite Quarterly Review* 53 (July 1979): 230.

148. *Congregational Order*, in *The Legacy of Michael Sattler*, trans. John H. Yoder (Scottdale, Pa.: Herald Press, 1973), 44–45.

149. MacGregor, *Central European Synthesis*, 13.

150. Michael Sattler, *Schleitheim Confession*, in *Legacy*, 36–37.

While the inextricable interrelationship between the sacraments and church discipline will be spelled out in chapter seven, suffice it to say here that the partakers of the Eucharist at any given moment constitutes the best visible approximation of the redeemed available to humanity.

Fourth, the Anabaptists practiced evangelism, a bottom–up approach quite different from the top–down compulsion advocated by the Magisterial Reformers, who made it their practice to convert the local magistrate, who would then impose (and, according to the Magisterial position, had an obligation to impose) the new belief system upon his subjects by law. Murray correctly points out that "the [Protestant] Reformers did not generally practice evangelism," for "[w]here they had state support, they relied on sanctions to coerce attendance."[151] Presupposing within Protestant territories the identity of church and state, the Magisterial leaders followed the policy of giving "legally converted" individuals spiritual guidance through the parish system rather than evangelizing them as unbelievers.[152] The Anabaptists, historically correct in recognizing this policy as the same taken by the post–Nicene Patristic Church upon the legal enforcement of Christianity as the state religion, strenuously opposed this conception of church and state and rejected all use of coercion. Instead, Anabaptists undertook a spontaneous missionary enterprise to evangelize Europe, traveling great distances, preaching in homes and fields, interrupting state church services, baptizing converts, and planting churches. Despite its contemporary prevalence, such evangelism was perceived as outrageous in the sixteenth century, since it was undertaken by formally untrained laity rather than clergy and disregarded official parish and national boundaries.[153] Thus it is directly to the Anabaptists that Christians today owe a deep debt of gratitude for restoring the missionary impulse of Jesus (Mt. 28:18–20; Acts 1:7–8) and the New Testament Way.

Fifth, Anabaptists endeavored to live as citizens of the Kingdom of God, which entailed their social deviancy and challenge of contemporary mores. Appealing to the New Testament example, seen especially in Acts 4:32–35, 2 Corinthians 8–9, and 1 Timothy 5:3–16, they disputed any interpretation of private property which left any believer in poverty. With the exception of the communitarian Hutterites, the Anabaptists retained personal ownership but asserted that their possessions were not their own but were available to any-

---

151. Murray, "Anabaptists," 16.
152. Diarmaid MacCulloch, *The Reformation* (New York: Penguin, 2003), 133–39.
153. Snyder, *History and Theology*, 190–93.

one as they had need.[154] As attested by the interrogators of German Anabaptist preacher Hans Hut, "He persuaded no one to sell his goods. However he taught, that whoever had a surplus should help the needy. True, some who were well–to–do sold some acres, vineyards and other property and shared it with the brothers who were poor. However there were no plans to move to any designated place."[155] The Anabaptist celebration of the Lord's Supper featured confirmation of this mutual commitment:

> Of all the brothers and sisters of this congregation none shall have anything of his own, but rather, as the Christians in the time of the apostles held all in common, and especially stored up a common fund, from which aid can be given to the poor, according as each will have need, and as in the apostles' time permit no brother to be in need.[156]

Moreover, while the teetering Holy Roman Empire faced the imminent threat of invasion by the Ottoman Turks, the Anabaptists decried violence and championed the pacifism and nonviolent resistance lying at the heart of the Sermon on the Mount. Hence Grebel portrayed the Swiss Brethren: "Neither do they use worldly sword or war, since all killing has ceased with them."[157] Here it should be noted that Anabaptism marked a return to the universal refusal of Christians in the pre–Constantinian era to participate in war or serve in the military, a refusal finally eroded with the just war theory of Augustine.[158] On the basis of Matthew 5:33–37, Anabaptists also refused to swear oaths or pledge loyalty to secular authorities, thus further causing them to be looked upon as seditionists even while reproducing the model of the Ante–Nicene Church. For these reasons, Anabaptist ethics aimed at building an alternative community which followed the example of Jesus regardless of social consequences, thus constituting the body of Christ and historically perpetuating the Incarnation by transforming society from the bottom up.[159]

Sixth, Anabaptists considered suffering for obedience to Christ as inevitable and biblical, such that it would be impossible for anyone to genuinely follow Jesus and avoid persecution. Anabaptist exegesis took quite literally

---

154. Estep, *Anabaptist Story*, 255.

155. *Interrogation of Hans Hut*, in *Anabaptism in Outline*, ed. Walter Klaassen (Scottdale, Pa.: Herald Press, 1981), 233–34.

156. *Congregational Order*, 45.

157. Grebel, *Letter to Müntzer*, 80.

158. Myron S. Augsburger, *The Peacemaker* (Nashville: Abingdon, 1987), 22.

159. Snyder, *History and Theology*, 47–50.

the Pauline alert: "But everyone who wants to live a godly life in Christ Jesus will be persecuted" (2 Tim. 3:12). That the Magisterial and Catholic Reformers by and large avoided persecution proved that they were not true disciples of Jesus and were constructing a counterfeit church.[160] Such an assessment was further reinforced by these Reformers' unswerving persecution of the Anabaptists, as illustrated by the lengthy denunciation of Dirk Philips:

> For this is the nature, character, and skill of Satan, that he transforms himself into an angel of light, 2 Cor. 11:14. Therewith he hides his guile and hypocrisy, disguises and conceals his ministers, and sets them before the world in a beautiful appearance of piety. For what has a more beautiful appearance than Satan in all hypocritical and unspiritual work . . . who pride themselves more of the gospel and Christendom, of true theology and knowledge of Holy Scripture than do the highly praised wise ones of the world. . . . So they alone are teachers and masters of Scripture and yet themselves have neither received nor . . . been in the school of Christ, and they have not had the true master teacher, namely the Holy Spirit. Yes, they have neither seen him nor known him. . . . Therefore then they are not ministers of Christ who are so great and highly regarded by the world, who are seated on high and who persecute others purposely. For that is far from Jesus Christ and from his gentle divine spirit, Matt. 13:28. It is also far from all Christians who have the mind and spirit of Christ. It is not Christlike but tyrannical to persecute, to expel, to strangle the people because of faith and religion. Those who do this are certainly a remnant of the pharisaical race [but] those who are true teachers must be tested with the cross.[161]

Although denying that they were apostles, as they regarded the apostolic office as foundational to the Church and thus non–repeatable (Eph. 2:20), Anabaptists believed themselves to be in precisely the same position in relation to the Church as were the apostles[162]—that is to say, the Great Commission was directly addressed to them, such that they bore the obligation, in strict adherence to the *ordo apostolis*, to gather the Church through preach-

---

160. Franklin Hamlin Littell, *The Anabaptist View of the Church* (Boston: Starr King Press, 1958), 63.

161. Dirk Philips, *The Sending of Preachers or Teachers*, in *The Writings of Dirk Philips*, 1504–68, trans. Cornelius J. Dyck, William E. Keeney, and Alvin J. Beachy (Scottdale, Pa.: Herald Press, 1992), 1:2, 16–17.

162. Estep, *Anabaptist Story*, 244.

ing, making disciples, baptizing, and teaching, all the while being hated and maltreated by the world for the sake of Christ (Mt. 10:22; Jn. 15:18–21). In short, Anabaptists viewed suffering as a necessary mark of the true Church. Tragically, their movement was nearly drowned out in blood, with over 10,000 Anabaptists martyred by Catholic, Lutheran, and Reformed authorities alike during the Reformation era (1517–1648).[163] Estep concisely explains the rationale behind these atrocities and the methods used to carry them out:

> Church and state were considered indivisible in both Catholic and Protestant areas. Any deviation from the established churches was considered a crime of treason. Rebaptism, sedition, anarchy, blasphemy, sacrilege, and hypocrisy were lumped together indiscriminately under the label of treason. Often there was not the slightest symbol of justice in the treatment of the accused. Frequently an accusation of Anabaptism was tantamount to condemnation. Imprisonment and torture were normally followed by death. Drowning, sword, and stake were all used to exterminate the hated movement.[164]

Notwithstanding this harassment, Anabaptism persisted and remains influential today through both its direct and indirect descendants. Direct or lineal descendants include the Brethren confessions (Church of the Brethren, Brethren Church, Brethren in Christ), the Mennonites, Hutterites, and Amish, while indirect descendants, which embody major features derived in some way from Anabaptism, encompass the Arminians, Baptists, and Methodists. In 1948 the World Council of Churches calculated that Anabaptist descendants accounted for nearly one–quarter of its membership.[165] Moreover, if the rapidly growing Pentecostal movement is designated as of Anabaptist descent, as forcefully argued by Kenneth R. Davis,[166] then Anabaptism constitutes a vital and powerful force in contemporary Christianity alongside its Catholic, Protestant, and Orthodox branches.

---

163. Goertz, *Anabaptists*, 121, 127.

164. Estep, *Anabaptist Story*, 29.

165. Huibert van Beek, ed., *A Handbook of Churches and Councils: Profiles of Ecumenical Relationships* (Geneva: WCC Publications, 2006), 382.

166. Davis, "Anabaptism as a Charismatic Movement," 219–34, provocatively goes on to postulate that the Anabaptists were charismatics and that Pentecostalism forms the closest contemporary equivalent to Anabaptism.

Objective of the
Molinist–Anabaptist Synthesis

The consistent testimony of the New Testament documents indicates that an inextricable weddedness between right thought and right action forms a necessary requirement for Kingdom living. Such an interrelationship runs decidedly contrary to modern fideistic definitions of relevance and practicality as "what helps people live right now" or "what gets results" regardless of their respective ontological bases in reality, both of which run the strong risk of fostering self–delusion.[167] Rather, we propose that a biblical understanding perceives relevancy as the overarching umbrella concept for a host of corollary concepts including practicality, such that anything biblically practical must already be relevant but not vice versa. Moreover, our perspective defines a thing or state of affairs as relevant if and only if it has the power to impart some good to its recipient, while it classifies as practical the subset of relevant things or states of affairs which comprehensibly shows individuals in general how to directly realize their power. According to the realist metaphysic upon which the biblical worldview stands, disciplines like theology, history, and philosophy and all acts of learning such disciplines constitute goods in and of themselves and so are relevant by their very natures, thus placing them within the highest dimension of relevancy. With this in mind, it is obvious that Christians—including many pastors—who make such derisive and false remarks as "I'm not interested in theology or church history, all products of dead white European males; I want something relevant for people today" are literally speaking nonsense and betraying the trust God has assigned them. As overseers of "the church of the living God, the pillar and foundation of the truth" (1 Tim. 3:15), ecclesiastical leaders must also avoid creating a false dichotomy between theory and application and teaching so–called "practical" messages for daily life without biblical substantiation, thus robbing these messages of true practicality and pulling the rug out from under their parishioners. On the contrary, it is the job of those who possess the discernment to realize the benefits of complex goods without simplification, such as pastors and scholar–teachers, to take that which is

---

167. The impulse, typically (whether rightly or wrongly) associated with postmodernism, to allege that "it doesn't matter whether a purportedly historical truth of Scripture actually happened; it only matters if belief therein enables people to better face the existential storm" is a disguise which furnishes its proponent the illusion of grasping valid goods. In actuality, this appearance is a thin veneer overlaying the ultimate pointlessness endemic to all antifoundationalist epistemology.

relevant and make it practical. In other words, Christian academics must use the raw materials of theology, history, and philosophy and present them in such a way that their goods are readily grasped through Kingdom obedience by the layperson or non-specialist. Nowhere is the cause–effect structure of this vocation better presented than by Paul: "We demolish arguments and every pretension that sets itself up against the knowledge of God, and we take captive every thought *to make it obedient to Christ*" (2 Cor. 8:5; emphasis mine). To this end, our systematic theology will be an exercise in "applied Christian thought," with the authentic discipleship embodied by Anabaptism fitting like a hand in the theoretical glove of Molinism. We shall thus fuse *scientia media*, quite possibly the single most fruitful theological construct ever discovered, with the sixteenth–century believers' church tradition which not only attempted but succeeded in implementing a Jesus–shaped Christianity requiring faithfulness to the Sermon on the Mount. The ultimate aim of our construction, therefore, is to illuminate Scriptural truth in a way that both magnifies its philosophical brilliance and equips individuals and congregations to grow in the grace and knowledge of Jesus by practicing "true and pure religion" (Jas. 1:27) under his Lordship.

Chapter 2

Scientia Media According to Molina, Not Arminius

A Genuine Rapprochement Between Sovereign Individual Predestination and Libertarian Human Freedom

Scientia media (middle knowledge), the second of three logical moments comprising divine omniscience, is God's knowledge of all true counterfactual propositions, or more precisely, conditional propositions in the subjunctive mood (*i.e.* statements of the following form: if something *were* the case, when in fact it may or may not be the case, then something else *would be* the case). Although anticipated earlier in the sixteenth century by the radical *doctor theologiae* Balthasar Hubmaier (1480–1528)[1] and the Jesuit philosopher Pedro da Fonseca (1528–1599),[2] this doctrine assumed its complete form under the second–generation Catholic reformer Luis de Molina (1535–1600) in his massive Latin tome *Liberi Arbitrii cum Gratiae Donis, Divina Praescientia, Providentia, Praedestinatione et Reprobatione Concordia* (The Compatibility of Free Choice with the Gifts of Grace, Divine Foreknowledge, Providence, Predestination, and Reprobation). Of this

---

1. Especially in his 1527 treatises *Von der Freiheit des Willens* and *Das andere Büchlein von der Freiwilligkeit*, as I demonstrated in Kirk R. MacGregor, "Hubmaier's Concord of Predestination with Free Will," *Direction: A Mennonite Brethren Forum* 35.2 (2006): 279–99.

2. Robert Merrihew Adams, "Middle Knowledge and the Problem of Evil," in *The Virtue of Faith and Other Essays in Philosophical Theology* (New York: Oxford, 1987), 91.

seven–part opus (611 pages), traditionally cited under the shortened title *Concordia*, only part four, "On Divine Foreknowledge" (113 pages, or 18.5% of the whole), has, by Alfred J. Freddoso, been translated into English. While this section introduces the concept of *scientia media*, placing it explanatorily between *scientia naturalis* (God's "natural knowledge" of all logical possibilities) and *scientia libera* (God's "free knowledge" of all true propositions in the actual world), and stipulates that God underwent an "absolutely complete and unlimited deliberation"[3] between his *scientia media* and his divine creative decree to decide which feasible world to actualize, it sheds virtually no light on either the content of or the factors which entered into this deliberation. For an elucidation of these pivotal nuances we must look instead to the untranslated part seven, "On Predestination and Reprobation" (158 pages), which reveals that Molina's account of this deliberation is inextricably intertwined with his exegesis of Romans 9, along with other related biblical texts.

Profoundly troubled by Calvin's doctrine of double predestination, the Dutch theologian Jacob Arminius (1560–1609) formulated an alternative theological system of creation and providence which he claimed was rooted in the theory of *scientia media*. Such an allegation is highly ambivalent, for it depends upon the narrowness or breadth of doctrinal substance one ascribes to this theory. On the one hand, if the theory simply denotes the doctrine of God's prevolitional counterfactual knowledge, then Arminius' system is undoubtedly based upon *scientia media*.[4] On the other hand, if the theory is taken as shorthand for the full range of divine cognitive activities posited by Molina from God's counterfactual knowledge to his creative decree, then Arminius' system is not grounded in *scientia media*, as it deviates quite sharply from Molina's depiction of God's complete and unlimited deliberation. This is a fact not sufficiently appreciated (if appreciated at all!) in the philosophical academy, which is all too quick to generalize that Arminius was a Molinist simply from his appropriation of middle knowledge,[5] despite his severe but little–known departure from Molina on the immediately

---

3. Molina, *Foreknowledge*, 4.52.13.

4. This has been verified by Richard A. Muller, *God, Creation, and Providence in the Thought of Jacob Arminius* (Grand Rapids, Mich.: Baker, 1991), 155–66.

5. Hence Eef Dekker answers affirmatively without reservation the title question of his article, "Was Arminius a Molinist?" (*Sixteenth Century Journal* XXVII:2 [1996]:337, 351–52), and William Lane Craig reports the high "degree to which Arminianism just *is* Protestant Molinism" ("Post–Debate Response to Edwin Curley," «http://www.leaderu.com/offices/billcraig/docs/craig–curley12.html», emphasis his).

ensuing issues of election and reprobation, and then to retroject Arminius' view of these matters back onto Molina. Contrary to Molina's affirmation of sovereign individual predestination,[6] Arminius regarded the predestination of Romans 9 as a group affair, in which each person freely joins the "children of the promise" through faith or the "children of the flesh" through unbelief.[7] Only at this point does God decree both to elect individuals whom he foreknows will embrace Christ and to reprobate those whom he foreknows will reject Christ. Ironically, this non–Molinist interpretation of Romans, which has been followed by such leading contemporary defenders of *scientia media* as William Lane Craig[8] and Paul Copan,[9] ranks among the primary reasons why many Reformed thinkers reject Molinism. Thus Richard A. Muller protests that *scientia media* undercuts God's sovereign determination of each individual's eternal destiny:

> The effect of such a doctrine upon soteriology is to allow an area of human choice, prior to the effective operation of divine grace, the results of which condition the divine activity or operation *ad extra*. God can elect individuals on the basis of his foreknowledge of their freely willed acceptance of the promises given in Christ, and this election will be based on no antecedent willing or operation in God. . . . [which] limits the sovereignty of grace in the work of salvation.[10]

---

6. Ludovici Molina, *Liberi Arbitrii cum Gratiae Donis, Divina Praescientia, Providentia, Praedestinatione et Reprobatione Concordia*, ed. Johannes Rabeneck (Madrid: Sumptibus Societatis Editorialis "Sapientia," 1953), 7.23.4–5. 1, 4.

7. Jacob Arminius, *Analysis of the Ninth Chapter of Romans*, in *Writings*, trans. James Nichols and W. R. Bagnall (Grand Rapids: Baker, 1956), 3:537.

8. In his debate with Edwin Curley, Craig explains, "What about the biblical passages on predestination? I suggest they be understood *corporately*. God has predestined a group, a people, for glorification and salvation. But who is it that is a member of the group? Those who freely respond to God's offer of forgiveness in Christ Jesus, and place their trust in him" («http://www.leaderu.com/offices/billcraig/docs/craig–curley04.html», emphasis his).

9. Copan exhorts: "Rather than embracing the view that God has picked out individuals for salvation and allowed (or destined) others to be damned, we can affirm that God has chosen a body of people in Christ, and they become part of the chosen people as they embrace Christ by faith. God does not choose individuals for salvation; he chooses a body of believers. His election is corporate and general rather than individual and specific" (*"That's Just Your Interpretation"* [Grand Rapids, Mich.: Baker, 2001], 89).

10. Muller, *Dictionary*, 274.

However, what modern defenders and critics of *scientia media* alike fail to realize is that this effect, far from being a necessary consequence of Molinism, was actually repudiated by Molina himself. The purpose of this chapter is twofold. First, from book seven of the *Concordia* I will present Molina's perspective on God's unlimited deliberation upon feasible worlds that intervenes between his *scientia media* and creative decree, spelling out the reformer's views on the pertinent factors influencing this deliberation—namely, predestination, election, and reprobation—which he exegetically derived from Romans 9 and its corollaries. Here it will be demonstrated that Molina formulated an account of unconditional election consistent with libertarian human freedom, thereby forging an uncompromised rapprochement between these respective Calvinist and Arminian hallmarks. Second, I will strengthen the significant contributions of Craig to the Molinist scheme, especially his solution to the problem of the unevangelized and his supposition that God actualized a world containing an optimal balance between saved and lost, by shifting its ground from Arminius' sparse reflections on divine deliberation to the far more versatile and sophisticated construction of Molina.

Molina's Conception of God's Unlimited Deliberation

In book seven of the *Concordia*, Molina queries "whether the cause of predestination may be ascribed to the part of the predestinate"[11] and "whether the cause of reprobation may be ascribed to the part of the reprobate."[12] Contra those who follow "the errors of Origen and Pelagius,"[13] he answers both questions decidedly in the negative. On the basis of the Pauline statement, "Before the twins were born or had done anything good or evil . . . not by works but by him who calls . . . [God said,] Jacob I loved, but Esau I hated" (Rom. 9:11–13), Molina declares that "foreseen faith cannot be the ground of justification or predestination,"[14] as affirming otherwise would undermine the *prima facie* implication that God's decree to elect Jacob and

---

11. "Utrum ex parte praedestinati detur causa praedestinationis"; Molina, *Concordia*, 7.23.4–5.1.
12. "Utrum ex parte reprobi detur causa reprobationis"; Molina, *Concordia*, 7.23.4–5.4.
13. "erroribus . . . Origenis et Pelagii"; Molina, *Concordia*, 7.23.4–5.2.
14. " . . . fides praevisa non sit ratio iustificationis ac praedestinationis"; Ibid.

reprobate Esau did not take into account their future good or evil works. Thus Molina deduces that God elects people "with his holy calling, not according to our works, but according to his own purpose and grace which was given to us in Christ Jesus."[15] Likewise, the reprobate person "is not reprobated because of foreseen sins, and truly he has neither the cause nor the ground of reprobation within him."[16] Molina insists that such constitutes the natural reading of Romans 9: "Behold in what way Paul teaches concerning Jacob that it was not on account of his works or his merits that he was beloved and predestined by God, so likewise he affirms concerning Esau that it was not on account of his works that he was hated and reprobated."[17] For Molina, therefore, the cause and ground of any person's election or reprobation is God's sovereign will: "The total effect of predestination . . . depends only on the free will of God,"[18] such that God could have predestined any "of the elect to have truly been reprobate" and any "of the reprobate to have truly been elect."[19] Molina proof–texts Romans 9:15–18 to substantiate this conclusion:

> Paul adds that God said to Moses: I will have mercy on whom I have mercy, and I will have compassion on whom I have compassion; that is, I will use mercy with whomever I wish and just as it gives pleasure to me. And Paul concludes: Therefore it is neither he who wills, nor he who runs, but God who shows mercy. . . . he has mercy on whom he wills, and whom he wills he hardens. . . . Therefore neither predestination nor reprobation is according to foreseen merits, but it leads back only to the free will of God.[20]

---

15. "Vocavit nos vocatione sua sancta, non secundum opera nostra, sed secundum propositum suum et gratiam quae data est nobis in Christo Iesu." Ibid.

16. "Ergo reprobatio non est propter peccata praevisa atque adeo nec causam nec rationem ex parte reprobi habet." Molina, *Concordia*, 7.23.4–5.4.

17. "Ecce quemadmodum Paulus de Iacob docet non propter opera sive merita sua fuisse a Deo dilectum et praedestinatum ita quoque de Esau affirmat non fuisse propter opera odio habitum ac reprobatum." Ibid.

18. "Totius effectus praedestinationis . . . ex sola libera Dei voluntate pendeat." Molina, *Concordia*, 7.23.4–5.1.

19. "illi electi . . . hi vero reprobi fuerint . . . illi reprobi . . . hi vero electi fuerint." Ibid.

20. "Subiungit Paulus Deum dixisse Moysi: Miserebor cuius misereor; et misericordiam praestabo cui miserebor; hoc est, utar misericordia cum quocumque voluero et prout mihi placuerit. Concluditque Paulus: Igitur non volentis, neque currentis, sed miserentis est Dei. . . . cuius vult miseretur, et quem vult indurat. . . . Ergo sicut praedestinatio non est propter merita praevisa ita neque

From these quotations, two very important conclusions can be drawn. First, Molina interpreted Romans 9 as teaching both individual predestination, since Jacob and Esau refer strictly to the persons in question and are not representatives of two different groups, and unconditional election, as God elects purely according to his pleasure without regard to any foreseen faith or merits and reprobates without regard to any foreseen unbelief or sins. Second, since God could have chosen to actualize sets of circumstances in which every elect person in the actual world would have been reprobate and every reprobate person in the actual world would have been elect, it follows that Molina would regard as unbiblical the conventional "Molinist" doctrine of transworld damnation, which affirms that anyone lost in the actual world would have been lost in any feasible world that God could create.[21] Moreover, as we saw in chapter one, the doctrine of transworld damnation is decisively proven false by Jesus' frank declaration that the citizens of Tyre, Sidon, and Sodom, who were lost in the actual world, would have been saved in a feasible world, only slightly different from the world which God in fact chose, where his miracles actually performed in Chorazin and Bethsaida had instead been performed in these former cities (Q; Mt. 11:21–24; Lk. 10:13–15). Admittedly realizing its *prima facie* significance, proponents of trans-

reprobatio, sed in solam liberam voluntatem Dei ea reducenda est." Molina, *Concordia*, 7.23.4–5.4.

21. While expounding the "middle knowledge perspective on the exclusivity of salvation through faith in Christ," Craig posits that "we may accordingly speak of the property of *transworld damnation*," through his cognizance of which God "has providentially ordered the world such that those who are lost are persons who would not have been saved in any world feasible for God in which they exist" ("'No Other Name': A Middle Knowledge Perspective on the Exclusivity of Faith in Christ," *Faith and Philosophy* 6 (1989): 172, 184; emphasis his). However, Craig elsewhere tacitly admits that such does not represent the perspective of Molina: "Molina held that God's choosing to create certain persons *has nothing to do with how they would respond to His grace*; He simply chooses the world order He wants to, and *no rationale for this choice is to be sought other than the divine will itself.* In this sense, predestination is for Molina *wholly gratuitous*, the result of the divine will, *and in no way based on the merits or demerits of creatures*" (*The Problem of Divine Foreknowledge and Future Contingents from Aristotle to Suarez* [Leiden: Brill, 1988], 204, emphasis mine).

world damnation who believe in biblical infallibility are forced to interpret this text in ways other than grammatico–historical.[22]

Molina's interpretation of Romans 9 along with its two aforementioned corollaries stand in sharp contrast to Arminius' exegesis of the same chapter. Arminius initiates his analysis by contending that if the cause of predestination is not found in the saved or lost subjects themselves, as Molina maintained, then divine justice is undermined:

> If God, without any respect of works, regards Ishmael and Esau with hatred and excludes them from the number of his children, but loves Isaac and Jacob, and considers them as his children, is he not unjust? It. . . . is true that, if the apostle was considering them in themselves, and not as types of certain characters . . . there would be an occasion for such an objection.[23]

Attempting to forestall the implication that "God has power *absolutely or unconditionally* to make . . . some *vessels of wrath*, others *vessels of mercy*,"[24] Arminius insists that "Esau and Jacob are to be considered, not in

---

22. Attempting to explain why his partially Arminianized rendition of *scientia media* cannot account for the pertinent text at face value, Craig insists, "The passage in Matthew 11 is probably religious hyperbole meant merely to underscore the depth of the depravity of the cities in which Jesus preached" (*The Only Wise God* [Grand Rapids, Mich.: Baker, 1987], 137). But Craig offers no exegetical substantiation for this assertion, which falls clearly outside the mainstream of Matthean scholarship. For instance, Matthean commentator D. A. Carson points out that one of the "three large theological propositions . . . presupposed by Jesus' insistence that on the Day of Judgment, when he will judge, things will go worse for the cities that have received so much light than for the pagan cities . . . is that the Judge has contingent knowledge: he knows what Tyre and Sidon would have done under such–and–such circumstances" (*Matthew*, in *The Expositor's Bible Commentary*, gen. ed. Frank E. Gæbelein [Grand Rapids, Mich.: Zondervan, 1984], 8:273). This verdict is echoed by Robert H. Gundry in his magisterial analysis of Matthew (*Matthew: A Commentary on His Handbook for a Mixed Church under Persecution*, 2nd ed. [Grand Rapids, Mich.: Eerdmans, 1994], 214–15). Hence Craig's interpretation of this text seems a clear case of allowing philosophical presuppositions to trump grammatico–historical exegesis rather than, as I advocate, utilizing a hermeneutical circle governed by the two poles of grammatico–historical exegesis and philosophical data derived deductively from Scriptural premises.

23. Arminius, *Romans*, 541.

24. Ibid., 559, emphasis his.

themselves, but as types, and so that which is attributed to them, is to be accommodated to the antitypes. . . . which had before been given in the phrases 'children of the flesh' and 'children of the promise.'"[25] Therefore Arminius, despite his appropriation of "middle knowledge" from Molina, departs from his predecessor by advocating corporate rather than individual predestination. For Arminius, membership within either group depends squarely on God's prescience of either personal faith or unbelief, not any secret decision of the divine will:

> [God's] decree to save and damn particular persons . . . has its foundation in the foreknowledge of God, by which he knew from all eternity those individuals who would, through his prevenient grace, believe, and, through his subsequent grace would persevere . . . and, by which foreknowledge, he likewise knew those who would not believe and persevere.[26]

Thus Arminius makes it clear that while God's predestinary decree is based upon his foreknowledge, the ground of such foreknowledge lies within created individuals themselves, thereby affording the saved immediate proof of their election:

> On this purpose, as it appears, depends the certainty of our salvation, and at the same time the assurance of it *in ourselves*. For we infer that assurance from this enthymene [truncated syllogism], "I am a believer," or "I believe in Christ; therefore I shall be saved," or, "I am elect." The strength of which depends on this proposition: "God has immutably determined from eternity to save those, who believe in Christ," in which words is contained the sum of that purpose.[27]

Hence Arminius, unlike Molina, deems anathema the doctrine of unconditional election, asserting that it is "repugnant to the nature of God," "hurtful to the salvation of men," and "injurious to the glory of God."[28] These soteriological differences between Arminius and Molina point to the respective narrow and wide functions *scientia media* plays in their respective systems.

Only two references to *scientia media* are to be found in the Arminius corpus—his public disputation on the nature of God and his private disputa-

---

25. Ibid., 536.

26. Jacob Arminius, *Declaration of Sentiments*, in *Writings*, 1:248, emphasis mine.

27. Arminius, *Romans*, 3:540.

28. Arminius, *Declaration of Sentiments*, 1:221–22, 230, 228.

tion on the understanding of God.[29] In both instances, *scientia media* serves the sole purpose of grounding God's foreknowledge of future contingents. Future contingents must be so grounded for Arminius because, in modern terminology, he (like Molina) is an A–theorist and not a B–theorist of time. Thus Arminius cannot construe God's foreknowledge on the analogy of sense perception, according to which God, living in an "eternal now," looks into the four–dimensional space–time block and views all events on the timeline as equally present.[30] Holding to the reality of temporal becoming and a privileged present moment, rather, Arminius predicates *scientia libera* upon *scientia media*: "Middle knowledge is that by which [God] knows that 'if *this* thing happens, *that* will take place'. . . . [Such knowledge] precedes indeed the free act of the divine will, but hypothetically from this act it sees that some particular thing will occur."[31] In a startling twist, however, Arminius claims that *scientia media* depends not upon God's infinite ability to discern all possible yet uncreated essences but upon created free will: "That 'middle' kind of knowledge must intervene in things which depend on the liberty of a created will. . . . [that is], in things which depend on the liberty of created choice or pleasure."[32] It is precisely this idea that the second moment of God's omniscience depends upon created beings, not a little insinuating that God needs created beings to be omniscient, which causes the Reformed to reject *scientia media* as undermining divine perfection. From his claim that God perceives "created will" or "created choice" through middle knowledge we see that Arminius, who lacks any discussion of the logical moment at which the divine creative decree occurs, seems to clearly presuppose that it transpired before (not after) God's *scientia media*. In other words, Arminius assumes that God has already settled on creating a particular group of individuals logically prior to his apprehension of *scientia media*, which knowledge then furnishes him the rational ground to elect or reprobate every such individual based upon what each would freely do in the actual world, rather than (as he characterizes Calvin's God) arbitrarily and hence unjustly electing or reprobating these individuals without reference to their future faith or unbelief.

---

29. Jacob Arminius, *Public Disputations*, in *Writings*, 1:448–49; Arminius, *Private Disputations*, in *Writings*, 2:38–39.

30. For a thorough exposition of these respective tensed and tenseless theories of time see John M. E. McTaggart, *The Nature of Existence*, ed. C. D. Broad (Cambridge: Cambridge University Press, 1927; rep. ed.: 1968), 5:33.

31. Arminius, *Public Disputations*, 1:448.

32. Ibid., 1:449; Arminius, *Private Disputations*, 2:39.

We are now in a position to spell out Arminius' interspersed succession of logical moments and divine decisions up to the creation of the actual world. First, not surprisingly, is God's *scientia naturalis*, which he defines as the knowledge "by which God understands himself and all things possible."[33] Having perceived all possible free individuals he could create, in his creative decree God chooses a particular subset of these individuals which will, at the moment of creation, comprise the actual world.[34] At this point God lovingly decrees to appoint Christ as Redeemer, Mediator, and Savior of all future created persons. Then God decrees both to save anyone who will receive Christ and to minister sufficiently and efficaciously the means (*i.e.* the Word, sacraments, etc.) for human appropriation of Christ.[35] Next comes God's *scientia media*, by which he apprehends who would make good use of these means by freely receiving Christ and who, contrariwise, would freely reject Christ. Consequently, God decrees to save or damn particular persons based on his middle knowledge of who would or would not believe. Finally, simultaneous with the moment of creation is God's *scientia libera*, by which his logically prior knowledge of all individuals in the actual world and his freely decreed dealings with them are now converted into foreknowledge. It is noteworthy that for Arminius, there is no divine deliberation (let alone Molina's "absolutely complete and unlimited deliberation") between God's *scientia media* and *scientia libera*, as the rubric for the intervening predestinary decree has already been determined by God's pre–counterfactual decree to elect believers and reprobate unbelievers. Rather, the divine deliberation transpires between *scientia naturalis* and *scientia media*, as it is there that God carefully ponders and decides upon which subset, if any, among the infinite range of possible individuals he wishes to actualize, the plan of salvation and the involvement of the second Trinitarian person within, and the means by which humans can appropriate his saving grace.

The ramifications of *scientia media* in Molina's system are far more widespread than for Arminius; not only does it furnish a basis for God's knowledge of future contingents, but it constitutes the nucleus of his conceptions, which couple full–blown divine sovereignty with libertarian free will, of predestination, election, and reprobation. Anticipating the misconstrual

---

33. Arminius, *Public Disputations*, 1:448.

34. Hence Arminius, when discussing the four divine decrees outlined in this paragraph, affirms that "the decree concerning creation is the first of all the decrees of God"; *Certain Articles To Be Considered and Weighed*, in *Writings*, 2:485.

35. Arminius, *Declaration of Sentiments*, 1:247.

that his theory compromises the *omnisufficientia et independentia Dei*, Molina vehemently denies that *scientia media* is in any way dependent on the future existence of free persons, but affirms that it stems entirely from the divine nature: "God does not get His knowledge from things, but knows all things *in* Himself and *from* Himself; therefore, the existence of things, whether in time or eternity, contributes nothing to God's knowing with certainty what is going to be or not going to be."[36] In his *scientia media*, God knows what each of the infinite possible individuals he could create would freely do in every conceivable set of circumstances. Molina emphasizes that God apprehends such knowledge despite that, at this point, none of these infinite individuals possess any existence whatsoever, and that the overwhelming majority of these individuals will never exist:

> *For prior to any existence* on the part of the objects, God has within Himself the means whereby He knows all things fully and perfectly; and this is why the existence of created things contributes no perfection to the cognition He has of them and does not cause any change in that cognition. . . . [and] God does not need the existence of those things in His eternity in order to know them with certainty.[37]

Since God possesses perfect middle knowledge of what an infinite array of never–future–existent individuals would freely do in any possible circumstances and apprehends middle knowledge about these never–future–existent individuals in precisely the same way as he does about the finite set of individuals now existing in the actual world, it becomes obvious that *scientia media* is predicated upon neither the existence nor the free decisions of created persons:

> Nor in this regard is there any difference between those future contingents that will exist in some interval of time and those that were able to exist but never will exist. For God knows each of them in the same way that it was or was not going to exist on the hypothesis and condition that He should have decided to create one or another order of things different from the one that He in fact created.[38]

Thus, created free will, just like uncreated free will, does absolutely nothing on Molina's scheme to cause or ground God's *scientia media*, and our free acts contribute nothing to God's middle knowledge of their occurrence. God

---

36. Molina, *Foreknowledge*, 4.49.12, 11, emphasis his.
37. Ibid., emphasis mine.
38. Ibid., 4.50.19.

does not, as many contemporary writers caricature Molinism,[39] therefore "wait" or "leave space open" in his omniscience for the future acts of free individuals and then, upon their acting, "middle–know" their decisions, as Molina would agree with his quasi–objectors that such a fallacious idea clearly undermines divine sufficiency and sovereignty. On the contrary, Molina grounds *scientia media* in God's cognitive ability to perfectly comprehend his own creative aptitude and power.

Among the necessary divine attributes, stipulates Molina, is supercomprehension, which he defines as God's unlimited intellectual capacity to infinitely perceive, within his own mind, the individual essence or pattern for every possible free person he could create. Molina insists that God obtains no knowledge from the persons which could be instantiated by these designs: "God acquires no knowledge *from things* but instead knows and comprehends everything He knows in His own essence and in the determination of His own will."[40] Since each essence is the product of the divine imagination, and God perfectly understands his own imagination, it follows for Molina that God can infinitely perceive each essence. This infinite perception includes knowing what each essence, if instantiated, would freely do in any possible set of circumstances in which it found itself:

> In Himself He comprehends all the things that exist eminently in Him and thus the free choice of any creature whom He is able to make through His omnipotence. Therefore . . . by virtue of the depth of His . . . . knowledge, by which He infinitely surpasses each of the things He contains eminently in Himself, He discerns what the free choice of any creature would do by its own innate freedom, given the hypothesis that He should create it in this or that order of things with these or those circumstances or aids—even though the creature could, if it so willed, re-

---

39. For example, Norman L. Geisler alleges, "Molinism assumes that God must 'wait' to know things are true. . . . God's omniscience 'waits' to see what a free creature does 'before' he selects those who will be saved. . . . Hence, God must wait (from a logical standpoint) the occurrence of free acts before he can know they are true" (*Baker Encyclopedia of Christian Apologetics*, s.v. "Molinism" [Grand Rapids, Mich.: Baker, 1999], 493–94), and Muller charges that since "God knows the future contingent relatively or hypothetically as a potential result of a prior creaturely act," *scientia media* "seems to introduce into the divine mind an element of potency or knowledge of possibility that is actualized by something external to God. . . . [which] raises a serious question about the extent of divine knowledge and its possible limitation" (*God, Creation, and Providence*, 156).

40. Molina, *Foreknowledge*, 4.52.19, emphasis his.

frain from acting or do the opposite, and even though if it was going to do so, as it is able to freely, God would foresee *that* very act and *not* the one that He *in fact* foresees would be performed by that creature.[41]

In other words, logically prior to his choice to create anything, the Designer knows all of his unactualized designs or patterns (of which a tiny minority would ever be actualized) so perfectly well to know how each would freely behave in any state of affairs if he proceeded to create it, thereby furnishing the ground for *scientia media*:

> Middle knowledge pertains to . . . objects that are uncertain in themselves, and yet because of the depth and eminence of His intellect God knows them with absolute certainty and hence has an absolutely unique knowledge of them which exceeds their nature. . . . Thus, what was in itself uncertain He knew with certainty, a certainty that stemmed not from the object, but from the acumen and absolute perfection of His intellect.[42]

Inherent to Molina's formulation of supercomprehension are two potent solutions to the so–called "grounding objection"—that no ground exists for counterfactuals of creaturely freedom—which, in my judgment, is the most prevalent (yet least substantiated) allegation levied against *scientia media* by philosophers of religion.[43] First, God, owing to his perfect knowledge of his own imagination and, therefore, the individual essences which were produced therefrom, knows what the instantiation of each essence would do under any set of circumstances. This insight gains dramatic confirmation from the fact that humans can apprehend the actualized essences of other humans well enough to gain a finite amount of counterfactual knowledge about them. From his intuition that his wife hates liver and onions, Craig provides the following analogy of human counterfactual knowledge: "If I were to offer my wife a plate of liver and onions and a plate of chocolate–chip cookies, I know which one she would choose as certainly as I know almost anything!"[44] So if we, with our finite intelligences and finite knowledge of the essences (which we did not excogitate) of some actual individu-

---

41. Ibid., 4.49.11, emphasis his.
42. Ibid., 4.52.33–35.
43. My appraisal is shared by Thomas P. Flint (*Divine Providence* [Ithaca: N.Y.: Cornell University Press, 1988], 123) and Craig ("Middle Knowledge, Truth–Makers, and the 'Grounding Objection,'" *Faith and Philosophy* 18 [2001]: 337).
44. Craig, *Only Wise God*, 139.

als, can know what they would freely do in some sets of circumstances, it seems eminently reasonable to hold that God, with his infinite intelligence and infinite knowledge of the essences (which he did excogitate) of all possible individuals, can know what each of them would freely do in any set of circumstances in which they find themselves. Second, since "the depth and perfection of the divine knowledge" includes innate knowledge of all truths, and there are true counterfactuals concerning possible essences, God simply discerns these truths as part of his omniscience.[45] It should be pointed out that neither of these solutions lead to theological fatalism because knowledge is not causally determinative—that is to say, God's knowledge of what a possible essence, if instantiated, would do in some set of circumstances does not in any way cause the instantiation to act as God knows, just as human knowledge of what other humans would do exerts no causal power over their choices (for example, Craig's counterfactual knowledge of his wife's tastes in food obviously does nothing to make her eat the chocolate–chip cookies instead of the liver and onions).

We are now in a position to delineate Molina's doctrine of predestination while spelling out the logical sequence of cognitive events intervening between God's *scientia media* and the divine creative decree. Confronted with his *scientia media* of what every possible individual would freely do in every conceivable set of circumstances, God commits himself, out of his love, to consider only the subset of those circumstances in which he offers sufficient grace for salvation to each individual. According to Molina, moreover, God perceives that for every feasible individual,[46] there is at least one compossible set of circumstances (*i.e.* one feasible world, or set of circumstances given creaturely freedom which are logically compatible with each other and thus accumulate into a world) in which the individual would freely appropriate his grace and be saved, and there is at least one compossible set of circumstances in which the individual would freely spurn his grace and be lost. Hence at this logical point God is faced with an infinite range (a lower–order infinity than the infinity of feasible worlds irrespective of salvific grace and the even higher–order infinity of possible worlds, but infinite

---

45. Molina, *Foreknowledge*, 4.49.11.

46. I say "feasible individual" rather than "possible individual" here because Molina was a traducianist regarding the creation of the soul rather than a creationist, and thus many logically possible individuals, who could have been generated by the procreative acts of other possible individuals, "drop out," so to speak, of God's knowledge when he perceives, through his *scientia media*, that the relevant procreative acts would never freely occur. See Molina, *Concordia*, 1.14.1–2.

nonetheless) of feasible worlds in which he grants all persons sufficient grace to be saved. Within this infinity of "all–gracious feasible worlds" is at least one world where every feasible individual would freely attain salvation, at least one world where that same individual would freely reach damnation, and at least one world where that feasible individual would not exist at all. Without consideration of any particular individual's salvation, damnation, or non–existence, God enters into an all–encompassing predestinary determination of what world to actualize, which arrives at completion through his sovereign creative decree. On Molina's view, then, predestination, comprising election and reprobation, are logically simultaneous with the divine creative decree, as predestination, in the words of Craig, "involves God's willing that aspect of the world comprising the natural circumstances and supernatural gifts of grace which form the milieu in which a person freely responds to God's gracious initiatives."[47] For by choosing which feasible world to actualize, God predestines to salvation, or elects, every individual in that world who would freely accept his prevenient grace, and he predestines to damnation, or reprobates, every individual in that world who would freely reject his prevenient grace. This is not to say that the compossible circumstances making up the feasible world determine whether one is saved or lost, as all such circumstances are freedom–preserving in character. Rather, God knows the essence of each feasible individual in that world so well that he knows, if instantiated, which way the individual would freely choose. Thus Molina's doctrine of predestination is entirely harmonious with libertarian human freedom.

However, we must not therefore think that predestination, for Molina, depends upon human free choice. For every elect person, God could have just as easily chosen another feasible world in which the same individual would have freely rejected his saving grace or not existed at all. Likewise, for every reprobate person, God could have just as easily chosen another feasible world in which the same individual would have freely embraced his salvation or not existed at all. As Craig points out,

> It is the case that had [the reprobate] been put in different circumstances or given other helps, they would freely have responded to God's grace and been predestined to salvation. Similarly, those who are predestined to salvation, if placed in different circumstances or given different helps, might not have responded and so been lost.[48]

---

47. Craig, *Foreknowledge and Future Contingents*, 206.

48. Ibid., 204; a surprising admission given his doctrine of transworld damnation.

Molina insists that no reason can be given concerning why God selected one feasible world over a host of others except for his sovereign will. Since this predestinary choice is in no way predicated upon how any person in that world would respond to his grace, Molina's theology, as well as his biblical exegesis, champions the doctrine of unconditional election. Thus God's choosing to elect or reprobate certain individuals by creating a world in which they would or would not attain to salvation rather than another world where they would freely do the opposite or not even exist has nothing to do with their merits or demerits; God simply, in his absolute sovereignty, selects the world he wants. At this juncture it must be emphasized that God is not guilty of foisting a "divine sting operation" upon the reprobate, as the circumstances in the world he chooses to actualize (as well as every other feasible world) are freedom–preserving and do nothing to cause either the reprobate to spurn prevenient grace or the elect to embrace it. Hence no one could legitimately complain before the throne of God, "Since I rejected you because of my unfortunate life circumstances, my condemnation is unfair." In this case God would reply, "While you freely chose to reject me in a world where you experienced various circumstances, those circumstances were irrelevant to your choice; you could have just as easily chosen to accept me under those same circumstances. So your condemnation is entirely fair as well as self–incurred." Consistently with his justice, then, God does not "set up" anyone for damnation in choosing to create a certain feasible world, as no feasible world is salvifically unfair. Edmond Vansteenberghe concisely summarizes Molina's synthesis of libertarian freedom with unconditional election:

> This is not to say that predestination depends on the individual, since it consists in the choice made by God of an order of things in which He foresaw that this individual will arrive at salvation. Precisely there is the delicate point, "the unfathomable depths of God's designs": God knew an infinity of providential orders in which the non–predestinated would freely arrive at eternal life and thus would have been predestinated; He knew as well an infinity of providential orders in which the predestined would have freely lost beatitude and would have been reprobate; and yet He chose for the one and for the other the order of providence in which He foresaw that the one would be saved and the other not. He did this by His will alone and without consideration of their acts, but without injustice, since he has provided them all the means of arriving at eternal life.[49]

---

49. *Dictionnaire de théologie catholique*, s.v. "Molinisme," by Edmond Vansteenberghe, 10.2., cols. 1028–29.

Given the truth of God's *scientia media*, it is *in sensu composito* impossible for the elect to be lost or for the reprobate to be saved; the elect will freely, yet infallibly, persevere to final salvation, while the reprobate will freely, yet infallibly, persevere in their resistance to God's sufficient grace until the moment of death. Nevertheless, since both the elect and reprobate are entirely free to accept or reject salvation, it is *in sensu diviso* possible for the elect to be lost and the reprobate saved; such a possibility is ruled out only by God's supercomprehension, by which he knows within himself the uninstantiated essence of each feasible person so well that he infallibly perceives how their instantiations would freely choose concerning salvation in every state of affairs, including the actual world. By coupling *scientia media* with the hypothesis that God could sovereignly actualize for any feasible individual a state of affairs in which that person was freely lost, freely saved, or non–existent, where the choice depends not at all on the feasible individual or anything therein but solely on God's good pleasure, Molina successfully reconciles full divine sovereignty with libertarian human freedom without undercutting the *prima facie* meaning of either doctrine.

The Unevangelized and Optimality Between Saved and Lost

In his noteworthy articles "Politically Incorrect Salvation" and "'No Other Name': A Middle Knowledge Perspective of the Exclusivity of Salvation Through Christ," William Lane Craig has offered several important lines of defense in behalf of the biblical portrait of Christian particularism amidst a prevailing climate of religious pluralism. Among these apologetics two directly pertain to our discussion of the cognitive events between God's *scientia media* and creative decree. First, from the biblical statements that "God wants all persons to be saved and to come to a knowledge of the truth" (1 Tim. 2:4) and that "the Lord is . . . not wanting anyone to perish, but everyone to come to repentance" (2 Pet. 3:9), Craig infers that God has actualized a world with an optimal balance between belief and unbelief, creating no more of the lost than is necessary to achieve the maximum number of the saved.[50] Second, Craig argues that all persons in the actual world who never hear the gospel and are lost would not have received salvation even if they had heard the gospel. Taking Romans 2:7, "To those who by persistence in

---

50. William Lane Craig, "Politically Incorrect Salvation," in *Christian Apologetics in the Postmodern World*, ed. Timothy R. Phillips and Dennis Okholm (Downers Grove, Ill.: InterVarsity Press, 1995), 84; Craig, "No Other Name," 176.

doing good seek glory, honor, and immortality, [God] will give eternal life," to be a *bona fide* offer of salvation, Craig reasons that persons who are uninformed, misinformed, or ill–informed about Christ can be saved by appropriately responding to God's general revelation in nature and conscience. Thus salvation is universally accessible to all humanity through general revelation, although Craig surmises that very few individuals actually appropriate salvation in this way (I am more optimistic than Craig on this score).[51] But then the inevitable question arises: Why doesn't God bring the gospel to those who, although failing to access salvation through general revelation, would have accessed salvation if they were only given special revelation? To this question, Craig ingeniously responds that there are no such people in the actual world, as God has providentially ordered the world through *scientia media* such that all who never receive special revelation and are lost would not have been saved even if they had received it.[52] While these two arguments are obviously consistent with Arminius' view of predestination, in which election was conditional upon human free acts (though not with his placement of the divine creative decree before God's *scientia media*), it remains to be seen whether they can be integrated with Molina's doctrine of unconditional election. The remainder of this chapter will attempt to effect such a synthesis by expanding Molina's series of cognitive events between *scientia media* and the divine creative decree.

At this juncture we may profitably list Molina's sequence of cognitive events as they transpire in the *scientia Dei*. (1) Through his *scientia naturalis*, God knows the infinite range of all possible worlds, which (2) is narrowed down to a lower–order infinite range of feasible worlds via his *scientia media*. (3) By factoring out all feasible worlds in which he does not give each individual sufficient grace for salvation, God further reduces the set of feasible worlds to a lower–order infinite range of all–gracious feasible worlds. (4) For every feasible individual P within this range of all–gracious feasible worlds, God perceives that there exists at least one world in which P freely receives salvation, at least one world in which P freely rejects salvation, and at least one world in which P does not exist at all. (5) Following his deliberation upon this range, God chooses one of these all–gracious feasible worlds to be actual. By inserting at least one step between (3) and (4) and another step between (4) and (5) while modifying steps (4) and (5), we can incorporate Craig's insights into the Molinist scheme. To begin, let us posit (3.1) that God reduces the infinite range of all–gracious feasible worlds to the lower–order infinite range of all–gracious feasible worlds that obtain to

51. Craig, "Politically Incorrect Salvation," 82–83.
52. Craig, "No Other Name," 185.

the optimal balance between saved and lost, thereby ensuring, as Craig suggests, that the world God chooses to actualize possesses such a balance. We can also extend this analysis to the problem of evil by inserting (3.2) that God then eliminates all worlds containing greater than the minimum amount of natural and moral evil found in any of the all–gracious feasible worlds that obtain to the optimal salvific balance, leaving a lower–order infinite range of worlds tied for the least cumulative evil. Thus prior to (4), God is confronted with an infinite range of equally good all–gracious feasible worlds reaching the optimal balance between saved and lost. Since each of these worlds includes no more evil than is logically and causally necessary, given libertarian human freedom, for any feasible world with the attributes of gracious universality and salvific optimality, we shall call these worlds "salvific–moral optimal worlds."

Modifying (4) to account for (3.1) and (3.2), we stipulate (4*) that for every P within the range of salvific–moral optimal worlds, there is at least one world where P is freely saved, at least one world where P is freely lost, and another world where P does not exist. It must be pointed out that the truth of (4*), as well as Molina's (4), is not uncontroversial. Nevertheless, all we need to illustrate here is the logical possibility of (4*), and it certainly seems logically possible that the scope of salvific–moral optimal worlds contains at least three such worlds. We are still faced, however, with the existence of many P (let us call them $P*$) who never hear the gospel in the between one world and some of the many worlds where they are lost and hear the gospel in the between one world and some of the many worlds where they are saved. If God were at this logical point to create one of the salvific–moral optimal worlds, then it is conceivable that many in the actual world who never hear the gospel and are lost would have been saved if they had heard the gospel, thus rendering their damnation the result of historical or geographical accident. Such a scenario recalls and greatly intensifies the previous dilemma concerning divine injustice, since the life circumstances of the reprobate would, in this case, be clearly causally determinative for their damnation. We can prevent this possibility by postulating (4.1) that, for every individual $P*$ who is lost in at least one salvific–moral optimal world where $P*$ receives only general revelation and is saved in at least one salvific–moral optimal world not on the basis of general revelation but only after receiving special revelation, God discards from the infinite range of salvific–moral optimal worlds *every* world where $P*$ exists (not just the at least two aforementioned worlds). This reduction leaves God with a lower–order infinite range of salvific–moral optimal worlds in which every remaining P is governed by one of two conditions. First, if P is lost in any world where P only receives general revelation, then P is also lost in every world where P

receives special revelation without first appropriating salvation through general revelation; hence the only world or worlds in which P is saved entail P appropriating salvation through general revelation either without or before hearing the gospel in the future. Second, if P is saved in any world only after receiving special revelation, then P is also saved in every world where P only receives general revelation; hence the only world or worlds in which P is lost entail P rejecting salvation through both general and special revelation. In other words, the resultant infinite set of worlds is defined by a diagonal asymmetry between the alternate types of revelation (general or special) received and the opposite salvific conditions (lost or saved) acquired by each individual P in various worlds, as displayed in the following chart:

P	Meeting first condition	Meeting second condition
Lost	• In at least one world where P only receives general revelation • In every world where P receives special revelation without first appropriating salvation through general revelation	• In at least one world where P receives special revelation without first appropriating salvation through general revelation
Saved	• In at least one world where P has only received general revelation at the moment of salvation (although P could receive special revelation at some point thereafter)[53]	• In at least one world where P receives special revelation without first appropriating salvation through general revelation • In every world where P only receives general revelation

---

53. We need not fear, therefore, evangelizing persons who have already responded to God's general revelation but have not yet received special revelation, as if they might reject Christ and so lose the salvation they once possessed. For Jesus himself presented this state of affairs as a logical impossibility: "But whoever already lives by the truth comes into the light (referring to himself as the light of the world) in order that it may be clearly seen that what that person has already done has been done in God. . . .If God were your Father, you would love me, for I came from God and now am here" (Jn. 3:21; 8:42). Hence everyone who has appropriated salvation through general revelation will accept special revelation if presented to them; Cornelius and his family are a case in point (Acts 10, esp. vv. 2–5, 15, 27–36).

Thus for every feasible person P, P's reprobation or election can only occur in what we now denominate "salvifically comparable worlds," where each P potentially freely lost upon never hearing the gospel would only be freely saved in other worlds where, at the moment of regeneration, P would not have heard the gospel, and each P potentially freely saved only after hearing the gospel would only be freely lost in other worlds where P heard the gospel. Upgrading (5) to account for this development, we hypothesize (5*) that God deliberates upon the range of salvifically comparable worlds and then, in his divine creative decree, chooses one of these worlds to be actual. (For those who are mathematically inclined, see the Excursus to this chapter for a numerical–analytic illustration of the reduction from higher to lower–order infinite sets in our revised Molinist scheme.)

Theologically, there is much ground to be gained from the conjunction of (4.1) and (5*). Without sacrificing God's sovereignty over the creation of individuals who owe their election unconditionally to God, such that God could have placed each elect individual in a salvifically comparable set of circumstances where that person would have been freely damned, (4.1) and (5*) preserve the fairness of God in ensuring that election and reprobation are never due to the accidents of geography or history, but hinge solely on the good pleasure of God. Hence on (4.1) and (5*), God, in deliberating upon and selecting a world, chooses for each feasible individual in that world to either be elect, reprobate, or non–existent, without respect to how any given person would respond to his grace. For every elect and reprobate individual essence whose instantiation would respond to or resist his sufficient grace in the actual world, it is entirely within God's power to have respectively reprobated or elected that essence by instantiating it in another equally good feasible world where it responded contrariwise to his grace or to have chosen not to create that essence at all by selecting another equally good feasible world in which it was not instantiated. At the same time, God's fairness to both the elect and reprobate is safeguarded by the fact that any such "equally good feasible world" in which they would possess the opposite predestinary status is salvifically comparable to the actual world. Thus no one who hears and responds affirmatively to the gospel need worry that she or he would have been lost if born in another space–time location where the gospel was unavailable. On our model, it is incoherent for those saved via special revelation to maintain that God showed them favoritism by placing them in lands where they heard the gospel, such that if their roles were swapped with persons in, say, a remote African tribe unreached by missionaries, they would have been lost. To be sure, God could have actualized a world in which they were lost—such is simply an affirmation of divine sovereignty—but in every such world, they would have heard the gospel and freely rejected it. Moreover, no one lost apart from the gospel could stand before God on the judgment day and object, "Although I failed to respond to your general revelation in nature and conscience, I would have received your salvation if you had only placed me in a world where I heard the gospel." For God would respond, "No—through my *scientia media*, I knew that for every feasible world in which you heard the gospel, you would have rejected it." Moreover, God's placing such a person in a world where she or he never hears the gospel actually turns out to be an act of mercy, since the person would have accrued much greater punishment for explicitly rejecting God in the gospel than she or he suffers for implicitly rejecting God in nature and conscience. Of course, God could have sovereignly decreed to create a world in which someone lost apart from the gospel would freely be saved, but in any such world, the person would have been saved without having heard the gospel. Hence without resorting to the un–Molinist (and perhaps unbiblical) doctrine of transworld damnation, we can preserve Craig's insight of God so providentially ordering the world that all persons in the actual world who never hear the gospel and are lost would still be lost even if they had heard the gospel.

Conclusion

Perhaps the greatest historical barrier preventing the Reformed from giving Molina a fair hearing is their viewing him as a philosophically more sophisticated version of Arminius and thus unworthy of serious consideration. However, this study has revealed that such a perception is extremely inaccurate. Unlike Arminius, Molina both interpreted Scripture (especially Romans 9) as teaching and constructed a theological system emphasizing the complete sovereignty of God to consign each individual he creates to salvation or damnation, irrespective of that person's merits or demerits in any conceivable set of circumstances but depending solely upon his good pleasure. Hence Molina concurred with Calvin on the sovereignty of God and his unconditional election of individuals. However, unlike Calvinism, in Molina's system God is completely sovereign over the eternal destinies of a world of libertarian free creatures who have, in Augustinian terminology, "free choice" and not merely "free will."[54] Remarkably, therefore, Molina's

---

54. For Augustine, "free choice" (*i.e.* libertarian free will) entailed the freedom to choose between opposites in both the physical and spiritual realms. Thus fallen humanity, by virtue of the *imago Dei*, can freely choose whether or not to respond to God's prevenient grace. By contrast, Augustine defined "free will" (*i.e.* compatibilist free will) as the ability to choose without any external con-

God is actually more sovereign than Calvin's, since a God who can infallibly determine the salvation or damnation of all individuals (and, in fact, providentially plan all of their actions down to the last detail) without compromising their libertarian freedom in any way is obviously superior to a God who can only determine the eternal destinies of created persons if they lack libertarian freedom and if he, in turn, premoves their bound wills toward his foreordained ends. While the sovereignty of Calvin's God seems threatened by libertarian human freedom, the sovereignty of Molina's God is greatly enhanced by it. Moreover, Molina's series of divine cognitive events between God's *scientia media* and his creative decree, by enumerating solely those events which the reformer regarded as biblically specified, is flexible enough to accommodate a host of insights stemming from contemporary philosophy of religion. In particular, Craig's hypotheses that God has providentially created a world which realizes the optimal balance between saved and lost and where all persons who are lost without hearing an accurate presentation of the gospel would have been lost even if they had received special revelation harmonize nicely with the Molinist scheme. Since Molina formulated a genuine rapprochement between sovereign individual predestination and libertarian human freedom, the respective hallmarks of Calvinism and Arminianism, I would commend his model of divine omniscience for serious consideration to all Calvinists and Arminians who interpret fidelity to their confessions as the quest to find biblically faithful and philosophically tenable foundations for their theological touchstones rather than the preservation of traditional defenses, in spite of their potential biblical or philosophical limitations, for these touchstones.

Excursus

Mathematically Depicting the Revised Molinist Scheme

Let us employ a mathematical analogy to elucidate the transition from higher to lower–order infinite sets of worlds on our revised Molinist scheme.

---

straint between the options compatible with one's nature. On this view, unregenerate humans, due to original sin, lack the ability to choose between spiritual good and evil. Just as a bad tree can bear bad fruit or no fruit at all, unregenerate humanity can either perform spiritual wickedness by actively rebelling against God or do nothing spiritual at all by displaying passivity toward God. See Augustine, *On Forgiveness of Sins and Baptism*, in *Nicene and Post–Nicene Fathers*, First Series, ed. Philip Schaff (Christian Literature Publishing Company, 1887; rep. ed., Peabody, MA: Hendrickson, 1994), 5:57–59, 74–76.

We shall compare the set of possible worlds that God apprehends in his *scientia naturalis* with the set of complex numbers. Through God's *scientia media*, the set of possible worlds is reduced to the lower–order infinite set of feasible worlds, just as the set of complex numbers can be reduced to the lower–order infinite set of real numbers. Next, in the same way that the negative numbers can be removed from the reals to yield the lower–order infinity of positive real numbers (greater than or equal to zero), so God eliminates the feasible worlds where each person does not receive sufficient grace for salvation from the feasible worlds to yield the lower–order infinity of all–gracious feasible worlds. God then narrows down the set of all–gracious feasible worlds to the lower–order infinite set of "salvific optimal worlds" (which obtain to the optimal balance between belief and unbelief), which set of salvific optimal worlds, by subtracting all worlds with more than the necessary amount of evil to achieve the optimal balance, is further narrowed down to the lower–order infinite set of salvific–moral optimal worlds. This procedure parallels the subtraction of all repeating decimal numbers (where the digit repeated is not zero) from the set of all positive reals to give the lower–order infinite set of all positive non–repeating–decimal reals, and then deleting all non–integer terminating decimal numbers (numbers with at least one nonzero decimal digit before the final zero) from the set of all positive non–repeating–decimal reals to give the lower–order infinite set containing all positive integers and all positive irrational numbers. Since we deem it "irrational," so to speak, for an all–good God to create persons who could be lost without hearing an accurate gospel presentation but would have been saved if they had only received special revelation, we associate with the infinite set of irrational numbers all salvific–moral optimal worlds containing any individual $P*$ who is lost in at least one salvific–moral optimal world where $P*$ is either uninformed, misinformed, or ill–informed about Christ and is saved in at least one other salvific–moral optimal world where $P*$ is correctly informed about Christ. Just as the set containing all positive integers and all positive irrationals can be reduced to the lower–order infinite set of all positive integers by removing the irrationals, so God, by discarding all salvific–moral optimal worlds containing any $P*$, reduces the set of salvific–moral optimal worlds to the lower–order infinite set of all salvifically comparable worlds. Finally, like a perfect mathematician who can pick any one of the infinite number of positive integers, God can sovereignly choose to create any one of the infinite number of salvifically comparable worlds, all of which are equally good in every respect, by nothing other than his own free will and good pleasure.

Chapter 3

A Molinist and Contra–Openness Approach to Scriptural "Anthropomorphisms"

Are These Being Misread by Biblically Centrist Christians?

Openness of God Theology (also known as "Open Theism" and "Openness Theology"), a position which made its entry into mainstream Christian thought in 1994 with the publication of the watershed collection of essays *The Openness of God*, endeavors to safeguard libertarian human freedom via the theory that it is logically impossible for God to possess foreknowledge of the truth–value of future contingent propositions, such as counterfactuals of creaturely freedom.[1] Such a theory is predicated upon the assumption (invalid in my estimation) that the only way God could know the truth–value of future contingents is to determine this truth–value in advance of their realization—namely, to cause them to happen or not happen beforehand—which would negate their character as contingent propositions. Openness thinkers typically defend this crucial presupposition with what, in logical form, is expressed in the following *reductio ad absurdum*:

1. Necessarily, if God foreknows some future contingent *C*, then *C* will happen.

---

1. Clark H. Pinnock, Richard Rice, John Sanders, William Hasker, and David Basinger., *The Openness of God: A Biblical Challenge to the Traditional Understanding of God* (Downers Grove, Ill.: InterVarsity Press, 1994); see especially Pinnock, "Systematic Theology," 101–25.

2. God foreknows C.
3. Therefore, C will necessarily happen, which contradicts the contingency of C.[2]

As stated, the argument commits the obvious fallacy in modal logic of distributing the necessary operator governing a conditional statement to the apodosis without distributing it to the protasis. This error serves to transmute the *necessity of the deductive inference* from the major and minor premises to the conclusion (from 1 and 2 to 3, respectively) into the *necessity of the conclusion* (3) itself, when no information concerning the conclusion's modality can be gleaned in this way.[3] So what follows validly from 1 and 2 is not 3, but

3*. Therefore, C will happen.

The legitimate conclusion, 3*, in no way undercuts libertarian freedom, as God's foreknowledge of C only implies that C will happen, which is consistent with a creature's freely doing C, not that C will necessarily happen. Undoubtedly a major source of confusion evident among Openness thinkers is their conflation of certainty, a property of creatures which bears no relationship to truth, with necessity, a property of statements ensuring that they cannot possibly be false.[4] For it is true that from 1 and 2 we can be absolutely certain that C will occur, but our certainty (which could possibly be misplaced) is entirely independent of C's occurrence, since knowledge is not causally determinative. Hence C will occur, and it will occur contingently. Lest the skeptic of this claim query as to the ground of C's truth and subsequently adjudge C groundless apart from its determination by God, my refutation of the "grounding objection" in chapter two is here germane, which revealed that divine supercomprehension affords C with two independent grounds of truth—God's perfect knowledge of his own imagination and his infinite discernment.

---

2. Clark H. Pinnock, "God Limits His Knowledge," in *Predestination and Free Will: Four Views of Divine Sovereignty and Human Freedom*, eds. David Basinger and Randall Basinger (Downers Grove, Ill.: InterVarsity Press, 1986), 150; Gregory A. Boyd, *Trinity and Process: A Critical Evaluation and Reconstruction of Hartshorne's Di-Polar Theism Towards a Trinitarian Metaphysics* (New York: Peter Lang, 1992), 296–341; Boyd, *God of the Possible: A Biblical Introduction to the Open View of God* (Grand Rapids, Mich.: Baker, 2000), 122.
3. Craig, *Only Wise God*, 72–74; Alvin Plantinga, *God, Freedom, and Evil* (Grand Rapids, Mich.: Eerdmans, 1977), 66–72.
4. Moreland and Craig, *Philosophical Foundations*, 519.

Realizing the fallaciousness of the foregoing form of the syllogism, some Openness theologians have tried to enhance its plausibility by repairing its structural incoherence—namely, by distributing the necessary operator to the conditional's protasis—thus replacing 2 with

2*. Necessarily, God foreknows C.[5]

Unfortunately, the intrinsic consistency acquired by 2* seems to be purchased at the high price of revising theology proper, for it robs God of his own free will, universally regarded as a necessary attribute of God throughout Christian history, whereby God could have created a different world in which C does not transpire or even no world at all.[6] In order to forestall this dilemma, proponents of 2* have attempted to show another way in which God could necessarily know C and yet retain his freedom—namely, through his entrance into time at the moment of creation. Since God and his beliefs are inseparable, and since God has known every C from the very first temporal moment, God's knowledge of all future contingents is said to be fixed in the past via "temporal necessity," as the past is now unalterable or unpreventable.[7] However, two fatal errors appear to plague this notion. First, it posits a constraint on temporal becoming which is simply unintelligible. For if past knowledge of future contingents destroys their contingency, then any time some human H_1 knows a future contingent about another human H_2 through H_1's finite apprehension of H_2's essence, as seen in the example of Craig's counterfactual knowledge concerning his wife's eating habits from chapter two, H_1 forces H_2 to do as H_1 knows by the mere fact of H_1's knowledge, which is not only absurd but also contradicts the self–evident principle that knowledge is not causally determinative. Second, it unjustifiably presupposes that the unchangeability of the past makes God's foreknowledge inevitable, as it is now fixed in the past. In defense of this assumption, its advocates have often pointed to the fact that backward causation is impossible. Nevertheless, this impossibility is relevant only if there does not exist any functional equivalent to backward causation by which present and future actions can render the past different than it would have been otherwise, and such a functional equivalent is readily provided by *scientia media*.

On the Molinist view, it lies within the power of every individual to

---

5. William Hasker, *God, Time and Knowledge* (Ithaca, N.Y.: Cornell University Press, 1989), 73–74; John Sanders, *The God Who Risks: A Theology of Providence* (Downers Grove, Ill.: InterVarsity Press, 1998), 220–22.

6. Moreland and Craig, *Philosophical Foundations*, 519–20.

7. Craig, "Middle–Knowledge View," 129.

freely perform any action *A* such that if *A* occurred, God's *scientia media* logically prior to the existence of time, and derivatively his foreknowledge within the temporal past, would have been different than it in fact was. To illustrate, suppose that God has always known that in the year 2006 I would submit an abstract to speak at a professional conference. Up until the submission deadline arrives, I possess the ability to avail or disavail myself of the opportunity. If the deadline passes without my writing an abstract, then the past would have included God's foreknowledge of my non–submission, instead of my submission, of the abstract. That God, in the past, would have held different foreknowledge than he in fact held results from the fact that different counterfactual propositions, which God would have discerned via his *scientia media*, would have been true.[8] So while God's foreknowledge of human decisions is chronologically prior to those decisions, human decisions are logically prior to God's foreknowledge of them and can thus acausally affect an essentially timeless God.[9] Hence without resorting to the incoherence of changing what the past *was* with regard to divine foreknowledge via backward causation, the acausal character of the Molinist relation between creaturely choices and their corresponding counterfactual propositions entails that humans can perform the precisely comparable task of changing what the past *would have been* by way of their free decisions.[10]

For these reasons, the philosophical efforts proferred thus far to demonstrate the logical impossibility of God's foreknowledge of future contingents have failed.[11] Therefore, Openness thinkers have turned to an exegetical strategy to convince biblically centrist Christians—namely, those committed to the authority of Scripture in (at least) matters of faith—that God does not know contingents of creaturely freedom. In a sound hermeneutical approach,

---

8. See Ibid., 131–32 for a similar example.

9. Molina, *Foreknowledge*, 4.52.1–8, 20–30.

10. This conclusion was first reached by Molina (Ibid., 4.52.38), and its ramifications have been fruitfully expanded by Flint, *Divine Providence*, 229–50 and Alvin Plantinga, "On Ockham's Way Out," *Faith and Philosophy* 3 (1986): 235–69.

11. Thus the deft judgment of Augustine still stands: "For to confess that God exists, and at the same time to deny that he has foreknowledge of future things, is the most manifest folly. . . . For one who is not prescient of all future things is not God" (*The City of God*, trans. Henry Bettenson [New York: Penguin, 1984], 5.9). Clearly such a cognitively limited deity would not be God on Anselm's standard definition as "that than which nothing greater can be conceived" or "the greatest conceivable being" (*Proslogion*, in *The Major Works*, trans. Brian Davies and Gillian Evans [Oxford: Oxford University Press, 1998], 87–89).

Openness thinkers insist, a biblical statement may be interpreted as metaphor only if there exists a literal truth which the statement figuratively expresses. Without such a literal truth at its core, the statement, by definition, cannot be metaphorical and must constitute either a literal truth itself or a meaningless combination of words. Since no divinely inspired statement can be pointless, the relevant description must relate an actual state of affairs.[12] Consequently, Openness proponents then apply this methodology to what I will dub "divine relational changeability" texts, or texts portraying God as altering plans or discovering truths due to his relationship with humans. Foremost among such passages are claims that God "changes his mind" (Ex. 32:9–14; Isa. 38:1–5; Jer. 18:4–11; 26:7–19; Joel 2:12–13; Jnh. 3:9–4:2), "repents of" or "regrets" decisions he himself made (Gen. 6:6; 1 Sam. 13:13; 15:10; 15:35; 1 Chr. 21:15), confronts situations other than or contrary to what he had expected (Isa. 5:2–5; 63:8–10; Jer. 3:3–20; 7:31; 32:35; Ezek. 22:30–31), and tests people to learn the level of their commitment to him (Gen. 22:12; Deut. 8:2–21; 13:1–3; Jdg. 3:4; 2 Chr. 32:31).[13] While these passages are typically explained away by biblically centrist scholars as anthropomorphisms, or metaphors depicting God in human terms,[14] Openness theologians protest, persuasively in my judgment, that it is impossible on such a reading to identify any literal truths to which these passages point, thereby evacuating the texts of any substance. Contrasting the divine relational changeability texts with procedurally valid anthropomorphisms, such as God's possession of physical features, Gregory A. Boyd asserts:

> Expressions like "the right hand of God" or "the eyes of the Lord," for example, communicate something true of God's strength and knowledge. But what does the concept of God's changing his mind communicate, for example, if indeed it is an anthropomorphism? If God in fact never changes his mind, saying he does so doesn't communicate any-

---

12. Boyd, *God of the Possible*, 54, 60, 67, 71–72, 120; Sanders, *God Who Risks*, 69–70.

13. Millard J. Erickson, *What Does God Know and When Does He Know It? The Current Controversy over Divine Foreknowledge* (Grand Rapids, Mich.: Zondervan, 2003), 17–38.

14. Bruce Ware, "An Evangelical Reformulation of the Doctrine of the Immutability of God," *Journal of the Evangelical Theological Society* 29 (1986): 442; Norman L. Geisler, *Creating God in the Image of Man? NeoTheism's Dangerous Drift* (Minneapolis: Bethany House, 1997), 90, 108; Klein, Blomberg, and Hubbard, *Biblical Interpretation*, 242–46; Erickson, *What Does God Know*, 61–62.

thing truthful: it is simply inaccurate.[15]

Hence, Openness theologians conclude, the texts cannot be interpreted as metaphorical, but must refer to literal facts about God. Since God, it is alleged, cannot express aspects of cognitive alterability or development in his dealings with humans if he previously foreknew everything that they would do, God must lack knowledge of future contingents, on pain of denying biblical infallibility.

To understand the standard biblically centrist response to the Openness interpretation of divine relational changeability texts, a brief excursion into the historical theology of late antiquity is beneficial. Influenced by the Platonic conception of the Form of the Good, or the perfect immaterial idea grounding all other immaterial forms (*e.g.* justice, love, knowledge), the first–century Jewish philosophical theologian Philo of Alexandria identified the Form of the Good as the nature of Yahweh and therefore posited that all Hebrew Biblical texts describing Yahweh in a manner inconsistent with his perfect nature, including those calling his omniscience into question, are metaphors rather than literal truths, just as Plato had argued concerning stories of the Greek gods.[16] Resulting in an anthropomorphic explication of divine relational changeability passages, this hermeneutical approach was imported into Christian thought with the tripartite methodology of the Alexandrian school (featured most prominently in the second–century treatises of Clement of Alexandria and the third–century systematics of Origen), according to which the primary meaning of each biblical text resided in one of three senses (φυσικός, ψυχικός, πνευματικός = literal, moral, spiritual).[17] Although this methodology and its Medieval successor, the *Quadriga*, have been largely discredited by contemporary biblical centrists in favor of the

---

15. Gregory A. Boyd, "The Open–Theism View," in *Divine Foreknowledge*, 39.

16. Philo of Alexandria, *The Contemplative Life, The Giants, and Selections*, trans. David Winston (New York: Paulist, 1981), 137–41; Plato, *The Republic*, trans. Allan Bloom, 2nd ed. (San Francisco: Basic Books, 1991), 1:377b–383c; Valentin Nikiprowetzky, *Le commentaire de l'écriture chez Philon d'Alexandrien: Son caractère et sa portée, observations philologiques* (Leiden: Brill, 1977), 134–47.

17. Clement of Alexandria, *The Stromata, Book II*, in *Ante–Nicene Fathers*, Vol. 2, trans. Alexander Roberts and James Donaldson, rep. ed. (Peabody, Mass.: Hendrickson, 1994), 363–64; Origen, *De Principiis, Book IV*, in *Ante–Nicene Fathers*, Vol. 4, 359–74; J. C. McLelland, *God the Anonymous: A Study in Alexandrian Philosophical Theology* (Cambridge, Mass.: The Philadelphia Patristic Foundation, 1976), 4:37–40, 122–23.

grammatico–historical approach (also rooted in the Patristic era and championed by the Antiochene school as the chief tripartite competitor), the former's general principle of allegorizing texts which seem to undermine divine perfection has persisted among centrists as a convenient "escape hatch." Not surprisingly, Openness theologians have accused biblical centrists of compromising their professed touchstone of *sola scriptura* by retreating to tradition driven by philosophical motivations.[18]

Concurring with the Openness disclosure of the exegetical problem but dissenting from its proposed solution thereof, I will posit a new interpretive approach which uses *sola scriptura* according to its original definition by Martin Luther—"the sufficient clarity of Scripture alone coupled with sound reason"[19]—to show precisely how the divine relational changeability texts convey more than mere metaphorical descriptions but signify real cognitive events transpiring in the divine life. Not only will this Reformation-grounded hermeneutic allow Scripture to interpret Scripture in the usual textual sense, such that unclear passages treating a given topic may be illuminated by clear passages treating the same topic, but it will also facilitate the self–interpretation of Scripture in the philosophical realm by shedding light on difficult texts with doctrines which, while never spelled out explicitly in any single text, can be validly derived by applying deductive logic to a collection of texts. As defended in chapter one, *scientia media* is one such doctrine. With this granted, my approach will implement *scientia media* in a fresh new way to reveal the significance of divine relational changeability statements in a way that does justice to the sacred text while maintaining the conclusion, unambiguously affirmed by passages every bit as clear as those denoting divine relational changeability, that God possesses foreknowledge of future contingents.[20]

---

18. Boyd, *God of the Possible*, 12; "God vs. God," *Christianity Today* 44.2 (7 February 2000): 35.

19. The formulation comes originally from Luther's *Bondage of the Will*, in *Luther's Works, American Edition*, ed. Jaroslav Pelikan (St. Louis: Concordia Publishing House, 1955–86), 18:616, and has received careful scholarly attention in Brian Albert Gerrish, *Grace and Reason* (Oxford: Clarendon Press, 1962), 168–71 and Mark D. Thompson, *A Sure Ground on Which to Stand: The Relation of Authority and Interpretive Method in Luther's Approach to Scripture* (Carlisle: Paternoster, 2004), 265–74. By "sound reason" or "evident reason" (*ratione evidente*) Luther meant the valid use of the laws of logic, as opposed to the dishonest fashioning of a logical veneer to blind the underinformed.

20. Erickson devotes an entire chapter to the enumeration of such texts in *What Does God Know*, 39–60; worthy of special mention is his skillful exegesis of Psalm 139:4, "Even before there is any word on my tongue, behold, O Yah-

Probing the Profundity of the First and Second Moments within the Structure of God's Omniscience

As delineated in chapter one, *scientia media* constitutes the center of the tripartite logical structure of divine omniscience, preceded by *scientia naturalis* and succeeded by *scientia libera*. To review, moreover, chapter two delineated the divine cognitive events—represented by (3), (3.1), (3.2), (4*), and (4.1)—transpiring between (2) *scientia media* and (5 or 5*) *scientia libera* on our revised Molinist scheme; however, unlike the biblically derived (1), (2), and (5), the intervening events (3.1), (3.2), (4*), and (4.1) as well as the upgraded (5*) are neither explicitly nor deductively taught in Scripture (although they are complementary to it) and so play no role in our interpretive approach. It is thus entirely possible to reject (3.1) through (5*) and embrace the hermeneutic found in this chapter, as their truth values are logically independent of one another.

At this juncture, we shall delve more deeply into the logical structure of God's omniscience. If God is, among other things, the supremely logical and rational mind, and if God apprehends the contents of his omniscience in logical (not, of course, temporal) sequence, then it follows that not only would the three broad moments of his omniscience flow in logical order, but also every fact apprehended during each moment would flow in logical order. Therefore in *scientia naturalis* (moment one), God gleans knowledge of all *possibilia* (*i.e.* all events that *could* happen) as they progressively unfold in logical sequence and thus accumulate into possible worlds, rather than obtaining his knowledge about all possible worlds logically simultaneously.[21] This distinction, I maintain, is pivotal for dissolving the prevalent misconception, evident among Openness adherents, non–Molinists, and most defenders of Molinism alike, that Molina's threefold architecture of omniscience entails that for each logical moment, God simultaneously apprehends a complete segment of knowledge "all at once."[22] We shall now

---

weh, you know כֻלָּה." By demonstrating that כֻלָּה means "both all of it and every one," Erickson proves that this text demands God's exhaustive foreknowledge of the psalmist, of which "any word" is an example. For confirmation of this exegesis see Franz Delitzsch, *Biblical Commentary on the Psalms* (Grand Rapids, Mich.: Eerdmans, 1955), 3:346.

21. God's logically sequential apprehension of knowledge within moments one and two is observed in Molina, *Foreknowledge*, 4.49.12–16, 50.15–20.

22. Gregory A. Boyd, *Satan and the Problem of Evil: Constructing a Trinitarian Warfare Theodicy* (Downers Grove, Ill.: InterVarsity Press, 2001), 126–29; Geisler, *Baker Encyclopedia of Christian Apologetics*, s.v. "Molinism,"

move to the logical ramifications of such a significant correction for moments one and two.

To start, it should be pointed out that God necessarily possesses initial intuition as a corollary to his libertarian freedom, and the integrity of this initial intuition is preserved by the fact that God, as a free agent, cannot supercomprehend himself.[23] Combining this insight with our expanded description of *scientia naturalis*, God would, logically simultaneous with his cognitive observation of successive events, naturally apply his initial intuition to these events, thereby yielding divine speculation as to which events and sequences of events would actually transpire in light of creaturely freedom. This means, moreover, that God, innately knowing his own character, would also intuit how he would react if the intuitively envisaged events and sequences actually transpired. But these suppositions entail, as admitted (either explicitly or implicitly) on all hands, that God has already made some basic decisions both as to what kind of creatures he would create and as to how he would treat his creatures.[24] For example, God would not apprehend his *scientia naturalis* without first deciding to reflect on the possibility of creating a world of libertarian free creatures existing in time and space. In addition, God would have already chosen, on the condition that he opted to create a world, to enter into time and space to sustain temporal relations with his creatures. If this is accurate, then it seems eminently reasonable to assume that God committed himself to other spatio–temporal principles in relating to humanity. But what exactly are these principles?

Notice that God, logically prior to apprehending his *scientia media*, has already conjectured as to how each possible individual human essence or pattern, if instantiated, would employ its libertarian freedom and how he

---

493–94; Muller, *God, Creation, and Providence*, 156; Alfred J. Freddoso, "On Divine Middle Knowledge," in *Philosophy of Religion*, ed. William Lane Craig (New Brunswick, N.J.: Rutgers University Press, 2002), 257–64.

23. As rightly perceived by Molina (*Divine Foreknowledge*, 4.52.11–13, 4.53.17–21) over against Francisco Suarez; for a thorough historical discussion of this debate in early modern Catholic philosophical theology see Johann Rabeneck, "De Vita et Scriptis Ludovici Molina," *Archivum Historicum Societatis Iesu* 19 (1950): 122–40.

24. Robert Adams, "Middle Knowledge and the Problem of Evil," *American Philosophical Quarterly* 14 (1977): 109–17; Richard Rice, "In Response to Nancy Howell," in *Searching for an Adequate God: A Dialogue Between Process and Free Will Theists*, eds. John B. Cobb, Jr. and Clark H. Pinnock, 94–95; Boyd, *Satan and the Problem of Evil*, 121; Clark H. Pinnock, *Most Moved Mover: A Theology of God's Openness* (Grand Rapids, Mich.: Baker, 2001), 139; Erickson, *What Does God Know*, 189–212.

would respond in turn. In other words, God, as the supremely rational mind, involuntarily and automatically senses what the content of his *scientia media* would probably include logically prior to his apprehension of what it actually includes. With this in mind, we are now in a position to disclose a subset of the principles entailed by God's choice to enter the spatio–temporal manifold of any possible world, if subsequently actualized, for the purpose of maintaining relationships with the humans therein. First, God becomes an actor in every possible, and derivatively feasible, set of circumstances. As previously implied, in his *scientia media* God apprehends the truth–values of all counterfactuals of creaturely freedom as they progressively unfold in logical sequence, thus disclosing to him all events that *would* and *would not* happen. Throughout this successive unfolding, God would literally experience various emotions across a wide spectrum, including surprise, regret, and frustration, as he discovers that respective events would turn out differently than he had anticipated. As an actor in each set of circumstances, moreover, God would literally change his plans with respect to free creatures as they confirmed or disconfirmed his expectations, and he would manage those circumstances as to examine and thus increasingly ascertain the character of his creatures. Hence there exists genuine reciprocity in the relationship between God and humanity, as human actions, such as prayer and prayerlessness, good and bad choices, and faithfulness and faithlessness under temptation, are logically prior to the divine responses and thus comprise the backdrop against which God's reactions take place. By virtue of the libertarian freedom of both parties, humans have the power to generate various situations in light of which God operates and vice versa. Accordingly, those trajectories comprised entirely of compossible events (those which logically cohere given human freedom) solidify into what we shall style "practicable worlds," while those trajectories containing at least one incompossible event drop out of further divine consideration.

Having already factored his initial intuitions, free creaturely decisions, and his original reactions thereto—in other words, the emotions which God experiences and the changes of plans and character–testing management of circumstances which God decides to implement when first confronted with the successive unfolding of creaturely choices—into the equation, God knows at this logical point everything that would transpire in each practicable world if actualized as is. Owing to the love he would have for his creatures if actualized and his consequent overarching plans for the world they would comprise, God providentially fine–tunes each practicable world through an exhaustive procedure of cognitively "trying out" various modifications on his original reactions in view of his ensuing comprehensive knowledge of that world. In the first step of this twofold algorithm, as it were, God would recursively alter his various original reactions, in all their possible permutations, to human choices in light of his complete knowledge of everything else that would happen in that world if the original reactions were left in tact. These permutations would encompass the full spectrum of possible alterations on the original reactions, from some to all, meaning that God's original reactions would sometimes be preserved and sometimes altered in view of their future ramifications. The alterations would subsequently give rise to new human choices followed by new original divine reactions, thus leading to further iterations of this step. After completing this all–encompassing first step, God would then compare his complete knowledge of each revised version of the practicable world generated by the various iterations to find the version optimally suited to achieve his sovereign aims for humanity. At this point God's *scientia media* is rounded out, as each optimal revision solidifies into a feasible world.[25] Via this thorough revision process God perfectly couples divine accommodation with divine sovereignty: he accommodates himself to human space–time limitations when choosing to preserve his original reaction to events without consideration of the future; and he sovereignly transcends those space–time limitations when choosing to act according to his knowledge of everything that would happen in that as well as any other revisionary iteration of its original paradigm, or practicable world, as in the cases of predictive prophecy, plans for individuals and groups requiring future and counterfactual knowledge, statements conveying counterfactual, conditional, or predestinary information, and the like.[26] Such a providential balance is rendered seamless by the

---

25. Not only is our logical extrapolation of this exhaustive fine–tuning of worlds fully consistent with Molina's thought, it actually appears to be latent in his description of the divine cognitive activities comprising *scientia media*: "[C]learly it should not be claimed that God knows before the determination of his own will which part that will is going to determine itself to, but it should rather be claimed that in that prior instant the divine intellect only shows him . . . those things that would come that would come to be because of any creatable faculty of choice on any hypothesis and within any order of things—so that, given an absolutely comprehensive deliberation on the part of the intellect, the will by its choice establishes and arranges all things, and, consistently with the freedom of created choice, provides for all things" (*Foreknowledge*, 4.52.15).

26. This is substantiated by the fact that, since there exists a major ontological difference between the Creator and his creation, "God's personal interaction with created personal beings must have a special *modus vivendi*, which takes into account the limitations of created person*ness* . . . whereby the eternal God operates relationally within the space/time context with a moral being less than Himself . . . [and] establishes the moral and physical parameters through which

criterion against which all accommodation–sovereignty decisions are made: God's most advantageous promotion, certified by the full scope of his counterfactual knowledge, of his omnibenevolent purposes for humanity in general and each individual in particular.

In sum, our dissection of *scientia media* has revealed that this second moment of divine omniscience is comprised of two layers: God's progressive apprehension of the truth–value of all counterfactuals of creaturely freedom as they unfold in logical sequence coupled with his original reactions to these counterfactuals; and God's transformation of each practicable world into a feasible world by fine–tuning it according to his full knowledge of everything that could or would happen in the entire history of that world as a result of different divine responses to creaturely choices. Our scheme thus beautifully explains the various aspects of counterfactual knowledge exhibited by Jesus in his denunciation of the unrepentant cities where he had performed most of his miracles:

> Woe to you, Chorazin! Woe to you, Bethsaida! For if the miracles that were performed in you had been performed in Tyre and Sidon, they would have repented long ago in sackcloth and ashes. Nevertheless I say to you, it will be more tolerable for Tyre and Sidon on the day of judgment than for you. And you, Capernaum, will you be exalted to heaven? No, you will descend to Hades; for if the miracles that were performed in you had been performed in Sodom, it would have remained to this day. Nevertheless I say to you, it will be more tolerable for Sodom on the day of judgment than for you (Q; Mt. 11:21–24; *cf.* Lk. 10:13–15).

For every possible divine action across the sweep of time and space, therefore, Jesus counterfactually knows in his subliminal Logos–consciousness the free creaturely response.[27] Our model also divulges why God chose to incarnately perform the miracles in the first–century C.E. Galilean cities of Chorazin, Bethsaida, and Capernaum rather than in the contemporaneous Syro–Phoenician cities of Tyre and Sidon or in nineteenth–century B.C.E. Sodom: because he knew, in the second layer of *scientia media*, that the state of affairs including the Galilean miracles and excluding miracles in Tyre, Sidon, and Sodom would better achieve his overall salvific

God is able to be involved dynamically and meaningfully in His creation" (Bruce A. Little, *A Creation–Order Theodicy: God and Gratuitous Evil* [Lanham, Md.: University Press of America, 2005], 136-37, emphasis his).

27. Such is precisely Molina's exegesis of this text (*Foreknowledge*, 4.49.9).

plans for humanity than any other conceivable state of affairs.

Our multilayered conception of *scientia media* furnishes us with an incisive hermeneutical strategy for successfully reading divine relational changeability texts as more than empty metaphors but as conveying literal truths—namely, the precise descriptions of God's original reactions to various situations logically prior to his apprehension of the full scope of truths about the world—without resorting to the unscriptural conclusion that God lacks knowledge of future contingents. On the other hand, passages depicting predictive prophecy, foreknowledge, counterfactual knowledge, election, reprobation, and foreordination literally express truths known or decisions made by God logically posterior to apprehending the full scope of truths about the world. In short, divine relational changeability passages could be said to be accurate on the first layer of *scientia media*, while passages entailing God's knowledge of "the end from the beginning" are accurate on the second layer of *scientia media*. Let us furnish some poignant applications of our hermeneutical strategy, which we will dub the "multilayered *scientia media* hermeneutic," which shed new light upon key scriptural texts.

Applying the Multilayered *Scientia Media* Hermeneutic to Representative Biblical Passages

From the perspective of our hermeneutic, rooted in the tradition of *sola Scriptura* plus sound reason, we shall now consider several passages representative of the four textual categories utilized by Openness theologians to support their position. Throughout these case studies it will be demonstrated that our hermeneutic possesses tremendous explanatory power to account for all these categories as well as greater plausibility and explanatory scope over the whole of the Scriptural canon than the Openness alternative. Our interdisciplinary hermeneutic thus synthesizes the best methods in biblical studies and philosophy of religion by respectively employing grammatico-historical exegesis to determine the original meaning of each text and then explaining the theological implications of that meaning via philosophical insights validly deduced from Scriptural premises.

I.   *Divine Changes of Mind*

In the famous golden calf incident, God's chosen people renege on their promise to keep the Mosaic Covenant through flagrant acts of idolatry and debauchery, violating at least three of the Ten Commandments. After the children of Israel manufacture and worship the golden calf, Exodus 32:9–14 relates the following conversation between Yahweh and Moses:

> Yahweh said to Moses, "I have seen this people, and behold, they are a stiff-necked people. Now leave me alone so that my anger may burn against them and that I may destroy them. Then I will make you into a great nation." But Moses entreated Yahweh his God, saying, "O Yahweh, why should your anger burn against your people, whom you brought out of Egypt with great power and a mighty hand. . . . Turn from your fierce anger; relent and do not bring disaster on your people" . . . So Yahweh changed his mind about the harm which he said he would do to his people.

On the multilayered *scientia media* hermeneutic, this passage describes God's original reaction to the possibility of the Israelites' worshiping the golden calf—only having apprehended the truth of the circumstances logically leading up to this, God literally wanted to destroy the Israelites and make from Moses a new nation, thereby fulfilling his covenant to Abraham. However, upon apprehending the logically successive knowledge that Moses, if apprised of this reaction, would implore God to spare the Israelites, God's mind, or planned reaction, literally changed to a new course of action which left the Israelites intact. However, our exegesis in no way compromises divine omniscience or immutability, as this divine relational changeability text only reflects the first level of God's *scientia media*, which is logically prior both to his complete knowledge of all counterfactuals on the second respective level and to his decree to create the actual world.

Similarly, consider the account of Hezekiah's illness in Isaiah 38:1–5 (*cf.* 2 Kgs. 20:1–6):

> In those days Hezekiah became ill and was at the point of death. The prophet Isaiah the son of Amoz came to him and said, "Thus says Yahweh: Put your house in order, for you shall die; you will not recover." Then Hezekiah turned his face to the wall and prayed to Yahweh, "Remember, O Yahweh, how I have walked before you in truth and with wholehearted devotion and have done what is good in your sight." And Hezekiah wept bitterly. Then the word of Yahweh came to Isaiah: "Go and say to Hezekiah, 'Thus says Yahweh, the God of your father David: I have heard your prayer, and I have seen your tears; behold, I will add fifteen years to your life."

In this fascinating text, pregnant with implications for Christian prayer, God's original reaction when confronted with Hezekiah's failing health was to give him forewarning through Isaiah about his impending death. This alert would ensure that the appropriate inheritance would be passed on to Hezekiah's family members, that the next king would be of the Davidic line, and that a smooth transition of monarchical succession would transpire. However, at the logically successive moment when God discerned that Hezekiah, upon such a revelation, would entreat him for a longer life, God's response to Hezekiah is to lengthen his life by fifteen years. All of this occurred in the first level of God's *scientia media*. But God knew all the truths concerning the situation, including his prediction of Hezekiah's passing, Hezekiah's entreaties for a longer life, and his miraculous renewal of Hezekiah's health for fifteen extra years, at the concluding second step of his *scientia media* and thus explanatorily prior to selecting the world in which we now live to be actual.

Understood in light of the distinction between how God "gains" his *scientia media* (in a logically cumulative way) and his full apprehension of all knowledge gleaned thereby, we now face stunning consequences which demonstrate the necessity and power of prayer. We can literally change what God would have done otherwise through our prayers, just as the prayers of Moses and Hezekiah changed the course of affairs God initially planned on taking when confronted with certain events. Hence we, through our prayers for others ("standing in the gap") and for ourselves, can have a tremendous impact on what God's "plan" is for our lives. This provides some much–needed revising of the typical concept of God's predetermined or foreordained "plan" for each person independent of his or her free will which the person in question must attempt to discover and follow. Rather, God's "plan" is developed in dialogue between himself and the individual believer. We can plead with God, as did Moses, for mercy upon the lives of the rebellious and unjust both within and outside the church, such that our pleading may well cause God to show mercy he otherwise would not have shown. Hence we, through our prayers, can literally quell God's anger against the godless.

Moreover, apart from the rare circumstances when God unmistakably reveals to us a specific purpose or unmistakably instructs us to do something (as he did in the cases of Moses and Hezekiah), God's will may be defined as our own will acting within the boundaries of God's moral and spiritual dictates when God does not prevent it from so acting, where God does prevent the will's actions when he, in light of the full scope of his omniscience, knows that these actions would give rise to some situation inimical to his "caus[ing] all things to work together for good to those who love him" (Rom. 8:28). An example will suffice to illustrate the point. Suppose a missionary is planning where she will carry out her next project and has not received any supernatural disclosure as to where God specifically wants her. Desiring to work in a certain place, she can rest assured that, wherever she decides to go, she will be in God's will since her choice is made within the confines of God's command to carry out the Great Commission. Thus she should not trouble herself with "figuring out" where God has willed for her to go, lest she waste her time trying to solve a literally self–contradictory problem. In other words, God's will is conditioned on his middle knowledge of where, if the missionary were to exist, she would freely desire to go, and God's will for her trip lacked all reality logically prior to such conditioning. However, she can also trust, in light of Romans 8:28, that if God in his omniscience knew that her traveling to the intended destination would be counterproductive to his working for the good of all believers, then God would sovereignly actualize circumstances that would prevent her from going there and cause her to go someplace else where her work would prove instrumental in God's omnibenevolent oversight of the world.

II.   *Divine "Repentance" or "Regret" for Decisions Made*

The first level of our multilayered *scientia media* hermeneutic allows us to readily understand texts where God experiences sorrow over certain choices as literal depictions of his original reaction when free creatures responded to these choices by violating his moral will. However, in light of the full range of counterfactual truths about our world, God chose to retain these choices, which he could have easily cognitively undone, as best suited for his providential plans. So although God's initial reaction to such decisions was regret, in retrospect (*i.e.* the second level of *scientia media*) God perceived that these decisions were actually the best of all the possible decisions he could have made and thus chose to retain them. Accordingly, texts such as Genesis 6:6, "Yahweh was sorry that he had made humanity on the earth," convey God's initial feeling of regret when he first apperceived the counterfactual of humanity's sinfulness in logical sequence, and thus in isolation from the counterfactuals following therefrom, rather than his regret given the full scope of knowledge he apperceived via the totality of his *scientia media* before choosing to actualize our world.

III.   *Divine Confrontation of and Frustration toward the Unexpected*

The poignancy of the multilayered *scientia media* hermeneutic is brilliantly illustrated in this class of texts, as it reveals how counterfactuals of creaturely freedom can be surprising to God when immediately ascertained on level one but unsurprising given his decision to create the world following level two. Jeremiah 3:3–20 features the elements of divine incredulity and frustration at Israel's brazen violations of the Mosaic Covenant and subsequent refusal to repent, sins amounting in severity to spiritual adultery:

> During the reign of King Josiah, Yahweh said to me [Jeremiah], "Have you seen what faithless Israel has done? She has gone up on every high hill and under every spreading tree and has committed adultery there. I thought that after she had done all this she would return to me but she did not. . . . I myself said, 'How gladly would I treat you like sons and give you a desirable land, the most beautiful inheritance of any nation. I thought you would call me "Father" and not turn away from following me. But like a woman unfaithful to her husband, so you have been unfaithful to me, O house of Israel.'"

This text should make us ponder the gravity of our own sins, as we can behave in ways that literally astonished and discouraged God when he first perceived them in counterfactual form. Nevertheless, nothing we say or do surprises God at the current time–space moment, as he foreknew all our free actions logically prior to his divine creative decree. Therefore, while God truly did not expect Israel to be faithless much less persevere in iniquity upon ascertaining his *scientia naturalis*, leading the counterfactual discernment of such wickedness to initially come as a surprise, he was certainly not caught unawares when the sins actually took place in space and time.

IV. Divine Testing of Human Character

The most famous testing passage in all of Scripture comes in Genesis 22, where God makes the unprecedented demand of Abraham that he sacrifice Isaac, the son of promise whose birth God had miraculously made possible, upon Mount Moriah. However, upon God's apprehension of the truth that Abraham had made the final decision to slay Isaac, seen in the Patriarch's taking out the knife for the sacrifice, God prevents Isaac's death via the instruction: "Do not lay a hand on the boy. Do not do anything to him. Now I know that you fear God, because you have not withheld from me your son, your unique son" (v. 12). This statement about God's obtaining the information that Abraham fears him is, on the multilayered *scientia media* hermeneutic, a literal non–apprehension of the degree to which Abraham was committed to him until, as an actor on the first level of *scientia media*, God discerned what the response of Abraham would be if created and asked to sacrifice Isaac. However, Genesis 22:12 does not imply that God gained knowledge of Abraham in time, as God's counterfactual and actual knowledge of Abraham were respectively exhaustive upon the second level of *scientia media* and the divine creative decree. But this passage does explain how God legitimately "tested" Abraham—namely, by initially discerning within the scope of his *scientia media* what Abraham would do if commanded to sacrifice the promised son and then choosing to actualize those states of affairs.

A Concluding Evaluation

We have seen that the multilayered *scientia media* hermeneutic enriches the study of Scripture by bringing stunning new insights to texts which, in recent times as well as periodically throughout Christian history, have been problematic. The problematic nature of these "divine relational changeability" texts is teased out by the fact that they are normally classified as anthropomorphisms, or metaphorical descriptions of God from a human viewpoint. However, the difficulty with this exegetical strategy is easily seen when compared with other texts which are clearly anthropomorphisms. Our hermeneutic thus concurs with Openness theology that for a text to classify as metaphorical, of which anthropomorphisms constitute a subset, there must be some literal truth which the metaphor is figuratively expressing. Such is clearly seen in obvious anthropomorphic texts describing God's bodily parts (such as eyes and ears), which are figures of speech pointing to the literal truths of God's being all–perceptive to what is said and done by humans. The reason why, for example, the LDS church is wrong in construing these texts as literal descriptions of God[28] is that they fit perfectly the definition of what it means to be a metaphorical text—for each one, an obvious literal truth can be stated as its referent. However, when it comes to the divine relational changeability texts, although biblically centrist exegetes typically state that these are anthropomorphic metaphors, we are never told the literal truth that stands behinds these metaphors. What is the literal truth of statements that "God changes his mind" or that "God regretted" or that "God was surprised"? In short, these statements fail as metaphors because they are metaphorical for nothing—simply by writing off such passages as anthropomorphisms is pointless unless one can state some literal truth which they express. Like the Openness view, therefore, our hermeneutic rigorously ap-

---

28. *Doctrine and Covenants* 130:22; Joseph Smith, *History of the Church of Jesus Christ of Latter–day Saints* (Salt Lake City: Deseret Book Company, 1973), 6:305–06; Brigham Young, *Journal of Discourses* (London: Latter–day Saints' Book Depot, 1854–56), 1:123.

plies the standards of grammatico–historical exegesis to the divine relational changeability texts, which standards demand their literal and *prima facie* construal, and thus possesses the explanatory power to coherently account for all such texts. Hence our hermeneutic is superior to the typical biblical centrist approach, which lacks such explanatory power.

In addition, our hermeneutic proves its superiority to the Openness approach in the realms of explanatory scope and plausibility. It exhibits greater explanatory scope than the Openness alternative in its universal applicability to all texts in the biblical canon—in particular, both the set of divine relational changeability texts and the set of texts positing exhaustive divine counterfactual knowledge and foreknowledge—rather than, in Openness fashion, championing the *prima facie* significance of the first set by denying the *prima facie* significance of the second. To delineate this second set, Openness thinkers find themselves forced into the precarious interpretation that God only knows some, but not all, counterfactuals and future events as well as, ironically, that God only knows those counterfactuals and future events which he deterministically caused to occur! Here the Openness method is snared on the same hook as the biblically centrist approach, as the same grammatico–historical standards that demand a straightforward reading of the first set also demand a straightforward reading of the second. Clearly a straightforward reading of the earliest chapters of Deutero–Isaiah (Isa. 40–49) indicates that the prophetic author regarded knowledge of all truths as no less than the essential attribute of God that distinguished him from all false gods:[29]

> "Set forth your case," says Yahweh; "present your arguments," the King of Jacob says. "Let the false gods bring forth and declare to us what is going to take place. Tell us the former things, what they are, so that we may consider them and know their outcome. Or declare to us the things to come; tell us what the future holds, so that we may know that you are gods. . . . This is what Yahweh says, the King and Re-

---

29. I know of no scholar of the book of Isaiah who interprets the Deutero–Isaianic prologue any other way; for verification of my assessment see John N. Oswalt, *The Book of Isaiah: Chapters 40–66, New International Commentary on the Old Testament* (Grand Rapids: Eerdmans, 1998), 43–443 *passim*; Claus Westermann, *Isaiah 40–66*, trans. David M. G. Stalker (London: SCM Press, 1969), 81–91, 138–43, 183–85; John D. W. Watts, *Word Biblical Commentary Vol. 25: Isaiah 34–66* (Nashville: Word, 1987), 109–20, 136–46, 163–68; Lawrence Boadt, *Reading the Old Testament* (New York: Paulist, 1984), 422–26; and Paul R. House, *Old Testament Theology* (Downers Grove, Ill.: InterVarsity Press, 1998), 286–88.

deemer of Israel, Yahweh Almighty: I am the first and I am the last; except me there is no God. Who then is like me? Let him declare and lay out before me what has happened since I established the ancient people and what is yet to come—yes, let him foretell what will come. . . . Remember the former things long past: I am God, and there is no other; I am God, and there is no one like me. I make known the end from the beginning, and from ancient times what is still to come" (41:21–23a, 44:6–8a, 46:9–10a).

According to the rules of grammatico–historical exegesis, both the definite article ה (the) and the relative pronoun אֲשֶׁר (what), seen in such phrases as *"the* things to come," *"the* future holds," "foretell *what* will come," "make known the end from *the* beginning," and "from ancient times *what* is still to come," encompass all elements in a particular class—in this case, all elements in the class of future events, or all facts about the future. Moreover, grammatico–historical exegesis dictates God's exhaustive counterfactual and future knowledge in the New Testament, especially in texts employing neologisms, such as προγινώσκω (foreknow; Rom. 8:29; 11:2), πρόγνωσις (foreknowledge; Acts 2:23; 1 Pet. 1:2), προοράω (foresee; Gal. 3:8), προκαταρτίζω (prepare in advance; Rom. 9:23; Eph. 2:10), προορίζω (predestine; Rom. 8:30; Eph. 1:5; 1:11), προμαρτύρομαι (foretell; Acts 3:18), and προκαταγγέλλω (announce in advance; Gal. 3:8), to specifically denominate such knowledge. Hence the multilayered *scientia media* hermeneutic, by accommodating both God's logically sequential apprehension of counterfactuals of creaturely freedom on the first level and God's cumulative knowledge of all counterfactuals on the second level, is able to use the same methodology for explaining all biblical texts and avoids the error, plaguing Openness and biblically centrist exegetes alike, of picking and choosing when passages should be interpreted grammatico–historically and when not.

By claiming that God only foreknows events he deterministically causes, the Openness model suffers from the implausibility of making God the author of sin, the ultimate incongruity since the model was proposed in 1994 largely to avert Calvinism and its implication of God as the author of sin! Thus God foreknew Joseph's slavery (Gen. 45:5; 50:20), Saul's suicide (1 Chron. 10:14; *cf.* 1 Sam. 31:1–6), Judas' betrayal of Jesus (Jn. 17:26; Acts 1:16–17), and Jesus' rejection by the Jewish religio–political leaders and subsequent crucifixion by the Roman authorities (Acts 2:23; 4:27–28), the prescience of which are granted by Openness theologians, only because he discerned that he would later compel the relevant human intermediaries to commit these sins. Since a perfectly good God cannot, by definition, compel humans to sin, much less punish them for acts over which they had no control, the Openness approach cannot be rationally sustained. On the contrary, the multilayered *scientia media* hermeneutic respectively upholds God's moral purity and magnifies his goodness through its level–one disclosure that sin is always committed contrary to the divine will by free creatures apart from any causal restraints and through its level–two illumination of how God marvelously utilizes the even the most heinous sins on the creaturely given landscape to providentially accomplish his salvific ends, thereby working all things together for good to those who love him.

In short, the multilayered *scientia media* hermeneutic surpasses its competitors both in terms of explanatory scope and plausibility while at least equaling (if not bettering) their explanatory power and is therefore to be preferred. Further, its central insight that divine relational changeability texts are not metaphors but instead refer to God's original reactions to feasible states of affairs when they first presented themselves in his *scientia media* fosters increased prayerfulness and righteousness in daily Christian living. Accommodating himself to our space–time limitations, God has graciously chosen to act with us in many cases (namely, those which would benefit us) according to his original reactions to feasible circumstances rather than always acting with us according to the full scope of his knowledge gleaned from the entirety of his *scientia media* and mediated through *scientia libera.* By choosing to actualize a world where he informs us of his original reactions to states of affairs, God gives us the opportunity to dialogue with him and change his original reactions, although he temporally already knows the entire dialogue and his final reactions in the completeness of his omniscience. This means that we, through our righteous actions and prayers, can change God's original reactions to ordinary circumstances in our lives, his wrath against the wicked, as well as a host of other states of affairs as they first present themselves to him within his *scientia media.* Moreover, it gives us a fresh new look at what "God's will" entails—something fully known by God in the second level of his *scientia media* plus his *scientia libera* which is formed in dialogue between any original reactions God may undeniably disclose to us, our prayers, desires, and deeds, and the full scope of God's omniscience. Such genuine reciprocity between humans and God should motivate us all to develop and nurture our relationship with him.

Chapter 4

The Coexistence of God and Genuinely Gratuitous Evil

For many people, the greatest obstacle to belief in God is the problem of evil and suffering in the world. This problem comes in two forms: logical and probabilistic. The logical version asserts that it is impossible for God, understood as an omnibenevolent (all–good) and omnipotent (all–powerful) being, to coexist alongside evil. However, it is now widely recognized by contemporary philosophers that neither any explicit nor implicit contradiction exists between the statements "God exists" and "evil exists," rendering the logical version simply invalid. Hence people who embrace the logical version are drawn thereto on emotional rather than rational grounds; their problem is pastoral (*i.e.* dissolving their dislike for a deity that can exist without eradicating evil) rather than academic. However, the probabilistic form contends that, while it is logically possible for God and evil in general to coexist, it is quite improbable for God to coexist with a particular strain of evil, namely, gratuitous evil, defined as evil which is pointless or morally unnecessary. The probabilistic version can be stated in the following syllogism:

1. If God exists, then gratuitous evil does not exist.
2. Gratuitous evil exists.
3. Therefore, God does not exist.

Both historically and presently, most theists have attempted to invalidate premise 2 through the so–called "Greater–Good Defense," which posits that God possesses morally sufficient reasons for permitting each one of the world's evils. Because God uses every evil to bring about a greater good, no evil is actually gratuitous even though it may seem gratuitous to humanity.

Notwithstanding its prevalence, the Greater–Good Defense is problematic on both rational and theological fronts. Rationally, the Greater–Good Defense is utterly counterintuitive in light of our innate moral insight that many of the world's evils are gratuitous. The typical reply of the Greater–Good defender here that such evils merely appear gratuitous due to our cognitive limitations in time, space, and intelligence proves vacuous, since humans perceive as properly basic the factuality of gratuitous evil.[1] In other words, the same species of argument could easily be made against any other properly basic belief, such as the existence of objective moral values, the external world, a veridical past, and so forth, all of which logically could, contrary to appearance, be false but are rationally maintained due to their nonfalsifiability via any defeaters. Obviously the mere supposition of greater good does not constitute a defeater for our properly basic apprehension, making the Greater–Good Defense yield inevitably to an unlivable skepticism. The absurdity of the Greater–Good Defense is multiplied by its transformation of the universe into a philosophically overdetermined system, where hidden benefits are needlessly assigned to all instances of evil therein. For example, every time I am bitten by a mosquito, stub my toe, get a headache, and the like, God allows it in order to bring about some secret greater good at some unspecified point in world history that would not have otherwise transpired, which proposition seems outrageously *ad hoc*. With such evils, we should, in accord with Ockham's Razor, refrain from multiplying causes beyond the necessary and sufficient mundane ones detectable by common sense.

Far worse than its implausibility are the noxious theological ramifications of the Greater–Good Defense. If God employs evils to bring about greater goods, then God operates according to the principle that the ends justify the means, despite that he explicitly denounces this principle as unethical in Scripture and punishes humans who act in precisely the same way as he purportedly does. As R. Z. Friedman rightly perceives, "[T]his is the complete antithesis of the moral task which religion gives to God."[2] Therefore, such a consequence greatly maligns the character of God, who either deceives humanity into misconstruing his moral nature, which we intuit as designating objectively morally false the principle of ends justifying means

---

1. Properly basic beliefs are those which flow naturally from our experience, thereby presenting themselves to us as given, but cannot be proved by that experience; consequently, in the absence of any defeaters (*i.e.* logical or empirical disproofs), these beliefs are rational to hold.

2. R. Z. Friedman, "Evil and Moral Agency," *Philosophy of Religion* 24 (1988): 7.

when it is in fact true, or flagrantly violates his moral nature which we have correctly construed. Since God would be guilty of immorality in any case, he would not be all-good, thus rendering the Greater–Good Defense self–contradictory, as it unwittingly negates the omnibenevolent God it aims to defend. Moreover, it presupposes a fallacious notion of sovereignty as divine planning of every action occurring in creation instead of divine governance over the creation. On the divine planning interpretation, God specifically ordains or purposes each action he permits in the universe, whether intrinsically good or evil, to further his ultimate ends. Not only does this notion further philosophically overdetermine the universe, as there is no independent reason to assume that every good fits into some overarching divine plan (much less every evil), but it also falsifies the moral goodness of God. To illustrate, suppose a person commits rape. If God ordains this rape for the purpose of its bringing about a greater good, then sin is the instrument of virtue, such that God ordains the very act he condemns. Rather, the biblical conception of sovereignty is explained and related to the problem of events *sans* divine intention by Bruce A. Little:

> Because God is sovereign, He is the supreme ruler since all His pre–creation and creation choices were not influenced by anyone or anything outside Himself. God's choice to create and to create the way He did, as well as His counsels concerning creation, are solely His choices....[H]ow should sovereignty be applied in the case of gratuitous evil? Does it necessarily mean that if something happens on this earth without a divine purpose, this somehow strikes at the truth of God's sovereignty? It seems to me that the answer is no.[3]

It may be objected at this point that Scripture teaches God's purposing every event he allows; however, such an interpretation goes well beyond what grammatico–historical exegesis of the relevant passages indicates. The two texts most commonly cited in favor of all–encompassing event ordination are Romans 8:28, "For we know that God causes all things to work together for good to those who love him, to those who are the elect according to his purpose," and Ephesians 1:11, "In him we were also chosen, having been predestined according to the plan of him who works out all things in conformity with the purpose of his will." But both texts are *a posteriori*, not *a priori*, portrayals of God's operation upon "all things"; in other words, they take as given the previous existence of "all things" and simply describe what God then does with these things, namely, working them together for the good of believers and for the purpose of his will. These texts do not state

---

3. Little, *Creation–Order Theodicy*, 106.

that God performs, ordains, or purposes all things for either the accomplishment of believers' benefit or his will; instead, they depict God as confronted with certain already performed events, with many of which he has absolutely nothing to do and are positively contrary to and outside of his will, and assure us of God's power and intelligence to take even these events and use them for our and ultimately his benefit. Little again shows keen insight into the exegetical situation, pointing out that these texts are "silent on causal issues with regard to suffering. . . .No matter how or when one understands the good obtaining—this life or in the life to come"—such verses do "not teach the meticulous providence and should not be quoted as support for the G–G (*i.e.* Greater–Good) theodicy."[4] Moreover, these verses in no way guarantee that God's good responses to earthly evils outweigh or counterbalance these evils, but simply ensure that God will thus positively react. To be sure, God's good responses may very well outweigh the provoking evils on many occasions, although it does not follow that the responses will necessarily or always outweigh these evils. Nor does it follow, when God responds to evil with greater good than would have transpired if events had followed their humanly predictable course, that responding to evil is the only way he could or would have brought about the same or an equally good effect. Hence, while evil is never necessary to God's producing a greater good than the good we would predict if events ran their normal course, he often responds to evil by doing precisely that. But if the evil had never occurred, then God would have produced the same good effect, an equally good effect, or even a better effect through entirely beneficent means.

All of these points are exemplified in the account of Joseph and his brothers. Several heinous sins were committed against Joseph, such as being sold into slavery by his own brothers, unjustly convicted of and imprisoned for adultery, and lied to by Pharaoh's cupbearer, which were totally contrary to God's will (Gen. 37:18–28; 39:11–20; 40:12–23). Certainly it would contradict God's holiness for his blessing on Joseph to depend on his brothers' sin! However, God, in his infinite intelligence, responded to these events by providentially "working in and behind the scenes" to make Joseph viceregent of Egypt and to save much of the Ancient Near Eastern world from a late eighteenth-century B.C.E. famine (Gen. 41:53–57; 45; 50). Certainly we cannot say that God "planned" the wicked events to produce this good effect without making God the author of evil; God could and would have produced the same, an equally good, or a better effect without any such atrocities by providentially responding to the usual course of affairs to create a greater good than would have predictably transpired from the life of a tribal nomad.

---

4. Ibid., 109-10.

In addition to its "ends justifies the means" presupposition defended by spurious biblical proof-texting, a slew of other problems plague the Greater–Good Defense, most of which follow as corollaries from its larger suggestion that evil is necessary to good. Not only is this thesis completely unprovable and so guilty of special pleading, but it leads to the unwanted implication that if there is a necessary good that can only occur through divine employment of evil, then there exists something logically possible that God cannot do—bring about a necessary good without evil—thus further pulling the rug out from under its apologetic for an omnipotent deity. Corollary difficulties surrounding the Greater–Good Defense include, as Little has convincingly argued, the undercutting of social justice, the untrustworthiness of God in prayer, the relativization of good as a concept, the distributive unfairness in who receives the good, its lack of objective criteria to measure good and evil, its failure to address wrong mental attitudes, and its non–logical limiting of God.[5] However, we maintain, in concert with the vast history of Christian theological reflection, that the only constraints on omnipotence are logical limits, such that God's omnipotence means that he can do anything that is logically possible. It does not mean that God can do the logically impossible (*i.e.* bring about logically absurd states of affairs), such as making $2 + 2 = 5$, a married bachelor, or a round triangle. With these considerations in mind, we are poised to tackle the problem of evil in a new way: by affirming premise 2 but denying premise 1. This has the advantage of preserving our cognitive insight that there really are gratuitous evils but showing on several grounds the logical invalidity of negative association between gratuitous evil and the existence of God.

Refuting Premise 1 in the Argument from Evil

First, we propose that perfection is an incommunicable and essential attribute of God. Thus it is logically impossible for God, in choosing to create anything, to impart to it perfection, for the simple reason that it constitutes contingent being which is ontologically dependent upon the Necessary Being. Since evil is, as Augustine points out, a *privatio boni* or privation of the good, it is not an independently existing thing, substance, or essence but rather a lack, limitation, or incompleteness in something that is good, namely, an absence of the complete limitless fulfillment which equals perfection. It follows deductively that evil is necessary to the creation, both to the natural order and to humanity, as God obviously cannot communicate an incommunicable attribute and, if he could, the universe would itself be

---

5. Ibid., 115-24.

perfect and therefore God, leaving us with the further contradictions of the existence of more than one God and of the universe as simultaneously a created and necessary being. However, God cannot be held responsible for evil, for as Little reminds us, "all created beings, of necessity, have this limitation, as anything created cannot be limitless in any or all respects, for such an attribute belongs only to God who is uncreated."[6] In other words, it is logically impossible for God to create a world without evil; if God chose to create anything at all, evil would necessarily come into existence, not because God created or caused it, but because whatever God created would not be God. Therefore, evil is ontologically necessary to contingent being every bit as much as perfection is necessary to Necessary Being.[7] This situation is summarized by Ed L. Miller:

> It would in fact be *logically impossible* to have a world without evil: Anything created by God would have to be *less* than God just by virtue of being *dependent* on him, and this means immediately that it must be less than perfect, and *this* means immediately the presence of various sorts of imperfections. How could God create something that was per-

---

6. Ibid., 50.

7. This argument was first proposed by Gottfried Wilhelm von Leibniz (1646-1716) in his 1710 treatise *Theodicy*. He reasoned that all created things are finite and imperfect, and that the resident imperfections in the very nature of such things lead to natural and moral evil. Hence there was original imperfection in humans and all other creatures prior to the events of Genesis 3. To summarize Leibniz' position, God could not, logically speaking, create perfect creatures; if he creates creatures at all they will be imperfect. Evil is thus a necessary result of creation. But, Leibniz emphasizes, this does not make God the author of evil or responsible for the limitation of his creation, since it is simply a point of logic that anything created cannot be limitless in any or all respects, for such an attribute belongs only to the uncreated God. Leibniz provides the analogy of a current moving a boat to illustrate the point: "The current is the cause of the boat's movement, but not of its retardation; God is the cause of perfection in the nature and the actions of the creature, but the limitation of the receptivity of the creature is the cause of the defects there are in his action. . . .[T]he current . . .is the cause of the boat's speed without being the cause of the limits to this speed. And God is no more the cause of sin than the river's current is the cause of retardation of the boat" (*Theodicy*, ed. Austin Farrer and trans. E. M. Huggard [LaSalle, Ill.: Open Court, 1951], 141).

fect, and therefore independent, and therefore uncreated? *It is logically impossible.*[8]

Such immediately solves the problem of natural evil; it is logically necessary to the universe, and God simply has to put up with it if he chooses to create a universe at all. As pointed out in chapter two, God also has to tolerate the level of natural evil in the universe if he chooses to create one as salvifically good as this universe. That is, we know that God, as an all–good and omniscient being, chose from the array of feasible universes with minimal soteriological evil a universe tied for the least natural and non–soteriological moral evil (*i.e.* he chose a salvific–moral optimal world). Hence it is logically impossible for God to have created a universe with less natural (and moral) evil than this one without lessening the balance obtaining in this universe between saved and lost. So natural evil is utterly gratuitous, but this fact does nothing to call into question God's existence.

Second, we propose that the logical structure of libertarian freedom entails that its holders possess not only the unconstrained ability to choose anything on the moral and spiritual spectrum from good to evil but also the unimpeded power to actualize their choices. Hence libertarian freedom, by its very nature, carries with it the possibilities for the greatest goods, the worst evils, and everything in between. Thus Hitler, if he possessed libertarian freedom, must have possessed not only the ability to choose to implement the Holocaust but the power to actually carry it out in all of its monstrosity. But such freedom is also necessary for humans to genuinely love God, as John Hick astutely observed in 1978.[9] Assessing the impact of Hick's insight upon contemporary scholars of theodicy, Little remarks, "Hick's point that human freedom is necessary for man to love God seems convincingly argued"; hence a valid theodicy "maintains that, without controversy, man loving God is man's highest calling. Next to it comes man loving his neighbor (Matt. 22:37–40). It is impossible for any human response that is coerced or compelled in any manner to be defined as love."[10] Moreover, we already know that God has created humanity with libertarian freedom and that humanity is, by definition, imperfect and limited. By vainly attempting to overcome their finitude apart from God and so to become gods themselves, humans commit the species of moral evil denominated soteriological evil, not accepting that the only way to experience

---

8. Ed L. Miller, *Questions that Matter*, 3rd ed. (New York: McGraw–Hill, 1992), 356, emphasis his.

9. John Hick, *Evil and the God of Love*, rev. ed. (San Francisco: Harper & Row, 1978), 272-74.

10. Little, *Creation–Order Theodicy*, 169.

evil, not accepting that the only way to experience infinitude is through spiritual marriage with God, consummated at the general resurrection where we, though still intrinsically imperfect, will obtain κοινονία (fellowship or union) with the divine perfection not our own (2 Pet. 1:4).

Despite that all such moral evils are gratuitous, even an omnipotent deity cannot stop them, for so doing would contradict the libertarian freedom he has given humans and thus be logically impossible. All that lies within God's power on this score is to choose a world with the lowest possible amount of soteriological evil in particular and then natural and moral evil in general, which is exactly what he has done. Hence it is just as impossible for God to prevent Teresa of Ávila from reaching the heights of spiritual ecstasy or to prevent the Anabaptist program of social justice (which he would not want to do if he logically could) as it is for him to prevent the Soviet Gulag or the 11 September 2001 World Trade Towers attack (which he would want to do if he logically could). For these reasons, the gratuitous nature of moral evil in no way invalidates the existence of God.

We here conclude that premise 1 in the problem of evil is simply false, since the existence of an all-good and all-powerful God implies absolutely nothing concerning the existence or nonexistence of gratuitous evil. Furthermore, we can modify premise 1 as follows to actually prove the coexistence of God and gratuitous evil:

1*. If God exists and has created a universe, then gratuitous evil exists.

While God cannot stop even the extreme negative applications of libertarian freedom (*i.e.* horrific evils) without violating logical limits, he freely chooses to respond to all such evils in positive ways, though the foregoing argument entails that his nature in no way obliges or compels him to do so. The biblical *Weltanschauung* stipulates that at the end of the age or seventh "day" of creation, there will come the "Day of Yahweh" (or eighth day) in which the souls of all those in Paradise and Gehenna will be reinfused into their resurrected bodies (Jn. 5:24–30), Christ will judge the persons formerly in Gehenna according to their deeds and consign them to the Lake of Fire (Rev. 20:11–15), God the Trinity will transfigure the physical universe by actualizing all its natural potentialities, collapsing the boundary between material and immaterial reality by inhabiting the transformed universe, and the persons formerly in Paradise will live timelessly with God in the "new heaven and new earth," *i.e.* new universe (Rev. 21:1–22:6).[11] However, we

---

11. Contra Jehovah's Witness theology, which anachronistically understands "new heaven and new earth" as denoting a new spiritual realm and a

know that often God graciously provides "foretastes" of the new universe by responding to evils before the Day of Yahweh. Examples would include all miraculous and non–miraculous answers to prayer, all biblical miracles, and all other strongly actualized divine events. Notwithstanding, God's "foretastes" do not overturn his logical inability to prevent these evils from occurring. Thus while God can raise Jesus from the dead as "the firstfruits of them that sleep" (1 Cor. 15:20), he cannot prevent Jesus' atonement via crucifixion, which logical impossibility is explicitly revealed in Jesus' prayer at Gethsemane: "My Father, *if it is possible*, may this cup be taken from me . . . My Father, *if it is not possible* for this cup to be taken away unless I drink it, may your will be done" (Mt. 26:39, 42; emphasis mine). Moreover, while God can defeat the Egyptians at the Red Sea, he cannot stop Pharaoh from pursuing the Israelites into the desert (Ex. 14:5–31). Further illustrations of this phenomenon abound in Scripture, such as Sennacherib's invasion of and public threats upon Jerusalem followed by the Angel of Yahweh's destroying his armies (2 Kgs. 18:17–19:35), Peter's mother–in–law coming down with a fever and then receiving healing (Mk. 1:30–31), and Eutychus' deadly fall out a window and resuscitation (Acts 20:9–12). So the question is not, "*Will* God respond to each evil"—the answer is an unambiguous yes—but rather, "*When* will God respond to each evil?" Will he respond at the end of the age, as with most evils, or will he give a "foretaste" of the new universe by responding immediately after the evil transpires or at some later point in time? In addition, one could ask why God responds when he does; for example, why did God choose to heal the Johannine paralytic thirty–eight years after he became an invalid (Jn. 5:1–15) rather than healing him when he first came to the Pool of Bethzatha or waiting until the general resurrection to restore his body? The answer to all such queries is simple: God chooses to respond to each evil at the point when it would best contribute to the optimal balance between saved and lost. This solution is implied by the healing of the paralytic, as it seems apparent that Jesus' specifically healing the man in Jerusalem led many people to place their trust in him who would not otherwise have done so, an observation reinforced by the miracle's iden-

---

separate new physical realm (*Reasoning from the Scriptures* [Brooklyn, N.Y.: Watch Tower Bible and Tract Society, 1989], 112–17, 161–68, 333–40). This view presupposes an Enlightenment–based definition of "heaven" unknown before the seventeenth century C.E. Rather, we simply find a distribution of the term "new" over the Genesis 1:1 phrase "heaven and earth" (universe) to yield "new heaven and new earth," as Revelation 21:1 explicitly shows: "Then I saw a new heaven and new earth, for the first heaven and the first earth had passed away."

tification as a σημεῖον, or special faith-engendering sign, in the pre-Johannine Σημεῖα source. Moreover, our solution is directly identified by Jesus himself as the reason he did not attend to Lazarus immediately upon the latter's death but waited four days before revivifying him: "Lazarus is dead, and for your sake I am glad I was not there, in order that you may believe. But let us go to him" (Jn. 11:14–15; *cf.* 11:41–46).

Scriptural Evidence In Behalf Of Gratuitous Evil

Let us propose a biblical case for the existence of gratuitous evil. First we shall consider the direct evidence, namely, Jesus' interpretation of two tragedies: Pilate's gruesome slaughter of Galileans offering a sacrifice in worship and the falling of a tower in Siloam which killed eighteen people. Such evidence is of *prima significatio* because it rests not on mere sinful human insight, but on the sinless perspective of the divine-human Christ. In contradistinction to the Greater–Good Defense, Jesus discloses no overarching divine purpose, such as punishment for sin, for these atrocities,[12] but

---

12. Jesus makes precisely the same point in John 9 when asked by his disciples concerning the blind man whether it was he or his parents who sinned to cause his blindness. In a passage which I have carefully rendered from the Greek, Jesus affirms that sin did not cause his sickness: "Neither this man nor his parents sinned. But in order that (ἀλλ' ἵνα) the works of God may be manifested in him, it is necessary (δεῖ) for us to work the works of him who sent me while it is day; night is coming when no one is able to work. As long as I am in the world, I am the light of the world" (vv. 3–5). Contrary to my rendering, many translations, unwittingly assuming Greater–Good thought, punctuate the passage differently, making God's working in the man's life the purpose for his blindness (*i.e.* the end of God's miraculous manifestation justifies the means of God's causing him to be born blind): "Neither this man nor his parents sinned; he was born blind so that God's works might be revealed in him. We must work the works of him who sent me while it is day..." (NRSV). However, this punctuation is grammatically infeasible for two reasons. First, the conjunction ἀλλά (elided with ἵνα into ἀλλ') is contrastive rather than connective; in other words, ἀλλά begins a new sentence while contrasting it with the previous sentence rather than initiating a new clause within a sentence that contrasts with the previous clause in that sentence (in which case the connective δέ would have been used instead of ἀλλά). Second, an ἵνα–clause followed by a δεῖ–clause constitutes a standard form of purpose–result statement, such that both clauses belong to the same sentence. This is clearly evident by the fact that the purpose of "the works of God" being "manifest in him" (the ἵνα–clause) is the result of working

insinuates their pointless character, testifying to the reality of human depravity and the absence of all security beyond the present moment: "Do you think these Galileans were worse sinners than all the other Galileans because they suffered this way? I say to you, no; but unless you repent, you will likewise perish. Or what about the eighteen who died when the tower in Siloam fell on them: do you think they were more guilty than all the others living in Jerusalem? I say to you, no; but unless you repent, you will all likewise perish" (Lk. 13:2–5). Hence Jesus maintains that the pertinent lesson is not that some good (much less a greater good) results from evil, but that life is highly precarious; never knowing when death may take a person, one must be prepared for life after death. Little judiciously remarks on this pericope: "These examples instruct the living in a very forceful way that today is the day of salvation. . . . There are no guarantees in this life."[13] But such galling instances of gratuitous evil often remind humanity of the potential bleakness of the human soul and the ambiguities of contingent existence, through which people resolve with increased tenacity to oppose moral and natural evil.

Second, we shall offer an indirect proof for gratuitous evil composed of Scriptural premises, based upon the dominical notion that "a kingdom . . . divided against itself . . . cannot stand" (Mk. 3:24; Lk. 11:17; Mt. 12:25):

1. God commands humans to prevent evil.
2. If gratuitous evil does not exist, then God permits every evil to bring about a greater good than would have been possible without that evil.
3. Thus if gratuitous evil does not exist, then God commands humans to prevent things which, if left unimpeded, are necessary for him to bring about greater goods than could have transpired without them, thus shortcircuiting his own ability to perform the maximal good.
4. But it is logically impossible for an all-good God to command humans to act in such a way to as shortcircuit the maximal good.
5. Therefore, gratuitous evil exists.

Lest God be divided against himself and so not stand—an obvious absurdity—it follows logically and inescapably from God's enjoinment of believers to fight against social injustice and all other forms of suffering that gratuitous evil exists.

"the works of him who sent me" (the δεῖ–clause). Since our translation reflects the only grammatically supportable option, it is to be preferred.

13. Little, *Creation–Order Theodicy*, 168.

Nevertheless, that God omnisciently and omnipotently responds to gratuitous evil with good enables us to avoid regret or guilt for past mistakes. Responding to his fearful brothers after being reunited with him in Egypt, Joseph carefully distinguishes between his brothers' sinful actions and God's "sending," namely, how God sovereignly responds to those evil actions with good for his sake and for the sake of humanity. Notice that Joseph never refers to God "selling him into slavery" or "meaning evil," lest he blasphemously claim that God ordained the sinful means to produce the positive effect; rather, every time the verb "to send" (שָׁלַח) is used, it denotes God's positive response to the evils carried out against him and not the evils themselves. Thus, since Joseph's brothers were responsible for the sin of selling him into slavery but God was responsible for the beneficent response of exalting Joseph in Egypt and, through him, sparing the Mediterranean basin from famine, Joseph can claim, "Now, therefore, *it was not you who sent me here, but God*, who made me father to Pharaoh, lord of his entire household, and ruler of all Egypt" (Gen. 45:8; emphasis mine). Although Joseph's brothers did not "send" him (*i.e.* play a role in any of the good), upon their repentance they should not blame themselves because of the compassionate divine response.

> Now do not be grieved or angry with yourselves because you sold me here, for God sent me ahead of you to save lives. . . .God sent me ahead of you to preserve for you a remnant on earth and to save your lives by a great deliverance. . . .As for you, you meant evil against me, but God meant it for good to accomplish what is presently being done, the saving of many lives (Gen. 45:4–5, 7; 50:20).

Granted our deductive biblical argument for *scientia media* in chapter one- and our aforementioned indirect proof for the necessity of gratuitous evil, Peter's logic for how the Jewish religio-political leaders and Roman authorities could join forces to engineer a judicial murder of Jesus, but that God employed this martyrdom to redeem the world, proves to be exactly the same as Joseph's logic. Preaching his famous sermon on the Day of Pentecost, Peter charges the Jewish authorities concerning Jesus: "This man, delivered over to you according to God's definite plan and foreknowledge, you crucified and killed with the help of wicked Gentiles" (Acts 2:23). That is, initially confronted with the counterfactual truth in the first level of his *scientia media* that if Jesus were in the circumstances of Holy Week, then he would be executed in the most ignominious fashion by the unholy alliance of Jewish and Roman elites. But God responds to this *ultimum peccatum* in the second level of his *scientia media* by fine-tuning the world where these circumstances transpire such that they would prompt his ultimate victory. When God chooses to actualize this world in his creative decree, he confounds the wisdom of the αἰών by using *in sensu composito* (but not *in sensu diviso*) its instrument of domination and oppression to culminate the redemption of all who wish to appropriate it. As Paul aptly declares:

> *For since, in the wisdom of God, the world through its wisdom did not know God, God was pleased through the foolishness of the kerygma to save the believing ones.* For Jews demand miraculous signs and Greeks desire wisdom, but we proclaim Christ crucified, a stumbling block to Jews and foolishness to Gentiles; but to the elect, Christ, the power of God and the wisdom of God. For the foolishness of God is wiser than human wisdom, and the weakness of God is stronger than human strength. . . . *But God chose what is foolish in the world to shame the wise; God chose what is weak in the world to shame the strong. God chose what is low and despised in the world, things that are not, to nullify things that are* (1 Cor. 1:21–25, 27–28, emphasis mine).

Notice in the italicized portions that it is not "in actuality" but "in the wisdom of God," *i.e.* in his omniscience, that "the world through its wisdom did not know God," thus corresponding in our explanation to the first level of his *scientia media*. But God responds, through the second level of his *scientia media* and his creative decree, by choosing what is foolish, weak, low, and despised in the world (namely, crucifixion, the epitome of foolishness and weakness) to shame the world in its supposed wisdom and strength. That our account, contra the Greater–Good Defense, shows itself quite harmonious with the Scriptural record further bespeaks its cogency and veracity.

Conclusion

God as the Only Solution to Gratuitous Evil

We have seen that the existence of gratuitous evil in no way stands as a disproof of the existence of God. It is highly ironic, moreover, that the very fact (gratuitous evil) which many wrongly feel threatens God's existence may be actually used to prove God's existence. Slightly modifying an argument offered by Craig, the syllogism runs as follows:

1. If God does not exist, then objective moral values do not exist.
2. Gratuitous evil exists.

3. Therefore, it doubly follows that objective moral values exist. (The acknowledger of premise 2 shows that objective moral values exist not only by recognizing the existence of evil but also by recognizing exactly what kind of evil she or he encounters.)
4. Therefore, God exists.[14]

Thus without God, there would be no metaphysical ground or basis by which to recognize as anything as evil, much less gratuitous evil. The recognition by non–theists of gratuitous evil, which proves twice over that God exists, is doubly contradictory to their antipathy toward theism.

This chapter carries enormous pastoral implications for those struggling with gratuitous evil. When believers face gratuitous evil, they should know that it is neither caused nor willed by God. Therefore, they should abandon any futile search to find the meaning of the evil and similarly futile queries about why God "allowed" the evil, which speculations wrongly presuppose that it is logically possible for God to stop the evil.[15] Instead, they should accept that there is absolutely no meaning to the evil, as it is simply a logically unavoidable necessity of contingent living that even an omnipotent being cannot prevent. However, believers should look to God for precisely those things an omnipotent being can furnish, such as comfort, strength, and companionship in the midst of evil. Moreover, believers should draw great hope both from God's awesome promise to use such unwelcome events for their good and from their knowledge that God will overcome and eradicate

---

14. William Lane Craig and Walter Sinnott–Armstrong, *God? A Debate Between a Christian and an Atheist* (Oxford: Oxford University Press, 2004), 125–26.

15. For this reason, people sin when blaming God for evil (Rev. 16:10–11). Other misguided pitfalls believers should avoid are thinking that evil is due to their sin, which contradicts the infinite magnitude of Christ's atonement (Heb. 8:12; 9:11–15, 26–28; 10:10–18; Jer. 31:34; Col. 2:13–15), or due to demonic attack, as Scripture promises that "the one who was born of God (*i.e.* the one who was miraculously conceived without any human father, namely, Jesus) keeps her or him safe, and the evil one cannot harm (ἅπτεται; lexical form ἅπτομαι) her or him" (1 Jn. 5:18). The Greek text renders this passage astonishingly stronger, as the verb ἅπτομαι refers to "causing even some relatively light physical, moral, and/or spiritual harm." Thus, as Johannes P. Louw and Eugene A. Nida point out in their authoritative *Greek–English Lexicon of the New Testament Based on Semantic Domains*, 2 vols. (New York: United Bible Societies, 1989), 1:230, the final clause is most accurately translated as "and the Evil One does not harm him at all" or "and the Evil One doesn't so much as touch him."

every past, present, and future evil in the new universe. At the end of the day, God proves to be the ultimate solution to the problem of gratuitous evil.

Chapter 5

Theology Proper

The Trinity and Christology

The questions of how God can be a Trinity and how Jesus could be both fully God and fully human are wrestled with by virtually all Christians and many non–Christians, especially those who are considering the Christian worldview. Moreover, faulty answers to these questions lie at the heart of various New Religious Movements (or NRMs) professing to be the "restored" or "true" version of Christianity, such as Mormonism and Jehovah's Witnesses. Likewise, several world religions proffer defective views concerning the nature of God and the person of Jesus, albeit not as central features of their doctrinal systems as for the quasi–Christian NRMs. But both of these aspects are *sine qua non* for the Christian faith, since the doctrines of the Trinity and Christology are obtained purely by the application of deductive logic to Scriptural premises and collectively constitute the irreducible essence distinguishing Christianity from other religions. Hence the Trinity and Christology are essential Christian doctrines comprising a subset of catechetical theology which an individual must, at least indirectly, believe in order to receive salvation. In other words, although knowledge of the fully developed philosophical–theological formulations of the Trinity and Christology are obviously not prerequisite to eternal life, adherence to the Scriptural premises from which these comprehensive doctrines deductively stem are, assuming special revelation, necessary for eternal life. For example, despite that the word "Trinity" and the precise philosophical formulation of it did not exist before the second half of the second century C.E., the earliest Christians believed in what would be later known as the doctrine of the Trinity and enjoyed salvation. To put it another way, while the earliest believers did not exhaustively construe the Trinity or Christology, their salvation was unhindered because they subscribed to the individual biblical teachings which, taken together, result in such exhaustive construals. It was only when controversies arose among groups within and without Christian ranks who either denied at least some of the aforementioned Scriptural premises or fallaciously combined these premises to yield false doctrines that Christians at large felt compelled to refute these errors by giving explicit philosophical expression to the doctrines they had always implicitly held. Incidentally, all such controversies are still alive and well today.[1] In order, therefore, to safeguard our minds, to cultivate our personal knowledge of God through understanding his triune nature and his means of relating to us in Christ, and to protect the flock and future generations from inevitably persistent aberrations, it is imperative that we can clearly explain and defend the biblical fidelity and logical consistency of these foundational doctrines.

Tragically, a widespread tide of anti–intellectualism in American Christianity since the late nineteenth century has discouraged rational investigation of the Trinity and Christology, even categorizing these doctrines as "mysteries" that cannot be unraveled by the human intellect and must be simply taken on "faith." In addition to its Kierkegaardian redefinition of faith as belief without evidence rather than the New Testament conception as personal commitment to Christ, this typical rejoinder misrepresents the notion of "mystery." Rightly defined, a mystery is not something illogical or paradoxical, but simply a topic for which the Scriptural data needed for an authoritative understanding is lacking or inconclusive. Examples of true biblical mysteries include the precise attributes of our resurrection bodies in the new heaven–earth, the mode in which Jesus' physical body is present outside the four–dimensional space–time universe, and whether the departed saints in Paradise can perceive events within the universe. Notice that distinguishing topics as mysteries does not mean we should avoid using philosophy and theology to formulate more or less probable answers to these questions—for that in fact is precisely what Christians are called to do, as an integral part of loving God with all our minds—but only that none of these answers can claim, in the absence of biblical adjudication, to be the only possible option. Instantly we see that, by definition, the overwhelming majority of themes which are commonly identified as "mysteries," such as the Trinity, Christology, the relationship between predestination and human

---

1. My doctoral adviser, Ralph Keen, encapsulated the principle which this fact exposes as "Keen's Law #3" of the history of religious thought. In class he articulated this principle: "All options are always present in a given religious tradition; even when they seem to disappear, they are just subsumed within the woodwork, ready to reemerge at any time."

freedom, and the problem of evil, are not mysteries at all but are simply misidentified as such to furnish an excuse for an unwillingness to think. Accordingly, the aims of this chapter are two. First, we will analyze the lines of biblical evidence which deductively imply the Trinity, revealing, in the process of delineating the emergent doctrine, that Scripture particularly substantiates a version of social trinitarianism known as Trinity monotheism. Second, we will demonstrate that the New Testament presents a Christology which can be retrospectively classified as "eclectic," weighted toward what would be known in post–Nicene theology as the Alexandrian view but also embracing aspects of the Antiochene view, especially those facets contrary to *communicatio idiomatum.*

Scriptural Argument for the Doctrine of the Trinity

There are five clearly and amply attested biblical premises which, when combined via deductive logic, collectively compose the doctrine of the Trinity. Thus, employing the nomenclature introduced in chapter one, the Trinity falls into the domain of biblical theology and not philosophical theology. Before proceeding to an examination of each one, we must first draw an important grammatical distinction which will come into play throughout our discussion. Koinē Greek has three basic types of statements (*i.e.* containing subject, main verb, and predicate) featuring the linking verb εἰμί (lexical/1st person singular form of "to be") as their main verb: indefinite identity statements, definite identity statements, and statements of predication (also called adjectival statements). Each of these types of statements is easily distinguishable by a fixed and unique grammatical structure. As their name suggests, indefinite identity statements are used to generically identify something as an instance of a certain class. Here the linking verb plays the role of an equals sign, such that what precedes the verb (the subject) and what follows the verb (the predicate) simply constitute two names for the same thing and so can be interchanged without any loss of meaning. Indefinite identity statements are accordingly translated "the Nominative is/was/will be a Predicate Nominative (abbrev. PN)" and possess the following construction:

Article + Nominative + Linking Verb + No Article + PN

Consider this indefinite identity statement and its interlinear translation:

ὁ	ἀπόστολος	ἦν		ἄνθρωπος.
The	apostle	was	a	human.

Equivalent to its converse "A human was the apostle," we would use this type of statement to state what species of being and how many of that species a certain apostle was.

Definite identity statements, like indefinite identity statements, employ the linking verb as an equals sign, rendering the subject and predicate interchangeable, but unlike their linguistic cousin they specifically identify something as the particular or special instance of a certain class. Thus definite identity statements are translated "the Nominative is/was/will be the Predicate Nominative" and possess the following construction:

Article + Nominative + Linking Verb +   Article + PN

We illustrate with this definite identity statement and its translation:

ὁ	ἀπόστολος	ἦν	ὁ	ἄνθρωπος.
The	apostle	was	the	human.

This statement would be found in a context of asking about a specific human and then identifying the apostle with that human; again, it means the same thing as its converse "The human was the apostle."

Performing a markedly different function than either the indefinite or definite identity statements is the statement of predication, otherwise known as the adjectival statement. Here the linking verb does not play the role of an equals sign, such that the subject and predicate cannot be reversed without destroying the meaning. The predicate, instead of being used as a noun identical to the subject, is used as an adjective which describes, but is not identical to, the subject. This type of statement "predicates" a quality or attribute to the subject, hence its name. English examples of statements of predication include "The shirt is yellow," "The suit is polyester," and "God is love." Rather than saying that the shirt is identical to the color yellow, that the suit is identical to the totality of the world's polyester, or that God is identical to the particular moral attribute of love, these statements affirm that the shirt, suit, and God possess the respective attributes or properties of yellowness, being made of polyester, and being loving. Obviously none of these statements can be reversed without meriting absurdity: the color yellow cannot be a shirt, the fabric polyester cannot be a suit, and the attribute of love is not God. Statements of predication are translated "the Nominative is/was/will be Predicate Nominative" and possess a construction quite unlike the identity statements:

No Article + PN   + Linking Verb + Article + Nominative

In statements of predication, the translation does not follow word order (as it does in the identity statements), which is displayed in the superscripts and consequent reordering:

$$\overset{3}{\text{ἄνθρωπος}} \quad \overset{2}{\text{ἦν}} \qquad \overset{1}{\text{ὁ}} \quad \overset{}{\text{ὀφθαλμός.}}$$

$$\overset{3}{\text{human.}} \quad \overset{2}{\text{was}} \qquad \overset{1}{\underline{\text{The}}} \quad \underline{\text{eye}}$$

= The eye was human.

Here the eye is obviously not identical to a complete human, but has the attribute of being human; moreover, the irreversibility of the statement is seen in the self–contradictory nature of any human simply consisting of an eye. While it is impossible just by looking at an English linking–verb sentence to determine which type of statement it is, fortunately Koinē Greek features separate constructions for each one so that it is impossible for the reader to confuse them. Let us now proceed to the Scriptural premises making up the doctrine of the Trinity.

Premise 1: There is only one God, or divine spiritual substance/essence/nature.

Monotheism is at the heart of the biblical concept of God. This fact is exemplified in Deuteronomy 6:4, the *Shema* or fundamental confession of Jewish faith: "Hear, O Israel! Yahweh is our God, Yahweh is one (אֶחָד)!" Here it must be emphasized that there are two different words for "one" in Hebrew: יָחִיד and אֶחָד. יָחִיד is the gendered form of "one" and so means "only one person (either male or female)," as illustrated by the account of Jephthah's daughter: "When Jephthah returned to his house in Mizpah, behold, his daughter was coming out to meet him with tambourines and dancing. She was his one (יָחִיד) child; besides her he had no sons or daughters" (Jdg. 11:34). Notably, God is never called יָחִיד in the Hebrew Bible; if God were described as יָחִיד, then he would be unitarian (Latin for "one God in one person"). However, אֶחָד is the neuter form of "one" and thus means "one entity." When referring to God's oneness, the Hebrew Bible always calls God אֶחָד, as seen in the Shema and elsewhere: "Has not one (אֶחָד) God created us? Why does each of us deal treacherously with his sisters and brothers so as to profane the covenant of our fathers?" (Mal. 3:10; *cf.* 2 Sam. 7:22; Isa. 37:20; 45:5; 46:9).

Koinē Greek also distinguishes between oneness in terms of persons and entities, even going farther than Hebrew by splitting male and female personal oneness. Hence Greek features three different words for "one": εἷς (one male person), μία (one female person), and ἕν (one entity). Thus the neuter ἕν is the Greek equivalent of the Hebrew אֶחָד. Leaving aside passages where the Greek form of "one" is predetermined by overarching grammatical rules and thus does not determine personhood or lack thereof, whenever the New Testament discusses God's oneness, it always uses ἕν rather than εἶς or μία. So when Jesus famously declared in John 10:30, "I and the Father are one (ἕν)," he was not asserting that he was the same male person as the Father (in which case the text would read εἶς) or (nonsensically) the same female person as the Father (in which case the text would read μία). Instead Jesus proclaims that he and the Father are the same entity. Now Jesus explains elsewhere that God is spirit (Jn. 4:24), and 1 Timothy 1:17 lists several other divine attributes: "Now to the King eternal, immortal, invisible, the only God (μόνῳ θεῷ, from which the term "monotheism" springs), be honor and glory for ever and ever." Hence the one entity comprising Jesus and the Father is an eternal, immortal, and invisible spirit.

Premise 2: Taken as a statement of predication (adjectival statement), the Father is God.

This fact is displayed throughout the New Testament. Thus Peter greets the Roman church, "Grace to you and peace from God the Father (ὁ θεὸς καὶ πατὴρ) and the Lord Jesus Christ" (1 Pet. 1:3), where the structure of "God the Father" is adjectival (*i.e.* first attributive position) and thus uses θεὸς (God) as an adjective to modify πατὴρ (Father). The same construction is found in John 6:27, Romans 1:7, 2 Corinthians 1:2, Ephesians 1:2, and several other texts, as evident in the following: "Paul, an apostle, sent not from humans nor by humans, but by Jesus Christ and God the Father, who raised him from the dead, and all the sisters and brothers with me" (Gal. 1:1). As a historical aside, monotheistic groups denying other premises in this argument (*e.g.* Jehovah's Witnesses) have never disputed the second premise.

Premise 3: Taken as a statement of predication (adjectival statement), the Son is God.

Among the most explicit testimonies to this verity is John 1:1: "In the beginning was the Word, and the Word was with God, and the Word was God (θεὸς ἦν ὁ λόγος)." Recalling our earlier explanation of the various types of linking–verb statements, we immediately observe that θεὸς ἦν ὁ λόγος is a statement of predication (adjectival statement), which uses θεὸς (God) as an adjective to describe ὁ λόγος (the Word). Hence the Elder John is not suggesting that the Word was identical to God as a totality (*i.e.* that the

Word was *the* God), any more than our example "The eye was human" suggests that the eye was identical to one particular human (*i.e.* that the eye was *the* human). In fact, the Greek makes such a suggestion impossible, since the only way the Elder John could have conveyed this idea was through the definite identity statement ὁ λογός ἦν ὁ θεὸς, which possesses a radically different structure than the statement of predication θεὸς ἦν ὁ λόγος. Moreover, the Greek renders equally impossible the notion that "the Word was a god" (as claimed in the *New World Translation* produced by Jehovah's Witnesses), for the only way the Elder John could have expressed this view was through the indefinite identity statement ὁ λογός ἦν θεὸς, which constitutes the semantic reverse of John 1:1.[2] Contra both of these identity connotations, the term θεὸς is not being used as a noun but an adjective, such that the Word has the property of being God; thus "the Word was God" just as "the eye was human" (the eye has the property of being human), "God is love" (God has the property of being love), or "the shirt was yellow" (the shirt has the property of being yellow). But "God" cannot be used interchangeably with "the Word"; claiming that "God is the Word" is just as mistaken as saying "human was the eye," "love is God," or "yellow was the shirt." In sum, John 1:1 is such a philosophically precise and powerful text that it alone establishes the truth of the third premise.

However, the New Testament contains several additional texts which also explicitly affirm the deity of Jesus. Having already revealed the Word as "the Only One (μονογενής) . . . [who] became flesh and tabernacled among us" (Jn. 1:14), the Elder John compares the unseen God the Father with the seen God the Word: "No one has seen God at any time, but God the Only One (μονογενής), who is in the bosom of the Father, has made him known" (1:18). Upon seeing him resurrected from the dead, Thomas declared to Jesus, "My Lord and my God!" (Jn. 20:28) In Romans 9:5, Paul employs a statement of predication to denote Jesus' deity: "To the Jewish people belong the patriarchs, and from them is traced the human ancestry of

---

2. Watchtower literature constantly draws the false dichotomy that John 1:1 is to be translated either "the Word was a god" (indefinite identity statement) or "the Word was the God" (definite identity statement); since the latter would require the definite article ὁ before θεὸς, it is argued that the only acceptable translation is the former. However, both of these options are equally wrong, analogous to suggesting that either "the eye was a human" or "the eye was the human" while avoiding talk that "the eye was human." Watchtower literature shows no cognizance of the correct third option (statement of predication), in which the predicate nominative both has no article and comes first in the clause.

Christ, who is God over all, forever praised."[3] That the author of the Pastorals regarded Jesus as God is made explicitly clear throughout the book of Titus; employing the Granville Sharp construction (article–substantive–καί–substantive, in which the two substantives must refer to the same antecedent), Titus 2:13 affirms that believers wait for the Parousia of "our–great–God–and–Savior (τοῦ μεγάλου θεοῦ καὶ σωτῆρος ἡμῶν), Jesus Christ." Peter also employs the Granville Sharp construction to affirm Jesus' deity: "Simon Peter, a slave and apostle of Jesus Christ, to those who through the righteousness of our–God–and–Savior–Jesus–Christ (τοῦ θεοῦ ἡμῶν καὶ σωτῆρος Ἰησοῦ Χριστοῦ) have received a faith as precious as ours" (2 Pet. 1:1). The anonymous Jewish–born author of Hebrews describes Jesus as "the exact likeness of the Father's ὑποστάσεως (person, center of self–consciousness)" (1:3), a term to which we will later return, and quotes the Father himself as proclaiming Jesus' deity: "But about the Son he says, 'Your throne, O God, is forever and ever, and righteousness is the scepter of your kingdom'" (1:8). We could go on, but enough has been highlighted to illustrate the clear biblical testimony in favor of the third premise.

Premise 4: Taken as a statement of predication (adjectival statement), the Holy Spirit is God.

Both the personality and deity of the Holy Spirit have historically been and are presently contested;[4] since the former is a necessary but not sufficient condition for the latter (*i.e.* while one must be a person to possess the property of being a personal God, obviously very few persons possess this property), we will proceed in logical sequence. Perhaps the best testimony to the personality of the Holy Spirit comes from Jesus himself. In Koinē Greek there are two terms for "another": ἄλλος, which means "another of the same kind"; and ἕτερος, which means "another of a different kind." Not only

---

3. Contra older translations which punctuate Romans 9:5 as two different sentences—". . . the human ancestry of Christ. God who is over all be forever praised"—the best and most recent critical editions of the Greek New Testament (UBS 4th rev. ed. and Nestle–Aland 27th ed.), based on the newest manuscript discoveries pertaining to Koinē Greek grammar, punctuate the two clauses as belonging to a single sentence.

4. The personality, and consequently deity, of the Holy Spirit was first denied by Macedonius (*c.* 314–62), the Arian founder of the Pneumatomachi (lit. "Spirit–fighters"). Today these attributes are denied by Jehovah's Witnesses, who regard the Holy Spirit as God's "active force" by which he performs deeds in the world, analogous to "divine electricity" (*Reasoning From the Scriptures*, 136–37, 361).

does Jesus call the Holy Spirit the παράκλητος (Defender, Counselor, Helper, Comforter, Provider of Evidence), which by definition must refer to a person (only a person can defend, counsel, provide evidence, etc.), but he also calls the Spirit ἄλλον παράκλητον, or "another Defender of the same kind" as himself: "If you love me, then you will obey what I command. And I will ask the Father, who will give you ἄλλον παράκλητον, the Spirit of truth, who will be with you forever" (Jn. 14:15–17). Since Jesus is a person and the Holy Spirit is "of the same kind," it follows inescapably that the Spirit is a person. (Granted the truth of the third premise, it also follows that the Spirit is God in an adjectival sense.) Moreover, Jesus employs the demonstrative masculine pronoun ἐκεῖνος in referring to the Spirit, despite that this is grammatically unnecessary and actually violates the rules of Greek grammar, which stipulate that pronouns must agree with their respective nouns in number and gender. In other words, since the noun "Spirit" (πνεῦμα) is grammatically neuter (which, as previously indicated, does not determine personhood or lack thereof),[5] it should be followed by the standard neuter pronoun αὐτό. If it were so followed, this would in no way detract from the Spirit's personhood. But in order to emphatically state that the Spirit is a person, Jesus not only uses a masculine pronoun but the demonstrative form thereof.

Substantiation of the Holy Spirit's personality actually comes from the Spirit, who employs personal pronouns for himself: "The Holy Spirit said, 'Set apart for *me* Barnabas and Saul for the work to which *I* have called them'" (Acts 13:2; emphasis added). Scripture indicates that the Spirit possesses a mind (Rom. 8:27), will (1 Cor. 12:11), and emotions (Eph. 4:30), each of which is an exclusive attribute of a person. Further, the Holy Spirit performs actions in Scripture that only a person can do: he teaches (Jn. 14:26), testifies (Jn. 15:26), prays in behalf of believers (Rom. 8:26), speaks (Acts 8:29), gives guidance to believers (Rom. 8:14), and persuades people

---

5. For nouns, grammatical gender has nothing to do with actual gender; the former is simply a function of word spelling and carries no implications for the latter. Thus "bread" (ἄρτος, actually neuter) is grammatically masculine, "head" (κεφαλή, actually neuter) is grammatically feminine, and "child" (τεκνόν, τεκνίον, actually masculine or feminine) is grammatically neuter. Moreover, grammatically neuter nouns frequently refer to actual persons, including infants (βρέφος; Lk. 1:41), girls (κοράσιον; Mt. 9:24–25), and angels (λειτουργικὰ πμεύματα; Heb. 1:14). It is only for adjectives which stand alone and function as nouns (*i.e.* substantive adjectives), the genders of which are therefore not predetermined by the grammatical genders of their antecedents, that grammatical and actual gender are identical (as in the substantive uses of εἷς, μία, and ἕν in the second premise).

not to sin (Gen. 6:3). Finally, the Spirit can be obeyed, as seen by Philip's witnessing to the Ethiopian eunuch (Acts 8:27) as well as by Peter's witnessing to Cornelius (Acts 10:19–23), and one cannot obey anything impersonal. In short, the evidence from Jesus, the Holy Spirit, and the Scriptural writers conclusively demonstrate the Spirit's personality.

Concerning the issue of his deity, several biblical texts explicitly show that the Holy Spirit possesses the attribute of being God. In Acts 5:3–4 Peter said to Ananias, "Why has Satan filled your heart to lie to the Holy Spirit . . . You have not lied to humans but to God." Since lying to the Holy Spirit is lying to God, logic demands that the Spirit is God. Moreover, in the *Nevi'im* (Prophets) the Holy Spirit designates himself as Yahweh, which is the most sacred covenant name of God. Accordingly, the Holy Spirit instructed Ezekiel to warn the rebellious Kingdom of Judah of the impending consequences of their social injustice and idolatry:

> Then the Spirit of Yahweh fell upon me, and he said to me, '*Say, thus says Yahweh*: This is what you think, O house of Israel; I know the things that come into your mind. You have killed many in this city, filling its streets with the slain. *Therefore, thus says the Lord Yahweh . . .* you have feared the sword; so I will bring the sword upon you, *declares the Lord Yahweh*. And I will bring you out of the midst of the city, deliver you into the hands of strangers, and execute judgment against you. You will fall by the sword; I will judge you to the border of Israel. *So you shall know that I am Yahweh*. . . . I will judge you at the border of Israel. *Thus you will know that I am Yahweh, whose statutes you have not followed, and whose ordinances you have not kept*, but you have acted according to the ordinances of the nations around you (Ezek. 11:5–12; emphasis added).

Against the backdrop of several similar Hebrew Bible citations (2 Cor. 3:7–16), Paul avers with a definite identity statement in 2 Corinthians 3:17 that the person calling himself Yahweh in these particular episodes was the Holy Spirit: "But ὁ κύριος is τὸ πνεῦμα (the Spirit)," where ὁ κύριος represents the consistent translation of Yahweh in the Septuagint, the Greek version of the Hebrew Bible used by virtually all first–century Jews (the rabbis were the solitary exception, who alone could read the Hebrew Bible in the original). This statement reveals that the Spirit is a person who is Yahweh, not specifying whether the linking verb denotes identity or predication; to clear up the ambiguity Paul follows this remark with an adjectival construction (first attributive position) utilizing κύριος as an adjective to modify Spirit: "And all of us, with unveiled faces . . . are being transformed into the same image from one degree of glory to another, for this comes from the κυρίου πνεύματος" (2 Cor. 3:18). Here κυρίου πνεύματος remarkably means "Yahweh Spirit," with the same construction as the very common "Holy Spirit"; just as "Holy" in the latter is an adjective which ascribes to the Spirit the quality of being holy, so "Yahweh" in the former is an adjective which ascribes to the Spirit the quality of being Yahweh. So as a statement of predication, "the Holy Spirit is God," thereby establishing the truth of the fourth premise.

Premise 5: The three persons, Father, Son, and Holy Spirit, are distinct.

This fact is abundantly evinced throughout the sayings and ministry of Jesus. During the Last Supper, Jesus repeatedly refers to and distinguishes between himself, the Father, and the Holy Spirit:

> I will ask the Father, who will give you another Defender, the Spirit of truth, who will be with you forever. . . . I have said these things to you while I am still with you. But the Defender, the Holy Spirit, whom the Father will send in my name, will teach you everything, and remind you of all that I said to you. . . . When the Defender comes, whom I will send to you from the Father, the Spirit of truth who goes out from the Father, he will testify about me. . . . But truly I say to you, it is to your advantage that I am going away. Unless I go away, the Defender will not come to you; but if I go, I will send him to you. When he comes, he will convict the world of guilt in regard to sin and righteousness and judgment: in regard to sin, because people do not believe into me; in regard to righteousness, because I am going to the Father, where you can see me no longer; and in regard to judgment, because the prince of this world now stands condemned. I still have many things to say to you, but you cannot bear them now. But when he, the Spirit of truth, comes . . . he will glorify me by taking from what is mine and declaring it to you. All that belongs to the Father is mine. This is why I said the Spirit will take from what is mine and declare it to you (Jn. 14:16–17, 25–26, 15:26, 16:7–15).

These *logia Jesu* directly refute the early trinitarian aberration of Modalism (also known as Patripassianism or Sabellianism after its third–century systematizer Sabellius),[6] which claims that the Father, Son, and Holy Spirit are

---

6. Present–day Modalist groups include the United Pentecostal Church (*i.e.* Oneness or "Jesus–Only" Pentecostals) and the Local Church, notable leaders of which include Watchman Nee (1903–72) and Witness Lee (1905–97).

three different names for the same person. Further evidence for the distinct-ness of the three divine persons appears at Jesus' baptism by John the Bap-tist, as the Son is baptized, the Father speaks from heaven, "You are my be-loved Son; in you I am well–pleased," and the Holy Spirit descends on Christ in the shape of a dove (Mk. 1:9–11; Lk. 3:21–22; Mt. 3:16–17; *cf.* 2 Cor. 13:14; Isa. 48:12-16). Therefore it is biblically incontestable that the Father, Son, and Holy Spirit are three different persons.

Conclusion: There is only one God, namely, one divine spiritual substance/essence/nature which comprises three distinct persons, Father, Son, and Holy Spirit.

Following logically from premises one through five is the deduction that the one entity we call "God" includes three persons, which is precisely the doctrine of the Trinity. Hence detractors of this doctrine who charge it with self–contradiction are simply ignorant of what it teaches. This doctrine does not hold that "three gods are one God," that "three persons are one person," or that "three gods are one person," all of which are just logical nonsense. Rather, God's oneness and threeness refer to two entirely different condi-tions: the oneness refers to the number of gods, or divine spiritual sub-stances, that exist; and the threeness refers to the number of persons which any particular divine spiritual substance contains. The oneness is on the level of God's spiritual substance/essence/nature (Greek οὐσία), while the three-ness is on the level of that substance's attributes, namely, the number of per-sons (Greek ὑπόστασεις) which the substance includes. Hence, as an iden-tity statement, God is one οὐσία containing three ὑπόστασεις, which was exactly the formula for the Trinity first articulated in Latin terms by Tertul-lian (*c.* 200 C.E.)[7] and later codified by the Second Ecumenical Council at Constantinople (381) in their famous Niceno–Constantinopolitan Creed (to-day somewhat anachronistically called the Nicene Creed). To put it another way, the doctrine of the Trinity claims, first, that a necessary attribute of any divine οὐσία is tripersonality—any god that exists must, by definition, be tripersonal—and, second, that there is only one God. Accordingly, the expli-cation of the Trinity here provided is known as "Trinity monotheism." Re-call from our discussion of the third premise that Hebrews 1:3 describes Je-sus as the exact likeness of the Father's ὑπόστασις, a philosophically

---

7. That is, one *substantia* containing three *personae*, articulated in his *Against Praxeas: In Which He Defends, In All Essential Points, the Doctrine of the Holy Trinity*, II.

precise term whose definition not only denotes "person" but also explains that a person is a "center of self–consciousness." Thus Jesus and the Father are persons whose distinct faculties mirror one another. Here we shall also point out that a soul, by definition, is a spiritual substance/essence/nature, such that the former is shorthand for the latter. Moreover, we know from both philosophy and Scripture that a center of self–consciousness, in turn, contains three irreducibly distinct cognitive rational faculties—the reason (νοῦς; also called the "intellect" or "mind"), the memory (μνήμη), and the will (θέλημα; also called the "spirit" in the sense not of "spiritual, immaterial substance" but of "the spirited, emotional, desiring component")—a discovery originally made by Plato, mediated into Judaism by Philo of Alexandria, and appropriated by Paul (*e.g.* in 1 Cor. 14).[8]

Drawing together these insights, we are now in a position to state with absolute precision the doctrine of the Trinity. The Trinity defines God as one infinite immaterial spiritual substance/essence/nature (*i.e.* one infinite soul) endowed with three complete sets of cognitive rational faculties, each sufficient for personhood.[9] Put in simplified form, God is one infinite immaterial spirit (*i.e.* one soul) endowed with three distinct centers of self–consciousness. Each of these centers of self–consciousness, or persons, possesses its own reason, memory, and will. This fact is surprisingly emphasized in the Hebrew Bible by its many divine multipersonality texts, in which God refers to himself as a community of persons. For example, after the primal human couple breaks the divinely instituted covenant, "Yahweh said, 'Behold, the human has now become like one of us, knowing good and evil'" (Gen. 3:22). After the unified Ancient Near Eastern populace erected the Tower of Babel,

Yahweh said, "Behold, they are one people, and they all have one language, and this is only the beginning of what they will do. And nothing

---

8. Thus in 1 Corinthians 14:14–17, Paul is not contrasting the immaterial soul with the material brain or arguing for two different immaterial substances (*i.e.* the spirit separate from the mind/soul), but he rather differentiates between the rational and emotional faculties of the immaterial human substance and encouraged the complementary use of both in worship: "For if I pray in a tongue, my spirit prays, but my mind is unfruitful. What shall I do then? I will pray with my spirit, but I will also pray with my mind; I will sing with my spirit, but I will also sing with my mind. Otherwise, if you are praising God with your spirit, how can people who do not understand say 'Amen' to your thanksgiving, since they do not know what you are saying? For you may be giving thanks well enough, but the other person is not edified."

9. Moreland and Craig, *Philosophical Foundations*, 594.

that they propose to do will now be impossible for them. Come, let us go down and confuse their language, so that they may not understand one another's speech" (Gen. 11:6–7).

When Isaiah received his prophetic commission, "Then I heard the voice of Adonai (one of the between 11–13 different names of God in the Hebrew Bible, meaning "Lord and Master") saying, 'Whom shall I send, and who will go for us?' And I said, 'Here I am; send me'" (Isa. 6:8). Structurally, the two clauses in the sentence "Whom shall I send, and who will go for us?" display synonymous parallelism, thereby equating the "I" with the "us" and ruling out the possibility that the "us" includes any entities other than "I."[10] Hence on the level of οὐσία God is "I," and on the level of ὑπόστασεις God is "us." Psalm 110:1, "Yahweh said to my Adonai, 'Sit at my right hand, until I make your enemies your footstool,'" is especially noteworthy among multipersonality texts since Jesus identified himself as David's Adonai to whom Yahweh spoke a thousand years prior to the events of the first century C.E., thereby necessitating Jesus' full deity and preexistence. Fittingly it should be underscored here that each of the Trinitarian persons is equal in

---

10. The old ploys to explain these "us" (first–person plural) texts away as either "plurals of majesty," which suffers from anachronistically and disingenuously imposing a device found in some Indo–European languages evolving in the medieval period upon an Afro–Asiatic language developed at least two thousand years earlier like ancient Hebrew that lacks this device, and as God speaking to angels or other divine powers, which is nothing more than a question-begging attempt to read these beings into monotheistic passages displaying no cognizance of them, have been exploded by Gleason L. Archer, *Encyclopedia of Bible Difficulties* (Grand Rapids, Mich.: Zondervan, 1982), 359, and Paul R. House, *Old Testament Theology* (Downers Grove, Ill.: InterVarsity Press, 1998), 61. Thus Archer profitably summarizes: "This first person plural can hardly be a mere editorial or royal plural that refers to the speaker alone, for no such usage is demonstrable anywhere else in biblical Hebrew. Therefore, we must face the question of who are included in this 'us' and 'our.' It could hardly include the angels in consultation with God, for nowhere is it ever stated that man was created in the image of angels, only of God. Verse 27 then affirms: 'and God [Elohim] created man in His own image, in the image of God he created him; male and female He created them' (NASB). God—the same God who spoke of Himself in the plural—now states that He created man in His image. In other words, the plural equals the singular. This can only be understood in terms of the Trinitarian nature of God. The one true God subsists in three Persons, Persons who are able to confer with one another and carry their plans into action together—without ceasing to be one God."

glory, power, honor, and divinity, but we call them "Father," "Son," and "Holy Spirit" because of the different roles they play in relationship to humanity throughout salvation history. The Father is the person who sends the Son to earth; the Son is the person who takes a human nature and becomes incarnate as Jesus of Nazareth; and the Holy Spirit is the person who stands in Christ's place on earth until the Second Coming. Summing up, the statement "God is the Trinity" constitutes an identity statement, as "God" and "the Trinity" are simply two names for the same entity, which means the same thing as the converse identity statement "the Trinity is God." But the statements "the Father is God," "the Son is God," and "the Holy Spirit is God" constitute statements of predication affirming that each one of the persons has the property or attribute of being God (*i.e.* of deity), not that each person is equivalent to God as a whole, rendering the converse of each statement false. Such a doctrine is logically consistent and therefore rationally unobjectionable.

A stunning verification of the Trinity, which encapsulates in advance the fully developed form of this doctrine, appears on the lips of Jesus himself in his Great Commission: "Go therefore and make disciples of all the nations, baptizing them in the name (τὸ ὄνομα) of the Father (τοῦ πατρὸς) and of the Son (τοῦ υἱοῦ) and of the Holy Spirit (τοῦ ἁγίου)" (Mt. 28:19). Here τὸ ὄνομα (the name) is in the singular followed by a plurality of persons represented as equal in dignity and authority. New Testament scholar Robert L. Reymond delineates the implications of this fact:

Jesus does not say, (1) "into the names [plural] of the Father and of the Son and of the Holy Spirit," or what is its virtual equivalent, (2) "into the name of the Father, and into the name of the Son, and into the name of the Holy Spirit," as if we had to deal with three separate Beings. Nor does He say, (3) "into the name of the Father, Son, and Holy Spirit," (omitting the three recurring articles), as if "the Father, Son, and Holy Ghost" might be taken as merely three designations of a single person. What He does say is this: (4) "in the name [singular] of the Father, and of the Son, and of the Holy Spirit," first asserting the unity of the three by combining them all within the bounds of the single Name, and then throwing into emphasis the distinctness of each by introducing them in turn with the repeated article.[11]

---

11. Robert L. Reymond, *Jesus, Divine Messiah: The New Testament Witness* (Phillipsburg, N.J.: Presbyterian and Reformed Publishing, 1990), 84; inserts added.

Hence, Jesus reveals, in a single clause loaded with theological import, that three distinct persons exist within the one divine being who is Yahweh (τὸ ὄνομα, "the name," is an obvious circumlocution for Yahweh, evident by the Jewish background of Matthew's Gospel).

Illustrating the Trinity

Probably the best way to elucidate the Trinity to another person is by exploring the implications of what it means for humans to be created in the *imago Dei* (the image of God). The term "image" (Hebrew צֶלֶם and Greek εἰκών) denotes a shadow or imprecise representation which lacks the essential characteristics of the original. Since God is an infinite immaterial spirit or soul, it logically follows that the image of God cannot be anything physical, such as our bodies or brains (which physicality we share with the animals) or our merely animal life. Rather, the *imago Dei* is the finite immaterial spirit or soul unique to the human species and which dualistically interacts with the physical brain. It is apparent that the human soul contains one center of self–consciousness, *i.e.* one set of cognitive rational faculties, including the reason, memory, and will. Now each finite soul endowed with three irreducibly distinct cognitive rational faculties (which accumulate to one person) imprecisely but clearly mirrors the one infinite soul comprising three irreducibly distinct and complete *sets* of such cognitive rational faculties (*i.e.* three sets of reason, memory, and will), each of which accumulate to one person, and which together total three persons in one being. This argument is greatly strengthened by the way the multipersonality of God is clearly linked in the creation narrative with humanity being made in God's image: "Then God said, 'Let us make humanity in our image, in our likeness'. . . . So God created humanity in his own image, in the image of God he created humanity; male and female he created them" (Gen. 1:26–27). As the great Protestant reformer Huldrych Zwingli rightly summarized:

> It remains then that it is in respect of the soul . . . that we are made in the image of God. . . . [T]he soul is the substance upon which that likeness is particularly stamped. . . . [T]he three faculties of intellect, will, and memory, which are distinct and yet constitute the one soul, are a similitude of the one God in respect of the existence and the trinity of the Persons.[12]

---

12. Huldrych Zwingli, *Of the Clarity and Certainty or Power of the Word of God*, in *Zwingli and Bullinger*, tr. G. W. Bromiley (Philadelphia: Westminster, 1953), 60–61.

Although appealing to our souls as the image of God represents the only means provided in Scripture of illustrating the Trinity, we may provide analogies for certain facets of this doctrine, as long as we remember that no analogy can explain all facets of the Trinity and avoid overextending any analogy beyond its limits. Good analogies for how three distinct and equal parts can make up one larger entity that is not identical to any of the parts, as in the case of three centers of self–consciousness making up one infinite soul or God, include a musical chord (three notes in one chord), a triangle (three angles in one figure), and an Irish clover (three leaves in one clover, a comparison famously used by the fourth–century St. Patrick to evangelize the Irish). Just as there are good analogies for various aspects of the Trinity, so there are bad analogies which misconstrue even the aspects they purport to explain. Particularly notorious is the "water analogy," which unfortunately is among the most widespread analogies allegedly showing how one entity can be composed of three equal parts. In this analogy, just as water can be a solid, liquid, or gas, so God can be the Father, Son, or Holy Spirit. However, this is not a depiction of the Trinity at all, for water is not composed of solid, liquid, and gas; rather, it is a depiction of Modalism, as the one entity of water plays the different roles of solid, liquid, and gas under changing conditions. According to Modalism, God is only one person (a unitarian entity) who reveals himself in three modes (Greek μῶδοι, "masks") at various times in salvation history, just as a single actor might play three different roles or parts and so wear three different masks in various parts of a theatrical production. Thus in the Old Testament God played the role of Father; in the New Testament he played the role of Son; and in the Church Age he plays the role of the Holy Spirit. Since the person who played the Father thus died on the cross (as he also played the Son), this view was branded by opponents as Patripassianism, Latin for "the Father suffers/underwent the Passion"–ism. Not as detrimental but still flawed is the "egg analogy" for the Trinity, in which the shell, white, and yolk compose one egg. While this analogy does illuminate how three distinct parts can make up one larger entity, it fails to show how three distinct *and equal* parts can do so, since the shell, white, and yolk are not equal. For the analogy to work, the egg would have to be composed of three different shells, three different whites, or three different yolks, as God comprises three equal centers of self–consciousness.

"Love" Argument for the Trinity

Having already proven the Trinity via revealed theology (*i.e.* the truths that God has revealed in Scripture), at this juncture let us turn our attention to natural theology (*i.e.* the truths which are naturally accessible to all humanity) to see if it furnishes any evidence that the God who exists must contain more than one person. Philosophers of religion William Lane Craig and Richard Swinburne have discovered one very persuasive argument, which is based upon the truth that "God is love" and attempts to logically extrapolate precisely what it means for God to be love. We start by pointing out that, by definition, God is the greatest conceivable being. As the greatest conceivable being, God must be perfect, for if there were any imperfection in God, then he would not be the greatest conceivable being. Now a perfect being must be a loving being, for love is a moral perfection. That is to say, it is obviously morally better to be loving than unloving. Therefore, God must be a perfectly loving being. However, it is of the very nature of love to give oneself away; love, by definition, reaches out to another person, rather than centering wholly in oneself. So if God is perfectly loving by his very nature, he must be perpetually giving himself in love to at least one "other." But who is this "other" or "others"?[13]

This "other" or "others" cannot be any created person, since creation is the result of God's free will, not the result of his nature; it belongs to God's very essence to love, but it does not belong to his essence to create. Hence God is necessarily loving but not necessarily creating. In other words, God would still be perfectly loving even if no created persons existed. Thus, created persons cannot be the sufficient explanation of whom God loves. Moreover, we know from science that created persons have not always existed from eternity, but God is eternally and timelessly loving. So again, created persons alone are not sufficient to explain whom the "other" or "others" is to whom God's love is necessarily directed. It follows, therefore, that the "other" or "others" to whom God's love is necessarily directed must be internal to God himself. In other words, God is not a single isolated individual.[14] Rather, God is a plurality of Persons, as the doctrine of the Trinity holds. While this argument does not show that God is specifically tripersonal (*i.e.* containing exactly three persons), it does disclose that God is multipersonal (*i.e.* containing more than one person) rather than unitarian (*i.e.* containing simply one person). In other words, if God is love (which is granted by virtually all who believe in God's existence whether Christian or non–Christians), it follows inescapably that God cannot be a single person (if God were a single person, then he could not be love.) Since there do not

---

13. Moreland and Craig, *Philosophical Foundations*, 594; Richard Swinburne, *The Christian God* (Oxford: Oxford University Press, 1994), 177–78.

14. Moreland and Craig, *Philosophical Foundations*, 594–95; Swinburne, *Christian God*, 179.

presently exist among religious groups any doctrines stipulating that God is composed of a number of persons other than one or three (there are no binitarians, quadrarians, pentarians, etc.), the Trinity proves to be the most plausible doctrine of God among the world's faith traditions.

"Transcendence" Argument for the Trinity

Another potent natural theological argument supporting the Trinity stems from the insight of Paul Tillich (1886–1965) that God, as that than which nothing greater can be conceived, must be greater than simply *a* person, even *a highest* person. Unfortunately, due to Tillich's antisupernatural presuppositions of logical positivism and that the universe was a closed system (both of which have since been respectively disproved by philosophy and cosmology), he failed personally to correctly apply his valid recognition. However, unshackled by these false assumptions, we are enabled to employ, and thus redeem, Tillich's recognition in tune with the genuine nature of the universe as an open system, as exhibited by the Big Bang discovery of the origin of the universe *ex nihilo* at a point in the finite past (approximately 13 billion years ago), and that the entity we call "God" thus, definitively speaking, lies outside of time and space. Tillich rightly saw that God, in order to be more than *a* person, must be suprapersonal—namely, he must transcend the duality between personhood and non–personhood by somehow standing in both categories simultaneously but not completely within either, yet without being in any sense impersonal or less than a person. But lacking the philosophical and scientific resources in his worldview to account for God's genuine suprapersonality, Tillich was forced into a sort of theological double–talk wherein suprapersonality inevitably collapsed into impersonality,[15] thus unwittingly contradicting his own insight that God must lie above and beyond, rather than below, the personhood and non–personhood dichotomy.

However, the doctrine of the Trinity portrays God as literally suprapersonal. On the one hand, it defines God as an infinite spiritual substance or soul which has non–personhood (*i.e.* this soul is not identical to any person). On the other hand, it further claims that this infinite spiritual substance contains three persons, thus rendering God superior to simply *a* highest person and assigning God triple the possession of personhood that *a* highest person

---

15. This is because, if the universe is all that exists with no reality lying beyond it, a suprapersonal God becomes at best a philosophical ground, basis, foundation, or principle of being which provides the structure for all interpersonal, or "I–Thou" relationships, thus carrying within itself the potentiality for personality without itself literally being personal in any sense.

would possess. Since God is identical not to a person but to a spiritual substance which comprises three persons, we find that God as Trinity simultaneously stands in both the categories of non–personhood and personhood while not completely within either. God has non–personhood on the level of his οὐσία (spiritual substance/essence/nature) while concurrently having personhood three times over on the level of his ὑπόστασεις, thus precluding absolutely the possibility of his being impersonal or less than a person in any sense. Hence God the Trinity is transcendent over the categories of "being a person" and "not being a person." Tillich himself recognized this point, although his antisupernatural worldview prevented him from embracing it as a viable option: "It should not be forgotten that classical theology employed the term *persona* for the trinitarian hypostases but not for God himself."[16] The Trinity is therefore unique among the doctrines of God postulated by world religions, for it alone substantiates the transcendence of God which his definition as the greatest conceivable being makes necessary. Due to its exclusive ability to show how God can be transcendent in a logically consistent fashion (rather than self–contradictorily ascribing transcendence to a being that does not transcend the duality between personhood and non–personhood), the Trinity is vastly intellectually superior to its doctrinal competitors and so warrants our acceptance.

The Christological Question and Its Solution

Christology is the theological category attempting to explain how Jesus of Nazareth could be fully God and fully human concurrently. Since our formulation of the Trinity has already illustrated Jesus' absolute deity, now the question arises: How could Jesus be fully human? The Fourth Ecumenical Council at Chalcedon (451) was convened to maintain the authentic deity and authentic humanity of Jesus in the face of sects such as the Apollinarians, founded by Apollinaris of Laodicea (*c.* 310–90), and the Eutychians, spearheaded by Eutyches (380–456). The Apollinarians argued that Jesus was fully God and possessed a human body, but shared in none of its limitations (such as those of the brain). The Eutychians claimed that Jesus of Nazareth was the purely divine combination of infinite divine and finite human elements, analogous to a drop of humanity being subsumed into an ocean of divinity, such that Jesus' humanity was deified (and so, for all practical purposes, negated) via absorption into the supernal sea. Not above resorting to duplicity, Eutyches exploited his powerful connections to Byzantine Emperor Theodosius II, Patriarch Dioscurus of Alexandria, and monastic lead-

---

16. Tillich, *Systematic Theology*, 1:244.

ers, in attempting to literally sneak his doctrine into ecumenical acceptance. The group conspired to secretly convoke a general (non–ecumenical) council at Ephesus in 449, inviting only fellow Eutychian leaders and preventing possible disruption or protest by other Christian leaders who somehow learned of the proceedings by guarding the doors of the meeting–house with armed soldiers. This council, appropriately branded the "Council of Robbers" or the "Robbers' Synod," pronounced Eutychianism as orthodoxy and anathematized all who affirmed the genuine humanity of Jesus. Outraged by this result, the majority of bishops throughout the Christian world aimed at the Council of Chalcedon to set Scriptural boundaries within which any doctrine of Jesus must fall to be legitimately orthodox.

With their Chalcedonian Definition, the Fourth Ecumenical Council established four interlocking boundaries which historical theologian Alan W. Gomes helpfully visualizes as the "Chalcedonian Box." Faithfulness to the biblical record requires that a given doctrine of Christ fall within the "box"; by contrast, any doctrine outside the box denies at least one biblical teaching so important as to constitute an essential Christian doctrine. The top side of the box maintains as a statement of predication (adjectival statement) that Jesus is fully God. This fact is balanced by the bottom side of the box, which maintains as a statement of predication that Jesus is fully human. The left side of the box stipulates as an identity statement that Jesus is one person. This truth is balanced by the right side of the box, which stipulates that Jesus possesses two natures—a divine nature and a human nature—which are distinct from one another. Containing a great deal of latitude, this box accommodates all possible doctrinal ways of affirming these four truths; hence it lays out the minimum criteria for a Christology to be Christian but without solving the problem of what the most probable view to take is.

To formulate such a solution, our Christology will start "from above" by working from Jesus' deity to his humanity; in the manner of Alexandrian or Word–Flesh Christology, we begin with the known Trinitarian datum that, prior to Jesus' birth, the Son or Logos—the Second Person of the Trinity— was timelessly a complete set of cognitive rational faculties within the spiritual substance that is identically God. Due to the infinitude of this spiritual substance, it follows that the Logos is an infinite immaterial set of cognitive rational faculties (person or self), thus rendering his reason, memory, and will as infinitely powerful. However, let us now shift to an analysis of human composition so that we may understand what it would mean for this infinite person to become flesh. Recall that a human is composed of a finite immaterial complete set of cognitive rational faculties—namely, a finite immaterial person or self comprising a human soul—conjoined to a finite material hominid body, including a finite brain. Now the capabilities of our finite immaterial selves, or human souls, are perfectly accommodated by our finite brains–bodies. Both philosophical and psychological evidence indicate not only that human souls exist, but that they mutually interact with their physical brains in a bi–directional manner known as dualism–interactionism. We may illustrate dualism–interactionism with the insight that the relationship between soul and brain is analogous to that between an organist and a partially "player" and partially "manual" organ. Based upon the human's genetic makeup and the input of the five senses, this "organ" performs a range of involuntary acts on its own, some of which cannot be controlled by the organist (heart beating, digestion, and so forth), corresponding to the "player" keyboards. Other keyboards play themselves only at the times when the organist does not touch them—thus, to mix metaphors, such keyboards are either on "automatic pilot" or controlled by the organist at any given time. Like a player piano, the main keyboard generates the "score" of music from the human's genetic makeup and the input of the five senses; however, unlike a player piano, the score does not automatically play, but the organist has the libertarian free will to play the score, to play something entirely different, or to not play anything at all.[17] The situation is poignantly illuminated by comparing humans with animals, which do not have souls. No matter how genetically close to humans, animals universally lack the personhood to reject the "score" of music generated by their genetic makeup and the input of their five senses, a score which includes sensations, thoughts, desires, purposes, and beliefs. Animals *must* act in accord with this information; they are entirely "player" organs without any organists or selves. Thus animals are electro-chemical automatons which are determined to act in the ways they do by their genetic influences and sensory data.[18]

---

17. Moreland and Craig emphasize the importance of libertarian free will, or the freedom from causal restraints to choose between opposite courses of action, for self-determination: "Given choices *A* and *B*, one can literally choose to do either one, no circumstances exist that are sufficient to determine one's choice; a person's choice is up to him, and if he does one of them, he could have done otherwise, or at least he could have refrained from acting at all" (*Philosophical Foundations*, 240).

18. In turn, the human possession of libertarian free will can only be explained by the existence of the soul. John Foster, in *The Immaterial Self* (London: Routledge, 1991), 266-80, articulates the argument in syllogistic form:

1. Human beings exercise libertarian freedom.
2. No material object (one which is such that all of its properties, parts and capacities are at least and only physical) can exercise libertarian freedom.
3. Therefore, human beings are not material objects.

One of the most exciting developments in contemporary psychology and neurobiology furnishing stunning evidence not only for the existence of human souls but also for dualism–interactionism surrounds the treatment of ego–dysontic disorders. Ego–dysontic disorders are brain disorders which arise apart from, and at odds with, the sufferer's intrinsic sense of self, the treatment of which depends on the sufferer's possession of a soul with libertarian freedom that can resist the seemingly coercive impulses of the brain. Hence research on such disorders throws new light on precisely what each of the physical brain and immaterial mind (*i.e.* soul) are, and are not, responsible for. In one of the best recent scientific defenses of the human soul and dualism–interactionism, entitled *The Mind & The Brain*, Jeffrey M. Schwartz, research professor of psychiatry at the UCLA School of Medicine, clearly discloses the separation of brain–roles and mind–roles using the case of obsessive–compulsive disorder (OCD), a genetic flaw and hence congenital defect creating a biochemical imbalance in the brain. For the patient with this ego–dysontic disorder, the orbital cortex (the underside of the front of the brain which functions as its "error-detection circuit") produces intrusive threatening thoughts (termed "obsessions") which trigger generation by the amygdala (the large, almond-shaped "fear center" of the brain located beneath the surface of the temporal lobe) of overwhelming instinctual urges to escape the perceived threat by performing mental or physical actions (dubbed "compulsions"). Since other areas of the brain work with the orbital cortex and amygdala to cause obsessions and compulsions, both of which combine sensations, thoughts, desires, purposes, and beliefs, to refrain from carrying out compulsions is literally to fly in the face of one's genetic makeup and sensory stimuli. It should be noted that the OCD sufferer derives no joy from performing compulsions, which the sufferer hates and from whose grip the sufferer is desperate to escape. This puts OCD in marked contrast to non–genetic and ego–ontic disorders like obsessive-compulsive personality disorder (OCPD), compulsive shopping, and com-

---

4. Human beings are either material objects or immaterial substances.
5. Therefore, human beings are immaterial substances.
Furthermore, these immaterial substances possess a wide spectrum of additional attributes which philosophical, psychological, and neurobiological studies have demonstrated lack any reasonable explanation in terms of the brain or DNA. Such attributes include personal identity at and over time, intentionality (the "of-ness" or "about-ness" humans impart to all mental states), the indexicality of thought, and the ability to apprehend an objectively existing and immaterial realm of moral values. For a detailed presentation of these arguments see Geoffrey Madell, *Identity of the Self* (Edinburgh: Edinburgh University Press, 1981) and H. D. Lewis, *The Elusive Self* (Philadelphia: Westminster, 1982).

pulsive gambling, where the person gains pleasure from the "compulsive" behavior. Hence OCD shows that the portions of the brain geared toward thinking, remembering, and desiring, which are respectively correlated with the reason, memory, and will of the immaterial mind (*i.e.* soul), can function independently of the mind to formulate and transmit messages diametrically opposed to the mind's desires. For OCD sufferers, the organ "score" is not only set before them, but the malfunctioning organ exerts tremendous pressure for them to play it.

Owing to the materialism then dominant in psychology, just forty years ago OCD was regarded as treatment-intractable. This is because it is impossible to treat animals genetically flawed with OCD, which always follow their instincts by performing compulsions (which, incidentally, only makes the obsessions worse and intensifies the vicious cycle). As an entirely "player" organ having no organist, the obsessive–compulsive score, determined by the animal's genetic makeup plus the input of its five senses, automatically plays itself. Since humans were regarded as the same as animals on this matter, Schwartz reports that advances in OCD treatment only emerged after "the very idea that the [human] brain can change at all, much less that it can change in response to mind, first [overcame] a century–old dogma," namely materialism, among a group of neurophysiologists and psychiatrists.[19] Dismissal of this faulty presupposition proved the key to developing methods of cognitive–behavioral therapy which directly depend for their success on the existence of an immaterial mind (*i.e.* soul) that dualistically interacts with the brain and which, by continually utilizing its freedom to resist the compulsive signals of the brain, actually has the power to change the brain's chemistry and alleviate the disorder. In this way, OCD is successfully treatable today. From his clinical results Schwartz draws the following conclusions regarding the mind–body problem, which are worth quoting in full:

> The demonstration that OCD patients can systematically alter their brain chemistry through cognitive–behavioral therapy . . . has inescapable implications for theories trying to explain the relationship between mind and brain. . . . For the first time, hard science—for what could be "harder" than the metabolic activity measured by PET scans?—had weighed in on the side of mind-matter theories. . . . a materialist explanation simply cannot account for these findings. To train people suffering from OCD requires tapping into their natural belief in the efficacy of their own willful actions. Explanations based exclusively on materialist causation are both infeasible and inappropriate for conveying to

---

19. Schwartz and Begley, *Mind & Brain*, 95.

OCD patients the steps they must follow to change their own brain circuitry systematically. In order to work, behavioral medicine . . . absolutely requires the use of the patient's inner experience, including the directly perceived reality of the causal efficacy of volition. The clinical and physiological results achieved with OCD support the notion that the conscious and willful mind cannot be explained solely and completely by matter, by the material substance of the brain. In other words, the arrow of causation relating brain and mind must be bi-directional. Conscious, volitional decisions and changes in behavior alter the brain.[20]

Such scientific evidence substantiates dualism–interactionism, which holds that mind and brain are irreducibly independent entities that interact with one another, such that the mind can cause states in the brain and vice versa. Thus in the case of OCD, while the brain can make the mind conscious of tremendous anxiety and exert pressure upon it to perform compulsions, the mind can progressively change the chemistry of the brain through free choices which run counter to its dictates.

Equipped with the knowledge of what the finite human soul is (identical to one complete finite set of cognitive rational faculties) and how this soul bi–directionally interacts with the finite human brain, we now possess the philosophical resources to unpack the implications of the events described by the primitive Christological hymn formulated in the 30s C.E. and quoted by Paul three decades later:

[Paul prefaces the hymn with the exhortation, "Let the same attitude be in you that was also in Christ Jesus:"]
Who, continually existing in the nature of God, did not regard equality with God as something to be exploited,
But emptied himself, taking the nature of a slave, having been born in human likeness.
And having been found in human form, he humbled himself and became obedient to the point of death—even death on a cross.
Therefore God also highly exalted him and gave him the name that is above every name,
So that at the name of Jesus every knee should bend in heaven and on earth and under the earth, and every tongue should confess,
That Jesus Christ is Yahweh (ὁ κύριος), to the glory of God the Father (Php. 2:[5], 6–11).

---

20. Ibid., 93-95.

This memorizable oral tradition reports that Christ, who continually bears the nature of God or μορφῇ (the Koinē equivalent of the Classical Greek οὐσία) θεοῦ, took for himself a human nature or μορφῇ (= οὐσία) ἀνθρώπων, rather than affirming that Christ took for himself a human being or ἄνθρωπος. A significant difference exists between an οὐσία ἀνθρώπων and an ἄνθρωπος. On the one hand, an οὐσία ἀνθρώπων is anhypostatic (lit. without a ὑπόστασις or "person"), *i.e.* lacking independent subsistence or personhood, and therefore refers to the set of attributes apart from the human soul/self/person which, when coupled with the soul, makes up a complete human being. This set of attributes is identical with a hominid body, including a hominid brain. On the other hand, an ἄνθρωπος is a complete human being, both body and soul, which is thus freestanding, *i.e.* possessing independent subsistence or personhood. Since the Second Person of the Trinity assumed for himself a human nature and not a freestanding human, we now perceive the necessity of Jesus' virginal conception. For, as body–soul composites, humans reproduce body and soul; so if Jesus had been conceived through sexual intercourse between Joseph and Mary, he would have been born a freestanding human being with a finite human soul and body, both generated wholly by human parents. In that case, the Incarnation could at best be reduced to the divine Christ setting up a moral or sympathetic union with the man Jesus, in which Christ would permanently indwell Jesus. The final product, Jesus Christ, would not be bipartite (soul and body) but tripartite, a human body, a human soul, and the divine Logos which controlled the human soul; hypothetically speaking, if the Logos were ever to stop indwelling (and so controlling) Jesus, then Jesus would be a normal, fully functioning human being like any other human with nothing divine about him. Thus God the Logos would not literally become flesh, as John 1:14 avers, but would, in an unprecedented manner, reside so utterly in a freestanding man so as to control his every thought and action. But if Jesus had no human father, then the Logos could take his very own anhypostatic human nature (not encompassing a human soul) from the Virgin Mary and hypostasize (*i.e.* personalize or instantiate) it.

Accordingly, this union between the Logos and the hominid brain–body for which the Logos furnishes the hypostasis (person) is denominated the "hypostatic union." At this juncture we shall logically analyze what would happen if an infinite immaterial self (the Logos) took for himself his very own hominid finite brain–body and conjoined himself to it. Recall that the Logos, as an infinite set of cognitive rational faculties, possesses an infinite reason, memory, and will. Since a human soul equals a finite set of cognitive rational faculties and thus a finite reason, memory, and will, the Logos is utterly more than sufficient to supply the human soul of Jesus; all that would be needed is simply a finite amount of each of his infinite cognitive rational faculties. This observation corresponds perfectly to what, logically speaking, must transpire if an infinite immaterial Self were conjoined to a finite brain. Only a finite amount of each of the infinite Self's cognitive rational faculties—namely, precisely the same amount as each of our cognitive rational faculties operating at full capacity—could be accommodated by this brain. To simplify, logic dictates that, from his virginal conception to his death, Jesus' finite brain continually limited the amount of his infinite immateriality that he could access to precisely the same finite amount of immateriality that any other human being would possess at each respective stage of life. Like the tip of an iceberg, the human soul of Jesus constituted the finite amount of his infinite immaterial Self that his finite human brain could handle, thus rendering Jesus' soul exactly identical to all other human souls. So Jesus' distinctly earthly immaterial consciousness came into existence, grew, and developed as the boy Jesus grew and developed. This consciousness drew its visual imagery from what the eyes of Jesus saw and its concepts from the languages he learned. In this way, Jesus' earthly immaterial consciousness was thoroughly human, Jewish, and first–century Palestinian in nature. During Jesus' earthly life, therefore, the vast majority of cognitive perfections belonging to his infinite Self, such as all the "omni" attributes (*e.g.* omniscience, omnipotence, omnipresence, etc.), could not be in his waking consciousness. Rather, they were resident in Jesus' subconscious, or what we may style the "divine subliminal," and temporarily reemerged at selected moments, such as when he performed miracles or displayed knowledge of past, counterfactual, and future truths. Moreland and Craig thoroughly illuminate how our Christology harmonizes beautifully with the New Testament depiction of the historical Jesus:

> Such a model provides a satisfying account of the Jesus we see in the Gospel portrait. In his conscious experience, Jesus grew in knowledge and wisdom, just as a human child does. One does not have the monstrosity of the baby Jesus lying in the manger possessing the full divine consciousness. In his conscious experience, we see Jesus genuinely tempted. . . . The enticements of sin were really felt and could not be blown away like smoke; resisting temptation required spiritual discipline and moral resoluteness on Jesus' part. In his waking consciousness, Jesus is actually ignorant of certain facts, though kept from error and often supernaturally illumined by the divine subliminal. Even though the Logos possesses all knowledge about the world from quantum mechanics to auto mechanics, there is no reason to think that Jesus of Nazareth would have been able to answer questions about such subjects, so low had he stooped in condescending to take on the human

condition. Moreover, in his conscious life, Jesus knew the whole gamut of human anxieties and felt physical hurt and fatigue. The model also preserves the integrity and sincerity of Jesus' prayer life, and it explains why Jesus was capable of being perfected through suffering. He, like us, needed to be dependent on his Father moment by moment in order to live victoriously in a fallen world and to carry out successfully the mission with which he had been charged. The agonies in Gethsemane were no mere show but represented the genuine struggle of the incarnate Logos in his waking consciousness.[21]

At this point some common Christological misconceptions, which our view helpfully avoids, need to be exposed. A common misconception is that Jesus needed to be virginally conceived, not to make it logically possible for God to become flesh, but for Jesus not to be conceived with the taint of original sin.[22] Hence, the argument runs, Jesus had a sin–free human nature, as did primal humanity before the Fall, whereas humanity since that time has been born in sin. This position ought to be rejected for three reasons. First, as shown in chapter one, the doctrine of original sin is unbiblical, meaning that the same libertarian human freedom that the primal human couple possessed is also possessed by all their posterity, such that all humans are born into the world with a human nature possessing the same strength to do good and avoid evil as the first humans. How this observation squares with the Genesis creation narrative will be delineated in the next chapter; suffice it to point out here that our observation is necessary both to God's distributive and punitive justice. Second, the logic of soteriology (the doctrine of how Christ saves humanity) demands that *quod non est assumptum non est sanatum* ("anything which is not assumed is not saved"), *i.e.* for Christ to redeem the type of human nature we possess, he must have assumed this same type of human nature. Had Christ assumed a purer type of human na-

---

21. Moreland and Craig, *Philosophical Foundations*, 612.

22. Historically, several attempts have been made by various Christian groups to explain how this could be possible. Solemnly defined as dogma by Pope Pius IX in his bull *Ineffabilis Deus* on 8 December 1854, Roman Catholicism posits the Immaculate Conception, namely, that Mary was conceived without original sin, thus enabling Jesus to be similarly conceived. Sixteenth–century Dutch Anabaptist leader Menno Simons conjectured the "heavenly flesh doctrine," according to which the Logos did not assume flesh from a sinful Virgin Mary but was clothed at the Incarnation with divine flesh by the Holy Spirit, such that Mary acted as simply the incubator for a child having no genetic relation to herself. It should be noted that this obviously controversial position has not been followed by Mennonites after the time of Simons.

ture than ours (a state of affairs which the denial of original sin renders self–contradictory), he could at best have redeemed that purer nature and not our human nature. In that case, as the Apostle Paul remarked, our "faith is futile," and we "are still in our sins" (1 Cor. 15:17). Third, and most importantly, the idea that Jesus was born with a purer human nature than ours is explicitly contradicted by Scripture. Recall from chapter one that Paul termed the Hebrew *yetzer ra*, or inclination naturally generated by the human body to follow one's sinful desires, the σάρξ (flesh, sinful nature), which inclination he opposed to the πνεῦμα (spirit, will) or *yetzer tov*, the soul's cognitive rational faculty inclining the person toward the performance of good. Due to its influence, this dichotomy between σάρξ and πνεῦμα dichotomy was followed by post–Pauline biblical writings. Confronted with the nascent (or proto–)Gnostic denial of Jesus' true humanity, Paul emphasizes that the human Jesus not only possessed σάρξ (the sinful inclination) but that this σάρξ genuinely contained the potential to commit sin (ἁμαρτία) had Jesus so chosen. This double insistence on Jesus' ownership of a human nature equally inclined to sin as ours Paul redundantly styles "the likeness of flesh/sinful nature of sin" (ὁμοιώματι σαρκός ἁμαρτίας):

> The law of the Spirit of life in Christ Jesus freed you from the law of sin and death. . . .God sent his own Son in *the likeness of flesh/sinful nature of sin* and, concerning sin, he dealt with sin in the flesh/sinful nature, in order that the righteous requirements of the law may be fulfilled in us, the ones who walk not according to the flesh/sinful nature but according to spirit (Rom. 8:2–4).

In addition, this passage attests to the *quod non est assumptum non est sanatum* principle, as God could only deal with our sin by Christ's assumption of the sinful inclination which provokes it. Writing after Paul's death, the Elder John penned a phrase which has since become so commonplace that we miss its significance—that the Logos became flesh (σάρξ; Jn. 1:14)—which we now perceive could equally well be translated "the Logos became sinful nature." Despite that he was born with a sinful human nature (one both inclined toward and actually able to commit sin), Jesus the Logos never sinned, a reflection that breathes powerful and awe–inspiring new life into the following affirmation:

> For this reason [Jesus] was obligated to become like his sisters and brothers *in all* (πάντα) *respects*, in order that he might become a merciful and faithful high priest in the service of God, to make atonement for the sins of the people. For because he has suffered, having himself been tempted, he is able to help those who are being tempted. . . . For

we do not have a high priest who is unable to sympathize with our weaknesses, but we have one who has been tempted *in all* (πάντα) *respects as we are, yet was without sin* (Heb. 2:17–18, 4:15; emphasis added).

Several pastoral implications immediately present themselves at this point. Although Jesus enjoyed no earthly advantage over us, having a nature like ours *in all respects*, he continually employed his libertarian freedom to resist every temptation of the σάρξ—exactly the same temptations we face—throughout an entire lifetime. Moreover, in terms of our organ analogy, the infinite Logos is like a musical virtuoso who superbly plays all the instruments in a symphony. Imagine that this virtuoso is locked in a room with a single organ and is thus consigned to play it without recourse to any other instrument. Obviously, the amount of the virtuoso's brilliance able to be displayed through the organ alone is vastly lower than the amount displayed through the sum total of all the instruments in the symphony. The organ will not allow the virtuoso to show, for example, his abilities to do so much as even play the trumpet, clarinet, flute, trombone, saxophone, and so forth, much less display his superiority to other performers on each of these instruments. However, there will be occasional moments where his technique on these instruments would have a chance to "leak through" or briefly manifest in his organ performance. At such points, the virtuoso could, if he so chose, to perform trumpet–like, clarinet–like, etc., devices on the organ within the constraints of what it will allow, which devices could not be performed by someone who exclusively plays the organ. However, knowing that the organ was never intended for the sounding of these devices, the virtuoso chooses not to perform such artificialities in his desire to safeguard the purity of his instrument, although he could perform them if he wished to simply show off his talents. But now imagine that a young child without any exposure to symphonic instruments was suddenly placed in the locked room with the virtuoso. The virtuoso, desiring for the child to get a sense of what not only the organ but also what other instruments could do, employs the limited capacities of the organ to create trumpet–like, clarinet–like, etc. sounds for the child's benefit, which he refrained from creating for his own benefit. In precisely the same way, Jesus never "cheated" as a human being by employing for his own advantage the limited divine abilities which his finite brain temporarily allowed to "leak over" from his subliminal into his waking consciousness. Thus Jesus never availed himself of these temporarily available abilities to keep from committing sin, to avoid hunger or tiredness, or any other temptation, trial, or suffering that we all face. On the contrary, Jesus compassionately used these abilities to help others, such as performing miracles and displaying supernatural knowledge, thereby meeting the physical and spiritual needs of otherwise lost and dying people.

The fact that Jesus, with an identical nature to ours and without use of any form of divine assistance that is unavailable to us, freely chose to live a sinless life proves that it is logically possible for any of us to similarly live a sinless life. Nevertheless, all of us freely choose to sin, even though it is entirely possible for us to never do so. This sordid predicament should humble us in the conviction that we, and we alone, are responsible for our sins; the primal human couple did nothing to cause them and share none of the blame. Nor does our humanity in any way compel us to commit them. As Ezekiel testified, "The soul who sins is the one who shall die. The son will not share the guilt of the father, nor will the father share the guilt of the son" (Ezek. 18:20). With this in mind, Jesus' earthly life proves to be a genuine, realistic example which we should all follow in our lives of discipleship. Thus Jesus was not speaking metaphorically when he challenged, "If anyone desires to come after me, let one deny oneself, take up one's cross, and follow me. For whoever wants to save one's life will lose it, but whoever loses one's life for my sake and the gospel's sake will save it" (Mk. 8:34–35). Moreover, Jesus' crucifixion is rendered all the more poignant for our own lives, since Jesus died as a propitiation not for some mythological "original sin" allegedly inherited from Adam but rather for our actual sins, namely, the sins we ourselves actually commit.

Our Christology also avoids the fallacy of reduplicative predication, which ascribes certain activities of Jesus to his divine will and other activities to his human will. Such a maneuver entails duothelitism, or Jesus' possession of two separate wills;[23] however, since a will is an exclusive and

---

23. In controversial fashion, the Sixth Ecumenical Council at Constantinople (680) affirmed duothelitism, despite the rightful championing of monothelitism (Jesus' possession of only one will) by the seventh–century Pope Honorius I, whom the council stunningly yet scathingly anathematized. Not surprisingly, many Christians throughout history have found this Council problematic on Scriptural grounds, along with Ecumenical Councils Five (Constantinople, 553) and Seven (Nicea, 787). (Obviously many contemporary Roman Catholics would find special difficulty recognizing Ecumenical Council Six in light of the Vatican I dogma of papal infallibility.) Even Pope Gregory the Great (*r.* 590–604), did not recognize as authoritative the far less contentious Fifth Ecumenical Council but asserted the validity of only the first four Ecumenical Councils, just as there existed only four Gospels: "I confess that I accept and venerate the four councils (Nicea, Constantinople, Ephesus and Chalcedon) in the same way as I do the four books of the holy Gospel" (*Registrum Epistolarum*, I:25). For these reasons, during the Reformation Catholics and Protes-

necessary rational faculty of an immaterial person, Jesus could only have two separate wills if he were two separate immaterial persons—one divine person and one human person—coexisting in a human body. Such a "schizophrenic" Jesus not only precludes a genuine Incarnation, as explained earlier, but also cannot be plausibly reconciled with the portrait of Jesus painted by the New Testament authors. The final misconception that our view forestalls is of a different kind than those aforementioned, for, unlike previously exposed errors, this inaccuracy has historically been associated with the type of Christology we are propounding (*i.e.* Christology from Above or Word–Flesh), despite that there is no logical connection between the two. Dubbed *communicatio idiomatum* (the "communication of attributes" doctrine), this position holds that at the virginal conception the Logos' divine attributes, such as his omniscience, omnipotence, and omnipresence, transfer over to the human nature he assumed, so that Jesus' human nature was also omniscient, omnipotent, omnipresent, and the like. While the fifth-century Alexandrians associated Word–Flesh Christology with *communicatio idiomatum*, this connection occurred solely through historical accident, as the goal of the Greek soteriology to which the Alexandrians were committed before the Christological debates equaled divinization, or human acquisition of divine attributes, a soteriology onto which the human Jesus was superimposed as a model. But this notion destroys the real humanity of Jesus, as a human nature is, by definition, finite in knowledge, power, and presence (*i.e.* only in one place at one time); therefore, an omniscient, omnipotent, and omnipresent human nature is simply not a human nature! Because the Logos can only save what he assumed, and this fallacy rules out his assuming a human nature, *communicatio idiomatum* negates both the Incarnation (the Logos becoming flesh, or human in the same way we are) and Christ's atonement for the sins of humanity. Owing to the fact that nothing in Word–Flesh Christology in any way implies *communicatio idiomatum*, we are logically entitled to affirm the first while rejecting the second.

Essential Christological Application: A Satisfaction Theory of the Atonement

We close our study of Christology by applying our model to one of the primary theological dilemmas which, if it be true, must solve—how Jesus

---

tants alike, in referring to the Ecumenical Tradition of the church, appealed exclusively to the *consensus quinquaesaecularis* (the first five centuries of Christian history, *i.e.* the period when Ecumenical Councils One through Four occurred).

could serve as an infinite sacrifice for the sins of humanity. Since Anselm's eleventh–century masterwork *Cur Deus Homo* (Why the God–Man?), the first systematic study of the Atonement in church history, most theologians have interpreted the necessity of Jesus' death in the fashion of divinely required violence, namely, the appeasement of God the Father's infinite wrath against human sin via the human sacrifice of his own Son. While this notion is often defended by appealing to God's justice, rightly arguing that it is logically necessary for an absolutely just being (which God must be as the greatest conceivable being) to rectify all wrongs, it is simply gratuitous to assert that punishment is the only possible way for this restitution to transpire. In fact, this appeal proves a *reductio ad absurdum*, for punishing a completely innocent person (even at his behest) for the crimes of the guilty while allowing the guilty to go free constitutes the epitome of injustice. By committing theological slight–of–hand in shifting from God's justice to the Father's justice, moreover, the violent model contradicts the doctrine of the Trinity, which requires all three persons comprising God (not merely the Father) to hold the attribute of perfect justice. If the violent model were valid, then the Son's justice and the Holy Spirit's justice would still require appeasement by, presumably, the sacrifice of another Trinitarian person. Incidentally, the violent nature of the Atonement first added by the Protestant Reformers to Anselm's theory (for which Anselm is typically blamed) parts company from Anselm himself, who did not regard the Father as punishing the Son for the sins of all humanity in place of the guilty human perpetrators; rather, Anselm vaguely posited that the Son rendered "satisfaction" for the totality of creaturely sin.[24] Here we shall provide the necessary substance to Anselm's insight concerning satisfaction by combining our Christology with metaphysical reflection upon the meaning of sin, thereby restoring and refurbishing a genuinely Anselmian theory of the Atonement.

Analyzing the internal logic of the Atonement, *Cur Deus Homo* inquires by its titular question, "Why is the life and death of a God–man necessary for the redemption of humankind? Why not the life and death of an angel? A mere man or woman? Or, apart from any time–space life, could God have saved humanity simply by an act of omnipotence?" In short, Anselm queries whether God could pardon sin without satisfaction and, if not, whether a God–man rather than some other rational being must serve as the mediator. Echoing the Old and New Testament witness (*e.g.* Ex. 29:36; Heb. 2:17), in which the former's animal sacrifices and other *mitzvoth* designate imperfect copies or shadows of the latter (Heb. 9:23), Anselm begins by asserting the absolute necessity of atonement if humanity is to be redeemed. Accordingly,

---

24. Anselm, *Cur Deus Homo*, 1.5.

Anselm rejects alternative Atonement theories, like Irenaeus' recapitulation theory, Origen's Ransom to Satan theory, and Abelard's moral influence theory that the death of Jesus is simply a manifestation of God's love to humanity, because they do not adequately explain this necessity. At this point we stipulate that the atonement comprised the fulfillment of two necessary attributes of the divine nature: perfect holiness coupled with perfect justice.[25] That the aforementioned amount to necessary divine attributes not only follow from God's definition as greatest conceivable being but also enjoy explicit biblical validation (Lev. 19:2; Deut. 32:4). In addition, we follow Augustine in defining sin as a *privatio boni, i.e.* a privation (lack) of good, having no being in and of itself but existing only as a defect or accident (nonessential property) imposed by persons upon created entities, such as themselves, other persons, and other animate or inanimate realities in the universe. Such an understanding expresses in metaphysical terms the biblical view of sin as active rebellion or passive indifference toward God, toward social justice, or both—in other words, any deviation from the two supreme commandments: "Love the Lord your God with all your heart and with all your soul and with all your mind and with all your strength. . . . Love your neighbor as yourself. There are no commandments greater than these" (Mk. 12:30–31). Whenever humans violate these laws, they incur damage (privation of good) to themselves, to one another, and to the created order.

While Anselm rightly points out that God cannot overlook this damage to his creation without being unjust, neither, we may add, can God blink at sin without compromising his holiness. For the essence of holiness is what

---

25. It is important to distinguish between the often wrongly conflated notions of holiness and justice. As Rudolf Otto showed, the term "holy" (Hebrew קָדוֹשׁ; Greek ἅγιος) originally denoted that which could be classed as *mysterium tremendum et fascinans,* apart from any moral connotations. On the contrary, "justice," designating fairness or righteousness, emanates exclusively from the ethical domain and in no way implies holiness. Thus Otto insisted that these two terms must be understood separately lest distortion and confusion inevitably result: "*[Q]ādôsh,* ἅγιος . . . mean beyond all question something other than 'the good.' This is universally agreed by contemporary criticism, which rightly explains the rendering of *qādôsh* by 'good' as a mistranslation and unwarranted 'rationalization' or 'moralization' of the term" (*The Idea of the Holy,* tr. John W. Harvey [Oxford: Oxford University Press, 1923], 5–11). Moreover, contra those who would oppose justice and love, Tillich reminds us that if God's justice were annulled, "he would cease to be love, for justice is the structural form of love without which it would be sheer sentimentality. The exercise of justice is the working of his love, resisting and breaking what is against love. Therefore, there can be no conflict between love and justice" (*Systematic Theology,* 2:174).

we shall denominate "complete functional unity and integrity," *i.e.* the conjunction of completeness, wholeness, soundness, and unity, which God possesses in perfect measure; but the damage of sin obviously destroys completeness and wholeness as well as fragmenting defective portions from sound or healthy portions of creation. So for a holy God to be in relationship with created persons (along with the rest of the created order), those persons must be first made holy, bearing complete functional unity and integrity, lest God, by virtue of relations with incomplete beings (and so unholy relations), cease to be holy. In addition to Anselm's biblical grounds, then, philosophical considerations also necessitate atonement, or full creaturely restoration, as the only possible avenue for the divine–human relationship. However, due to his evaluation of its magnitude, Anselm correctly discerns that humans are unable to make satisfaction for sin. Anselm realizes that the gravity of any sin (*i.e.* the damage which it exacts upon the sinner) depends upon the value of the being whose belongings, construed broadly to include all personal, impersonal, material, and immaterial entities that one possesses, are harmed. To give an example from the animal world, if a dog bites some other animal (whose value is less than or equal to itself), thus harming the body belonging to the animal, it is unlikely that a law court would demand for the dog to be put to sleep. But if the dog bites, and so harms the body belonging to, a human being (whose value is much greater than itself), then it is quite likely that the court would order the dog to be killed. Likewise, logic demands that any sin, as a violation of the moral character of God himself, is of infinite gravity, since God is a being of infinite value. Hence we find ourselves confronted with the sobering reality that, for each sin we commit, we inflict infinite, and therefore irreparable, harm upon ourselves, not to mention whatever finite harms we inflict upon others and the natural world. This is why "the wages of sin is death" (Rom. 6:23a), where "death" in this context refers to spiritual separation from God. Even if humans began to fully submit their will to God and henceforth render God perfect obedience, they would merely be doing what God has required from the beginning, thereby preventing future self–inflicted wounds but doing nothing to heal those already suffered. As Jesus told his disciples, "So you also, when you have done everything you were told to do, should say, 'We are unworthy servants; we have only done our duty'" (Lk. 17:10). Therefore, it is beyond the power of humanity to make compensation for its sin.

The infinite gravity of sin outweighs anything in the world, except God himself. In other words, since the damage humanity has inflicted upon itself is greater than all created things, it follows that the redeemer must be capable of making an infinite satisfaction for such damage. Hence, it is necessary for the redeemer to be God. But the redeemer must also share in the human condition in order to transmit his restoring benefits to humanity, in accordance with the logical principle *quod non est assumptum non est sanatum*. Thus the redeemer must also be human, yet himself without sin, so as not to deface the holiness and justice necessary to his deity, on which the infinite power of his saving work depends. In Tillichian language, the redeemer needed to be the bearer and inaugurator of the "new being" or transfigured creation exemplified by essential or complete humanity—humanity that is whole, fully actualizing its potentialities to maximally love God and neighbor, and thus rightly related to the divine—under the conditions of existence.[26] As N. T. Wright reveals, an integral part of Jesus' perceived divinely ordained mission or "messianic job description" was to personally fulfill the vocation entrusted to Israel at Mount Sinai, *i.e.* to be the light of the world by engaging in Spirit–powered loving service to the nations beyond itself and thereby inviting outsiders to join the community of God, but which Israel had collectively failed to accomplish.[27] Serving as its representative, Jesus aimed to bring Israel's history to its climax and finally make Israel the divinely intended light shining in the midst of sin's darkness. Moreover, Jesus intended to bring about in his own person Israel's true return from exile, namely, its liberation from the kingdom of the world, or philosophical system of top–down domination controlled by Satan according to which the world operates, and into the Kingdom of God, an alternative philosophy of life according to which God is the king over all earthly affairs which will, at the end of the age, manifest itself as the reign of God over the fully transfigured creation.[28] By reopening the gateway for all persons, regardless of ethnic heritage, to become part of the family of God marked by the Abrahamic Covenant, Jesus explicitly extended the abolition of exile to all humanity who wished to be grafted into the tree of Israel. Hence Jesus instituted a new entity which he dubbed the ἐκκλησία (Mt. 16:18; 18:17), the standard English translation of which, "church," hides its exactingly literal meaning: "the called–out–of–exile people," intended to include all ἔθνη, or ethnic groups (Mt. 28:19).

Not only for these reasons must the redeemer be ὁ θεάνθρωπος, "the God–man," but his full deity alongside his full humanity also powerfully reveals precisely why Jesus, through his life, was able to set in motion an unstoppable and supernaturally powered Kingdom program which is continually repairing, and will culminate by totally repairing, the damage of sin

---

26. Tillich, *Systematic Theology*, 2:120–21.
27. N. T. Wright, *Jesus and the Victory of God* (Minneapolis: Fortress, 1996), 530–31.
28. Ibid., 537–39.

caused by humanity. If Jesus had simply been a sinless human, then his life would possess only the finite power to preserve himself from the clutches of the Kingdom of the World, which is impotent to heal the infinitely deep wounds of sin of any other person. But since Jesus is also God, the greatest conceivable being, it follows logically that his life is of infinite value, rendering his ministry a work of supererogation, or possessing a power far above and beyond what is possible for a solely human life. Through his infinitely powerful divine–human Kingdom ministry, Jesus produced in time and space an endless storehouse of power forever accessible to any person who enters the Kingdom through the bond of personal commitment to him, *i.e.* biblical faith.[29] This indissoluble bond, traditionally depicted as the spiritual marriage between Christ and the believer in both biblical and ecclesiastical tradition, carries a number of monumental consequences. These stem from the fact that, like common property in a human marriage where the formerly individual possessions of each spouse belong equally to both spouses, the infinite treasury of restorative power, a power otherwise termed "grace" and "merit," that properly belongs to Jesus now becomes eternally linked to the believer. By virtue of this link, Jesus' infinite restorative power automatically and constantly flows into each believer's soul from the moment of personal commitment, immediately healing all the believer's infinite (and so humanly incurable) wounds of sin as well as immediately canceling out and thereby negating the deleterious force of future sin before it may harm the soul. In this way, the believer's soul is instantly regenerated, the believer's past and present sins are instantly forgiven, and the believer's soul is "sealed" or protected from future sinful damage, thus causing all future sins to be forgiven as soon as they are committed. Since these benefits automatically impact every new believer without any additional human action, we may dub them the "passive benefits" of Jesus' life, summarized in the Pauline transition from a natural human to a spiritual human (1 Cor. 2:15–16). Other passive benefits include the transformation of believers' bodies at the general resurrection into "spiritual bodies" free from the effects of sin, sickness, disease, and death (1 Cor. 15:42–49). Moreover, a number of "active benefits" of Jesus' life, requiring further action on the part of believers, are permanently accessible whenever the faithful so will to appropri-

---

29. Picking up on the mathematical and set–theoretic language of chapter two, the type of infinity which Christ's earthly life and ministry was invested would be of the highest order, namely, an infinitely high order. Such an observation gives new meaning to Paul's remark concerning "how wide" and "high is" the mystery of Christ (Eph. 3:18), whose power is not only infinite in breadth but infinite in depth.

ate them. Such benefits are encapsulated in the process of sanctification, whereby each believer chooses to draw upon the supply of infinite power to increasingly transform her or his mind and lifestyle into the image of Christ. In philosophical terms, Christ's deity renders his earthly life infinitely valuable and thus his earthly ministry infinitely powerful to restore every infinite and finite privation of good, or every sin and sinful consequence, throughout the entire time–space universe. By identifying such restoration as satisfaction, we furnish Anselm's theory with precision while simultaneously drawing attention to its profound significance.

With believers now "made perfect" (Heb. 10:14), and with the sin that they perpetrated against themselves and against the universe, by Jesus' atoning work, respectively undone or infallibly guaranteed to be undone on the Day of Yahweh, the righteous demands of God the Trinity's justice are fully met, for no unaccounted wrong remains to be punished. Due to their present spiritual completeness or holiness, God is able to now enjoy personal relationship with the redeemed, taking up residence in their souls (Jn. 14:23; *cf.* 1 Cor. 15:50–54), without compromising his holiness. When their physical bodies along with the physical cosmos are likewise restored at the general resurrection, God will enter into material fellowship with his saints in the new heaven–earth, fulfilling his ultimate sovereign end of a holy creation rightly related to a holy God. In our scheme, the earthly ministry and death take on a dramatically new and poignant focus. No longer is merely the death of Christ related to his atonement, such that the specific Jewish Kingdom–inaugurating activities of his earthly career were unnecessary to his advent of salvation (as any sinless life, no matter what its particular contents, would suffice).[30] Rather, it is the entire ministry of Jesus, composed of the specific historical words and deeds through which he, in his own person, brought the Kingdom of God to humanity which is infinitely powerful. However, Jesus' advent of the Kingdom was not dependent upon his crucifixion; in other words, if the Jewish religious aristocracy had received his teaching and Israel had adopted his way of being the light of the world, then humanity would no less have been redeemed from sin. Thus we see that the emphasis of Jesus' redemptive work has, since the Reformation, been put in the wrong place: what was necessary for humanity's redemption was Jesus' inception of the Kingdom of God, regardless of how his contemporaries responded to that inception, and not his contemporaries' negative reaction of brutally executing him. (In other words, Jesus' role as Savior was not predi-

---

30. A problem that, as N. T. Wright incisively demonstrates, has plagued most theories of the Atonement since the Reformation, which can only explain why Jesus died but are powerless to explain why he lived as he did (*Jesus*, 14).

cated upon inciting others to crucify him.) Converse to most assessments, we conclude that it was not Jesus' crucifixion that invested his earthly ministry with value, but his earthly ministry that substantiated his crucifixion. This insight is easily verified via *reductio ad absurdum*; if the crucifixion was necessary for God to instantiate humanity's salvation, then a monstrous human evil was necessary for God to accomplish the ultimate good.[31] Not only would this undercut the omnipotence of God, who then could not perform the clearly logically possible state of affairs of saving humanity apart from the judicial murder of his second person, but it would also destroy the justice of God, who then would be guilty of the supreme employment of ends to justify the means. But since God is able to accomplish all logically possible states of affairs and, as an all–just being, could never ordain the greatest possible injustice—the crucifixion of one who deserved precisely the opposite treatment—to carry out good (as we explicitly demonstrated in chapter four), it follows that Jesus' crucifixion was not essential to his redemptive work; rather, Jesus turned this ultimate evil into good by using it to accomplish his redemptive work. For these reasons, our satisfaction theory may equally well be dubbed a "non–violent theory of the Atonement," as a wrathful Father did not require the ultimate human sacrifice of his own Son to forgive humanity, nor was violence in any way necessary for the holiness and justice of God to be satisfied. On the contrary, such violence stands as testimony to the depths of wickedness in the human heart and was ultimately engineered by Satan. But given the counterfactual truth that, upon Jesus' Kingdom inauguration, the Jewish and Roman political leaders would freely crucify him, God turned Jesus' crucifixion into the instrument by which all humanity might be reconciled to himself. Hence our non–violent nature theory in no way compromises the substitutionary nature of the Atonement but actually safeguards and enhances it, for Jesus' suffering the wrath of Satan plus his power of death on the cross and thereby defeating him with his αἰών (world–controlling philosophical system) once and for all ensures that we will never suffer the wrath of Satan or his power of death. Since Jesus bore Satan's wrath and power of death in our place, we stand as "more than conquerors" over his dark empire (Rom. 8:37), such that we need no longer fear the evil

---

31. At a lecture at First United Methodist Church in Waterloo, Iowa on 7 October 2006, John Dominic Crossan aptly remarked concerning the Mel Gibson film *The Passion of the Christ*, which perpetuates a violent view of the Atonement, that while he heard many people coming out of the theater professing how much they loved Jesus, not once did he hear anyone say how much they loved God.

one's power to "cast body and soul into Gehenna" (Mt. 10:28).[32] Thus, as the most ancient Christian tradition relates on this score,[33] Jesus literally died "in behalf of our sins" (ὑπὲρ τῶν ἁμαρτιῶν ἡμῶν), breaking the self–inflicted bonds to Satan's domination which our sins represent. Our analysis is verified by the book of Hebrews, whose logical outline we not only replicate but fill out with substance:

> Therefore, since the children have shared in flesh and blood, he likewise shared in the same things, in order that through death he would destory the one having power over death, that is the devil, and free those who all their lives were being subject to slavery by their fear of death. . . . For this reason he was obligated to become like his sisters and brothers in all respects, in order that he might become a merciful and faithful high priest in the service of God, to make atonement for the sins of the people (Heb. 2:14–15, 17).

Therefore, our Atonement model possesses great explanatory power and scope concerning the Scriptural claims that Jesus made atonement for human sin precisely in his defeating the devil, which explanatory advantages are not enjoyed by its competitors.

In addition to its ability to reconcile biblical texts long assumed *prima facie* incompatible, our Atonement model lends itself to the best philosophical analyses on the nature of sin and the ὀργή θεοῦ, or "wrath of God." The Bible affirms that death entered the world through sin which, as a privation of good, is intrinsically self–destructive (Gen. 2:16–17; Rom. 5:12–21), a deduction confirmed by Aristotle. Aristotle perceived that while truth is linear, such that it always remains self–consistent regardless of how far it is pressed, falsehood is circular and thus eventually refutes itself. Since sin is self–curved in upon itself, sin bears within itself the seeds of its own destruction. For this reason, God does not have to judge sinners proactively but, as Jesus pointed out, "those who do not believe have been judged already . . . this is the judgment, that the light has come into the world but humans loved darkness rather than light because their works were evil" (Jn. 3:18–19). Hence those who reject Christ are permitted to exercise their libertarian freedom and so remain in their self–inflicted spiritual death and dark-

---

32. That the one who has power to cast body and soul into Gehenna refers to Satan and not God is proven from the context of the pericope by Wright, *Jesus*, 454.

33. Kirk R. MacGregor, "1 Corinthians 15:3b–6a, 7 and the Bodily Resurrection of Jesus," *Journal of the Evangelical Theological Society* 49.2 (2006): 225–28.

ness. Paul concurs in his delineation of how "the wrath of God is revealed from heaven against all ungodliness and wickedness of humans who suppress the truth in unrighteousness" (Rom. 1:18). The governing idea which thrice appears in his account of humanity's downward spiral into condemnation is "Therefore, God gave them over" (1:24, 26, 28). In other words, God respected human freedom by allowing his creatures to leave his presence and experience the self–destructive course of sin. Enslaving themselves to that which God detests, humanity fell ever deeper into the black hole of idolatry, sexual immorality, every manner of wickedness, and ultimately death (1:24–32). Thus C. Norman Kraus contends that the ὀργή θεοῦ

> is not retaliatory nor vindictive . . . [but] points to the objective, intrinsic consequences of sin in the created order as God's judgment. The very concept of a rational creation implies an order of existence in which consequences are inherent in the actions themselves.[34]

So it is simply a logical necessity for any sin to intrinsically embody the potencies for its own punishment, which unleash themselves after the sin is committed. Philosophically speaking, then, we see that the Scriptural references to God's pouring out his wrath are descriptions of God's activity not *in sensu diviso* but rather *in sensu composito*. In other words, the wrath that human beings experience is inherent in their committing the sinful actions and is inflicted upon humans by themselves and by Satan. That humans suffer such wrath is not directly caused by God and, in fact, lies outside his perfect will; God does not personally dispense punishment upon sinners nor has any desire to do so. In fact, God literally pleads with humans to turn back from their self–destructive ways and experience his salvation:

> "Do I take any pleasure in the death of the wicked?" declares Yahweh Elohim. "Rather, am I not pleased when they turn from their ways and live?. . . If a wicked person turns away from the evil he has committed and does what is just and right, he will save his life. Because he considers all the sins he has committed and turns away from them, he will surely live; he will not die. . . .Repent! Turn away from all your wrongdoings; then sin will not be your downfall. Rid yourselves of all the wrongdoings you have committed, and get a new heart and a new spirit. For why will you die, O house of Israel? For I take no pleasure in the death of anyone," declares Yahweh Elohim. "So repent and live!" (Ezek. 18:23, 27–28, 30–32)

---

34. C. Norman Kraus, *God Our Savior: Theology in a Christological Mode* (Scottdale, Pa.: Herald, 1991), 210–11.

Jesus echoed the Hebrew Biblical response during his final visit to Jerusalem when he reflected on the impending judgment for sin the city would experience at the hands of the Roman Empire:

> As he came near, having seen the city, he cried over it, saying, "If you, even you, knew the things leading to peace this day; but now it is hidden from your eyes. Therefore, days will come upon you when your enemies will construct an embankment against you and will surround you and will hem you in from all directions. And they will dash you to the ground and your children with you, because you did not know the time of your visitation from God" (Lk. 19:41–44).

Nevertheless, such wrath is ultimately caused by God in the sense that God freely chose to create a universe where he counterfactually knew that, if he were to create that universe, humans would freely sin therein and experience its corresponding wrath. By denoting this punishment as "the wrath of God," Scripture simply follows its consistent pattern of attributing to God events which he weakly actualizes by setting in motion courses of free creaturely action which he knows, if instantiated, would lead to the pertinent events. For example, 2 Samuel 24:1 pictures God as "inciting David" to sinfully take a census because he weakly actualized this event, although 1 Chronicles 21:1 reveals that Satan was responsible for its strong actualization. God weakly actualized and so caused the Fall of Samaria in 722 B.C.E. while denouncing Assyria's strong actualization of this event by making war upon the Northern Kingdom. God "hardened the heart of Pharaoh" (Ex. 7:3; Rom. 9:18) by weakly actualizing his condemnation while desiring him not to perish but to receive salvation and come to the knowledge of the truth (2 Pet. 3:9; 1 Tim. 2:4).[35] But since God neither compels his creatures to sin nor doles out their punishment (*i.e.* he does not strongly actualize either), he is not morally responsible for them. In other words, God's choice to create a universe where he knows that humans would freely choose iniquity and suffer the logically necessary punishment in no way makes them so choose and suffer, as knowledge is not causally determinative. Consequently, God is indirectly responsible for humans suffering wrath; God weakly actualizes its outpouring while we ourselves and Satan strongly actualize its outpouring. For these reasons, we see how punishment for sin is indeed "the wrath of

---

35. For a complete explication of God's hardening Pharaoh *in sensu composito* but not *in sensu diviso*, or in such a way that he is not the author of evil, see MacGregor, "Hubmaier's Concord," 286–88.

God" without God personally dispensing such punishment and so violating his own dictates concerning forgiveness.

Although all humanity followed the αἰών and therefore became slaves to sin, Jesus believed that the worst possible sin was trying to make human wrath and military zeal the means to the victory of God over evil. It was precisely this situation that the vast majority of first–century Jews, led by their religio–political authorities, found themselves in, as they longed for a political messiah who would execute holy violence against their Roman oppressors, restore the boundaries of Israel back to their original expanse under Joshua and David, purify the land from all pagans, and make Israel the superpower of the Ancient Near East, thereby preventing them from ever being enslaved again and enabling them to spread Judaism and its ideals throughout the world via its own devices. This sin would ultimately carry the punishment, Jesus warned, of ultimate defeat and crucifixion at the hands of the Romans. When these atrocities transpired, Jesus alleged that they were not to be seen as merely political accidents, but rather represented the wrath of God against the nation of Israel for their *supremum peccatum*. In order to save his people from this fate, Jesus bore the punishment for their sin by undergoing it himself in the sight of all, thereby making the point clearer than any words ever could: if the Romans are mercilessly executing him in spite of the common knowledge that he was a pacifist who uniquely commanded his Jewish nation to love, pray for, and compassionately serve the Romans, then how could those fomenting violent revolution even hope to survive? As Jesus warned the women of Jerusalem on the way to the cross:

> Daughters of Jerusalem, do not cry for me, but cry for yourselves and for your children, because behold, days are coming in which they will say, "Blessed are the barren and the wombs which did not bear and the breasts which did not nurse." Then they will begin to say to the mountains, "Fall on us," and to the hills, "Bury us." For if they do these things while a tree is full of moisture, what will happen while it is dry? (Lk. 23:28–31)

At the cross, Jesus brought to a climax his ministry of identifying with sinners in order to bring them God's salvation. He had touched lepers, corpses, and people suffering from impurities, and he had celebrated meals with infamous sinners. But instead of him contracting impurity, the diseased and sinners found new life. Thus in his crucifixion, Jesus identified at last with the worst possible sinners, the rebels exacting holy violence, in order to save them and all other, lesser sinners. Just as Jesus saved Barabbas' physical life

by suffering "the extreme penalty," as Tacitus called it,[36] quite literally in
Barabbas' place, so he saved Barabbas' spiritual life and that of all other
persons willing to embrace his call by suffering the logically necessary tor-
ments of Satan associated with that *supremum peccatum* on the cross, thus
explaining his despairing cry: "My God, my God, why have you forsaken
me?" (Mk. 15:34) Olin A. Curtis poignantly captures a glimpse into Jesus'
plight:

> There alone our Lord opens his mind, his heart, his personal conscious-
> ness to the whole inflow of the horror of sin, the endless history of it,
> from the first choice of selfishness on, on to the eternity of hell, the
> boundless ocean of desolation, he allows wave upon wave to over-
> whelm his soul.[37]

At the cross Jesus bore the full brunt of the sin of the αἰών, both in terms of
its temporal penalty and in terms of its very worst spiritual consequences,
thereby defeating the αἰών and ensuring that we would never have to face
any of those consequences.

The portrait painted thus far fits beautifully with the current state of historical Jesus scholarship, especially Jesus' own interpretation of his death.
Following his revolutionary actions in the Temple, symbolically announcing
its destruction, Jesus discerned that, due to the hostility of his hearers among
the Jewish and Roman political elites, his crucifixion was imminent. In a
stroke of brilliant and world–inverting ingenuity, Jesus decided to use his
impending death as the culminating symbol of everything his Kingdom message and life stood for. Turning the wisdom of the αἰών on its head, Jesus
used the world's utmost symbol of defeat, powerlessness, and shame—the
cross, the Roman Empire's most ignominious instrument of execution reserved only for treasonists and slaves—as the vehicle for concluding his un-
paralleled and infinitely valuable life, thereby finalizing the victory of God
over the world. Hence Paul, Jesus' greatest interpreter, explains: "The message of the cross is foolishness to those perishing, but to us being saved it is
the power of God. . . . For the foolishness of God is wiser than human wisdom, and the weakness of God is stronger than human strength" (1 Cor.
1:18, 25). We may therefore see Jesus' entire life as a living sacrifice, not in
the violent terms of the Father punishing his Son instead of punishing humanity via tortuous execution but as a "fragrant offering" to God (Eph. 5:2),

---

36. Tacitus, *Annals of Imperial Rome*, 15.44.
37. Olin A. Curtis, *The Christian Faith* (Grand Rapids, Mich.: Kregel,
1971), 325.

which offering was consummated by his crucifixion. As Wright masterfully draws together the logic of Jesus heading to the cross:

> [Jesus] would be the means of the kingdom's coming, both in that he would embody in himself the renewed Israel and in that he would defeat evil once and for all. But the way in which he would defeat evil would be the way consistent with the deeply subversive nature of his own kingdom–announcement. He would defeat evil by letting it do its worst to him. . . . Jesus therefore took up his own cross. He had come to see it . . . in deeply symbolic terms: symbolic, now, not merely of Roman oppression, but of the way of love and peace which he had commended so vigorously, the way of defeat which he had announced as the way of victory. . . . It was to become the symbol of victory, but not of the victory of Caesar, nor of those who would oppose Caesar with Caesar's methods. It was to become the symbol, because it would be the means, of the victory of God.[38]

Summation: The Trinitarian God

The God of the Christian tradition is most precisely defined as one infinite, immaterial spirit or soul containing three complete sets of cognitive rational faculties, each sufficient for personhood. The second of these three persons or selves, whom Scripture calls the λογός, took for himself his very own anhypostatic human nature from the Virgin Mary and personalized it. Thus the human soul of Jesus of Nazareth was comprised of a finite amount (exactly the same "size" as each of our finite souls) of his infinite immaterial self and, in particular, of a finite amount of each of the Logos' three infinite cognitive rational faculties. So the soul of Jesus was the Second Person of the Trinity, but in such a way as not to allow Jesus to "cheat" as a human being by drawing upon divine attributes that his fellow human sisters and brothers lacked recourse to. Considered along these lines, the incarnation of an immaterial infinite self proves no harder to understand than the incarnation of an immaterial finite self in our own case. Finally, this holy Trinity is not, and logically cannot be, dependent upon sin in order to accomplish human redemption. Rather, precisely because Jesus is fully deity and fully human, his earthly life was of infinite value, and thus his Kingdom–launching ministry was of infinite power in both scope and degree. Therefore, all who receive Jesus as Lord are instantly saved by this power, the *summum bonum* (ultimate good) which completely repairs all privations of good (sins) in their souls and thereby provides satisfaction of God's holiness and justice.

---

34. Wright, *Jesus*, 565, 610.

Chapter 6

Inerrancy and the Importance of Reading Scripture Biblio–Critically

Since the tragic and widespread disconnect between biblical–theological scholarship and pastors–laity in North American Christianity, instigated by a two–century train of events including the Thirty Years' War, Pietism, the Enlightenment, the American Revolution, and the Second Great Awakening,[1] reached its zenith in the mid–nineteenth century, the historic Christian doctrine of biblical inerrancy has served as a frequent target for indirect as well as direct attack from within and without the Christian community. Indirect attack typically comes in the form of unwittingly misconstruing inerrancy as the belief that, when taking literally every Scriptural pericope, or discrete unit of text, that it is possible to take literally (regardless of its original literary genre), the Bible contains no errors. From its emergence in the fundamentalist movement of the late nineteenth century, this redefinition of inerrancy has been propagated by pastors among the populace, such that most people know nothing of the doctrine's original substance. This situation has led well–educated laypeople (including some academic scholars of religion) broadly trained in church history but not expertly trained in periods prior to the Enlightenment to launch the direct attack on inerrancy. Identifying inerrancy with its revisionary definition and cognizant that such a definition received no subscription before the modern era, many of the church's best contemporary minds have denied that the *ecclesia universalis* at any

---

1. Justo L. González, *The Story of Christianity*, 2 vols. (San Francisco: HarperCollins, 1985), 2:257–58; Sydney Ahlstrom, *A Religious History of the American People*, 2 vols. (Garden City, N.Y.: Image, 1975), 1:443; George Marsden, *Religion and American Culture* (San Diego: Harcourt Brace Jovanovich, 1990), 29.

point embraced the inerrancy of the Scriptures.[2] So with, on the one hand, churchgoers unaware of even the faith's historical contours accepting both the accuracy and validity of a specious understanding of inerrancy and, on the other hand, with churchgoers aware of only these contours and not its particulars wrongly accepting the accuracy but rightly denying the validity of the fallacious doctrine, the preexisting lines of demarcation between liberal and conservative Christians were redrawn, with the intelligentsia largely redistricted out of the latter into the former. Owing to the academic vacuum plaguing a sizeable segment of conservative Christianity for the last 150 years, many desiring to preserve their faith in the Scriptures have fallen prey to a veritable mare's nest of difficulties when attempting to reconcile their fallacious exegeses with findings from other disciplines, such as the biological, physical, and social sciences, archaeology, and philosophy, spawning a host of alleged contradictions between special and natural revelation. Not surprising but equally troubling is the consequent rift pervasive among Bible–believing Christians between the "heart and head" or the "spirit and mind," an artificial fragmentation of the life of discipleship which handicaps the academic integrity and transformational potency of the Gospel.[3]

Throughout the Ancient (30–100), Patristic (100–590), Medieval (590–1517), and Reformation (1517–1648) eras of Christian history, an intellectually defensible and persuasive doctrine of inerrancy persisted as the backbone of Scriptural interpretation, as easily demonstrable by examining a representative sample of the primary sources. The classic doctrine of biblical inerrancy stipulates that, for each pericope within every document of the Scriptural canon, when we first take into consideration that pericope's original literary genre and the rules for what does and does not constitute an error in that genre, the pericope contains no errors.[4] Although this definition does not demand the conformity of all biblical interpretation to literary genre (just that errors stemming from readings disaccording with genre cannot be charged to the text itself), it fits naturally with a grammatico–historical her-

---

2. Jack B. Rogers, ed., *Biblical Authority* (Waco, Tex.: Word, 1977), 18–23, 45; Rogers and Donald K. McKim, *Authority and Interpretation of the Bible: An Historical Approach* (San Francisco: HarperCollins, 1980), 89–176; Dewey M. Beegle, *Scripture, Tradition and Infallibility* (Ann Arbor, Mich.: Pryor Pettengill, 1988), 174.

3. Rick M. Nañez, *Full Gospel, Fractured Minds?* (Grand Rapids, Mich.: Zondervan, 2005), 19–26, 112–31.

4. This is both a recension and expansion of the definition provided by the 1978 *Chicago Statement on Biblical Inerrancy*, with which I am sympathetic; for the complete text of the statement see Norman L. Geisler, ed., *Inerrancy* (Grand Rapids, Mich.: Zondervan, 1980), 493–502.

meneutic which employs objective literary and historical criteria to extract from any pericope the meaning reflective of authorial intent and original comprehension.[5] When such a grammatico–historical hermeneutic replaces the erroneous methodology required by the revisionist version of inerrancy, then the substance of all alleged contradictions generated by the latter are evacuated, thereby drawing all realms of knowledge into a coherent and integrated worldview. This fact serves as powerful corroboration for the truth of Christianity, since one would expect to find on the hypothesis of Christianity's validity that God, as the supremely rational mind, must have created all fields in such a way that all truth emanating from each is God's truth, such that data from one helps us understand the others, and that, when combined in an interdisciplinary vein, a unified perspective emerges which points back to God as its creative source.

In this chapter we will analyze two of the most familiar but least understood passages of Scripture biblio–critically, by which I mean an interdisciplinary approach which arrives at accurate interpretation by coupling grammatico–historical exegesis with data gleaned from all other fields. The validity of this approach is inescapably guaranteed by the common divine origin and consequent trustworthiness of every cognitive realm. We shall first examine the creation narrative of Genesis 1–3 in light of contemporary biology, cosmology, and astrophysics, illustrating in the process that the sacred text and latest scientific discoveries harmonize to furnish a mutually complementary view of the cosmos and the divine relationship with it. Contending that God actualized in his *scientia media* a fully gifted creation with the innate capacities to naturally proliferate from unicellular to multicellular life in all its complexity, our exegesis will dismantle the caricatured war between "science and religion" generally and "creation and evolution" particularly. Then we shall turn to Jesus' parable of the Good Samaritan (Lk. 10:25–37) and, without in any way undermining (but in fact strengthening) its ramifications concerning compassion and social justice, revealing an astonishing underlying subtext which summons the listener to proper discernment and wisdom in rightly understanding and, most of all, in properly applying the biblical text. As the contemporary socio–political climate shows, the lesson promoted by this parabolic infrastructure is imperative for the integrity and vitality of the witness carried out among churches today.[6]

---

5. Walter C. Kaiser, Jr., "Legitimate Hermeneutics," in Geisler, ed., *Inerrancy*, 115–47.

6. Wes Avram, ed., *Anxious About Empire: Theological Essays on the New Global Realities* (Grand Rapids, Mich.: Brazos, 2004), 143–86.

The Genesis Creation Narrative

The opening three chapters of Genesis constitute one of the best loved, frequently referenced, and yet most controversial accounts in all of Scripture. For many, its truth or falsity, equated with the choice between its scientific accuracy as a journalistic account of cosmic origins or its pre–scientific and primitive legendary nature, is the crux on which the truth of the Christian faith, and even the existence of God, stands or falls. Tragically, the popular media proliferates and thus seemingly validates this dilemma through presentations which limit their attention to Christian special creationists and atheistic evolutionists.[7] Contrary to the media, however, from the historian's perspective it is simply a false dichotomy to claim that the biblical creation account in Genesis is either history or mythology. Rather, Genesis 1–3 is a poetic–structural narrative, a common literary genre in the Ancient Near East in which truths are reported in highly figurative and poetic ways within a strophic or chiastic literary framework. A strophic framework follows a $x_1 x_1 y$ or $x_1 \ldots x_n x_1 \ldots x_n y$, $n > 1$, pattern such as ABCABCD, while a chiastic framework adheres to a $x_1 y x_1$ or $x_1 \ldots x_n y x_n \ldots x_1$, $n > 1$, pattern like ABCDCBA. In both patterns, the y section serves as the foundation upon which the narrative is built, and therefore as the pivot or climax upon which the primary meaning of the narrative hangs. These configurations served the purpose of memory in an oral culture where most people could not read but had sharp memories for what was transmitted to them.[8] In addition, the primary thrust of Genesis is not scientific but theological; it serves as a critique of and a corrective for the mythologies of the Ancient Near East. Unlike pagan creation epics like the Babylonian *Enuma Elish*, which feature successions of rival deities that are coexistent with cosmic matter and war against one another, Genesis teaches creation *ex nibilo* (out of nothing) by a monotheistic deity not reducible to nature who made the sun, moon, and stars (in other words, the biblical text is asserting that these bodies are not gods in their own right but rather owe their existence to the sole God).[9]

---

7. A dilemma rightly exploded by Howard J. Van Till in "The Fully Gifted Creation," in *Three Views on Creation and Evolution*, gen. eds. J. P. Moreland and John Mark Reynolds (Grand Rapids, Mich.: Zondervan, 1999), 161–73.

8. Birger Gerhardsson, *Memory & Manuscript* (Lund, Sweden: C. W. K. Gleerup, 1961), 20–23.

9. Gordon J. Wenham, "Genesis," in *New Bible Commentary*, ed. Gordon Wenham *et al.* (Downers Grove, Ill.: InterVarsity Press, 1994), 57.

Moreover, the seven "days" (Hebrew יוֹם) of creation refer to literary periods or logical moments with no temporal significance, thus rendering any correlation with time stages coincidental, rather than 24–hour days. Following the description of the six "days," the author of the creation account uses the word "day" for a temporally indefinite period—namely, the entire creative process from "day" one through "day" six: "These are the generations of the heavens and the earth in the day (יוֹם) Yahweh God made earth and heaven" (Gen. 2:4).[10] The successive biblical writers also interpreted the seven "days" as temporally indefinite. For example, the anonymous author Hebrews, a follower of the Jewish Way writing in the 60s C.E., explicitly asserts that the seventh "day" of creation refers to the indefinite period from the beginning of the human race to the end of the world.

> Therefore, let us be careful that, because the promise of entering his rest still stands, none of you be found to have fallen short of it. . . . Now we who have believed enter that rest . . . although God's work has been finished since the creation of the world. For he has said somewhere concerning the seventh day, "And God rested on the seventh day from all his work". . . . God defined a certain day, namely Today, when he later spoke through David, as has been previously indicated: "Today, if you hear his voice, do not harden your hearts". . . . Hence there remains a Sabbath–rest for the people of God; for those who enter God's rest also rest from their own work, just as God did from his. So let us make every effort to enter that rest (Heb. 4:1, 3–4, 7, 9–11).

Exhorting believers to enter into the divine rest exemplifying the seventh "day," this loaded theological passage discloses that there exists a direct tie between the entire domain of human history and the Sabbath day: the former is the overarching Sabbath of God's rest during which God invites humanity to partake of that rest in communion with and reliance upon him, while the latter constitutes the weekly human reminder that the purpose of all temporal existence is confidently reposing in the eternal life which he supplies. In short, the seventh "day" is "Today," the era in which we presently live, and the "big Sabbath," memorialized by the "little Sabbath" on the final day of each week. By implication, if the seventh "day" is not twenty–four hours long but independent of temporal measurement, then the same is true of the other six "days." It is not commonly realized that, in fact, Genesis 1–3 has almost universally been regarded as poetic–structural narrative throughout

---

10. Blocher, *Beginning*, 50–52.

the history of Judaism and Christianity.[11] Even Jesus himself interpreted the creation account as poetic–structural narrative, as demonstrated by two famous sayings. First, in an argument with the Jewish religious leaders, who accused him of breaking the Sabbath, Jesus reasoned that since the seventh "day" of creation, God's Sabbath, was still ongoing and his Father is constantly working on his Sabbath, as the Son he was entitled to work on the day of the week that commemorates it (Jn. 5:16–18).[12] Second, Jesus encouraged the Galilean crowds to follow him with the promise that he would personally supply them with the rest of the seventh creative "day":

> Come to me, all who are weary and heavy–laden, and I will give you rest. Take my yoke upon you and learn from me, for I am humble and gentle in heart, and you will find rest for your souls. For my yoke is easy and my burden is light (Q; Mt. 11:28–30).

These literarily independent texts prove via multiple attestation that Jesus did not regard the "days" of creation as either 24–hour periods or lengthy temporal moments, but rather as logical and literary moments depicting various ways that God creatively interacts with the world.

The Hebrew Biblical prophetic tradition, in whose stead the Way pursued, indirectly but clearly conveyed their non–temporal understanding of the creative "days" with their predictions of the "Day of Yahweh" (Isa. 13:9; Lam. 2:22; Ezek. 30:3; Joel 2:31; Amos 5:18–20; Zeph. 1:8–18; 2:3; Mal. 4:5) following the present "day." Assuming terminological consistency, since the Day of Yahweh utterly explodes temporal categories, *i.e.* a literally timeless state in the new universe (new heaven–earth), it follows that the prophets regarded the previous days as no more related to time than this one. Insofar as Jesus (Mk. 13:32; 14:24; Lk. 21:34; Mt. 24:36, 50; 25:13) and the New Testament church (Acts 2:20; 1 Cor. 5:5; 1 Thess. 5:2; 2 Thess. 2:2; 2 Pet. 3:10) propagated this conception of the Day of Yahweh, they tacitly bore witness to their poetic–structural understanding of the creation narrative. In addition, the poetic–structural genre of Genesis 1–3 has been enunciated by several major biblical interpreters of the Jewish and Christian traditions, including Philo, Augustine, Bernard of Clairvaux, Maimonides,

---

11. M. J. Lagrange summarizes the consensus view of the Genesis creation narrative: "It has always been understood in the church that this story was very true but was not like any other, a story full of figures of speech, metaphors, symbols or popular language" ("L'innocence et le péché," *Revue Biblique* 6 [1897]: 361); *cf.* By Ceuppens, *Genèse I–III* (Paris: Desclée de Brouwer, 1946), 72–74; Van Till, "The Fully Gifted Creation," 186.

12. Blocher, *Beginning*, 56–57.

Aquinas, Luther, and Calvin.[13] Interestingly enough, in his commentary on Genesis, the fourth–century church father Augustine postulated 1,500 years prior to Darwin that God did not perform special acts of creation to make each species but created a world endowed with certain potencies that unfolded on their own over the progress of time (a theory which sounds strikingly like evolution).[14] Beginning in the 1860s, however, Genesis 1–3 increasingly received interpretation as historical narrative by American fundamentalists as a reactionary movement against the philosophy of naturalism, which they incorrectly associated with Darwin's theory of evolution. But this poor genre identification will not stand in light of many other examples of poetic–structural narrative from the Ancient Near East contemporaneous with the composition of Genesis.[15]

Through careful analysis of Ancient Near Eastern documents, historians of religion have deduced that a text belongs to the genre of poetic–structural narrative if (1) it possesses a strophic and/or chiastic framework and contains four of the following elements: (2) repetition of traditionally symbolic numbers like 3, 7, and 10; (3) word plays throughout the narrative; (4) parallelism on the sentence level; (5) rhyme and meter; (6) imagery; and (7) similes and metaphors.[16] It is relatively easy to show that Genesis 1–3 contains all the indicators of poetic–structural narrative and thus not only belongs to this genre but is an exemplar of the genre. Let me discuss each of these indicators in turn.

---

13. Philo, *De Opificio Mundi*, 13–14; Howard J. Van Till, "Basil, Augustine, and the Doctrine of Creation's Functional Integrity," *Science & Christian Belief* 8.1 (1996): 21-38; Bernard of Clairvaux, *De diligendo Deo*, 2.2–6; Maimonides, *Guide for the Perplexed*, 2.27, 30 (the latter section states concerning Genesis 1–3: "The following is also a remarkable passage, most absurd in its literal sense; but as an allegory it contains wonderful wisdom, and fully agrees with real facts"); Aquinas, *Summa Theologica*, 1.74.1–3; Martin Luther, *Genesisvorlesung*, in *D. Martin Luthers Werke*, eds. J. K. F. Knaake, G. Kawerau, *et al.* (Weimar: Hermann Böhlaus, 1883), 52.5.15–18; John Calvin, *Genesis*, tr. John King (Grand Rapids, Mich.: Baker, 1984), 86–87.

14. Augustine, *De Genesi ad litteram*, 1.42–43.

15. Kenneth A. Kitchen, *Ancient Orient and the Old Testament* (Downers Grove, Ill.: InterVarsity Press, 1966), 89.

16. Derek Kidner, *Genesis*, Tyndale Old Testament Commentary (Downers Grove, Ill.: InterVarsity Press, 1967), 54; Meredith G. Kline, "Because It Had Not Rained," *Westminster Theological Journal* 20 (May 1958): 155–56; Kline, "Space and Time in the Genesis Cosmogony," *Perspectives on Science and the Christian Faith* 48 (1996): 2–15; Bruce Waltke, "The Literary Genre of Genesis, Chapter One," *Crux* 27 (December 1991): 2–10.

Fulfillment of Hermeneutical Indicators

(1) Genesis 1–3 divides into two halves (1:1–2:4a and 2:4b–3:24), where the framework of the first half is strophic and the framework of the second half is chiastic. Regarding the strophic parallelism of the "creation week" in Genesis 1:1–2:4a, day 1 corresponds to day 4, day 2 to day 5, and day 3 to day 6, as days 1–3 give "form" to the cosmos (light, sky, dry land), while days 4–6 fill the form with content. Day 7 comprises the foundation on which the being and significance of the previous days depend. We may thus style days 1–3 "days of forming," where God forms certain realms, and days 4–6 "days of filling," where God places appropriate inanimate and animate entities in each one:[17]

Days of Forming	Days of Filling
Day 1: Creation of the luminous domain heralded by the proclamation, "Let there be light," and separation of light from darkness (1:1–5)	*Day 4*: Filling of the luminous domain heralded by the proclamation, "Let there be lights," which separate day from night (1:14–19)
Day 2: Creation of the sky and sea (1:6–8)	*Day 5*: Filling of the sky with birds and filling of the sea with marine life (1:20–23)
Day 3: Appearance of dry land and creation of seed–bearing plants (1:9–13)	*Day 6*: Filling of dry land with animals and humans who eat seed-bearing plants (1:24–31)
Day 7: God rests from his work (2:1–4a)	

Here we learn the theological truths that God intelligently and purposively creates all realms: rather than making domains haphazardly without planning how they would unfold, God imbues each domain with innate potentialities and, precisely in so doing, promises or covenants to the domain that he will do everything possible to actualize all its potentialities.[18] In this way, the text demonstrates the tremendous care and providence of God for all his creations (*cf.* Eph. 1:9–10). More than that, it displays God's extraordinary care for human beings; not only are they created in his image (*i.e.* finite souls), thereby providing in advance for their spiritual needs, but he previsions fulfillment of their material needs by specifically forming seed–bearing plants for them to eat long before they ever existed (*cf.* Gen. 2:9). As discerned

---

17. Blocher, *Beginning*, 50–51, 54–55.

18. Paul Beauchamp, *Création et séparation: étude exégétique du premier chapitre de la Genèse* (Paris: Aubier–Montaigne, 1969), 67–68, 385.

from its position, furthermore, the key application of Genesis 1 proves to be the Sabbath. Since we live in a perpetual state of Sabbath, the seventh day of the week commemorating it constitutes the seal of being in covenant with God and the foundation of Jewish life, as it embodies the twin foci of worshiping God authentically (a right horizontal relationship) and social justice (a right vertical relationship). In other words, by reserving one day per week exclusively for worship of Yahweh, humans are reminding themselves that the purpose of their whole existence is being in fellowship with God— namely, entering God's rest—as well as cultivating their relationship with him through praise, study, and contemplation. Communion with God is rightly depicted as participating in his rest, for the human partner in this spiritual marriage ceases trying to earn right standing before God, which standing is imputed simply by virtue of the relationship, and ceases worrying about the future, as God promises guidance and companionship throughout the earthly life and ultimate protection in the hereafter (Paradise followed by the new universe) guaranteed regardless of what the earthly life might bring. Thus Jesus instructed, "Do not fear those who kill the body but cannot kill the soul" (Q; Mt. 10:28). Moreover, by disallowing all persons from working on the Sabbath, humans ensure that everyone regardless of social class, from slaves and peasant farmers to the upper classes, have sufficient bodily and mental rest to labor the rest of the week without suffering exhaustion.[19]

With structural similarity but organizational inversion to Genesis 1:1–2:3, the chiastic parallelism of the Adam and Eve story in Genesis 2:4–3:21, where 2:4–18 corresponds to 3:20–27, 2:18–25 to 3:14–19, and 3:1–5 to 3:9–13, displays geometric symmetry in the shape of a parabola:

Humanity Within Initial Covenant	Humanity Outside Initial Covenant
A: God places humanity in the Garden of Eden (2:4b–18)	A': God banishes humanity from the Garden of Eden (3:20–27)
B: God speaks; He brings "all the beasts of the fields" towards Adam; creates Eve; discussion of ideal relationship between husband and wife in the covenant (2:18–25)	B': God speaks; He curses the snake "amongst all the beasts of the fields"; negative implications for husband–wife relationship outside the covenant (3:14–19)
C: Temptation to forsake God and warning of spiritual death (3:1–5)	C': Consequences of forsaking God and experience of spiritual death (3:9–13)
D: Man and woman break their initial covenant with God (3:6–8)	

19. Marva J. Dawn, *Keeping the Sabbath Wholly: Ceasing, Resting, Embracing, Feasting* (Grand Rapids, Mich.: Eerdmans, 1989), 67–68.

It follows from Genesis 1 that, by creating humanity, God automatically entered into a covenant with them to work for the fulfillment of their panoramic potentialities in every way possible. Thus human existence begins, as illustrated by the diagram above, within this initial covenant with God. Paul, intertextually referring to this covenant, describes its terms as follows: "He who began a good work in you will bring it to completion until the Day of Christ Jesus" (Php. 1:6). But, since an essential faculty of the *imago Dei* is libertarian free will and since God's omnipotence does not enable his doing the logically impossible, humanity possesses the free choice to either remain under God's loving guardianship in the covenant or live self–sufficiently outside the covenant. This choice is seen figuratively in the endless plethora of trees from which humans should eat, each representing an option where God nourishes and cultivates one of their numerous innate capacities, versus the tree of the knowledge of good and evil, representing the option of humans attempting to usurp the singular authority of God to judge between good and evil and so formulate their own system of what is right and wrong without reference to God.[20]

With primal humanity (and every human thereafter) selecting the latter, the position of the D or foundational section graphically depicts the magnitude of both the monstrous blasphemy committed against God by and the self–destructive nature of this act. These insights are easily disclosed by comparing how the text following the temptation to break the initial covenant would have been arranged if humanity had resisted the temptation with how the text is actually arranged. Understanding the internal logic of Genesis 1:1–2:3, we know that if humanity had remained faithful to God, the second half of 2:4–3:28 would have unfolded in exactly the same manner as its predecessor, *viz.* sequentially portraying the fulfillment of each human potency described in the A, B, and C sections and closing with humanity grounded in the rest of God, which rest comprises their source of completion.[21] To elaborate, the C section would have been followed by an A' section where humans ate from and cultivated all the trees in the Garden, fulfilling the A section's caretaking mandate (2:15). Next the B' section would have depicted God in perfect spiritual intimacy with humanity and, in turn, the wife and husband living out the ideal marriage in perfect physical intimacy. Then the C' section would have contained a testament to the primal couple's resistance of temptation, starting with the husband's display of self-

---

20. Blocher, *Beginning*, 111–21.

21. Note also the inversion from "the heavens and the earth" (1:1) to "the earth and the heavens" (2:4) which illustrates the change in perspective between the two halves of the creation narrative; Ibid., 31.

less love for his wife as he protects her from the serpent's attempted exploitation and warns her of the fatal consequences of godless autonomy. After buffeting the serpent's temptation, the narrative would have concluded with the D section in its proper seventh place, where humans enter into "the peace that passes all understanding" (*cf.* Php. 4:7) by experiencing the full divine tranquility or "Sabbath–rest."[22]

However, the author brilliantly shows that primal humanity "moved," in effect, the Sabbath from its most exalted position to the lowliest possible position—squarely in the middle of the "week" as the fourth day, the epitome of normality (such that even the third or fifth day would not have been as "average" as the fourth)—by violating everything the Sabbath stood for.[23] By this structural device of debasing the D section from its favored place as an endpoint of the "week" to its most common "day," the author exposes how humanity literally took that which was most sacred (*i.e.* "set apart") and rendered it most profane (*i.e.* "mundane"). Hence sin, at its very essence, comprises active rebellion against and/or passive indifference toward God and/or social justice. We thus visually apprehend from the text's structure that the first humans committed not simply a minor infraction, as when a child breaks his father's somewhat arbitrary rule not to eat out of the cookie jar, but the supreme act of treason against God.[24] This fact serves as the literal turning point or principal thrust of the account which, not surprisingly, carries the profound consequence of turning everything else on its head. Since treason against God inverts and disorders every domain of human life, we find the D section followed by, rather than the A' section, the C', B', and A' sections tracing the self–destructive consequences for the divine–human relationship (C': spiritual death or alienation from God), the marital relationship (B': difficulty in men materially providing for their families; sinful male domination and exploitation of women), and the physical world at large (A': expulsion from the Garden). In diametric opposition to God's plan, this human self–imposed disordering does nothing to actualize any of humanity's potencies but causes them all to regress.[25]

---

22. Paul K. Jewett, *The Lord's Day* (Grand Rapids, Mich.: Eerdmans, 1971), 157.

23. An observation further amplified by the fact that "the woman saw that the fruit of the tree was good" (3:6) on her own prerogative in the same way that "God saw that it was good" (1:4, 9, 12, 18, 21, 25, 31) with the authority exclusively belonging to him, portraying how primal humanity arrogated to themselves the place of God (3:5).

24. Blocher, *Beginning*, 135–54.

25. Ibid., 121–34.

(2) The "creation week" (1:1–2:4a) is tightly packed and highly structured, using the symbolic numbers 3, 7, and 10.[26] Genesis 1:1 contains 7 Hebrew words, and the first section of Genesis is divided into 7 sections. Genesis 1:2 contains 14 (twice 7) words. The two key words in Genesis 1:1 occur in Genesis 1:1–2:4a in multiples of 7: God (Hebrew אֱלֹהִים) occurs 35 times, and earth/land (Hebrew אֶרֶץ) is found 21 times. The paragraph on the Sabbath has 35 words. The prologue of Genesis, anticipating the ten "words" or commandments in Exodus 20, is carefully arranged around 10 divine commands.[27] In addition, other occurrences fit into this numerical symbolism: "And God said" (10 times); "Let there be" (7 times); "make" (7 times); "firmament" (21 times = 7 times 3); "according to their kind" (10 times); "and it was so" (7 times); "and God saw that it was good (Hebrew טוֹב)" (7 times, where טוֹב is a contrasting wordplay or pun on תֹהוּ [desolate] in 1:2); God "blessed" (3 times); and God "creates" (3 times).[28] Given this tightly knit structure of the early portion of Genesis, it seems sensible to consider this passage something other than straightforward historical narrative.

(3) There are several word plays throughout the creation account, including "naked" (Hebrew עֲרוּמִּים, the plural of עָרֹם) in 2:25 with "cunning" (Hebrew עָרוּם) in 3:1 and 3:14 and "tree" (Hebrew עֵץ) with "pain" (Hebrew עֶצֶב) in 3:16ff.[29] (4) Parallelism on the sentence level is exhibited in the threefold repetition of Genesis 1:27: "So God created man in his own image, in the image of God he created him; male and female he created them."[30] (5) The following 10 lines (corresponding to the 10 divine commands) adhere to the same Hebrew meter and rhyme scheme: 1:3, 1:6, 1:9, 1:11, 1:14, 1:20, 1:24, 1:26, 1:28, and 1:29.[31] (6) The creation account is replete with vivid and dramatic imagery, including the description of the earth as "formless and empty, with darkness over the face of the deep" (1:1), the Tree of Life contrasted with the Tree of the Knowledge of Good and Evil (2:9), the serpent symbolizing Satan (3:1), and the flaming sword flashing back and forth (3:24).[32] (7) Finally, the text paints its rich portraiture through similes, such as "you will be like God, knowing good from evil" (3:5), and

---

26. Umberto Cassuto, *A Commentary on the Book of Genesis*, 2 vols. (Jerusalem: Magnes Press, 1992), 1:13.

27. Beauchamp, *Création*, 33.

28. Copan, *"Interpretation,"* 147.

29. Blocher, *Beginning*, 35–36.

30. Ibid., 83–84.

31. Beauchamp, *Création*, 59.

32. Luis Alonso–Schökel, "Wisdom and Covenant Motifs in Genesis," *Biblica* 43 (1962): 295–315.

metaphors, like the picture of an immaterial God "walking in the garden in the cool of the day" (3:8).[33]

For these reasons, the majority of Hebrew Bible scholars agree that Genesis 1–3 belongs to the literary genre of poetic–structural narrative and therefore was never intended as either historical narrative or mythology.[34] Therefore, the biblical creation account teaches *that* God created the universe, not *how* various species of life originated within the universe. Hence, the theory of evolution, if true, is perfectly consistent with Genesis 1–3 and the Christian faith.

Evolution as Evidence for God's Existence

While, at worst, biological evolution is irrelevant to the truth of the Christian faith, we shall now argue that, it, in tandem with philosophy and mathematics, in fact supplies concrete and tangible evidence for the existence of God and so supports the validity of Christianity. At this juncture we need to briefly discuss the role of science as pertaining to theistic arguments. Since the fields of science, by definition, make up a discipline whose subject matter is the natural and physical world, it is impossible for scientific finds in and of themselves to say anything about the existence or nonexistence of God or about the truth or falsity of religious claims. Hence it would be disingenuous for a chemist or biologist, for example, to claim that science proves God's existence, as this assertion is a contradiction in terms; obviously no field restricted to studying the natural world can validate what realities, if any, do or do not exist outside the natural world. (Such would be analogous to a chemist claiming that science proves aesthetic truths, such as the beauty of a piece of artwork, or that science proves ethical truths, like the solution to a moral dilemma, which logical howlers fail to recognize that any discipline may only adjudicate over its own particular domain of study.) But while the scientist *qua* scientist cannot corroborate religious claims, the scientist as well as every other human being searching for the meaning and value in life should take an interdisciplinary approach to these questions, not artificially restricting themselves to just one discipline but integrating what is learned from all disciplines to draw conclusions.[35] Thus, whereas evolu-

---

33. Blocher, *Beginning*, 37.

34. Kidner, *Genesis*, 28.

35. A parallel point is made by Craig concerning the historian *qua* historian versus the "historian in his off–hours" in *Assessing the New Testament Evidence for the Historicity of the Resurrection of Jesus* (Lewiston, N.Y.: Edwin Mellen, 1989), 419.

tion by itself says nothing about God's existence or any other religious teaching, evolution coupled with other disciplines becomes part of a cumulative case corroborating theism.

Unlike those in the minority fundamentalist "creation science" movement, much of which I feel is pseudoscience,[36] the majority of Christians engaged in either scientific or biblical scholarship espouse the theory of evolution and correctly regard it as not in any way contrary to the Christian faith.[37] While popular culture regularly links the philosophy of naturalism

---

36. Unlike "creation science," the so–called "intelligent design" (ID) movement, although basing itself on legitimate mathematical and scientific data, draws philosophically illegitimate conclusions therefrom through the fallacy of opposing one field of knowledge to another field of knowledge. Thus ID proponents often correctly point out the extraordinarily low probability that evolution should occur given naturalism but then invalidly appeal to this fact as an excuse for bypassing the evidence from genetics and biology that it did occur. This is precisely the same fallacy made by the atheist in rejecting, for instance, the resurrection of Jesus: pointing out the extraordinarily low probability on the naturalistic hypothesis that a dead man could return to life, the atheist invalidly appeals to this fact as an excuse for ignoring the historical evidence that the resurrection occurred. Paradoxically, both the ID proponent (unexpectedly) and the atheist (expectedly) irrationally suppose, by showing that something could not happen on a naturalistic worldview, that they have demonstrated its impossibility on worldviews other than naturalism. Rather, all realms must be taken into account when formulating a conclusion and, as we shall see, such an interdisciplinary approach actually furnishes powerful evidence for the existence of God. So in a further irony, the ID adherence to this fallacy and the invalid argument for God produced thereby blind ID supporters to the valid argument for God emanating from sound methodology.

37. Christians who deny biological evolution based on a literalistic misinterpretation of Genesis 1–3 would do well to consider the virtually prophetic remark of Augustine: "Usually, even a non–Christian knows something about the earth, the heavens, and the other elements of this world, about the motion and orbit of the stars and even their size and relative positions, about the predictable eclipses of the sun and moon, the cycles of the years and seasons, about the kinds of animals, shrubs, stones, and so forth, and this knowledge he holds to as being certain from reason and experience. Now, it is a disgraceful and dangerous thing for an infidel to hear a Christian, presumably giving the meaning of Holy Scripture, talking nonsense on these topics; and we should take all means to prevent such an embarrassing situation, in which people show up vast ignorance in a Christian and laugh it to scorn. The shame is not so much that an ignorant individual is derided, but that people outside the household of the faith think our sacred writers held such opinions, and, to the great loss of those for

(that the natural world is all there is) with biological evolution, Alvin Plantinga, the foremost philosopher of religion now writing, has argued on both scientific and philosophical grounds that if biological evolution is true, then naturalism must be false, and if naturalism is true, then biological evolution is false.[38] Like Plantinga, many Christian scholars would argue for the same conclusion along the following scientific lines: first, the genetic evidence coupled with the fossil record proves beyond reasonable doubt that biological evolution occurred; and second, the probability that evolution should occur is fantastically low. They point, for example, to the recent findings of physicists John Barrow and Frank Tipler (both endorse biological evolution and, interestingly enough, both deny the existence of God). In their celebrated book *The Anthropic Cosmological Principle*, Barrow and Tipler list ten steps necessary to the course of human evolution, each of which is so improbable that before it should have occurred the sun would have ceased to be a main sequence star and would have burned up the earth. Further, Barrow and Tipler estimate the odds of the evolution of the human genome by chance and natural selection to be on the order of one chance out of 4 to the power of 360 times 110,000.[39] Remarkably, then, the fossil record and genetic data provide hard evidence that an event occurred whose probability is virtually zero and thus should not be able to transpire in a naturalistic world. In other words, if evolution occurred, it would be a miracle, so that, viewed in an interdisciplinary light, evolution is actually evidence for the existence of God.[40]

We may summarize our argument in the following syllogism:

---

whose salvation we toil, the writers of our Scripture are criticized and rejected as unlearned men. . . . Reckless and incompetent expounders of Holy Scripture bring untold trouble and sorrow on their wiser brethren when they are caught in one of their mischievous false opinions and are taken to task by these who are not bound by the authority of our sacred books. For then, to defend their utterly foolish and obviously untrue statements, they will try to call upon Holy Scripture for proof and even recite from memory many passages which they think support their position, although they understand neither what they say nor the things about which they make assertion" (*The Literal Meaning of Genesis*, tr. John Hammond Taylor, 2 vols. [New York: Newman Press, 1982], 1:42–43). I shudder to think about the untold damage done to evangelism worldwide by the contemporary antecedents of Augustine's quotation.

38. Alvin Plantinga, "Methodological Naturalism?" in *Philosophical Analysis, Origins and Design* (1997): 18.1.

39. John Barrow and Frank Tipler, *The Anthropic Cosmological Principle* (Oxford: Clarendon Press, 1986), 561–65.

40. Craig and Sinnott–Armstrong, *Debate*, 14–15.

1. If biological evolution occurred, it would undoubtedly have been extraordinarily improbable, beyond scientific ability to explain *why* it happened (although science certainly has the ability to show *that* it happened).
2. By definition, events beyond scientific ability to explain why they happened constitute miracles, whose reality demand the existence of God.
3. If biological evolution occurred, it would have been a miracle requiring the existence of God.
4. Beyond reasonable doubt, genetic evidence primarily and fossil evidence secondarily establishes the reality of biological evolution (*that* evolution happened).
5. Beyond reasonable doubt, God exists.

Not only does this reasoning reflect a Kingdom worldview, in which all realms of knowledge complement and cohere with each other to point back to their divine ground, but it also reveals the accurate (and astonishing) way to view the physical evidence supporting biological evolution. Each new genetic breakthrough and fossil discovery in fact constitutes physical evidence for the existence of God, since the probability that these genetic and fossil findings would even exist are virtually zero and yet, obviously given our possession of them, do exist! By employing philosophy to synthesize the mathematical and biological sciences, we reach an interdisciplinary conclusion that powerfully indicates the existence of God. Moreover, we should now query what our conclusion discloses concerning the nature of the Deity. With its extraordinarily lengthy chain of remote probabilities, the evolutionary schema could only unfold in time–space if the God who exists knew what would contingently happen in every possible (not merely actual) set of circumstances and then proceeded to create a universe in which precisely those innumerable contingencies necessary for the evolution of intelligent life would naturally transpire. In short, the genesis of our fully gifted cosmos requires a God with counterfactual knowledge or *scientia media*.[41]

Here it should be noted that even if someone rejects the argument for God from evolution, one is not justified in thinking that atheism is true. If the evolutionary argument is unsuccessful, then evolution is simply irrelevant to the question of God's existence and does nothing to support or deny either theism or atheism. As previously noted, evolution is a scientific theory which explains how the various species, from unicellular to multicellular life

---

41. Del Ratzsch, "Design, Chance, and Theistic Evolution," in *Mere Creation*, ed. William Dembski (Downers Grove, Ill.: InterVarsity Press, 1998), 289–312.

in all its complexity, originated on planet Earth and not a philosophical theory about the existence or nonexistence of God. Further, the objector betrays misunderstanding of the scope of evolutionary theory itself, as evolution does not (and has never purported to) answer the more fundamental questions of why the universe exists or why the universe that exists is life–permitting.[42] Clearly, both of these are needed for the evolutionary process to take place (*i.e.* evolution depends upon there being a universe and for the initial conditions of that universe to permit the rise of intelligent life). On this score, a host of arguments are available in the literature of philosophy of religion which illustrate that both the origin of the universe and its finely tuned life–permitting initial conditions require the existence of God.[43]

The Parable of the Good Samaritan

Undisputably Jesus' parable of the Good Samaritan (Lk. 10:25–37) encapsulates the themes of compassion, love, generosity, self–sacrifice, and the obliteration of racial and ethnic boundaries so poignantly that it has both directly and indirectly spearheaded influential religious and socio–cultural reforms throughout the globe during the past two millennia. Due to scholarly unanimity on this assessment and its widespread elaboration elsewhere,[44] we shall shift our attention to one crucial element whose identification nowhere currently appears in the literature but which seems to me both evident and vitally important for the health of the twenty–first century church. This element is the blueprint for sound biblical application which comprises the underlying subtext of the parable. In other words, Jesus intentionally conveyed to the questioning Torah scholar a method for validly applying Scripture to

---

42. Van Till, "Fully Gifted Creation," 216–17.
43. William Lane Craig, *Reasonable Faith*, rev. ed. (Downers Grove, Ill.: Crossway, 1994), 76–125, Craig, *The Kalām Cosmological Argument* (New York: Macmillan, 1979), 61–174; Stephen T. Davis, "The Cosmological Argument and the Epistemic Status of Belief in God," *Philosophia Christi* 2 (1999): 5–15; Craig, "The Kalam Cosmological Argument," in *Philosophy of Religion* (New Brunswick, N.J.: Rutgers University Press, 2002), 92–113; John Leslie, "The Prerequisites of Life in Our Universe," in G. V. Coyne, ed., *Newton and the New Direction in Science* (Vatican City: Speculo Vaticana, 1988), 97–119; Craig and Sinnott–Armstrong, *Debate*, 3–30, 53–78; Moreland and Craig, *Philosophical Foundations*, 463–500.
44. Robert W. Funk, "The Old Testament in Parable. A Study of Luke 10:25–37," *Encounter* 26 (1965): 251–67; John Dominic Crossan, ed., *Semeia* 2 (1974); J. Dwight Pentecost, *The Parables of Jesus* (Grand Rapids, Mich.: Kregel, 1982), 67–71.

all realms of life which he, given his impeccable knowledge of the Hebrew Bible, could not have missed.

The background to the parable features the expert in Torah asking Jesus, "What must I do to inherit eternal life?" (v. 25) By turning the question back around on the scholar (v. 26), who answers with the two great commandments (v. 27), Jesus now forces him to wrestle with the implications—especially in the realms of the purpose and interpretation of Torah—of his own admission that these two laws are all that are necessary for eternal life (v. 28).[45] If this is true, then all of the other 621 *mitzvoth*, or commandments, in Torah (623 total) are merely commentary on these themes (as explicitly stated in the Synoptic parallels of Mk. 12:28–34 and Mt. 22:35–40), rather than the other way around. In other words, Jesus makes the radical claim that all other laws in Torah are only valid insofar as they do not contradict or undermine the laws of הֶסֶד / ἀγάπη (divine love flowing from a right relationship with God), which then constitute the only objective (*i.e.* unchanging in all circumstances) lenses through which the other *mitzvoth* are qualified. This claim flies squarely in the face of typical first–century C.E. rabbinic exegesis (as attested, for example, in the proto–Tannaitic materials of the Mishnah) where the laws of הֶסֶד / ἀγάπη are no more important than the other *mitzvoth* (an argument denominated the "equality of divine injunctions"), which then constitute the boundary channels through which we must love God and neighbor.[46] The intent to issue such a watershed directive is clear from the context that Jesus is speaking to someone who has memorized Torah in its totality and knows its fine points like "the back of his hand." Hence the key questions raised by the parable are: (i) Why did the priest and the Levite pass by, and (ii) why did the Samaritan stop?

(i) The Torah expert would immediately know why the priest and the Levite passed by—it was not that they were necessarily (if at all) indifferent to the wounded man's plight, but because the prevailing reading of Torah (all *mitzvoth* are equal and must be kept to the letter) barred them from helping a half–dead man, as the books of Leviticus and Numbers repeatedly forbade such an act because it would render the religious functionaries ceremonially unclean.[47] Thus, paradoxically, precisely because they knew Scripture so well and applied its teachings through their "equality of divine injunctions" theory did the priest and Levite refuse to help the man (we can imagine them thinking, We love you and really want to help you, but we love

---

45. This challenge also forms the basis of Jesus' validation of Mary and admonishment of Martha in the succeeding account (vv. 38–42).

46. Holstein, *Jewish Experience*, 176–77, 182–86.

47. See, *e.g.*, Lev. 21:1–3; Num. 5:2; 19:2–13; *cf.* Ezek. 44:25–27.

God more than we love you, and our love for God compels us to keep the requirements in Leviticus and Numbers). Jesus is suggesting that love for God cannot be defined by or interpreted through the other *mitzvoth* (such "love for God" is not love for God at all); rather, love for God is a self–defined and irreducible quality which, coupled with love for neighbor, furnishes the necessary perspective for applying the other *mitzvoth*.

(ii) The Samaritan stopped not only due to his compassion, but because he was completely ignorant of Torah and hence was not subject to its poor exegesis then propounded by the Jewish religious authorities. Thus Jesus is making the point that not knowing Scripture at all (and relying on one's innate apprehension of the moral law "written on our hearts" via conscience; *cf.* Rom. 2) is better than knowing it backwards and forwards but reading it through the wrong interpretive lenses. We could say it like this: in the ethical realm (as well as many others), relying on natural revelation is better than relying on special revelation when it is misunderstood or misapplied.

A good modern–day example will suffice to drive home all of Jesus' points. Imagine an ordinary person pulled over to the side of the road with major car problems on a Sunday morning ten minutes before the local church service (which church subscribes to a literalist hermeneutic) begins. First, the church's devoted pastor drives by and thinks, I love you and really want to help you, but Scripture (especially the Pastoral Epistles and Acts) compels me to preach to my congregation this morning; since my duty to God trumps my duty to you, I'd better get to church. Five minutes later, a devoted Christian family drives by and thinks, I love you and really want to help you, but Hebrews 10:25 commands us not to forsake the assembling of believers together, so I'll put Jesus first and attend the service. Then, the town atheist (with the "Darwin" quasi–fish and bumper stickers saying "God is dead" on his car) pulls over and spends the next few hours helping the person with car problems, both because of his innate compassion and because he knows nothing about the Bible (and thus is disabused of its poor interpretation among the locals).[48] The problem with the pastor and family is the same as that with the priest and Levite: they know the text of the Bible but predicate its application upon a false presupposition (*i.e.* that each of its teachings comprise an equally weighty command) rather than upon divine love, where the mandate to love God and neighbor holds supremacy over, and serves as the guiding principle for correctly applying, all other teachings. It seems, in sum, that Jesus' points are quite shocking and profound

---

48. A variant on this example is found in Gordon D. Fee and Douglas Stuart, *How to Read the Bible for All Its Worth*, 2nd ed. (Grand Rapids, Mich.: Zondervan, 1993), 147.

and have just as much to say about Scriptural application as they do about compassion.

A Concluding Biblio–Critical Summons

Analogous to his providential oversight of evolution, God employed his *scientia media* to construct a world in which he placed just those individuals who could freely write exactly the message he wanted to be revealed to all humanity in just those circumstances where they would freely write it.[49] In this way, God ensured, without violating but in fact working through libertarian human freedom, that the Bible, a fully divine yet fully human product, was inerrant, or free from all mistakes as defined by its various literary genres and rules thereof. Interpreting this absolutely authoritative revelation in a biblio–critical vein illuminates the reign of God over the unified and cohesive set spanning all fields of learning. The interdisciplinary reading of the Genesis creation narrative revealed, on the textual level, that the truths intentionally conveyed by the author and understood by the original audience were theological in character. Principal among these are the concepts that only one God, who exists beyond and is not reducible to nature, created the universe (1:1–2:3) and that humanity sinned against God by choosing to turn away from fellowship with him (2:4–3:24). On the scientific level, we perceived that biological evolution was not merely consistent with the account's poetic–structural literary genre but actually functioned as powerful evidence for theism when examined within the broad spectrum of human knowledge.

Grammatico–historical exegesis further disclosed the provocative subtext underlying the dominical parable of the Good Samaritan: Scripture is correctly applied only insofar as it is empowered by and predicated upon the love springing from the Divine fountain; all biblical applications not resonating with הֶסֶד / ἀγάπη are necessarily false and deleterious to the doer's spiritual life. Such is tantamount to turning the Gospel into Law, as Martin Luther rightly cautioned: "[B]eware lest you make Christ into a Moses . . . the gospel demands no works to make us holy and to redeem us. . . . Thus it is not by our own works, but by His work . . . that he makes us righteous."[50] Referring to Jesus' command to "love one another as I have loved you" (Jn.

---

49. The details of this position are delineated by William Lane Craig, "'Men Moved By the Holy Spirit Spoke From God' (2 Peter 1.21): A Middle Knowledge Perspective on Biblical Inspiration," *Philosophia Christi* 1 (1999): 71–82.

50. Martin Luther, *Preface to the New Testament*, in *Martin Luther: Selections from his Writings*, tr. John Dillenberger (New York: Anchor, 1962), 17.

15:12), Peter powerfully synthesizes the ramifications of our subtext: "It would be better for them not to have known the Way of righteousness, than to have known it and then turn their backs on the holy commandment passed on to them" (2 Pet. 2:21). Since nothing is therefore more dangerous (and spiritually lethal) than professing allegiance to the Way while seemingly "keeping the teachings of God" outside the superintendence of חֶסֶד / ἀγαπή, it is paramount that we remember our calling to live as beacons through whom Christ's cruciform love flows out toward others,[51] a calling grounded upon the biblio–critical interpretation and love–driven application of Scripture.

---

51. Michael J. Gorman, *Cruciformity: Paul's Narrative Spirituality of the Cross* (Grand Rapids, Mich.: Eerdmans, 2001), 387–400.

Chapter 7

The Sacraments and
Church Discipline

For the earliest followers of the New Testament Way, the sacraments of
baptism and the Lord's Supper proved indispensable to the respective expansion and purity of the church. While other ceremonies may or may not
also qualify as sacraments (a query irrelevant to the present task), it is historically certain that Jesus took up the central symbol of John the Baptist by
commanding his disciples to baptize all converts to his Kingdom program,
as multiply attested by John 3:22–4:3 and Matthew 28:19. Part of the purpose of baptism was to publicly pledge allegiance to Jesus and his redemptive community, analogous to a wedding ceremony heralding the spiritual
marriage between God and the believer. It is also historically incontestable
that, on the night he was arrested by the Jewish religious authorities, Jesus
instituted a meal designating the spiritually and morally redeemed community his life, culminating with his impending crucifixion, had inaugurated
and would continue to establish. This fact is guaranteed by multiple attestation in three independent sources—the pre–Markan passion narrative, the
Eucharistic creed, and John 13–17, the first two of which[1] form criticism
discloses to have been formulated so early (*i.e.* in the 30s C.E.) that the reliability of each is assured even without the other's corroboration. As the Way
spread throughout the Mediterranean Basin, Paul insisted that only those
committed to Jesus' agenda of mutual forgiveness, love for God, and social
justice could partake of the Lord's Table (1 Cor. 10:14–22; 11:17–22, 27–

---

1. When the New Testament was later composed, these sources were respectively enscripturated in Mark 14:12–26 and 1 Corinthians 11:23–26.

34).[2] Not surprisingly, both baptism and the Eucharist were inextricably intertwined with church discipline, as broadly devised by Jesus (Mt. 18:15–35) and specifically applied by Paul (1 Cor. 5; 2 Cor. 2:5–11; 7:5–16; 2 Thess. 3:14–15; 1 Tim. 5:19–20; Tit. 3:10).

Accordingly, the purpose of this chapter is pluriform. First, we shall draw ecumenically upon the wealth of Christian history to define what precisely constitutes a sacrament. Second, we shall treat the purpose of baptism, in the process proposing a powerful relationship between baptism and accountability to church discipline and clearing up perennial misconceptions about this sacrament. Third, we shall lay out the New Testament model of church discipline. Finally, we shall craft a Eucharistic theology which synthesizes the strengths but avoids the weaknesses of existing formulae, such as transubstantiation, consubstantiation, and sacramentarianism, and which includes a praxis celebrating, perpetuating, and safeguarding the ultimate aim of the church. It is the author's hope that, as believers figuratively become Christ to others, nonbelievers will be attracted to Jesus and the community walking as he walked (1 Jn. 2:6), enter the visible church through baptism, and come to ontological communion with Jesus through the Lord's Supper.

What is a Sacrament?

Since there are many different understandings of the term "sacrament," it would be helpful at this point to outline its technical meaning. Following the consensus of the three main branches of Christianity—Catholic, Orthodox, and Protestant—a sacrament is conceived as both a sacred symbol and a container of grace instituted by Christ which actually gives the grace it symbolizes to its recipient. To fill out this conception with its multifaceted dimensions of theological substance, we shall appropriate a host of representative insights reflecting the richness and diversity of the Christian tradition. At the pinnacle of the Catholic Reformation stood the Council of Trent (1545–63), which proclaimed that "a sacrament is something presented to the senses, which has the power, by divine institution, not only of signifying, but also of efficiently conveying grace."[3] For Luther, sacraments were the Word of God communicated visibly rather than simply orally. Just as with

---

2. Notice that lack of this commitment, not any quasi–perfectionistic absence of residual or unconfessed sin, is how Paul categorizes partaking "unworthily" (ἀναξίως), as evident from the context.

3. J. Waterworth, trans. and ed., *The Canons and Decrees of the Sacred and Oecumenical Council of Trent* (London: C. Dolman, 1848), 235.

the Word, moreover, sacraments possess an objective character, through which the agency of the Holy Spirit works, and cannot be caricatured as allegories or bare symbols of the Christian life any more than the Word can. Drawing upon his *theologia pactum*, Zwingli complemented this depiction with the notion that sacraments also function as covenant signs which God has graciously provided to inform the church in general who belongs to the community of faith, while providing their individual recipients with grace. Here we shall follow Zwingli (and later Calvin) by defining grace broadly both as the unmerited favor of God and as a divine quasi–substance which empowers believers to perform works of righteousness. Calvin helpfully added that a primary function of the sacraments was to confirm to the individual believer that she or he is one of the elect. The common thread running throughout this entire discussion is that sacraments constitute means of grace in and of themselves. Taking the totality of these pivotal contributions into account, we may define a sacrament as a holy rite appointed by Christ through which, by means of an external and visible sign, grace is imparted to the believing individual and to the believing community.

The Sacrament of Believers' Baptism

Baptism, as practiced by John the Baptist and the primitive church, was an appropriation in form and transformation in meaning of the Jewish *mikvah*, or ceremonial immersion in water prerequisite to offering animal sacrifices at the Temple and so coming into the definitive presence of God.[4] Retaining the mode of immersion (βαπτίζω literally means "to immerse"), the followers of the Way reconceptualized the significance of baptism around the death and resurrection of Jesus. While baptism is usually taken today to denote salvific initiation, there is no New Testament evidence that receiving the gift of eternal life originally represented the purpose of baptism. Rather than a sacrament of initiation, then, I propose that we view believers' baptism as a sacrament of identification, where the believer specifically identifies with Jesus' burial when she or he goes down into the water and specifically identifies with Jesus' resurrection when she or he rises up from the water. This certainly represents the perspective of the Apostle Paul, who explained to the Roman followers of the Way:

> Or do you not know that all of us who have been baptized into Christ Jesus have been baptized into his death? Therefore we have been buried

---

4. Ralph Keen, *The Christian Tradition* (Upper Saddle River, N.J.: Prentice Hall, 2004), 70.

with him through baptism into death in order that, just as Christ was raised from the dead through the glory of the Father, we too may live a new life (Rom. 6:3–4).

The Deutero–Pauline Epistles affirm precisely the same point; believers are "buried with Christ in baptism, in which you were also raised up with him through faith in the power of God, who raised him from the dead" (Col. 2:12). Moreover, Scripture unanimously presents baptism as one's outward identification with the visible family of the redeemed. Thus Luke relates the response of those Samaritans who placed their faith in Jesus as a result of Philip's mission: "But when they believed Philip as he preached the gospel of the kingdom of God and the name of Jesus Christ, they were baptized, both women and men" (Acts 8:12; *cf.* 9:18; 16:31–34). Such represents precisely the logic used by Peter concerning Cornelius and his family: after the Holy Spirit furnished unmistakable evidence that these Gentiles had received salvation and thus already belonged, in Zwinglian terminology, to the "invisible church," they must identify themselves with the "visible church" through baptism: "Then Peter said, 'Can anyone prevent these people from being baptized with water? For they have received the Holy Spirit just as we have.' So he commanded that they be baptized in the name of Jesus Christ" (Acts 10:46–48).

At this juncture we must turn to the proper recipients of baptism. Careful exegesis of the Greek New Testament illustrates the consistent fivefold logic of baptism in the primitive church consisting of word, hearing, change of life or recognition of sin, baptism, and good works. Because infants cannot understand the message of the Gospel, much less repent of sin, it follows that baptism is for believers only, namely, people who have made a free and voluntary life commitment to Jesus. Not surprisingly, the New Testament exclusively portrays believers as receiving this sacrament and, through its grammatical conventions, disallows texts which may seem vague in translation, such as the "household baptisms," from including infants. Considering the parallel Synoptic accounts of John baptizing the crowds in the Judean wilderness (Mt. 3:1–12; Mk. 1:3–8; Lk. 3:2–17), we point out that (1) "the word of God came to John" (Lk. 3:2), who was (2) "preaching" for people to (3) "[r]epent, for the kingdom of heaven is near" (Mt. 3:1). Upon their confession of sin, the people (4) "were baptized (Greek ἐβαπτίζοντο) by [John] in the Jordan River" (Mt. 3:6) and subsequently instructed to (5) "bear fruit worthy of repentance" (Lk. 3:8). Here the verb ἐβαπτίζοντο is in the passive voice and literally means "they let themselves be baptized." Since infants cannot "let themselves be baptized," the verb presupposes that only adults were baptized by John. This conclusion is strengthened by the fact that the people who were baptized then asked John what they should do, and John responded that whoever has two shirts should give to the one who has none and whoever has food should do the same (Lk. 3:10–11). Balthasar Hubmaier, almost universally regarded by Reformation scholars as the greatest sixteenth–century theologian of believers' baptism,[5] sarcastically yet rightfully deduces that since infants obviously could not have asked John how to live, they could not have been baptized by him:

> Note well, the evangelist Luke has overlooked the little children because he does not report them asking what they should do. . . . Instead the Scripture says: "The people asked him." Little children cannot speak, lest John would have replied: "The child with two diapers must give one to the child who has none."[6]

From this set of texts, Hubmaier concludes that even "if there were no other passage on earth," still no one should be so impudent and bold to imagine "that John also baptized little children."[7]

Undoubtedly the central New Testament proof–text for believers' baptism is the Great Commission (Mt. 28:18–20). As first illustrated by Hubmaier, this text subscribes to the fivefold *ordo salutis* of *Wort, Gehör, Glaub, Tauff,* and *Werk*:[8]

> Then Jesus came to them and said, "All authority in heaven and on earth has been given to me. Therefore (1, 2) go and (3) make disciples of all the nations, (4) baptizing them in the name of the Father and of the Son and of the Holy Spirit, and (5) teaching them to obey everything I have commanded you."

---

5. MacGregor, "Hubmaier's Concord," 279.

6. "Hye merck: der Euangelist Lucas hat der jungen kindlin vergesen, das er nit anzeygt jr frag, was sye thûn sollent. . . . Die gschrifft sagt: Das volck fragt jn. Die kindlen kündten nit redden, oder es müßt auch Johannes geantwortet haben: Welches kindlin zwů windlen hatt, das gebs dem, welches keyne hat." Balthasar Hubmaier, *Von der christlichen Taufe der Gläubigen*, in Gunnar Westin and Torsten Bergsten, eds., *Balthasar Hubmaier Schriften* (Gütersloh: Gütersloher Verlagshaus Gerd Mohn, 1962), 129.

7. "[W]enn sunst keyn gschrifft were dann die auff erden, so solt doch ye keyner so vnuerschampt vnnd freuel seyn, das er jm traumen liesse . . . wie Johannes auch kindlich täufft habe." Ibid.

8. Ibid., 128.

This passage chronologically lists the principal events in the Christian life, namely, discipleship, baptism, and obedience stemming from lifelong training in Jesus' commands. Here the order demands that one must become a disciple prior to baptism, where discipleship entails understanding the gospel and committing one's life to Christ. Since infants can do neither of these things, they should not be baptized. To the objection of his sixteenth–century Catholic, Lutheran, and Reformed contemporaries that believers' baptism was heretical, Hubmaier responded in rare form by making a positive argument that the text reinforces the first four steps of our *ordo salutis*:

> For if baptism of people who have previously been instructed and believe is a heresy, then Christ is the first archheretic. For he commanded that one should first hear the Gospel preached (word and hearing), afterward believe (change of life), and third, be baptized.[9]

Filling out the foundation here provided, we shall now analyze the concrete examples of baptism in the life of the apostolic church.

For all instances of the apostolic model of baptism, baptism adheres to our fivefold *ordo salutis* and thus followed personal faith on the part of adults. In Acts 8:4–13, only after the people of Samaria turned away from Simon Magus and believed Philip's preaching on the kingdom of God, they "let themselves be baptized, men and women alike." When for a short period of time Simon Magus assented to the message, he then "let himself be baptized and followed Philip." Continuing in the same chapter with the account of the baptism of the Ethiopian eunuch (8:26–39), Philip first preached the gospel of Jesus to the eunuch, then the eunuch requested baptism from Philip when they came to water along the road, and finally Philip went down into the water with the eunuch and baptized him. One of the most powerful texts from the book of Acts supporting the entirety of our argument is the conversion narrative of Cornelius' household in Acts 10:30–48. After Peter preached a rather complete sermon to them, including the lordship, miracles, death, and resurrection of Jesus, which culminated with the promise that "everyone who believes in him receives forgiveness of sins through his name" (v. 43), the Holy Spirit "came on" (v. 44) and "was poured out on" (v. 45) all who believed the message (prior to their being baptized) such that they spoke in tongues and praised God. It goes without saying that the

---

9. "Wann ist Tauffen die vor vnderrichten vnnd glaubigen ein ketzerey, so ist Christus der erst ketzermaister. Er hat es also geordnet, das man zum ersten predigen, darnach glauben, zum driten tauffen solle. . . .Wort, Gehör, Endrung des lebens." Balthasar Hubmaier, *Ein Gespräch auf Zwinglis Taufbüchlein*, in Westin and Bergsten, *Schriften*, 175; Hubmaier, *Von der christliche Taufe*, 128.

Spirit's actions guarantee the pre–baptismal salvation of Cornelius' family, as it would be logically impossible for the Spirit to come upon or pour himself out upon anyone not already regenerated without losing his holiness and violating the human instruments' free will. We highlight that it was only at this point, following these Gentiles' reception of the Holy Spirit, that Peter asked, "Can anyone keep these people from being baptized with water? They have received the Holy Spirit *just as we have*" (v. 47; emphasis added). Since Cornelius and his family received the Spirit in exactly the same way as Peter and his entourage had, the latter of whom no one would deny salvation, it follows that the former were equally recipients of salvation and should thus fittingly undertake the sacrament of identification with Christ, of whose death and resurrection they had just learned, and with his visible community of like–minded disciples.

We round out our discussion of the book of Acts with an examination of two passages used by proponents of pedobaptism to argue that infants were baptized in the early church. On the basis of Acts 16:15 and 16:33–34, in which the respective households of Lydia and the Philippian jailer were baptized, proponents of pedobaptism deduce that infants and small children probably belonged to these households, and therefore it was more likely than not that the apostles baptized infants and small children. Even before our exegesis, we must immediately point out that such reasoning amounts to an *argumentum ex silentio*, and therefore insist that only a definitive statement of Scripture can validly settle such a pivotal issue as baptism. Worse than that, however, two features of these Greek texts decisively preclude infants from belonging to the baptized households. Woodenly literal translations reveal that "Lydia and her household let each of themselves be baptized (ἐβαπτίσθη)" (16:15) and that "the jailer and all the ones of his family let each of themselves be baptized (ἐβαπτίσθη)" (16:33), where the verb is in the third–person singular rather than the expected third–person plural form. To understand why Luke chose the singular form, recall that the verb already means "to let oneself be baptized," which entails a personal choice that young children cannot make. But to further emphasize that each individual in these texts *chose for herself or himself* to submit to baptism rather than submitting to baptism in behalf of the family at large, Luke ingeniously employs a device which renders each person a separate subject receiving the action of the verb. In addition, the rules of Greek grammar dictate that the Philippian jailer's entire household, not simply the jailer, believed in God, an act of faith impossible for infants: "Then he brought Paul and Silas into his house, set them at the table, and he was overjoyed, with the whole household (πανοικεὶ) having believed (πεπιστευκὼς) in God" (16:34). Since the noun πανοικεὶ and the participle πεπιστευκὼς agree in gender and number (both masculine singular), and since the clause contains no other terms agreeing with πεπιστευκὼς (*i.e.* there is no masculine singular term "he" underlying the translation "he was overjoyed," as "he" is implied by the verb), it is grammatically necessary that πεπιστευκὼς modifies πανοικεί. Thus the subject "having believed" comprises "the whole household," as shown by the above punctuation, and not simply the Philippian jailer. The idea that everyone in a household could commit their lives to Jesus at once is confirmed by Acts 18:8, where "Crispus, the synagogue ruler, and his entire household believed in the Lord." For these reasons, the "household" texts do nothing to undermine and, in fact, strengthen the abundant and clear Scriptural testimony that personal faith must precede baptism.

Before turning to perennial misunderstandings of what baptism accomplishes, we must examine two further texts which have historically been cited in favor of pedobaptism. In 1 Corinthians 1:16, Paul incidentally remarks, "I also baptized the household of Stephanas," impelling advocates of infant baptism to invoke the probabilistic argument concerning children belonging to that household. But to so appeal here takes this aside out of context, as the main point of the text to which Paul appended the aside was to prevent people from boasting about their baptizer, as shown by the preceding three verses: "Did you let yourself be baptized into the name of Paul? I am thankful that I did not baptize any of you except Crispus and Gaius, so no one can say that you let yourself be baptized into my name" (vv. 13-15). Since Paul's parenthetical comment that "I also baptized the household of Stephanas" occurs in this context, and since children could not boast about their baptizer, it follows that the household of Stephanas could not have included children. Further, the pronouncement at the close of the Synoptic account of Jesus blessing the children (Mk. 10:13–16; Lk. 18:15–17; Mt. 19:13–15) is often misparaphrased, "Let the little children come to me (Jesus), and forbid them not, for theirs is the kingdom of God," in order to reason that if Jesus admitted children into the Kingdom, then no one can justly forbid them the Kingdom sign of baptism. However, the Greek text does not say "for theirs is the kingdom of God," but "for of such as these (τοιούτων) is the kingdom of God....whoever does not receive the kingdom of God as a child may by no means enter into it" (Mk. 10:14–15), meaning that the kingdom belongs to those who receive it like children—namely, with utter humility (*cf.* Mt. 18:1–4)—rather than children themselves. Hence this text furnishes no justification for the baptism of young children. Substantiating our exegesis of the New Testament baptismal texts, Kurt Aland has conclusively demonstrated, via careful analysis of the biblical and extrabiblical primary sources, that the church in neither the first nor the second centuries baptized infants; moreover, even in the third and fourth centuries pedobaptism was by no means normative but was practiced intermittently when specially requested by parents.[10]

The Disanalogy of Circumcision to Baptism

A frequent line of reasoning made by proponents of infant baptism underscores the originally medieval notion that Jewish circumcision is functionally equivalent to Christian baptism in the New Covenant. Just as admittance to the Old Covenant was extended to the children of Jewish believers through circumcision on the eighth day, so God, who is certainly no less gracious in the New Covenant than the Old, initiates children of Christian believers into the New Covenant through infant baptism.[11] In order to confute this allegation, we contend that circumcision of the heart (*i.e.* regeneration), not baptism, is unanimously presented by the New Testament documents as parallel to physical circumcision in the Old Covenant. Romans 2:28-29 serves as the classic articulation of our position: "A person is not a Jew if he is only one outwardly, nor is circumcision merely outward and physical. No, a person is a Jew if he is one inwardly; and circumcision is circumcision of the heart, by the Spirit, not by the written code." Even the Hebrew Bible prophecies concerning the redemption by the Messiah show that literal circumcision would be replaced by spiritual circumcision under the New Covenant. For instance, Deuteronomy 30 promises that after biblical Israel breaks the Mosaic Covenant and then repents of their sin, God will restore the people and "circumcise your hearts and the hearts of your descendants, so that you may love him with all your heart and with all your soul, and live" (v. 6). And Jeremiah, who anticipates the "new covenant with the house of Israel" (31:31), commands the Israelites to "circumcise yourselves to the Lord, circumcise your hearts" (4:4). By contrast, baptism has nothing to do with circumcision; it is rather the New Testament analogue of the Hebrew Biblical *mikvah* and, as we have already seen, directly symbolizes the believer's public identification with Christ. In particular, it illustrates sharing in Jesus' death as one is immersed in the water and sharing in Jesus' resurrection as one comes up from the water.

---

10. Kurt Aland, *Did the Early Church Baptize Infants?* (London: SCM Press, 1961), 42–99.

11. Jaroslav Pelikan, *Reformation of Church and Dogma (1300–1700)*, Vol. 4 of *The Christian Tradition: A History of the Development of Doctrine* (Chicago: University of Chicago Press, 1971), 283.

The Fallacy of Baptismal Regeneration

Clearly the most common misconception surrounding baptism through-out church history as well as in the present day is the notion of baptismal regeneration, according to which the Holy Spirit regenerates and so forgives the sins of individuals in and through their baptism. Obviously this fallacy offers powerful support for the practice of pedobaptism, as it implies that children cannot be saved unless first baptized. Contemporary advocates of baptismal regeneration typically appeal to four passages for support—Acts 2:38, 22:16, 1 Peter 3:21, and Mark 16:16—where, among these texts, the first plays the pivotal role. Thus we shall focus our attention on Acts 2:38 and then shift to the secondary passages.[12] The most common rendering of Acts 2:38 is an essentially literal translation which follows the word order of the Greek text: "Peter replied, 'Repent and be baptized, each one of you, in the name of Jesus Christ for the remission of your sins. And you will receive the gift of the Holy Spirit.'"[13] Although the literal strategy is praiseworthy, we shall argue that this text contains an underlying structure essential for deciphering its meaning which is destroyed when non–inflected English words follow the order of inflected Greek words, which approach thereby yields an inaccurate translation. To perceive why, we need to remember two pertinent rules of Greek grammar. First, word order is irrelevant to the trans-lation since Greek is an inflected language,[14] *viz.* the subject, direct object, indirect object, and possessive are determined by the endings of nouns (called case endings) rather than their positions in a sentence. Therefore, the sequence in which clauses are translated must be based on semantic agree-ment rather than word order. Second is the basic rule of concord, which stipulates that a personal pronoun, if it has an antecedent, must agree with its

---

12. However, it should be noted that the doctrine of baptismal regeneration was not originally derived from Acts 2:38 or any other scriptural text, but was adopted as Christian dogma in the early fifth century by Pope Innocent I as a corollary to Augustine's extremist doctrine of original sin, formulated in reac-tion to the Pelagian controversy. Only after the idea came to prominence that the stain of original sin must be washed away by the sacrament of baptism, at which point the person is "born again" or regenerated, did theologians in ensuing cen-turies ransack the New Testament to find proof–texts in its support.

13. So, with minor variations, NIV, NRSV, NASB, and ESV.

14. As the great grammarian A. T. Robertson commented, "The freedom of the Greek from artificial rules and its response to the play of the mind is never seen better than in the order of words in the sentence" (*A Grammar of the Greek New Testament in the Light of Historical Research* [Nashville: Broadman, 1934], 417).

antecedent in gender and number.[15] With this in mind, we observe that Acts 2:38 has two imperatives, μετανοήσατε ("repent," second person plural) and βαπτισθήτω ("be baptized," third person singular), and two instances of the second person plural pronoun in the genitive case, ὑμῶν. Found in the phrase "each one of you (ὑμῶν)," the first ὑμῶν is a partitive genitive, which by definition carries no antecedent but rather indicates the group from which something (in this case, each person) derives. However, the second ὑμῶν, located in the clause "for the remission of your (ὑμῶν) sins," is a subjective genitive, which must have an antecedent and here indicates whose sins are involved in the remission. Therefore, we must ask the question: what is the antecedent of the second person plural ὑμῶν ("your")? There are only two options, the second person plural verb μετανοήσατε ("repent") and the third person singular verb βαπτισθήτω ("be baptized").

According to the basic rule of concord, the only possible option is to associate the second person ὑμῶν ("your") with the second person μετανοήσατε ("repent").[16] This interpretation is reinforced by the syntactical break in thought between "repent" and "be baptized," which is indicated in the Greek by the redundant and otherwise grammatically unnecessary φησίν ("he said") between "repent" and "let each of you": the text reads Πέτρος δὲ πρὸς αὐτούς, Μετανοήσατε, φησίν, καὶ βαπτισθήτω ἕκαστος, literally, "But Peter said to them, Repent, *he said*, and let each of you be baptized." In Koinē Greek, such a syntactical break is often accompanied by an intercalation or ABA "sandwich–like" structure, as seen, *e.g.*, in Mark 3:19–35, 5:22–43, 11:12–21, 12:38–13:2, 14:66–72, John 18:13–27, and Ephesians 4:26–27, where the B section comprises a parenthetical insert (the "meat" of the sandwich) not syntactically related to the A phrases (the "two slices of bread").[17] In other words, the A section begins, the B section begins and ends, and finally the A section ends. Owing to its nature as an inflected language, the original hearers and readers of a Greek text would immediately notice any intercalation, link the A phrases together into one section, and afterwards consider the B section. Obviously, however, this device is lost in translation when English uninflected words replace their Greek inflected originals, potentially leading to profound misinterpretation. Against this backdrop, we see that Acts 2:38 is indeed an intercalation, as easily revealed through the following diagram:

---

15. Luther B. McIntyre, Jr., "Baptism and Forgiveness in Acts 2:38," *Bibliotheca Sacra* 153 (1996): 54–55.

16. McIntyre, "Acts 2:38," 54.

17. John Dominic Crossan, *Who Killed Jesus?* (San Francisco: HarperSan-Francisco, 1995), 62–63, 100–04.

A begins: Repent (second person plural)
> **B begins and ends**: he said, and let be baptized (third person singular) each (third person singular) of you in the name of Jesus Christ
> **A ends**: for the remission of your (second person plural) sins and you (second person plural) will receive the gift of the Holy Spirit

This structure demonstrates that the command to be baptized is parenthetical and not syntactically linked to the remission of sins.[18] In other words, when Peter commanded the people to repent, he was speaking to the crowd. Then the command to be baptized was directed to each individual. Finally, Peter again directed his words to the crowd collectively in the "remission of your sins" phrase. Since the English language cannot accommodate intercalations without creating potential confusion, the only way to accurately convey what the original audience at Pentecost heard Peter say, what Luke intended in writing Acts, and what the book's original hearers and readers detected, is by translating the text to exhibit verb–pronoun concord, with the A phrases combined into one section followed by the B section:

> But Peter said to them, "Repent (second person plural) for the remission of your (second person plural) sins and you (second person plural) will receive the gift of the Holy Spirit," he said, "and let each (third person singular) of you be baptized (third person singular) in the name of Jesus Christ."

Properly translated, then, this passage teaches that remission of sins and reception of the Holy Spirit is predicated exclusively upon repentance, which is defined as a single action of turning away from or releasing one's grip upon the αἰών—the "power–over" philosophy of selfishness (or, more bluntly, self–deification) that ultimately generates all sin and serves as the *modus operandi* of the world—and turning to or clutching onto Jesus as Lord and his Calvary–patterned "power–under" way of life.[19] Not only is this rendering the only grammatically defensible option, but it is also the only one consistent with the remainder of Acts and the rest of the New Testament. The pattern that repentance alone brought forgiveness of sins and the gift of the Holy Spirit, which was subsequently followed by believers' baptism, is exemplified by the account of Cornelius' family:

---

18. McIntyre, "Acts 2:38," 57.
19. Grudem, *Systematic Theology*, 713–14; Boyd, *Myth*, 18, 28.

While Peter was still uttering these sayings, the Holy Spirit fell upon all the ones embracing the Word. And all the believers of the circumcision who accompanied Peter were amazed that the gift of the Holy Spirit had been poured out upon the Gentiles, for they were hearing these Gentiles speaking in tongues and exalting God. Then Peter answered, "Can anyone keep these people from being baptized with water? They have received the Holy Spirit just as we have." And he commanded them to be baptized in the name of Jesus Christ (Acts 10:44–48).

We see that this narrative precisely agrees with our translation of Acts 2:38. Our translation of Acts 2:38 proves consonant with the Pauline Epistles and the book of Hebrews, which unambiguously affirm that salvation is accessed by God's grace through faith in Christ and not by works, especially religious rituals, of which baptism—the Jewish *mikvah*—was one.

For the sake of contradiction, let us examine the alternative, that the antecedent of "your" in Acts 2:38 is "be baptized." Then the verse translated into English—"Let each (third person singular) of you be baptized in the name of Jesus Christ for the remission of your (second person plural) sins"—yields the absurdity of each individual person being baptized for the remission of the entire group's sins rather than simply her or his own sins. Thus, it is grammatically impossible for the remission of sins clause to be affiliated with the baptismal command.

We close our discussion of Acts 2:38 by refuting the allegation that the following verse, "For the promise is for you, for your children (τέκνοις), and for all who are far away, everyone whom the Lord our God calls to him" (v. 39), means that baptism should be administered to infants. It is evident from the context that "the promise" refers to the entirety of verse 38. So even if verse 38 were for infants, it still renders repentance, which infants cannot yet perform, the necessary prerequisite to salvation, reception of the Holy Spirit, and baptism, thus promising infants the aforementioned benefits upon their future act of repentance. However, the assumption that verse 38 pertains to infants is lexigraphically dubious since the term in verse 39 for "children" (τέκνοις) is the generic term for one's immediate offspring without reference to age and not the specific term for "young children" or "infants" (παιδίοις). Hence the context demonstrates that Peter's offer of repentance followed by forgiveness, the Spirit, and baptism "for you, for your children, and for all who are far away, everyone whom the Lord our God calls to him" simply means that the promise of salvation is universal for all humanity and carries no implications for infant baptism. This fact is reinforced by Luke's explicit statement that "those who accepted his message let themselves be baptized" (Acts 2:41), thereby indicating that acceptance of the gospel was required for baptism (*i.e.* that only believers were baptized at Pentecost).

Acts 22:16 is another oft–cited verse *pro* baptismal regeneration, whose standard translation essentially follows Greek word order and is reflected by the NIV: "And now what are you waiting for? Get up, be baptized and wash your sins away, calling on his name." But careful examination of the verb and participle tenses suffices to show that the verse supports not baptismal regeneration but believers' baptism. Thus on linguistic grounds, the meaning of this text cannot be accurately conveyed by following the Greek word order in English translation. We illustrate why by disclosing the tenses that would be evident to a Greek listener or reader but disappear in translation:

> Now (νῦν) what do you intend (μέλλεις, present tense verb) to do? Be arising (ἀναστάς, present tense participle) to be baptized (βάπτισαι, infinitive modifying ἀναστάς), and to wash away (ἀπόλουσαι, infinitive modifying ἐπικαλεσάμενος) your sins having called (ἐπικαλεσάμενος, aorist = past tense participle) upon his name.

To establish the true significance of this text, word order should accordingly be eschewed by the translator in favor of chronological order, *i.e.* when the various tenses reveal that the reported events transpired from first to last. Since the passage contains two tenses, past and present, the past–tense clause "and to wash away your sins having called upon his name," which arranged in English idiom yields "and having called upon his name to wash away your sins," should be placed at the beginning of the translation, followed by the remainder of the clauses, all in the present tense. When the verse is properly arranged in chronological fashion, the following translation emerges: "And having called upon his name to wash away your sins, now what do you intend to do? Be arising to be baptized." Therefore Ananias, reminding Paul that he had already accepted the Lordship of Jesus over his life and so received forgiveness for his previous persecution of Jesus' disciples, exhorts him to receive the public sign of this newfound identification with Jesus and his cause. This conclusion, reached purely on exegetical grounds, is independently confirmed by the preceding verses, which show that Paul had recognized the errancy of his "holy violence" against followers of the Way and, in light of his acknowledgment of Jesus as Lord, sought to make amends for his persecution:

> I fell to the ground and I heard a voice saying to me, "Saul, Saul, why are you persecuting me?" But I answered, "Who are you, Lord?" And he said to me, "I am Jesus the Nazarene, whom you are persecuting". . . And I said, "What shall I do, Lord?" And the Lord said to me, "Having

arisen, go into Damascus, and there you will be tild everything that has been assigned for you to do" (Acts 22:7–8, 10).

Moreover, when Ananias first sees Paul (*i.e.* before he admonishes Paul to be baptized), he describes Paul as Σαοὺλ ἀδελφέ (Brother Saul), where "brother" (ἀδελφός) is exclusively used in Acts as a designation for a follower of the Way in contradistinction to simply an ethnic Jew (*cf.* Acts 9:30; 10:23; 11:1, 12, 29; 12:17; 15:1, 3, 7, 13, 23, 32–33, 36, 40; 16:2, 40; 17:6, 10, 14; 18:18, 27; 21:7, 17; 28:14–15). In these ways, the context of Acts 22:16 indicates that Paul first received admission into Christ's redeemed community and subsequently received baptism, a pattern verifying the early church *praxis* of believers' baptism.

Appeal to 1 Peter 3:21 in support of baptismal regeneration is a classic case of pulling a passage out of context, in this case citing only the first third of the verse while ignoring its explanatory second part. The full verse reads: "Corresponding to this, now baptism saves you—not as a removal of dirt from the body but as an appeal to God for a clear conscience—through the resurrection of Jesus Christ." Wayne Grudem skillfully explains the meaning that emerges from considering the entire verse rather than taking its first of three clauses in isolation:

> [W]hat about 1 Peter 3:21 . . . does this not give clear support to the . . . view that baptism itself brings saving grace to the recipient? No, for when Peter uses this phrase he continues in the same sentence to explain exactly what he means by it. He says that baptism saves you "*not as a removal of dirt from the body*" (that is, not as an outward, physical act which washes dirt from the body—that is not the part that saves you), "*but as an appeal to God for a clear conscience*" (that is, as an inward, spiritual transaction between God and the individual, a transaction symbolized by the outward ceremony of baptism). We could paraphrase Peter's statement by saying, "Baptism now saves you—not the *outward* physical ceremony of baptism but the *inward* spiritual reality which baptism represents." In this way, Peter guards against any view of baptism that would attribute automatic saving power to the physical ceremony itself.[20]

Therefore, the personal commitment to Christ publicized in baptism is what saves and not the act of baptism itself, just as the exchanging of vows publicized in a wedding ring seals the marriage of husband and wife and not the wedding ring itself. Nonetheless, it should be underscored that 1 Peter 3:21

---

20. Grudem, *Systematic Theology*, 974.

portrays a link between discipleship and baptism every bit as strong as between marriage and a wedding ring. Since we would have the right to presume that someone not wearing a wedding ring was unmarried or separated, we likewise have the right to assume that an unbaptized person is not a follower of Jesus. So we arrive at a counterfactual probabilistic doctrine concerning the relationship between salvation and baptism: while baptism plays no role in salvation, particularly justification, anyone who is persuaded that Christ commands baptism for believers, has someone available who is willing to baptize her or him, and still refuses to be baptized has probably never been regenerated in the first place; if the person claims to "believe in Jesus," it is quite likely that such belief is *assensus* (intellectual assent to certain propositions about Jesus) and not *fiducia* (personal commitment to following Jesus as Lord).

Although there is no reason to doubt the salvation of people who are either unaware of or, from our perspective, misunderstands the New Testament teaching about baptism, *i.e.* those who have never been baptized and fail to realize its importance and those who were baptized as infants and regard their infant baptism as valid, those who are legitimately persuaded that Scripture insists upon believers' baptism and yet fail to receive the sacrament may well not be saved. For further insight on this matter we turn again to Hubmaier. In his classic *Von der christlichen Taufe der Gläubigen* (On the Christian Baptism of Believers), Hubmaier stresses the indispensability of believers' baptism and reinforces it with a counterfactual illustration based on the Ethiopian eunuch in Acts 8.

> But to those who say, "Yes, we believe, yes, some of us have already received the Holy Spirit as well. We have no need of baptism". . . . Not at all! The person who believes submits to baptism and does not keep arguing, for where water and a person to baptize him are available, he has the command of Christ before his eyes . . . . which Christ demands and wants us to fulfill . . . . Consider an example. If the treasurer who sat beside Philip in the chariot and who had come to faith had died suddenly before they reached the water, then he would not have been saved less than after baptism . . . . When now the treasurer had both the baptizer and the water available, then according to the dictate of Christ, he was required to be baptized. If he had not done so, then Christ would have regarded him as a scorner and violator of his words, and he would have been punished accordingly.[21]

---

21. "Warlich sye . . . sagen: Ja, wir glauben, ja, wir haben zum teyl auch den heyligen geyst schon empfangen, was bedürffen wir des tauffs . . . . Neyn nit also. Sonder welcher glaubt, der laßt sich täuffen vnd disputiert nit weytter, dann

Due to accusations against Hubmaier by other sixteenth–century reformers of propagating a baptismal theology which consigned to damnation many great saints throughout church history, Hubmaier attempts to straighten out this misunderstanding with reference to the bandit on the cross as an example of someone assuredly saved but lacking the opportunity to identify with Christ through baptism.

> The thief on the cross believed and was in Paradise with Christ on the same day, but he was absolutely not baptized. . . . The person who has the same excuse as the thief on the cross is absolutely at peace with God even though he has never been baptized in water. But when one does not have this excuse, then let the person examine the reality of his own faith.[22]

In *Von der christlichen Taufe*, Hubmaier is also careful to safeguard the Scripturally guaranteed fact that the historic church has always performed its redemptive function (Mt. 16:18; Eph. 3:21), such that a multitude of persons have legitimately been saved down through church history although not baptized as believers: "Undoubtedly many thousands have been saved who were not baptized, since they had no opportunity to be baptized."[23] To summarize, while believers' baptism does not save, among people cognizant of its status as a dominically commanded sacrament of initiation it proves an excellent though not infallible indicator of those who have and have not been re-

---

er sycht die ordnung Christi vor augen, vnd das, wo wasser vnnd der täuffer mögen gehabt werden. . . . den eruordert er vnd will jn von vns haben. . . . Nymm ein exempel. So der Schatzmeyster, auff dem wagen neben dem Philippo sitzend, vnd glaubend, gehling gestorben wer, ee sye zů dem bach kamen, wer er nit weniger selig worden, dann nach dem tauff. . . . Da nun der Schatzmeyster den täuffer vnnd das wasser hett bey einander, ward er schuldig nach dem beuelch Christi, sich zů täuffen lassenn. Wo er das nit thon, hätte jn Christus für ein verschmeher vnd übertretter seiner worte gehalten, vnd wer also gestrafft worden." Hubmaier, *Von der christlichen Taufe*, 142–43, 145.

22. "Der Schacher am Creütz hat glaubt, vnd ist des selben tags mit Christo in Paradeyß gewesen, vnnd gar nicht Getaufft mit kainem eüsserlichen Tauff. . . Wölcher Mensch die entschuldigung hat des Schächers am Creütz, der ist mit Got wol zů friden, ob er schon nymmermer Wassertauff wirdt. Wo aber dise entschuldigung nicht ist, da lüge ein yegklicher zů jm selber." Hubmaier, *Gespräch auf Zwinglis Taufbüchlein*, 185.

23. "Dann on zweyffel vil tausendt selig worden, die nit täufft seyndt, dann sye haben nit mögen darzů kümmen." Hubmaier, *Von der christlichen Taufe*, 143.

deemed. Anyone aware of the baptismal directive who professes allegiance to Jesus yet remains unbaptized ought to carefully consider the reality of this allegiance. As Jesus pointed out, "Every good tree bears good fruit, and a bad tree bears bad fruit; a good tree cannot bear bad fruit, nor can a bad tree bear good fruit" (Mt. 7:17–18), where believers' baptism constitutes a biblically provable good fruit.

A final text cited by exponents of baptismal regeneration is Mark 16:16, "The person who believes and is baptized will be saved; but the person who does not believe will be condemned." Two major problems plague this verse, of which the first alone disqualifies it from any Scriptural authority, much less any authority concerning salvation: it is inauthentic, *i.e.* neither written by Mark nor originally part of his Gospel; and it logically does not convey any relevant information on either side of the baptismal regeneration issue. First, during the sixteenth century the Markan Appendix (Mk. 16:9–20) was presumed as authentic on all hands and was printed as part of the Gospel of Mark in Erasmus' 1516 *Greek New Testament* (who had only a dozen manuscripts at his disposal, none of which predated the twelfth century).[24] This first critical edition of the *Greek New Testament*, otherwise known as the *Textus Receptus*, underlies the New Testament translation of the 1611 King James Version, which became the dominant English Bible from thence until the mid–twentieth century. However, with the advent of biblical archaeology in the late nineteenth century and the thousands of New Testament manuscripts it has since unearthed (the current total is 5,686),[25] biblical scholars quickly learned on the basis of far superior manuscript evidence reaching back to the second century that the Gospel originally ended at 16:8 and that the Appendix was a spurious addition made in the fifth century.[26] Since Jesus simply never uttered the words which Mark 16:16 attributes to him, all appeals to this passage are at best invalid and at worst dishonest. Second, Mark 16:16 taken at face value does not state that anyone unbaptized will be condemned nor imply that baptism is required for salvation. It simply affirms that *if* someone believes and is baptized, *then* her/his sins are forgiven; however, the statement says nothing one way or the other about the status of a person who has only believed but is not baptized. It is simply a logical error (a form of the inverse error) and an argument from

---

24. Norman L. Geisler and William E. Nix, *A General Introduction to the Bible*, rev. ed. (Chicago: Moody Press, 1986), 565–67.

25. The figure comes from the Institute for New Testament Textual Research, Münster and Westphalia, Germany.

26. Bruce M. Metzger, *The Text of the New Testament: Its Transmission, Corruption, and Restoration* (Oxford: Oxford University Press, 1964), 122–28.

silence to reason from this text that if someone believes but is not baptized, then she/he is damned. Hence even granted the inauthentic Mark 16:16, we still know nothing about the eternal destiny of someone who has believed but is not baptized. Thus we must turn to other Scriptures to settle the issue, which over 200 times insist that faith in Jesus is sufficient for salvation with no religious ceremonies in view.[27]

An additional apologetic can be launched toward proponents of baptismal regeneration who (mis)regard baptism as the New Testament analogue of circumcision. Here Paul's argument in Romans 4:9–17 identifying the moment in time when Abraham was saved is applicable, where the Apostle discloses that Abraham was justified prior to his circumcision and that circumcision served as a "seal of the righteousness that he had by faith while he was still uncircumcised" (v. 11). Thus for the sake of argument, if circumcision and baptism were functional equivalents, and if circumcision was not necessary to salvation although a prescribed religious ritual in the Hebrew Bible, then it follows inescapably that baptism is not necessary to salvation despite that it ought to be undertaken by believers.

Relationship between Baptism and Church Discipline

From the advent of the Patristic era to the official replacement of believers' baptism with infant baptism by Pope Innocent I in 407, candidates for baptism were required to take a baptismal vow immediately prior to receiving the sacrament. The vow would minimally consist of two essential elements: a pledge of faith addressed to Christ; and a pledge to submit to fraternal discipline addressed to the members of the church.[28] For the second through fourth century church, then, both vertical and horizontal promises were viewed as prerequisite to believers' baptism and essential for the neophyte to be included within the visible church but not the invisible church. Our baptismal theology proposes that the Church should return to this ancient practice. In this case, when one is baptized the candidate makes final confirmation of the vertical pledge to live a saintly life according to the rules of Christ and of the horizontal pledge that if she or he should stray from this

---

27. Consider, *e.g.*, John 3:15; 5:24; 11:25; 12:46; 20:31; Eph. 2:8–9; Tit. 3:5; Rom. 3:20; Gal. 2:16.

28. MacGregor, *Central European Synthesis*, 131; Pelikan, *Emergence of Catholic Tradition*, 317–18. Eleven years later the Synod of Carthage (418) went so far as to decree: "Anyone who denies that newborn infants are to be baptized . . . let him be anathema."

intent, she or he will voluntarily submit to fraternal discipline by the church. Thus, in the act of baptism, believers give the church the right to discipline and excommunicate them if the church deems this necessary. To find historical instances of such a model of baptism successfully implemented which are more recent than the Old Catholic Imperial Church, one need look no further than the Radical Reformation. Nowhere are all the elements of our discussion encapsulated more concisely than in Hubmaier's baptismal liturgy, where the officiant's lines (in this case a bishop, which for Hubmaier is the same as an elder) are marked "B" and the recipient's lines "R":

> Here the bishop lays out the baptismal vow to the baptizand in the following manner:
> [Statement of faith in the Father, Son, and Holy Spirit from the Apostles' Creed]
> B: Will you lead your life and walk according to the Word of Christ from this day forward, as he gives you grace? If so, speak:
> R: I will.
> B: If now you sin and your brother is aware of it, will you allow him to admonish you once, twice, and the third time before the church, and voluntarily and submissively accept fraternal admonition? If so, speak:
> R: I will.
> B: Do you now desire, in light of your faith and vow, to be baptized in water according to the institution of Christ, and to be inducted and thus enrolled in the visible Christian church for the forgiveness of your sins? If so, speak:
> R: I desire it in the power of God.
> B: I baptize you in the name of the Father and of the Son and of the Holy Spirit.[29]

---

29. "Hie helt der Bischoff dem menschen für die Tauffglubd vnnd also. . . . Wiltu füran dein leben vnd wandel fieren nach dem wort Christj, als vil er dir gnad verleyhet, so sprich: JCH WJL. So du nun füran sündest vnd dein brüeder waiß es, wilt du dich von im zum ersten, andern vnd zum dritten mal vor der Kirchen straffen lassen vnd brüederliche straff willigklich vnnd gehorsamlich auff nemen, so sprich: JCH WJL. Begerstu nun auff disen glauben vnnd pflicht im wasser nach der einsetzung Christi getaufft, eingeleibt vnd also in die eüsserlichen Christenlichen Kirchen eingeschriben werden zů verzeyhunng deiner sünnden, so sprich: Jch begeers auff die krafft Gottes. Jch Tauff dich in dem namen des Vatters vnd Sons vnd des heiligen geysts." Balthasar Hubmaier, *Eine Form zu taufen*, in Westin and Bergsten, *Schriften*, 349–50.

In this way, no one is admitted to the visible church without first understanding and accepting the disciplinary rules of the visible church laid down by Christ, its founder and head. Jesus instituted these rules in the following pericope, which, it must be bluntly admitted, is one of the most ignored and flagrantly disobeyed texts in the entire New Testament.

> But if your brother or sister sins against you, you may go and show the person his or her fault between you and that person alone. If that person listens to you, you have regained your brother or sister. But if that person does not listen to you, take one or two others along with you, so that every word may be confirmed by the evidence of two or three witnesses. And if the person refuses to listen to them, tell it to the church; and if the person refuses even to listen to the church, let such a person be to you as a pagan or a tax collector. Truly I say to you, whatever you bind on earth will have already been bound (δεδεμένα, future perfect passive; not the future passive δεθήσεσθε, "will be bound") in the heavens, and whatever you loose on earth will have already been loosed (λελυμένα, future perfect passive; not the future passive λυθήσεσθε, "will be loosed") in the heavens.[30] Again, truly I say to you, if two of you agree on earth about anything that you ask, it will be done for you by my Father in heaven. For where two or three are gathered in my name, I am there among them (Mt. 18:15–20).

The application of this text is straightforward. An individual in the church has the right (but not the obligation or duty) to approach a fellow believer who is sinning against that individual personally—but let it be emphasized that the text neither states nor implies that an individual has any business approaching a fellow believer over other sins that were not directly committed against that individual. This text thus supplies no license for individuals

---

30. "In the heavens" is a reverential circumlocution for "before God." As the grammar shows, this text is not stating that the congregation in the excluding stage of church discipline has the authority to forgive sins (*i.e.* loose in the heavens) or to refuse forgiveness of sins (*i.e.* bind in the heavens); such a prerogative belongs to God alone (Mk. 2:6; Lk. 4:21). Instead, it affirms that the excluding stage of church discipline, when validly performed, reflects the condition of the miscreant before God, to which Christ's presence bears witness. If the miscreant repents before the congregation, such repentance comprises concrete proof that she or he has already repented before God and has thus "already been loosed in the heavens." Conversely, if the miscreant fails to repent before the congregation, such hardness comprises concrete proof that she or he has henceforth refused to repent before God and has thus "already been bound in the heavens."

to act as "morals police" for the remainder of the community or to search for the faults of others; elsewhere the New Testament condemns such actions as meddling, gossiping, and not minding one's own business (1 Pet. 4:15; 2 Cor. 12:20; 1 Thess. 4:11). Not addressed by the passage is the further question of how the church should handle non–interpersonal sins, especially public scandals; for answers we will turn in the next paragraph to the Proto–Pauline and Pastoral Epistles. If the offender repents when encountered face–to–face, then the matter is over, and the wronged individual must genuinely forgive the offender.[31] If the offender refuses to repent, then the

---

31. Even if the offender commits the same sin against the person a limitless number of times yet repents each time she or he is approached by the wronged individual, then the matter must be dropped each time: "Then Peter came up to Jesus and asked, 'Lord, how many times shall I forgive my sister or brother when that person sins against me? Up to seven times?' Jesus answered, 'I say to you, not seven times, but seventy–seven times" (Mt. 18:21–22). So as long as the offender repents upon confrontation, the wronged individual has no right to move on to the next step of church discipline or to tell anyone else in the church about the matter, as such would not only constitute gossip but also betray a hypocritical and unforgiving spirit. This is because the wronged individual has done the same thing to God to a far greater degree than the offender has done to the wronged individual. In other words, the wronged individual has committed certain sins of infinite gravity against God repeatedly and yet has expected and received God's complete forgiveness each time she or he repents. God has never replied, "I have already forgiven you for this same sin time after time, just to see you commit it again. Therefore, I will no longer forgive you for this sin! Moreover, I will supernaturally tell your sin to other members of your church." Since God has treated the wronged individual with infinite undeserved kindness, so the wronged individual must treat the offender with finite undeserved kindness. Thus Jesus concluded when addressing this precise situation in his parable of the unmerciful servant: "For this reason the kingdom of the heavens (a reverential circumlocution for God) is like a king who wished to settle accounts with his servants. But having begun to settle accounts, one debtor of ten thousand talents (equivalent in modern currency to millions of American dollars) was brought to him and, as he could not pay, the lord ordered that he and his wife and his children and all that he had to be sold to repay the debt. So the servant fell on his knees before him, saying, 'Have patience with me, and I will pay back everything to you.' And having had compassion, the lord of that servant pardoned him and forgave him the debt. But having gone out, that servant found one of his fellow servants who owed him one hundred denarii (equivalent in modern currency to a few American dollars) and, having seized him, was choking him, saying, 'Pay back what you owe!' Therefore, having fallen, the fellow servant begged him, saying, 'Have patience with me, and I will repay you.' But he was

wronged individual, in accordance with Jewish legal regulations, should take one or two others along to ensure that the offender receives fair treatment and to serve as witnesses for the church lest the offender persist in obstinacy. Again, the matter must be dropped if the offender repents; but if the offender again spurns the plea to repentance, the wronged individual and the confirming witnesses should bring the matter before the church, which then as a body exhorts the offender to have a change of mind. If such an extreme measure fails to produce repentance, then the offender is to be treated as an outsider to the believing community, which treatment has historically been designated as "banning."

Non–interpersonal sins, such as matters of public scandal, for which repentance has not been forthcoming must be immediately exposed by the leadership of the church at the first available assembly. Here we must underscore that church leaders are not to muckrake into their parishioners' faults but only so address *publicly committed sin for which the sinner is unrepentant*, as the Pastoral Epistles clearly dictate: "Those sinning before all, expose before all (here ἐνώπιον πάντων, 'before all,' functions as the direct object of both ἁμαρτάνοντας, 'sinning,' and ἔλεγχε, 'expose'), in order that the rest may take warning" (1 Tim. 5:20; *cf.* Tit. 1:13; 2:15). It is also commanded that leaders carry out any such public disclosure "with great patience" (2 Tim. 4:2). The logic is simple: unrepented public sins undermine the ethical fiber of the entire community and so require public redress. If the miscreant repents before the congregation, then the person is to be immediately forgiven without penalty. But if the miscreant persists in unrepentance, then she or he must be banned. Paul furnishes an example of how leaders must sort out scandal with the case of a Corinthian man who both was sleeping with his mother or stepmother (obviously a public sin) and already displayed flagrant unrepentance before the local congregation.

> It is actually reported that there is sexual immorality among you, and of a kind not even found among the pagans: a man is sexually having the

---

not willing; then he went and threw him into prison until he could repay the debt. Therefore, with his fellow servants having seen what took place, they grieved greatly and went and reported to their lord everything that had happened. Then the lord summoned the unforgiving servant and said to him, 'You wicked servant! I forgave you all that debt because you begged me. Was it not necessary also to have mercy upon your fellow servant, as indeed I had mercy on you?' And having been angry, his lord handed him over to the jailers until he should repay everything he owed. Thus also my heavenly Father will do to you, unless each one of you forgive one's sister or brother from your hearts" (Mt. 18:23–35).

wife of his father. And you have been proud! Should you not have been grieved instead, so that the one doing this deed would be taken out of your midst? For indeed I myself, being absent in body but present in spirit, have already judged, as being present, the man so having done this thing. When you are gathered together in the name of our Lord Jesus and my spirit is present with the power of the Lord Jesus, hand over such a person to Satan for the destruction of his flesh, *in order that his spirit may be saved by the day of the Lord.* Your boasting is not good. Don't you know that a little teast leavens the entire batch of dough? Purge out the old yeast, so that you may be a new batch, as you are really unleavened (1 Cor. 5:1–7; emphasis added).

Amidst these instructions to the Corinthian leaders, Paul illuminates that the purpose of banning is not retaliatory but the rehabilitation and salvation of the offender, so that the offender may come to her or his senses and repent while there is still time.

At this juncture of any discussion of church discipline, it is obligatory to call attention to a necessary caveat, one which cannot be overemphasized since failure to regard it will spell not only failure to regulate behavior but far greater eternal consequences. Church discipline is only open to biblically provable sin; no disputably sinful matters, personality conflicts, or differences in customs or habits may be regulated by this means. In this matter believers are thus controlled by the highest ontological standard. In other words, unless the matter at hand is a violation of an objective moral value rooted in the nature of God, such that God could no longer be God if the matter were permissible in his sight, then we have no right to subject that matter to church discipline. In that case, we would, in the words of Martin Luther, be turning Christ into another Moses,[32] and we would fall prey to the literally damnable heresy of subjecting ourselves to a humanly fabricated yoke of slavery and thus separating ourselves from the light and easy yoke of Christ (lest one think our evaluation is too harsh, one need only review Galatians 5:1–4). So unless one can *explicitly demonstrate* from Scripture[33]—note that we did not say "render probable" or "implicitly demonstrate" from Scripture—that it is logically impossible for God to tolerate the matter in question on the Day of Judgment, then the matter cannot be judged as sin and cannot be disciplined (hence ruling out all "gray areas" from the disciplinary arena).

---

32. Luther, *New Testament*, 17; see p. 184 for the full quotation.
33. This is why 2 Timothy 3:16 claims that only the God–breathed Word is sufficient for "rebuking and correcting."

By baptism, in sum, each believer voluntarily places herself or himself under the disciplinary authority given to the church by Christ and pledges to resolve all otherwise intractable conflicts with fellow believers exclusively through the church's disciplinary channels. For this reason Paul forbids believers from taking each other to court, as such a sordid predicament spells renunciation of the Lordship of Jesus:

> Dare any one of you having a dispute with another take it to court before the unrighteous and not before the saints? Or do you not know that the saints will judge the earth? And if the earth will be judged by you, are you incompetent judges of the smallest matters? Do you not know that we will judge angels, not to mention the things of this life? Therefore, if you have a case concerning things of this life, how could you appoint as your judges such persons having no standing in the church? I say this to your shame. Is there not even one wise person among you who would be able to make judgment between his brothers or sisters? But brother or sister goes to court against brother or sister—and this before unbelievers? Therefore, to have lawsuits with one another at all means that you have already altogether been defeated. *Why not rather be wronged? Why not rather be cheated?* But you yourself do wrong and cheat, and this to your brothers and sisters! Or do you not know that the unrighteous will not inherit the kingdom of God? Do not be deceived (1 Cor. 6:1–9a; emphasis added).

We see in the italicized portion of the Pauline prohibition that even church discipline is a "concession and not a command" (*cf.* 1 Cor. 7:6); that is to say, if one believer sins against another, it is not compulsory for the maltreated believer to approach the other via discipline. The maltreated believer is certainly free to accept being wronged or cheated or to settle the dispute in a non–disciplinary way and is under no obligation to begin the disciplinary process against his sister or brother. Rather, Paul exhorts maltreated believers to invoke their right to discipline as a last resort when all else has failed. It appears obvious that the aforementioned teachings would render impossible hypocrisy and flagrant sin in the church; hence such deleterious consequences represent the direct failure of the contemporary church to implement the dominical model of church discipline.

With the relation of baptism and church discipline established, we shall now accordingly consider the theological significance and disciplinary import of the Eucharist, in the process drawing together the two sacramental threads into a coherent fabric.

The Sacrament of the Eucharist

Any model of the Eucharist is necessarily grounded upon a prior Christology, whose conception of the *praesentia Christi* provides the boundary channels for the suppositions which the model may logically stipulate. In particular, one's Christology answers the question, How is Jesus present in the Lord's Supper? Given this primary answer, one's formulation of all other facets of the Eucharist may rationally proceed along any line not contradicting it. Since our Christology denies all *communicatio idiomatum*, the physical body of Jesus possesses a finite and limited (*i.e.* localized) presence, as his divine attribute of omnipresence or ubiquity does not transfer over to the hominid body which he assumed and personalized in the Incarnation. This consequence serves as corroborating evidence for the veracity of our Christology, for an omnipresent human body is a contradiction in terms; localized presence is a necessary attribute of the human body, whether in its glorified (πνευματικός) or corrupted (ψυχικός) state. Thus contending that Jesus' humanity is present everywhere, the *sine qua non* presupposition of both transubstantiation and consubstantiation,[34] seems unwittingly to both deny the Incarnation itself and replace it with docetism. Our Eucharistic theology will thus proceed on the assumption that it is logically impossible for Christ's physical body to be present in the Supper. This is not in any way to demean the presence of Christ in the Eucharist, but rather to simply affirm that Christ's bodily presence on the table is self–contradictory; hence our view no more denigrates the *praesentia Christi* than denying a round square denigrates a square or than denying 2 + 2 = 5 denigrates arithmetic. Hence transubstantiation and consubstantiation, in point of fact, are not more exalted forms of Christ's presence than that which we shall delineate; it is rather that these Eucharistic doctrines posit forms of Christ's presence which are not forms at all but comprise meaningless combinations of words (a "married bachelor" is not a type of bachelor at all but a meaningless combination of words). However, we must emphasize it is entirely logically possible for Christ's divinity, naturally endowed with omnipresence, to be present in the Supper, and that such a divine presence may manifest itself in any

---

34. Though, it needs to be emphasized, not to be immediately equated with the physical presence affirmed by either of these views. In other words, these views do not teach that Christ is present in the Eucharist just as he is present everywhere. But reasoning from the greater to the lesser, these views argue that if Christ's humanity can be present everywhere (ubiquity), then no logical restraints exist which prevent that humanity from being specially present in the Eucharist (real bodily presence).

possible way, as there are by definition no logical constraints on this presence.

Given our Christological underpinnings, we may now formulate a model of the Eucharist which owes its structure to John Calvin (1509–64). Although Calvin was certainly neither Molinist nor Anabaptist (in fact, he would and/or did strenuously object to both groups), the present construction is unconcerned with allegiance to particular strands of Christian thought over against others but only endeavors to seek truth on each point. While the majority of our construction historically constitutes an outgrowth of Molinist and Anabaptist trajectories, here we claim that Calvin's Eucharistic theology comprises the trajectory in church history having the most to commend it, and we will thus proceed to build upon it. Expanding on Calvin's treatment in book four of his classic *Institutio Christianae Religionis* (Institutes of the Christian Religion), we stipulate that in the Supper, the soul of the believer literally feeds on the omnipresent divinity of Jesus in exactly the same way and at precisely the same time that the body feeds on the bread and wine. Thus a genuine eating and drinking of Jesus' infinite divine spirit by the finite human spirit transpires in the Eucharist,[35] which consumption we know is possible from Jesus' twofold description of his spirit as "the bread of life" (6:35, 51) and the wellspring of "living water" (4:10, 14; 7:37–38). That these passages refer to Jesus' spirit and not his body is evident by their depiction of the living bread and living water as "coming down from heaven" (6:32, 38), a portrayal which could only apply to Jesus' eternally preexistent divinity and not to the anhypostatic humanity which he acquired and hypostasized on earth in the womb of Mary. The divine import of Jesus' statements were immediately recognized by his hearers, including his opponents among the Jewish religiopolitical elite who regarded it as blasphemous: "At this the Jewish religious leaders started to grumble about Jesus…they said,

---

35. Calvin, *Institutes*, 4.17.5, 10. As Calvin explains: "Christ feeds our souls, just as bread and wine support our bodily life. There would be no point in the signs, if our souls did not find their nourishment in Christ. . . . Although it seems an incredible thing . . . we have to remember the immense power of the Holy Spirit and how stupid it is to try to measure its immensity by our feeble efforts. . . . the Spirit really does unite things separated by space. Christ transfuses his life into us by that sacred communion of flesh and blood. . . . because of it, believers have Christ living in them. In the same way, Christ chose to call himself the bread of life (John 6:51), not only to teach that our salvation is treasured up in the faith of his death and resurrection, but also, because of real communion with him, his life passes to us and becomes ours, just as bread gives strength to the body."

'Is this not Jesus, the son of Joseph, whose father and mother we know? How can he now say, 'I came down from heaven'?" (6:41–42).

Although from a source critical perspective, which demonstrates Johannine literary independence from the Synoptics and Q,[36] I find highly improbable the thesis that the authorial intent of John 6 bore any connection with the Eucharist, the Eucharistic character of John 6 would not undermine but actually furnish strong verification for our Eucharistic theology. For our theology would then resolve the seeming paradox between Jesus' assertions that a genuine eating and drinking takes place indispensable for eternal life but that such life comes not from the flesh but from the spirit:

> Jesus said to them, "Truly, truly, I say to you, unless you eat the flesh of the Son of God and drink his blood, you have no life in you. Whoever eats my flesh and drinks my blood has eternal life, and I will raise him up at the last day. For my flesh is real food and my blood is real drink....Does this offend you? What if you see the Son of Man ascend to where he was before? The spirit gives the life; the flesh counts for nothing. The words I have spoken to you are spirit and they are life" (6:53–55, 61–63).

Through the believer's soul literally eating and drinking the infinite spirit of Jesus while physically eating the bread and wine, our view reveals how one can receive eternal life by eating Jesus' flesh (metonymous for the bread) and drinking his blood (metonymous for the wine) when the infinite divine spirit of Jesus and not his finite human body gives that life.[37] Such explanatory power is not possessed by any other Eucharistic theology, which opt for one of the two polarities and open themselves to the charge of disingenuousness in explaining away the other polarity in a way contrary to its grammatico–historical meaning.

The Highest Possible Form of *Praesentia Realis*

From the perspective of Christian Platonism, our Eucharistic theology must be classified as a form of real presence. Far from the notion that our model posits merely the spiritual presence of Christ in the Supper, a conse-

---

36. Leon Morris, *The Gospel According to St. John*, rev. ed., in *New International Commentary on the New Testament* (Grand Rapids, Mich.: Eerdmans, 1995), 43–45, 118; Merrill C. Tenney, *John*, in *The Expositor's Bible Commentary*, gen. ed. Frank E. Gæbelein (Grand Rapids, Mich.: Zondervan, 1984), 9:20.

37. Brian Albert Gerrish, *Grace and Gratitude: The Eucharistic Theology of John Calvin* (Minneapolis: Fortress, 1993), 176–78.

quence which seems scarcely distinguishable from the repletive presence of Christ that is accessible to the believer at all times, we shall argue that our model actually mediates the highest possible form of real presence.[38] For what radically separates our model from either spiritual presence or its theological cousin sacramentarianism is that the soul of the believer literally eats and drinks the infinite divine spirit of Jesus, thus respectively satisfying the soul's literal hunger and quenching the soul's literal thirst. Astonishingly, our view thus stipulates that uniquely in the sacrament the divine spirit of Jesus becomes literally consumable such that the redeemed human soul can eat it and literally potable such that the redeemed human soul can drink it. Such a transformation of Christ's divinity into consumable and potable forms is literally supernatural and, on our model, never occurs outside the sacrament.[39] This alone renders the Eucharist of utmost importance in the Christian life and remedies the low view of the Supper that has especially plagued modern Protestantism and sadly seeped into more liberal sectors of Catholicism. Hence believers eat Jesus' spirit with their souls concurrently as they eat the bread with their bodies, and believers drink Jesus' spirit with their souls concurrently as they drink the wine with their bodies.

A brief excursion into the *Weltanschauung* of Christian Platonism is at this point instructive for enhanced comprehension of our model. The Christian Platonist worldview divides reality into the immaterial or spiritual realm of perfect ideas or essences and the derivative realm of their imperfect physical copies. On this worldview, the spiritual realm is ontologically superior, or greater in being or reality, to the physical realm, since the former exists necessarily and the latter exists contingently. Plato identified the greatest possible idea as the "Form of the Good," the πεγέ (logically prior, but not chronologically prior, source or wellspring) for all other immaterial ideas.[40] For instance, ideas such as holiness, love, and justice, while existing necessarily and thus co–eternally with the Form of the Good, are timelessly generated by the Form of the Good.[41] With the exception of the Form of the Good, which alone possesses the attribute of aseity, all other ideas exist necessarily only because they naturally flow out of the Form of the Good. Not surprisingly given its theistic overtones, Plato interchanged the Form of the

---

38. Thus Calvin insisted that his view, contra transubstantiation, consubstantiation, and sacramentarianism, accurately depicted and magnified "the true and substantial communication of the body and blood of the Lord" (*Institutes*, 4.17.19).

39. Gerrish, *Grace and Gratitude*, 182–84.

40. Plato, *Republic*, 6.504–11.

41. Ibid., 6.512–20.

Good with the term "God,"[42] leading Christian thought from the second–century Greek Apologists to follow suit by regarding the Form of the Good as the very nature of God himself.[43] Such a theology proper came to explicit expression in Anselm's celebrated definition of God as "that than which nothing greater can be conceived," or "the greatest conceivable being."[44] Therefore, the necessary being of God is the tripersonal ground or foundation for all other necessary being as well as for all contingent being. Concerning the Second Person of God, the divinity or spirit of Jesus, possessing not only necessary existence but also aseity, provides the ground for the humanity of Jesus. Hence the spirit of Jesus possesses an ontological value not merely higher than but infinitely higher than the humanity of Jesus, making Jesus' divine spirit infinitely more real than his physical body. Since we propose that the faithful actually partake of Christ's spirit, supernaturally transformed into consumable and potable forms, rather than partaking of his material flesh and blood, our Eucharistic theology features an even more real presence than that proposed by transubstantiation or consubstantiation—indeed, the highest conceivable form of real presence that could possibly exist.

Relation between the Eucharist and Church Discipline

At this juncture we shall again follow Calvin, whose exegesis of the Pauline Epistles deduced an antithetical relationship between the Lord's Supper and the excluding stage of church discipline; it is worth pointing out that Hubmaier reached the identical conclusion two decades prior to Calvin (however, Calvin is not dependent on Hubmaier for his view). As I have concluded elsewhere,

> withholding the Eucharist from miscreants proved to be a central mechanism in Hubmaier's Waldshut and Nikolsburg and Calvin's Geneva for the inculcation of new habits which the reformers viewed as compliant with their respective Radical and Reformed faiths.[45]

Turning to what precisely "banning" in the New Testament means, we are faced with two possible options. Whether church discipline means not allow-

---

42. Ibid., 1.379a–383a.
43. Pelikan, *Emergence of Catholic Tradition*, 230, 247–49.
44. Anselm, *Proslogion*, 2–4.
45. MacGregor, *Central European Synthesis*, 222.

ing the banned to have any involvement with church affairs or barring the person from the Eucharistic meal depends on the exegetically debatable interpretation of the Pauline admonition "with such a person do not even eat" (1 Cor. 5:11) and the dominical instruction to "let such a person be to you as a pagan or a tax collector" (Mt. 18:17). Personally I favor the latter option since it makes more sense of the fact that pagans and tax collectors were allowed into and encouraged to visit the worship service (1 Cor. 14:22–25); thus treating the banned as a pagan or a tax collector would not seem to disqualify them from attending the worship service. Indeed, the Pauline perspective is that the worship service should serve as evangelism for such persons, who thus have more need of attending the worship service, where they are most likely to be convicted of their sin and come to repentance, than anyone else! Of course implementation of my suggestion would demand returning our churches to the first–century practice of practicing the Eucharist weekly and holding a separate Eucharistic service from the general worship assembly.[46] Independent confirmation of this fact is furnished by a most hostile source, Pliny the Younger (62–113), a Roman governor of Bithynia and ruthless persecutor of Jesus' followers. In addition to identifying bread and wine as the antecedent of "food of an ordinary and innocent kind," we also underscore Pliny's unlikely admission of the high moral standards displayed by the early Jesus movement:

> They were in the habit of meeting on a certain fixed day before dawn, when they sang in alternate verses a hymn to Christ, as to a god, and bound themselves by a solemn oath, not for any criminal purpose, but to abstain from theft, robbery, and adultery, never to falsify their word, nor deny a trust when they should be called upon to deliver it up; *after which it was their custom to separate, and then reassemble to partake of food—but food of an ordinary and innocent kind.*[47]

At the very least, therefore, "banning" for the Jewish Way spelled exclusion from the Eucharist (if not exclusion from all congregational affairs) unless and until the miscreant repents of the relevant sin before the congregation. When straying members return to the fold, the church must welcome them back with open arms, holding no grudges and reaffirming their love for their penitent sisters and brothers. Thus Paul directed the Corinthian congregation

---

46. This constitutes the reference of "breaking bread (in their homes)," the homes alluding to house churches (Acts 2:42, 46), and the ἀγάπαις or "love-feasts" (Jude 12). See Brown, *New Testament*, 288–89, 522–23 and Gundry, *New Testament*, 365–66.

47. Pliny the Younger, *Letters*, Vol. 2, X:96; emphasis added.

when the believer who had been sleeping with his father's wife publicly repented:

> But if anyone has caused grief, he has not so much grieved me but all
> of you to some extent, not to put it too severely. The punishment which
> was inflicted by the majority is sufficient for such a man. Now, on the
> contrary, you ought to forgive and comfort him, lest perhaps such a
> person be swallowed up with excessive sorrow. Therefore I urge you to
> reaffirm your love to him. . . . Now if you forgive anyone, I also for-
> give that person. For indeed what I have forgiven, if there was anything
> for me to forgive, I have forgiven for your sakes in the presence of
> Christ, lest Satan should take advantage of us; for we are not ignorant
> of his devices (2 Cor. 2:5–8, 10–11).

For a person who desires to repent of a sin at any stage of church discipline
but finds oneself unable to break away from it, Hubmaier helpfully provides
pastoral counsel by laying out the steps to victory as well as a useful self–
test of one's sincerity regarding the achievement of freedom.

> True repentance and remorse over sin consists in this: that one forsakes
> all performance of the relevant sin and thereafter flees, lays aside, and
> refrains from anything that might entice him and draw him again into it,
> including gluttony, drunkenness, gambling, anger, sexual immorality,
> and bad company. The contrition of any person who refuses to do this
> stems not from the heart, regardless of the mouth might utter. *For he
> who claims to be sorry about his sins but does not flee enticements to
> those sins is a liar. He is acting like someone who claims he wants to
> avoid being dirty but spends all his time with coal and old kettles.*
> However, the father receives the prodigal son with great joy when he
> returns wholeheartedly and admits that he sinned against both heaven
> and his father. Although he realizes that he no longer deserves to be
> called his son, he asks for forgiveness. He will never commit it again,
> which is the best repentance. [To] never commit [the sin again] is the
> best repentance.[48]

---

48. "Das ist aber ein rechte büß vnnd rew vber die sünd. So der mensch der
selben sünden mit der that absteet vnd fürhin alles fleücht, hinweg thůt vnd
meydt, als vberessen, trunckenhait, spill, zorn, hůrerey, böse gselschafft vnd
alles das, dardurch er widerumb in die sünd mecht geraitzt vnd gezogen werden.
Wölher aber das nit thůt, den selben rewen sein sünd nit von hertzen, geb was er
mit dem mund schwetze. Dann wölher redt, jm seyend sein sünd layd, vnd ver-
meydt aber die vrsachen der sünnden nit, der ist ein Lugner vnd thůt gleich wie
ainer, der sich nit verromigen will vnd doch sein gsellschafft teglich hat mit

All believers, regardless of disciplinary status, would do well in taking to heart the italicized portion, for one's actions prove the best determinant of one's motives. As Paul contends on this score: "Bad company corrupts good character" (1 Cor. 15:33).

On our sacramental conception, frequent reception of the Eucharist exhibits supreme importance for three major reasons. First and foremost is its affording believers the most intimate possible earthly communion with Jesus—just as intimate as when Jesus walked the earth with his apostles—which cannot be otherwise acquired. So, while Christ is not *on* the Eucharistic table, we insist that *he is uniquely present in the supreme possible way at* his table. Second, we posit that Jesus grants believers a measure or supply of grace during the Supper; such *gratia cooperans* (cooperating grace) should be conceived as a divine substance which cannot operate in and of itself but requires human free consent to be effective. Thus the grace poured out in the Eucharist must not be confused with the non–substantive *gratia operans* (operating grace), or God's unmerited favor toward sinners which clearly operates in and of itself, dispensed at the moment of personal faith in Christ. This grace distributed in the Eucharist is therefore "potential grace," which is converted by recipients into "actual grace" when they choose to carry out works of charity toward God and neighbor. Upon this conversion, the actual grace supplies the faithful with the divine energy needed to carry out the works they choose to undertake, thereby fostering harmony between grace and free will. Hence Paul can in the same breath assert: "I worked harder than all of the other apostles, nevertheless it was not I, but the grace of God that was with me" (1 Cor. 15:10). In this way the Eucharistic elements display, in addition to the matchless *unio Christo*, a deep ethical symbolism, as the potential grace mediated through the vehicles of bread and wine is transformed by the soul into the energy necessary for spiritual life. This is why reception of the Eucharist is indispensable for living the Christian life and progressing toward sanctification; no one wanting to live consistently as a disciple of Christ can avoid the Supper. Therefore, for Calvin and Hubmaier, the Eucharist assumed a preeminent place in the life of the church which

---

kolen vnd allten kösslen. Ja den verlornenn Son nimbt der vater an mit grossen freüden, der von hertzen widerkhert vnd bekennt sich, das er in den himel vnd in Jn gsünd hab. Er sey nit wirdig sein Son genennt zů werden. Aber er solle jm verzeihen. Er wölle es fürbaß nymmer thon, wölhes die höchst büß ist. Nimmer thon die gröst büß." Balthasar Hubmaier, *Von dem christlichen Bann*, in Westin and Bergsten, *Schriften*, 377; emphasis added.

desperately needs to be recovered for the vitality of the body of Christ and the coherence of church discipline.[49]

Third, despite our rejection of the Roman Catholic notion that Christ is literally sacrificed by the priest celebrating the Eucharist, we affirm that the Supper causes Christ's body to be figuratively sacrificed in a new way. Insofar as the Kingdom message of Jesus impels us to be loving servants to all (Mk. 10:44), so we must sacrifice ourselves for one another and for the world as did our Lord. Since it is the power mediated by the Eucharist that makes this sacrifice possible and believers constitute the body of Christ (1 Cor. 10:16; 12:12–27; Eph. 5:23; Col. 1:24; 3:15), Christ is figuratively sacrificed not in, but as a result of, the Eucharist. As Hubmaier explains:

> Because we now, as a result of eating the bread and drinking the wine in memory of the passion and shed blood of our Lord Jesus Christ for the forgiveness of our sins . . . have all become one loaf and one body, and our Head is Christ, we ought to fully conform ourselves to our Head . . . by each of us offering his own flesh and blood.[50]

In this reconceptualization of the Eucharistic sacrifice as the self–offering of the worshiping community empowered by the Eucharist, we maintain that Christ's sacrifice for humanity becomes the transforming power of history when those who appropriate it for themselves imitate its sacrifice. The element of ἀνάμνησις, "Do this in remembrance of me" (Lk. 22:19), places believers in unbroken contact with the original disciples and summons them to the same life of selfless compassion as Christ led:

> Do you know what I have done to you? You yourselves call me the Teacher and the Lord, and well you say, for I am. If therefore I washed your feet, being the Lord and the Teacher, you yourselves also ought to

---

49. It is probably for this reason that Hubmaier's churches in Waldshut and Nikolsburg practiced the Eucharist weekly, a practice that Calvin desired to adopt in Geneva but was prevented from implementing by the Genevan city government. For a complete discussion of these issues see MacGregor, *Central European Synthesis*, 200–08.

50. "Wie wir nun yetz all mit dieser essung des brots vnd trinckung des trancks in der gedechtnuß des leidens vnd blůtuergiessens vnsers herrens Jesu Christj zů nachlassung vnserer sünden . . . vnd seind all ain brot vnd ain leib worden, vnd vnser haubt ist Christus, also sollen wir billich vnserm haubt gleichförmig werden . . . einer . . . sein fleisch und blůt darspannen." Balthasar Hubmaier, *Eine Form des Nachtmals Christi*, in Westin and Bergsten, *Schriften*, 363.

wash the feet of one another. For an example I gave you, in order that as I did to you, also you yourselves may do (Jn. 13:12b–15).

Here the evangelistic thrust underlying our doctrine of the Supper is exposed: as believers figuratively become Christ to others (the literal meaning of the term "Christian"), nonbelievers will be attracted to Jesus, enter the visible church through baptism, and ultimately come into absolute communion with Jesus in the Eucharist. On our construction, the sacraments thereby facilitate the salvific work of God the Son in the church. In sum, the Eucharist, whose consumption was made possible by the Christian's right relationship with God, encompasses three historical points of reference, as it points backward to the suffering of Christ, to the present in experiencing Jesus in the preeminent metaphysically possible mode, and forward to the righteous living, evangelism, and suffering of Christ's people. The Lord's Supper thereby indicates that the incarnation is being carried on in the church.

The Biblically Intended Synthesis of the Sacraments and Church Discipline

The teachings of Jesus on baptism, the Lord's Supper, and church discipline function as an organic unity which can only be separated at the expense of each otherwise incomplete part. Through this dominical synthesis, Jesus ensured that, for all congregations choosing to subscribe to it, those assemblies would not only experience freedom from strife, division, and hypocrisy but also serve as living lights radiating his beautiful Calvary–quality love and inimitable resurrection power to a desperately seeking world. The initial pole of this network is believers' baptism, predicated upon the baptizand demonstrating commitment to Christ by pledging to live by the rules that Christ laid down for his Kingdom community, namely, through expressing willingness to be fraternally disciplined if one wanders from the path of discipleship and to resolve all insoluble conflicts with one's sisters and brothers exclusively via fraternal discipline. Upon taking the baptismal vow, the believer publicly identifies with Jesus' death and resurrection through the act of baptism and so associates with Jesus' visible community. The second pole of this network is the Eucharist, where it follows that the recipients of which comprise at any given moment the best visible approximation of the redeemed. In the New Testament, the Eucharist was administered on a weekly basis as a separate service from the broader worship assembly; only community members in good standing could participate in the former while all persons regardless of faith in Christ could attend the latter. When offered weekly, the Supper service thus takes on three profound qualities: all in the church recognize the privilege of receiving the sacrament and long to receive at every possible opportunity; members in good standing view their reception as tangible evidence of their salvation; and banned members are forced to come to grips with the fact that they may well not be among the saved and are thereby strongly drawn to a point of repentance. It is therefore not surprising that Paul associates proper church discipline with keeping the Eucharistic feast of Christ, our Passover Lamb:

> For indeed our paschal lamb, Christ, was sacrificed. So let us keep the feast not with old yeast, the yeast of malice and evil, but with unleavened bread of purity and truth. . . . But now I am writing to you not to mix with any sister or brother being called a fornicator or greedy or an idolater or a reviler or a drunkard or a swindler; do not eat with such a person (1 Cor. 5:7b–8, 11).

The magnetic force that binds the two poles of baptism and Eucharist together is church discipline. Employing an equivalent analogy, Hubmaier identifies the two sacraments as the garments with which Jesus has clothed his bride and discipline as the belt holding them together. The removal of the belt or either of the two garments, Hubmaier points out, is tantamount to debasing the pure church to a shameful adulteress who ceases to be the bride of Christ:

> O my Lord Jesus Christ, institute once again the two bands, namely water baptism and the Supper, with which you have outwardly girded and bound your bride. For unless these two elements are again instituted and practiced according to your appointment and order, we have among us neither faith, love, church covenant, fraternal admonition, ban, nor exclusion, without which it may never again be well in your church.[51]

For these reasons, the New Testament has bequeathed to us a network inextricably intertwining baptism, the Lord's Supper, and fraternal discipline, which enables the visible church to directly participate in the divine life and

---

51. "O mein herr Jesu Christe, richte widerumb auff die zway band, namlich den Wassertauff vnd das Nachtmal, mit wölhen du dein Praut außwenndig vmbgürtet hast vnd gebunden. Wann es sey denn sach das die zway stuckh nach deiner einsetzung vnd ordnung wider auffgericht vnd gebraucht werdent, haben wir vnder vns weder Glauben, liebe, Kirchenn glübd, Brüderliche straff, Ban noch auß schliessung, on wölhe dinng es nimmer mer wol steen mag in deiner Kirchen." Balthasar Hubmaier, *Die zwölf Artikel des christlichen Glaubens*, in Westin and Bergsten, *Schriften*, 219.

ongoing Kingdom work of Jesus. As we have seen, these elements are separated at their own peril. Moreover, this network furnishes believers visible marks by which they may recognize one another and find assurance that they are among the redeemed, thereby supplying them vital motivation and support to grow ever more faithful to their high calling. If we would return to the biblical conception of the sacraments and church discipline, then the problems among biblically centrist congregations in the West would simply not exist.

Chapter 8

Women in Ministry

A New Testament Proposal

The exegetical question of deciphering the possible offices women may hold in the church, in itself a relatively innocuous query, has unfortunately become obscured by cultural phenomena since the 1960s, from which many expositors have failed to objectively distance themselves before handling the sacred text. Prominent among such phenomena is the woman's liberation movement, at its core a socio–political critique of culturally constructed Western gender roles which attempted not only to admirably remedy unequal treatment of women in the workplace but also to, from a biblical perspective, disadmirably undermine the distinct gender roles created by God as part of the natural order and amply attested in Scripture. Spearheaded by Mary Daly and Rosemary Radford Reuther, the women's liberation movement had by the 1970s extended itself into the mainstream of the American religious studies academy, under the appellation of feminist theology. In the context of mainly liberal Protestant seminaries, the unbiblical nature of feminist theology has grown ever more pronounced, going so far as to deny the Incarnation on the grounds that the Second Trinitarian Person could not have taken human form as a man, to redefine God as a "Goddess" that projects a feminine ideal, and to replace all male symbols and offices, both culturally and ecclesiologically, with female equivalents. Recent developments have seen feminist theology become closely allied with gay theology, as the dissolution of distinctive female and male relational attributes readily facilitates the legitimation of same–sex couples. These extreme developments have rightly provoked outrage among practitioners of historic Christian orthodoxy, who now find themselves under the Pastoral mandate to uphold biblically defined gender roles and to refute the contrary arguments advanced by alternative versions of Christianity (Tit. 1:9).

It is precisely in the midst of such an emotionally charged cultural crisis that special attention must be paid to conveying fairly and accurately the position of Scripture and then prayerfully trusting the Holy Spirit to utilize the truth in convicting non–believers of sin and in drawing them to Jesus, rather than responding to the extreme of feminist theology by developing an equally extreme rebuttal that commits the same methodological error as its opponent—namely, going beyond the allowable limits of grammatico–historical exegesis. Such a method of "fighting fire with fire" seems in actuality a subtle distrust of the Holy Spirit, wherein believers indirectly doubt the Spirit's ability to work through the vehicle of truth and, therefore, attempt to supplement this intangible divine means with the tangible means of human sophistry. Notwithstanding its Pauline critique (Gal. 3:3), this strategy has become the standard and predictable response to clashes of theology and culture throughout church history; distressing but hardly surprising, then, is the development in historic Christian circles of a reactionary movement to feminist theology termed "complementarianism," which encompasses far more than the suggestion of its name that men and women naturally complement each other in their differing God–ordained roles. Not content to merely deny the wrong conclusions reached by feminist theology, complementarianism aims to prevent the feminist theological enterprise from even getting off the ground. In addition to affirming that wives should be submissive to their husbands and execute their motherly duties toward their children, complementarians insist that women should be barred from leadership positions in the church and have even departed from the *consensus quinquesaecularis* by introducing into Trinitarian theology a quasi–Arian eternal subordination of the Son to the Father, which is then conveniently turned round to justify the ecclesiastical and marital subjection of women to men. Complementarians make their revisionist doctrine of the Trinity deceptively appealing through the citation of lengthy references originally pertaining to the economic Trinity (*i.e.* how God acts in time–space relations with humanity, or *deus pro nobis*, "God for us") from Patristic, Medieval, and Reformation authorities (such as Tertullian, Athanasius, Augustine, Aquinas, Luther, Calvin, and Arminius) in favor of positions concerning the immanent Trinity (*i.e.* the internal constitution of God, or *deus in se*, "God in and of himself"). What makes this selective reading of leading historical theologians even more tragic than a prolonged contextual blunder is that none of these figures actually held to the eternal subordination of the Son to the Father but in fact strenuously opposed this teaching as logically entailing the heresy of the Son's inferiority to the Father. While complementarians universally subscribe to the equal divinity of the Father and the Son, I cannot help but agree with Kevin Giles that they do so inconsistently, which logical error we cannot reasonably expect our posterity to follow. In his outstanding historical critique of eternal subordinationism, Giles incisively summarizes the dangerous effects and the culturally conditioned causes of the complementarian predicament:

> For the fourth–century Arians, subordination in being, work, and authority were inextricably linked. One implied the other two. The dominant evangelical view is that it is possible to have *eternal* subordination in function and authority without implying subordination in being. It is my case that this is not possible. If my argument is compelling, then by implication all evangelicals who endorse the eternal subordination of the Son in function and authority embrace—without realizing it, and even often denying it—the subordination of the Son in being. . . . Are then my debating opponents twenty–first–century Arians? The answer to this question is no. . . . All those with whom I am debating insist that they are not Arians and that they say they accept the creeds and confessions. . . . My charge is rather that in arguing for the *eternal* subordination of the Son to support the doctrine of the *permanent* subordination of women, my debating opponents' primary and consuming concern, they have in ignorance broken with how the best of theologians and the creeds and confessions have concluded the Scriptures should be read and understood. Unintentionally they have embraced fundamental aspects of the Arian heresy in its varied forms, producing a strange amalgam of truth and error.[1]

Holding true to typical historical form,[2] in this case an extreme initial response by the Christian community to a cultural crisis with theological ramifications was quickly met by others within the community, who proceeded, without committing the more egregious errors made by the culture, to swing the church's ideological pendulum in the opposite direction. Termed "egalitarianism," this alternative position not only claims that the Bible presents all church governing and teaching positions as open to

---

1. Kevin Giles, *Jesus and the Father: Modern Evangelicals Reinvent the Doctrine of the Trinity* (Grand Rapids, Mich.: Zondervan, 2006), 306–09, emphasis his.

2. Notable examples of this pattern include the counter–response of the late–Augustine to the response of Pelagius to cultural immorality infiltrating the Latin Church and the eventual counter–response of Arminius to the predestinarian response of late medieval theologians to the Black Death.

women and men alike but also alleges that the Bible does not stipulate differing roles for women and men in marriage based on gender alone, thus debarring husbands from holding a unique leadership role. But this latter allegation is, from a hermeneutical perspective, highly problematic, since it flies in the face of several clear texts whose *prima facie* message is both confirmed and strengthened upon their grammatico–historical exegesis. Including Colossians 3:18–19, Titus 2:5, 1 Peter 3:1–7, and the Genesis creation narrative itself, the overarching position on marriage which this set of texts delineates is encapsulated by Ephesians 5:21–32.

> Be subject to one another out of reverence for Christ. Wives, be subject to your husbands as to the Lord. For the husband is the head of the wife as Christ is the head of the church, his body, and is himself its Savior. As the church is subject to Christ, so also wives should be subject to their husbands in everything. Husbands, love your wives, as Christ loved the church and gave himself up for her, that he might sanctify her, cleansing her by the washing of water with the word, in order to present the church to himself in splendor, without spot, wrinkle, or anything of the kind, so that she indeed may be holy and without blemish. In the same way, husbands must love their wives as they do their own bodies. He who loves his wife loves himself. For no man ever hates his own body, but nourishes and cherishes it, as Christ does the church, because we are members of his body. "For this reason a man will leave his father and mother and be united to his wife, and the two will become one flesh" [Gen. 2:24]. This is a great mystery, and I am applying it to Christ and the church. However, each of you should love his wife as himself, and the wife must respect her husband.

Consistent with my avoidance of polarities thus far, such as either–or perspectives on Calvinism and Arminianism and on Openness of God theology and full–blown metaphorization of texts denoting divine cognitive changes, and consistent with my previous discernment that truth often lies in mediating positions between extremes, I propose that the frequently offered choice between complementarianism and egalitarianism is a false dichotomy. Thus I contend that truth concerning gender roles and relationships lies between these two camps rather than exclusively within either one. In particular, although not agreeing with all the exegetical details advanced by each camp on these issues, I believe that the complementarian position essentially reflects the biblical teaching on marital gender roles, while I equally believe that the egalitarian position essentially reflects the biblical teaching on church polity. Thus I see marital gender roles and the admissibility of women to church leadership positions as completely separate and intrinsically independent issues that have through historical accident, namely the contemporary feminist movement, become entangled. Since robust Scriptural defenses of distinctly ordained gender roles in marriage have been made elsewhere,[3] this fact will simply be taken as given throughout the chapter. Rather, our attention will here be occupied with the second issue, where both negative and positive evidence will be adduced for the thesis that the New Testament places no gender restrictions on the holding of offices within the church. Accordingly we shall first show that for each of the ecclesiological passages to which complementarians appeal, a close examination of the Greek text furnishes no support for the notion that women should be excluded from the pastorate, eldership, or any other ecclesiastical office. Secondly, we shall demonstrate that the New Testament both portrays first-century women filling the highest church leadership positions and encourages women to serve in these positions.

1 Corinthians 14:33–38

The NIV reflects the standard translation of this text, including the paragraph breaks and punctuation, found in most other modern English versions (*e.g.* NASB, NAB, ESV):

> For God is not a God of disorder but of peace.
>
> As in all the congregations of the saints, women should remain silent in the churches. They are not allowed to speak, but must be in submission, as the Law says. If they want to inquire about something, they should ask their own husbands at home; for it is disgraceful for a woman to speak in the church.
>
> Did the word of God originate with you? Or are you the only people it has reached? If anybody thinks he is a prophet or spiritually gifted, let him acknowledge that what I am writing to you is the Lord's command. If he ignores this, he himself will be ignored.

The standard translation should be praised for its division of the text into three paragraphs, which follows the consensus of commentators on 1 Corin-

---

3. Exemplary treatments include Ken Campbell, *Marriage and Family in the Biblical World* (Downers Grove, Ill.: InterVarsity Press, 2003), Susan Hunt, *By Design* (Wheaton, Ill.: Crossway, 1994), R. Kent Hughes, *Disciplines of a Godly Man* (Wheaton, Ill.: Crossway, 1991), Barbara Hughes, *Disciplines of a Godly Woman* (Wheaton, Ill.: Crossway, 2001), and Weldon M. Hardenbrook, *Missing from Action: Vanishing Manhood in America* (Nashville: Nelson, 1987).

thians and is readily verified by an examination of the original text. This is seen in the isolated presence of Ὡς, a particle which introduces new discourse when found alone, and the interjection ἤ followed by a question, where each of these grammatical elements initiates a shift in thought corresponding to the start of a new English paragraph. These paragraph breaks are independently indicated by transitions in subject matter that would naturally signal shifts in thought even without grammatical markers. Following is the Greek text, with the aforementioned terms italicized, accompanied by an interlinear formal (*i.e.* precisely word–for–word or "woodenly literal") English equivalent:

οὐ γάρ ἐστιν ἀκαταστασίας ὁ θεὸς ἀλλα εἰρήνης.

Ὡς ἐν πάσαις ταῖς ἐκκλησίαις τῶν ἁγίων αἱ γυναῖκες ἐν ταῖς ἐκκλησίαις σιγάτωσαν· οὐ γὰρ ἐπιτρέπεται αὐταῖς λαλεῖν, ἀλλὰ ὑποτασσέσθωσαν, καθὼς καὶ ὁ νόμος λέγει. εἰ δέ τι μαθεῖν θέλουσιν, ἐν οἴκῳ τοὺς ἰδίους ἄνδρας ἐπερωτάτωσαν· αἰσχρὸν γάρ ἐστιν γυναικὶ λαλεῖν ἐν ἐκκλησίᾳ.

ἤ ἀφ᾽ ὑμῶν ὁ λόγος τοῦ θεοῦ ἐξῆλθεν, ἤ εἰς ὑμᾶς μόνους κατήντησεν; Εἴ τις δοκεῖ προφήτης εἶναι ἤ πνευματικός, ἐπιγινωσκέτω ἃ γράφω ὑμῖν ὅτι κυρίου ἐστιν ἐντολή· εἰ δέ τις ἀγνοεῖ, ἀγνοεῖται.

[4]not [1]For [3]is [5]of disorder [2]God [6]but of peace.

As in all the assemblies of the holy ones the wives [2]in the assemblies [1]should keep silent; [6]not [3]for [5]are [7]permitted [4]they (f.) [8]to speak, but should be in submission, just as the Law says. [2]if [1]But [5]anything [4]to learn [3]they desire, [8]at home [7]their own husbands [6]let them ask; [10]shameful [9]for it is [11]for wives to speak in an assembly.

Or [4]with you (pl.) [2]the word of God [1]did [3]originate, or to you (pl.) only (masc. pl. = "men only") has it come? If anyone seems [2]a prophet [1]to be [3]or spiritual, [4]let that one recognize [6]what I write to you (pl.) [5]that [8]of the Lord [7]is a commandment; [10]if [9]but [11]anyone [13]this [12]disregards, [14]let that one be disregarded.

Before proceeding it should be noted that Greek is an inflected language, meaning that nouns, pronouns, adjectives, and nominals possess gender, case, and number and that verbs possess person, number, tense, voice, and mood. Thus Greek adjectives have gender, which is the same gender as the nouns or pronouns they modify. Our translation discloses several noteworthy features of the Greek text. First, the bolded adjective μόνους is the masculine accusative plural form of μόνος ("only") and must therefore be rendered "men only." That "men only" is here the sole possible translation of μόνους is confirmed by the rules of Greek grammar, which demand the employment of different forms of μόνος if referring generally to people irrespective of gender or particularly to women. If Paul wanted to connote both women and men, he would have used the neuter accusative plural μονά, which means "only" without making any gender distinction; moreover, Paul would have used the feminine accusative plural μονάς to connote "women only." Second, since the gender of μόνους is the same as the term it modifies, namely the second–person plural accusative pronoun ὑμᾶς ("you"), ὑμᾶς is masculine as well, denoting "you men" rather than the generic "you." These two observations disclose Paul's intended meaning of the Greek sentence in which the terms under discussion appear: "Or did the word of God originate with *you men*, or to *you men only* has it come?" This sentiment provides the key to exegetically unlocking the remainder of the passage, for it indicates in no uncertain terms that Paul disagreed sharply with the preceding thought–unit or paragraph. Far from attempting to silence women, therefore, Paul was rebuking the Corinthian men for prohibiting women from speaking in the assemblies, as he regarded such a restriction as tantamount to alleging that the Word of God belonged properly to the men and merely derivatively to any woman who was married to one of them. Paul summarily exposed the absurdity of this allegation with our key sentiment, a two–part rhetorical question whose form (not to mention the context) required a negative answer for each part. Obviously the Word of God neither originated with men nor has come only to men; hence it is ridiculous, and contrary to the character of the Gospel, to act as though the Word belonged properly to men by disallowing women from discoursing about it or asking questions about it in church. For these reasons, the preceding thought–unit is shown not to belong to Paul, but is rather Paul's quotation of the Corinthians' position from the letter they had previously sent him, his response to which letter constituted in large part the purpose of 1 Corinthians. This conclusion explains perfectly the aforementioned paragraph breaks, as Paul would clearly compose two shifts in thought when alternating from his own counsel to the position of the Corinthians back to his own counsel again.

Moreover, the accuracy of our conclusion is guaranteed by the undisputed presence of this device five other times in 1 Corinthians (6:12–13; 7:1–2; 8:1; 8:8; 10:23), in which Paul quotes a position from the Corinthians' letter with which he disagrees and then refutes it. We shall abbreviate this quotation–refutation device accordingly as *QRD*. Assessing the grammatical structure of these five instances, one more explicitly and four less explicitly evince the presence of *QRD* than 14:33–38, such that the certainty of *QRD* in the latter four logically necessitates the presence of *QRD* in 14:33–38. The most explicit instance is 7:1–2, the recognition of which led to the scholarly discovery of the other four instances during the last century: "But concerning (Περὶ δὲ) that which you wrote about (ὧν ἐγράψατε), 'It is good for a man not to have sex with a woman.' But because of (διὰ δὲ) sexual immorality, each man should have sex with his own wife and each woman should have sex with her own husband." Here Paul employs the phrase Περὶ δε, which introduces new discourse when found alone, then clearly identifies the extra–Pauline source of this discourse as ὧν ἐγράψατε (for the purpose of this and the remaining instances of *QRD*), and finally shifts to his refutation with the interjecting phrase διὰ δε. 8:1 is similar but far less overt: "But concerning (Περὶ δε) food sacrificed to idols, 'We know that we all have esoteric knowledge.' Esoteric knowledge causes conceit, but love builds up." With the exception of the new discourse introduction Περὶ δε, the presence of *QRD* is indicated by content alone apart from any grammatical markers. Likewise, the *QRD* in 6:12–13 and 10:23 is substantiated largely by contrast in content with only one grammatical indicator, here the indicator—the interjection δέ alone or the interjection ἀλλά conjoined with the negator οὐ(κ)—qualifying Paul's rebuttal rather than the Corinthians' stance as in the former instances. Thus the original shift from the position of Paul to that of the Corinthians goes initially undetected and is only perceived in retrospect after reading or hearing the Pauline interjection:

> "Everything is permissible for me," but not (ἀλλ᾿ οὐ) everything is beneficial. "Everything is permissible for me," but I will not (ἀλλ᾿ οὐκ ἐγὼ) be mastered by anything. "Food for the stomach and the stomach for food," but (δὲ) God will destroy them both (6:12–13).
>
> "Everything is permissible," but not (ἀλλ᾿ οὐ) everything is beneficial. "Everything is permissible," but not (ἀλλ᾿ οὐ) everything is constructive (10:23).

In the same way, the *QRD* in 8:7–8 goes undetected until Paul's interjection οὔτε:

> Since some have become so accustomed to idols, they still think of the food they eat as having been sacrificed to an idol, and their conscience, being weak, is defiled: "Food will not bring us close to God." Neither are we worse off if we do not eat, nor are we better off if we do (οὔτε ἐὰν μὴ φάγωμεν ὑστερούμεθα, οὔτε ἐὰν φάγωμεν περισσεύομεν).

Of special note is the Pauline two–part refutation, which comprises a direct structural parallel to the two–part refutation in 14:36: "ἢ ἀφ᾿ ὑμῶν ὁ λόγος τοῦ θεοῦ ἐξῆλθεν, ἢ εἰς ὑμᾶς μόνους κατήντησεν." The double interjection οὔτε... οὔτε ("neither . . . nor") qualifying both halves of the 8:8 refutation is analogous to the double interjection ἤ... ἤ ("or . . . or") qualifying both halves of the 14:36 refutation.

In sum, 14:33–38 features both of the two possible species of grammatical indicators possible in *QRD*s—an introducer of new discourse governing the Corinthian quotation and an interjection governing the Pauline refutation— while each of the four established *QRD*s in 6:12–13, 8:1, 8:8, and 10:23 contains only one of these species. Only the foundational *QRD* in 7:1, like 14:33–38, features both, along with the unique frank acknowledgment of the Corinthian correspondence as the source material of this and all other *QRD* quotations. The linguistic evidence, then, permits no doubt that 14:33–38 is a *QRD* and hence that the prohibition against wives speaking in church is non–Pauline, a conclusion which can only be avoided by denying, in an incoherent recourse of desperation, the existence of four of the five firmly attested *QRD*s in 1 Corinthians.

This grammatically necessary conclusion is independently attested by the contextual evidence, which also decisively rules out Pauline authorship of 14:33–35. In 11:3–16 Paul argues that women should have their "heads covered" when praying or prophesying in church, which covering he identifies as "long hair" (v. 15):

> Every woman who prays or prophesies with her head uncovered dishonors her head. . . . Judge for yourselves: Is it proper for a woman to pray to God with her head uncovered? Does not nature itself teach you that if a man has long hair, it is degrading to him, but if a woman has long hair, it is her glory? For long hair is given to her as a covering. If anyone wants to be contentious about this, we have no other practice, nor do the churches of God (vv. 5, 13–16).

While the ramifications of this text for present church life are highly controversial, one historical element is transparently obvious, namely, Paul's view that women should pray and prophesy in church. Such explicit advocacy by Paul of religious speech by women in church illustrates the impossibility of Paul's expressing his own perspective in 14:33b–35, as it would render Paul guilty of self–contradiction. Further, we shall now call attention to the basis on which 14:33b–35 restricts women from speaking in the assemblies, namely, adherence to the ceremonial *mitzvoth* of the Torah: "They are not allowed to speak, but must be in submission, just as the Law says" (v. 34). However, this rationale flies in the face of one of the dominant themes running throughout the entire Pauline corpus: the freedom of believers from the Torah's ceremonial *mitzvoth*, *i.e.* "the works of the Law." Far from exhorting believers to keep these *mitzvoth*, Paul consistently admonished his congregations not to observe them, even going so far as to state that embracing the *mitzvoth* spelled rejection of Christ. Examples of these points are legion, of which the following portions of Paul's epistle to the Galatians, whom Paul severely upbraided for considering adoption of the *mitzvoth*, are representative.

> You foolish Galatians! Who has bewitched you? It was before your eyes that Jesus Christ was clearly exhibited as crucified! I want to learn just one thing from you: Did you receive the Spirit by doing the works of the Law, or by believing what you heard? Are you so foolish? After beginning with the Spirit, are you now trying to achieve your goal with human effort? Have you experienced so much for nothing, if it really was for nothing? Does God give you his Spirit and work miracles among you because you do the works of the Law, or because you believe what you heard?....For all who rely on observing the Law are under a curse, for it is written: "Cursed is everyone who does not observe and obey all the things written in the Book of the Law". . . . Before faith came, we were imprisoned by the Law, locked up until faith should be revealed. Therefore the Law was our pedagogue until Christ came, so that we might be justified by faith. But now that faith has come, we are no longer under a pedagogue. . . . Now, however, that you have come to know God, or rather to be known by God, how can you turn back to the weak and miserable rudiments, whose slaves you want to be once more? You are observing special days, months, seasons, and years! I am afraid I have labored over you in vain. . . . It is for freedom that Christ has set us free. Stand firm, then, and do not let yourselves be burdened again by a yoke of slavery. . . . You who want to be justified by the Law have cut yourselves off from Christ; you have fallen away from grace (3:1–5, 10, 23–25; 4:8–11; 5:1, 4).

In light of Paul's emphasis on liberation from the Law coupled with his warning that the *mitzvoth* could only be observed on pain of alienation from Christ, it is unthinkable that Paul would have demanded the ecclesiastical silence of women by virtue of obedience to the *mitzvoth*. Among the Corinthians, rather, it seems clear that 14:33b–35 originated in the Judaizing faction of their church, which stressed obedience to the *mitzvoth* as necessary for salvation and which Paul vehemently opposed. Regarding these Judaizers who identified themselves as "belonging to Cephas" (1:12) and disputed Paul's apostleship (4:1–5; 9:1–18), Paul inveighed against them as "false apostles and deceitful workmen who masquerade as apostles of Christ" (2 Cor. 11:13) and warned their fellow Corinthians that such self–proclaimed "super–apostles" (2 Cor. 11:5; 12:11) preach a "different Jesus," a "different spirit," and a "different gospel" than the Way which lead only to damnation (2 Cor. 11:3–4).

The foregoing evidence conclusively demonstrates that in 1 Corinthians 14:33–38 Paul was not forbidding women to speak in church, but in the opposite vein was harshly reprimanding the Corinthian men for their arrogance in attempting to ecclesiastically silence their female equals and was insisting as a commandment of the Lord that women play the same roles in worship as men. It is one of the most tragic ironies in the history of Bible translation that the very text Paul penned to guarantee the unrestricted ecclesiastical participation of women has been unwittingly yet effectively falsified to deny women this right. From the Latin Vulgate to the KJV, the preexisting cultural stereotype that men ought to hold authoritative, and women subservient, positions has been all too hastily read into Scripture, thereby blocking the presuppositionless approach (wherein the translator assumes no knowledge of what the original "must have said" before rendering it in the receptor language) necessary for the close reading of the Greek text which discloses its rejection of this stereotype in ecclesiastical matters. Then in the last few centuries, a somewhat different problem has blinded translators to the passage's true meaning: the unbroken, unquestioned, and therefore either consciously or unconsciously reverenced, tradition of how 14:33–38 has been rendered since the fourth century, along with the corollary of popular disquiet over perceived scholarly alterations in the meaning of the biblical text to suit contemporary leanings. Today we face the further irony that Western society, which stresses "female liberation from male domination" to such a degree that it unbiblically blurs gender roles and thus undermines the natural complementarity between the sexes, actually inhibits popular Christian acceptance of the grammatico–historical exegesis of the pertinent text, as its implication that women ought to perform functions in the church which they have traditionally been denied raises lay suspicion that scholars have tampered with Paul to make him "politically correct." While there are cases where such suspicion is rooted in fact (homosexual ordination, abortion advocacy, etc.), in this instance it is based sheerly on popular ignorance of the original language of the New Testament. Regardless of whatever tension may exist at any time between church and culture, we must follow the authorial intent of 14:33–38, which Paul reminds us stems not from his own opinion but was commanded by Jesus himself.

1 Timothy 2:8–15

Again the NIV presents the usual rendering, of which other English translations (NASB, NAB, ESV) are only negligibly different:

I want men everywhere to lift up holy hands in prayer, without anger or disputing. I also want women to dress modestly, with decency and propriety, not with braided hair or gold or pearls or expensive clothes, but with good deeds, appropriate for women who profess to worship God. A woman should learn in quietness and full submission. I do not permit a woman to teach or to have authority over a man; she must be silent. For Adam was formed first, then Eve. And Adam was not the one deceived; it was the woman who was deceived and became a sinner. But women will be saved through childbearing—if they continue in faith, love and holiness with propriety.

The integrity of this pericope as a single paragraph is unanimously attested by New Testament scholars and thus all versions. In order to avert the prohibition of women from leadership positions in the church which many believe follows from the traditional rendering, some scholars resort to the extreme position of denying the authority and authenticity of 1 Timothy as the Word of God. Appealing to the marked divergence between the writing styles of the Pastoral Epistles and of the undisputed or Proto–Pauline Epistles, these scholars not only reason that Paul did not pen the Pastorals, a hypothesis in no way inimical to a proper understanding of biblical inerrancy, but proceed to contend that the Pauline disciple who composed these works drastically parted company from his teacher on the issue of female ecclesial equality and thus failed to faithfully represent the position of Paul. Unlike the former supposition, the latter claim flies directly in the face of biblically inerrancy and, even assuming an uninspired Bible for the sake of argument, proves to be far too extreme and harmful a literary procedure for solving the dilemma, analogous to the quack who cures the headache by decapitating the patient! Before analyzing the Greek text, we shall lay out what seems to be the most plausible solution to the question of the authorship of the Pastorals in light of the historical evidence, stressing the important caveat that ours is certainly not the only possible stance for a Christian committed to the doctrine of inerrancy to take; any stance is viable which conforms to the criterion of apostolicity and recognizes the Pastorals as Scripture.

Significant new light has been thrown on the distinct writing style of the Pastorals by recent archaeological finds, which render it probable that for these epistles Paul employed an amanuensis, to whom he gave great compositional freedom.[4] Richard Longenecker has illustrated that extrabiblical nonliterary Koinē Greek papyri from the first century C.E.—*i.e.* ordinary documents rather than literary classics which thus show how the language was used in common practice—reveal the work of several different kinds of

---

4. Brown, *New Testament*, 663.

amanuenses: some who wrote by dictation, and others who composed with substantial freedom.[5] Thus, the papyri suggest that the responsibilities of an ancient secretary could range from taking dictation to expanding an outline of thought.[6] Paul's own practice likely varied with the special circumstances of the case and the particular companion whom he employed at the time.[7] Because Paul was in prison when 2 Timothy was reportedly written with his freedoms greatly restricted over his first Roman imprisonment, and the Pastorals, which unquestionably share a common literary style and thus a common author, are the last writings attributed to Paul, it is very probable that his long–time companions could be increasingly trusted to modify an annotated outline rather than copy down a verbally dictated letter. Still, Paul would be responsible for the final product, and his customary personal note at the end of each epistle shows that he carefully read them before being sent.[8] Since 2 Timothy 4:11 declares that "only Luke is with me" and striking linguistic and grammatical similarities exist between Luke–Acts and the Pastorals, the hypothesis that Luke was the amanuensis for these letters is extremely plausible.[9] The Greek text of the passage under examination, as accompanied by its interlinear formal equivalent, runs as follows:

Βούλομαι οὖν προσεύχεσθαι τοὺς ἄνδρας ἐν παντὶ τόπῳ ἐπαίροντας ὁσίους χεῖρας χωρὶς ὀργῆς καὶ διαλογισμοῦ. ὡσαύτως καὶ γυναῖκας ἐν καταστολῇ κοσμίῳ μετὰ αἰδοῦς καὶ σωφροσύνης κοσμεῖν ἑαυτάς, μὴ ἐν πλέγμασιν καὶ χρυσίῳ ἢ μαργαρίταις ἢ ἱματισμῷ πολυτελεῖ, ἀλλ' ὃ πρέπει γυναιξὶν ἐπαγγελλομέναις θεοσέβειαν, δι' ἔργων ἀγαθῶν. γυνὴ ἐν ἡσυχίᾳ μανθανέτω ἐν πάσῃ ὑποταγῇ· διδάσκειν δὲ γυναικὶ οὐκ ἐπιτρέπω οὐδὲ αὐθεντεῖν ἀνδρός, ἀλλ' εἶναι ἐν ἡσυχίᾳ. Ἀδὰμ γὰρ πρῶτος ἐπλάσθη, εἶτα Εὔα. καὶ Ἀδὰμ οὐκ ἠπατήθη, ἡ δὲ γυνὴ ἐξαπατηθεῖσα ἐν παραβάσει γέγονεν· σωθήσεται δὲ διὰ τῆς τεκνογονίας, ἐὰν μείνωσιν ἐν πίστει καὶ ἀγάπῃ καὶ ἁγιασμῷ μετὰ σωφροσύνης·

5. Richard Longenecker, "Ancient Amanuenses and the Pauline Epistles," in *New Dimensions in New Testament Study*, eds. Richard Longenecker and Merrill Tenney (Grand Rapids, Mich.: Zondervan, 1974), 283–88.

6. Longenecker, "Ancient Amanuenses," 285.

7. Luke Timothy Johnson, *The Anchor Bible: The First and Second Letters to Timothy* (New York: Doubleday, 2001), 58–59.

8. Longenecker, "Ancient Amanuenses," 289–90.

9. Johnson, *Timothy*, 89; Longenecker, "Ancient Amanuenses," 291.

²I desire that ¹Therefore ⁵should pray ⁴the husbands ³in every place, lifting up holy hands without wrath or quarreling. ²in the same way ¹And ³wives should adorn ⁵in modesty ⁷with decency and propriety ⁶adorned ⁴themselves, not in elaborate hairstyles and gold or pearls or ²attire ¹expensive, ³but ⁷which is appropriate for wives who profess religion ⁴through ⁶deeds ⁵good. ²a wife ⁴in silence ¹Let ³learn ⁵in all obedience; ¹⁰to teach ⁶but ⁸a wife ⁹neither ⁷I permit ¹¹nor to domineer a husband, but she must be in silence. ²Adam ¹For ⁴first ³was formed, then Eve; and Adam ²not ¹was ³deceived, ⁵the ⁴but ⁶wife was deceived and ⁸in transgression ⁷became; ⁹she will be saved ⁸but through the bearing of children / the childbirth, if they (pl. verb = "the husband and wife") remain in faith and love and holiness with propriety.

In Koinē Greek, the noun γυνή doubles for "woman" and "wife," while two nouns exist which may be translated "man": ἄνθρωπος, which also denotes "a human being" or "humanity"; and ἀνήρ, which also means "husband." Although typically simple to determine, it is not always apparent which meaning is intended when any of these terms are used individually. Fortunately, however, no such ambiguity exists in a combination of γυνή and one of the masculine identifiers. The rules of Greek semantics stipulate that the concurrent use of ἄνθρωπος and γυνή generically denotes members of the male and female genders, *i.e.* "man" and "woman," while the concurrent use of ἀνήρ and γυνή specifically denotes a "husband" and a "wife." There are no exceptions to this rule in the tens of thousands of nonbiblical Koinē Greek manuscripts from the first century C.E.; furthermore, in each of the other 54 New Testament pairs of ἀνήρ and γυνή outside the passage under investigation, the terms always mean "husband" and "wife" rather than "man" and "woman."[10] Since 2:8–15 repeatedly juxtaposes ἀνήρ and γυνή without a single occurrence of ἄνθρωπος, etymologically it is both inescapable that this paragraph is discussing husbands and wives in particular[11] and

---

10. G. P. Hugenburger, "Women in Church Leadership," in *The International Standard Bible Encyclopedia*, rev. ed., ed. Geoffrey W. Bromiley (Grand Rapids, Mich.: Eerdmans, 1988), 4:1099. We have already evaluated one Pauline example in 1 Corinthians 14:33–38, where the Corinthian Judaizers endeavored to silence wives in the church and pressured them to ask any questions they had about the Word of God to their husbands at home.

11. Attempting to balance this recently discovered fact, which emerged via the massive papyrological finds previously alluded to, with popular opposition to perceived academic alterations in the Bible, the NRSV and TNIV have retained the traditional renderings of "man" and "woman" in the body of the text but

impossible for it to be discussing men and women in general.[12] But the inference that 2:8–15 forbids women from holding teaching or authority posi-

---

have called attention to the actual renderings "husband" and "wife" in a marginal note.

12. The attempt by the eminent commentator Douglas Moo to argue that 1 Timothy 2:8–15 constitutes the exception to this rule is fraught with problems: "If Paul had wanted to confine his prohibition in verse 12 to wives in relationship to their husbands, we would have expected him to use a definite article or possessive pronoun with *man*: 'I am not permitting a woman to teach or to exercise authority over *her* man.' (Paul readily made a similar distinction elsewhere in writing of male/female relationships. Women, he said, are to submit to "their own [*idiois*] husbands" [Ephesians 5:22, NASB; cf. Colossians 3:18].) And the context (verses 8–9) clearly addresses men and women generally as members of the church, not (as in Ephesians 5:22–33; Colossians 3:18–19) as husbands and wives, as members of family units; it is not only husbands who are to lift holy hands in prayer, but all the men, and not only wives who are to dress modestly, but all the women (verses 9–10). Therefore, the prohibitions of verse 12 are applicable to all women in the church in their relationships with all men in the church" ("What Does It Mean Not to Teach or Have Authority Over Men? 1 Timothy 2:11–15" [Louisville: Council on Biblical Manhood and Womanhood, 1997], 9). Moo's response fails to convince on several levels. His claim that Paul would have used a definite article or possessive pronoun with ἀνήρ if he meant to connote the husband–wife relationship is based on selective use of evidence; while the verses he cites from Ephesians and Colossians, as well as 1 Corinthians 14:35, indeed satisfy this requirement, equally many Pauline texts which unmistakably deal with the marital relationship do not. Thus in 1 Corinthians 7:10, Paul exhorts on the basis of the dominical oral tradition, "To the married I give this command (not I, but the Lord): A wife must not separate from a husband (γυναῖκα ἀπὸ ἀνδρὸς μὴ χωρισθῆναι)," which contains neither definite article nor possessive pronoun and, contra Moo, where the husband in question obviously belongs to the wife! Similarly, 1 Corinthians 11:7 (like 1 Tim. 2:8–15) appeals to the first married couple, Adam and Eve, in its account of why husbands should wear short, and wives long, hair: "A husband should not cover his head, since he is the image and glory of God, but the wife is the glory of a husband (ἡ γυνὴ δὲ δόξα ἀνδρος ἐστιν)"; again, despite that no definite article or possessive pronoun accompanies ἀνδρος, no one would deny that the wife is the glory of her own husband and not someone else's husband. To cite an example from the Pastorals, Titus 2:4 instructs women to be φιλάνδρους ("lovers of husbands"), a conjunction of the infinitive φιλειν ("to love") and the anarthrous accusative plural ἀνδρους ("husbands") which cannot be formed if ἀνδρους is accompanied by the definite article τούς or the possesive pronoun ἰδιους. Moreover, even if it were true, Moo's claim would carry

tions in church depends for its validity upon the premise that the paragraph presents guidelines for proper relations between men and women in general and so between men and women in church. Instead the paragraph lays down

---

no weight for three reasons. First, it does not deal seriously with the significant possibility that Paul wrote neither Ephesus nor the Pastorals, in which case the Proto–Pauline Epistles, Ephesus–Colossians, and the Pastorals would have three different authors, thus abnegating any implications of a grammatical argument from the first two epistolary groups to the third. Second, even if Paul personally penned all three epistolary groups, the argument both arbitrarily and implausibly reads significance into Paul's slightest departure from his previous use of grammar—the absence of a definite article or possessive pronoun—when such departures are commonplace in the Pauline corpus and are never elsewhere assigned any significance, let alone such powerful significance as to overturn a previously unfalsified etymological rule. Third, if, as I have argued, Paul used Luke, who provided substance to an annotated outline based on his knowledge of Paul's teachings, as an amanuensis to produce the Pastoral Epistles, then no conclusion follows from any grammatical difference between the Pastorals and other Pauline writings. In this case, one could actually reverse Moo's argument in favor of 1 Timothy 2:8–15 treating the marital relationship, as Luke would then simply be following his stylistic convention of *not* accompanying the γυνή–paired ἀνήρ with the definite article or possessive pronoun when discussing husbands and wives (a convention seen throughout Luke–Acts; for instance, Lk. 2:36 describes the prophetess Anna as having "lived with a husband [ζήσασα μετὰ ἀνδρὸς] seven years after her marriage," where the ἀνήρ in question obviously refers to her own husband and not some other unspecified "man"). As for Moo's further allegation that the context shows that the etymological "husband–wife" rule does not apply here, this is simply flawed reasoning, since the general applicability of any moral imperative does nothing to determine the size of the audience to whom the imperative was addressed. The fact that lifting holy hands in prayer and dressing modestly are moral imperatives which respectively pertain to all men and all women in no way implies that the author could have only issued such imperatives to men and women in general and not to husbands and wives in particular, any more than the general applicability of "whatever you do, work at it with all your heart, as working for the Lord, and not for humans" (Col. 3:23; *cf.* Eph. 6:7) to all believers implies that this imperative could not have been specifically addressed to slaves, as it in fact was (Col. 3:22–25; *cf.* Eph. 6:5–8), but rather must have been generally addressed to all Christians. Hence it is impossible to legitimately argue from the obvious universality of the moral imperatives in vv. 8–10 to the disregarding of an established grammatical rule to the universality of an otherwise far from obviously universal moral imperative in v. 12. One suspects that when a scholar as

the regulations for a healthy marital relationship based upon the very nature of marriage itself, a fact clearly evidenced by the appeal to the primal married couple, Adam and Eve, focusing specifically on the consequences of their breaking the Edenic covenant for the marital relationship (*cf.* Gen. 3:15–16). Moreover, it is obvious that for followers of the Way "the bearing of children" can only legitimately transpire in the binding relationship between wife and husband, thus leaving the textual remark on childbearing inexplicable if the passage were referring to women and men in general. Since no implications concerning the admissibility of women or men to ecclesiastical offices can be validly drawn from these directives for married life, 1 Timothy 2:8–15 is shown to be independent of and therefore irrelevant to questions of church polity.

Having articulated what this passage does not indicate, we are now in a position to explore its true significance. Here the author is giving instructions to remedy the problems plaguing marital relationships in the church at Ephesus, to which all scholars agree the epistle was written regardless of authorship or date of composition. Contemporary historical accounts of from extrabiblical sources disclose that the prevailing religious climate in Ephesus placed strains on married life not found elsewhere in the Mediterranean basin. Ephesus was the only city in ancient times where the Greek goddess Artemis (Roman name Diana) was worshiped as the primary deity and not merely a secondary one, as evidenced by the city's magnificent Temple of Artemis, one of the Seven Wonders of the Ancient World.[13] Artemis was assigned several attributes socioculturally uncharacteristic for a female deity: she governed the hunt, wild animals, and the wilderness, thus causing her to be most frequently depicted in cult statues as a huntress with her bow and arrows. But since she also served as the goddess of fertility, the personality of Artemis gave rise in Ephesus to a unique and syncretic feminine ideal which blended seemingly mutually exclusive elements, namely, the traditionally masculine functions of hunting and killing with the traditionally feminine functions of childbearing and motherhood.[14] Therefore, the myths of Artemis portray an unusually aggressive and possessive female who

---

careful and thorough as Moo offers such a surprisingly weak argument, the scholar is unwittingly examining the text through the lenses of confessional presuppositions rather than examining it as though nothing were at stake in the outcome.

13. Sharon Hodgin Gritz, *Paul, Women Teachers, and the Mother Goddess at Ephesus: A Study of 1 Timothy 2:9–15 in Light of the Religious and Cultural Milieu of the First Century* (Lanham, Md.: University Press of America, 1991), 11-27.

14. Ibid., 28–36.

unleashed her wrath on anyone who disobeyed her wishes, slaying the female children of Niobe with her bow and arrow and demanding, on pain of defeat in the Trojan War, that Agamemnon sacrifice his daughter Iphigenia as punishment for killing a stag in her sacred grove. Distinctive to Ephesus was a religious climate where all young girls were initiated into the cult of Artemis at puberty and taught to emulate her, which lessons included exerting disciplinary mastery over their future husbands, as Artemis did with all males in her life, and relegating these husbands to a servile role.[15] Not surprisingly, the author of 1 Timothy regards the Ephesian feminine ideal as flagrantly violating the order of marriage naturally prevailing since the events of Genesis 3. Endeavoring to restore and yet transform the natural order in accord with the redemptive work of Jesus, the author offers his solution by way of a Christocentric commentary on the following text from Genesis 3:15–16:

> So Yahweh God said to the serpent, "Because you have done this, cursed are you above all cattle and above all wild animals; upon your belly you will crawl, and you will eat dust all the days of your life. And I will put enmity between you and the woman, and between your seed and her seed; he will crush your head, and you will strike his heel." To the woman he said, "I will greatly increase your pain in childbearing; in pain you will give birth to children. Your desire will be for your husband, and he will have dominion over you."

While the import of the commands for wives to dress modestly and to clothe themselves with good deeds, reflective of their worship of God, rather than with luxurious garments are self-evident (vv. 9–10), the commands and exegetical remarks in vv. 11–15 require further explanation. Quite significant is the infinitive διδάσκειν ("to teach") in the phrase "I permit a wife neither to teach nor to domineer a husband," which when paired with any other term of authority refers not to "teaching" or "being a teacher" in the general sense but rather in the specific sense of the master–disciple relationship. Here the clear term of authority αὐθεντεῖν ("to domineer") guarantees that teaching as a master would a disciple is in view. Such teaching included the right to correct, chastise, and orient the disciple toward desired behavior through the implementation of punishment, thereby setting the disciple's mind in the order the master deemed proper. On two occasions Jesus illustrated the master–disciple relationship connoted by διδάσκειν. In Matthew 23:8–12 Jesus uses the noun form διδάσκαλος as a synonym for "Rabbi":

---

15. Ibid., 37–49.

But you are not to be called "Rabbi," for you have only one Teacher
(διδάσκαλος) and you are all sisters and brothers. And do not call anyone on earth "Father," for you have one Father, who is in the heavens.
Nor are you to be called "Master," for you have one Master, the Christ.
The greatest among you will be your servant. For whoever exalts oneself will be humbled, and whoever humbles oneself will be exalted.

In conjunction with the terms "Rabbi," "Father," and "Master," the connotation of power and authority in διδάσκαλος is so strong that Jesus forbids his
disciples to invoke the title for anyone besides himself. Recall from chapter
one, however, that when used by itself διδάσκαλος means "scholar-
teacher" and is one of the four permanent church offices which the Pauline
Epistles stipulate must be filled (Eph. 4; 1 Tim. 3); hence the dominical prohibition that a believer cannot be a διδάσκαλος in a master–disciple context
does not prohibit a believer from holding the ecclesiastical office of διδάσκαλος or serving as a διδάσκαλος in an ordinary instructive context.
This understanding is reinforced by Mark 10:42–43, where Jesus admonishes his disciples to be servants rather than "to rule over"
(κατεξουσιάζουσιν, a synonym of διδάσκειν coupled with a term of authority) one another like rulers outside the Kingdom of God. Confirming our
interpretation of the dominical texts, Charles Powell observes, "What is especially instructive about these two accounts is that the cautions of Jesus are
not simply set against being 'teachers' or 'rulers' in a general sense but
rather condemn the kind of un–Christian practices one might expect to find
among unbelievers."[16]

Due to their upbringing, however, many believing wives in Ephesus
naturally followed in the stead of Artemis by "teaching" their husbands like
a master teaches a disciple, taking it upon themselves to reprove and punish
their husbands for unwanted behavior, and "domineering" over them by
playing the dominant gender role in the relationship.[17] The author of 1 Timothy perceives such actions as diametrically opposed both to the created order
as originally intended by God, who he created man before woman, and to the
created order after the breaking of the initial covenant by Adam and Eve,
because God specifically ordered Eve that "he [Adam] will have dominion
over you" (Gen. 3:16) as a result of her being deceived by Satan into violating the covenant. Instead, the wife, as a disciple of Jesus, must learn in silence with all obedience, where it is especially noteworthy that the author

16. Charles Powell, "Paul's Concept of Teaching and 1 Timothy 2:12," presented at the 49th annual meeting of the Evangelical Theological Society in November 1988.

17. Gritz, *Paul, Women Teachers, and the Mother Goddess*, 106–17.

refrains from committing the opposite fallacy by demanding that she learn from her husband in silence with all obedience. Rather, the author omits the indirect object of the verb μανθανέτω (imperative form of μανθάνω) altogether, which practice in biblical usage consistently comprises a reverential circumlocution for God. That God is the implied yet obvious being from whom the wife must learn in silence with all obedience is further indicated by the fact that μανθάνειν ("to learn"; infinitive form of μανθάνω) constitutes the direct counterpart to διδάσκειν paired with a term of authority; in other words, μανθάνειν means "to learn" as a disciple in the master–disciple relationship, which learning Jesus insisted could only be validly done from him. As indicated by Matthew 23:8–12, making the husband the "teacher" over his wife in a master–disciple relationship would be just as sacrilegious as making the wife the "teacher" over her husband, since only Jesus may be the "teacher" over his disciples, believing husbands and wives alike. At this point we may validly draw the textual application that in a marital relationship, a wife must not take the place of Christ for her husband, and a husband must not take the place of Christ for his wife. While not allowing the husband to be "teacher" over his wife, the author clearly commands that the wife submits to her husband ἐν ἡσυχίᾳ ("in silence"), which does not mean "never saying a word" but "quietly listening in a respectful attitude of stillness and receptivity"; note, for instance, that the same term characterizes the believer's relationship to God in the preceding paragraph— "that we may live peaceful and quiet (ἡσύχιον) lives in all godliness and holiness," which "pleases God our Savior" (2:2–3).

Finally, we must discuss the meaning of the enigmatic phrase "but she will be saved through the bearing of children / the childbirth (τῆς τεκνογονίας)," which, as my translation indicates, is a brilliant double entendre. Both meanings refer back to Genesis 3:15–16 and show how, through the redemptive work of Christ, believing wives are spiritually delivered from the curse imposed on Eve while extending the benefits of such deliverance to their believing husbands. This extension is apparent in the remarkable shift from singular to plural, seen in the transition from the singular verb σωθήσεται ("she [antecedent: 'the wife'] will be saved") to the plural verb μείνωσιν ("they remain"), whose antecedent is necessarily "the husband and wife" since the preceding vv. 11–14 only use singular forms of ἀνήρ and γυνή. Moreover, the conditional phrase "if they (the husband and wife) remain in faith and love and holiness with propriety" shows that the deliverance accomplished through Jesus is not automatically extended to all men and women but only comes to those who display spiritual perseverance, the mark of sincere commitment to Christ. First, the connotation of τῆς τεκνογονίας as "the bearing of children" indicates that the believing wife is saved from the eternal judgment of God against sin, despite the fact of her birthpains, the experience of which originally stemmed from God's punishment of sin. The "they" here denotes that both she and her husband may rest assured that she is spiritually secure, as her pain in giving birth to children does not contradict her salvation. [18] Second, the connotation of τῆς τεκνογονίας as "the childbirth" refers to the birth of Jesus and signifies that, in fulfillment of the *protoevangelium* in Genesis 3:15 that the woman's "seed" would crush the serpent's heel, the curse which began with the transgression of the faithless Eve was objectively undone by the birth accomplished through the faithful Mary. [19] In this case, the "they" denotes that the spiritual liberation from the penalty and power of sin, a blessing which emanates from Mary's childbirth of Jesus, stretches not only to wives but to their husbands as well.

Positive New Testament Evidence for Female Leadership in the Church

In addition to 1 Corinthians 11:3–16 and, as we have demonstrated, 14:33–38, there are several texts which explicitly show that women held leadership positions in the New Testament church. Proceeding in chronological order via date of probable authorship, we shall begin with the lengthiest Pauline enumeration of female leaders in Romans 16:1–7, 12.

> I commend to you our sister Phoebe, who is a deacon (διάκονον) of the church in Cenchrea, that you receive her in the Lord in a manner worthy of the saints and that you give her any help she may need from you; for she herself has also been a great help to many people, including me. Greet Prisca and Aquila, my fellow-workers (συνεργούς) in Christ Jesus, who risked their own lives to save mine. Not only I but all the churches of the Gentiles give thanks to them. Greet also the church that meets at their house. . . . Greet Mary, who has worked very hard (πολλὰ ἐκοπίασεν) for you. Greet Andronicus and Junia (fem.), [20] my

---

18. Robert H. Gundry, *A Survey of the New Testament*, 3rd ed. (Grand Rapids, Mich.: Zondervan, 1994), 414.

19. Irenaeus would famously pick up on this line of reasoning in his doctrine of recapitulation; see his *Against Heresies*, 3.18.1, 22.1–3, 23.1; 4.38.1, 40.3; 5.1.2, 14.1, 16.2, 23.2, 36.3.

20. That the nominative form of the accusative Ἰουνίαν was the feminine Ἰουνία is attested by the more than 250 instances of Ἰουνία in contemporary Koinē manuscripts without a single instance of a masculine variant of this name.

relatives who have been in prison with me; they are outstanding among the apostles, and they were in Christ before I was. . . . Greet Tryphena and Tryphosa, those women who are the hard–workers (τάς κοπιώσας) in the Lord. Greet my dear friend Persis, another woman who has worked very hard (πολλά ἐκοπίασεν) in the Lord.

From this passage we see that women not only played prominent roles in the first–century Way, but that their leadership was indispensable to the spread of the Gospel in general and Paul's missionary journeys in particular. Paul revealed that Phoebe was a διάκονον (accusative of διάκονος) at the church of Cenchrae, the only Koinē term for "deacon" and thus exactly the same noun used to denote deacons known to be male (*cf.* 1 Tim. 3:12). The wife–husband pair Prisca (same as the variant spelling Priscilla) and Aquila were Paul's συνεργούς, fellow–workers in the sense of being "people of the same trade" and "colleagues," in the Lord. A grammatico–historical exegesis of this text would strongly imply that Prisca was engaged in exactly the same kind of work as Paul, including teaching and preaching.[21] This implication is independently confirmed by Acts 18:26: "Apollos began to speak boldly in the synagogue. When Priscilla and Aquila heard him, they invited him to their house, and *they explained* to him the Way of God more accurately." Two observations are worthy of note: both Prisca and Aquila, as indicated via italics, explained the Way to Apollos rather than simply Aquila; and both Paul and Luke listed Prisca ahead of Aquila, a severe departure from Koinē literary practice, in which the husband would always be listed ahead of his wife, and thus stands in need of explanation. According to the majority of contemporary scholars as well as that of past exegetes, the only plausible explanation is that Prisca served as leader of the ministry team comprising herself and Aquila. Prisca's spiritual prominence over Aquila is underscored by Linda L. Belleville:

For the first 1500 years of church history Paul's reference to a female apostle was accepted without question; it is only after the Reformation that translators starting with the KJV, finding unthinkable the then countercultural idea that Paul could have termed a woman as an apostle, attempted to masculinize the name "Junia" to "Junias" (unbeknownst to them, a failed attempt because Junias, despite its English appearance, would not be a masculine name in Koinē, but is rather the genitive form of the feminine Junia).

21. Aída Besançon Spencer, *Beyond the Curse: Women Called to Ministry* (Nashville: Nelson, 1985), 118–19, points out that in the Pauline corpus a συνεργούς "is someone whom Paul considers a colleague placed in a position of authority similar to his own position."

What is unusual, however, is that when Luke refers to their occupation as tent makers, the order is "Aquila and Priscilla" (Acts 18:2; cf. 1 Cor. 16:19), but when Luke and Paul speak from a ministry point of view, the order is always "Priscilla and Aquila." This would suggest that of the two, it was Priscilla who possessed the dominant ministry and leadership skills.[22]

Such was also the conclusion reached by John Chrysostom (347–407), perhaps the greatest Greek New Testament exegete in church history, in his gloss on Paul's placement of Prisca before Aquila: "He did not do so without reason: the wife must have had, I think, greater piety than her husband. This is not simple conjecture; its confirmation is evident in the Acts."[23] The text discloses that a church met in the house of Prisca and Aquila; thus, in modern terminology, we would say that this married couple "co–pastored" a church.[24]

Employing various forms of the verb κοπιάω ("to work hard, to labor"), Paul then praised four women—Mary, Tryphena, Tryphosa, and Persis—for their service to the church, with the intensity of the labors of Mary and Persis acknowledged by the adverb πολλά (idiomatically "very"; literally "strongly" or "greatly"). Although the sort of labor these two performed cannot be discerned from this text, more can be gleaned concerning Tryphena and Tryphosa, for whom Paul shifted from his standard use of the verb κοπιάω (ἐκοπίασεν is simply the aorist form) and transformed it into the aorist substantive participle τάς κοπιώσας. Τάς κοπιώσας thus functions as a verbal noun meaning "the hard–workers," a different significance than that connoted by the verb ἐκοπίασεν ("has worked hard") used with Mary and Persis; the former seems to denote an official vocation within the Roman church, while the latter does not necessarily entail more than individual acts of hard work. To give an English analogy, the difference between τάς κοπιώσας and ἐκοπίασεν is thus the same as between "the fishers," for whom fishing is a permanent occupation, and "she/he has fished," which

---

22. Linda L. Belleville, *Women Leaders and the Church* (Grand Rapids, Mich.: Baker, 2000), 68; for an extended discussion of this topic see Ben Witherington III, *Women and the Genesis of Christianity* (Cambridge: Cambridge University Press, 1990), 218–25. Assuming that 2 Timothy originated with Luke and Paul, 2 Timothy 4:19 illustrates the same point.

23. John Chrysostom, *Homilies on the Epistle to the Romans*, XXXI.6.

24. Although certainly not agreeing with all aspects of Gilbert Bilezikian's egalitarianism, on this score his analysis is correct (*Beyond Sex Roles: What the Bible Says about a Woman's Place in Church and Family*, 2nd ed. [Grand Rapids, Mich.: Baker, 1985], 201).

discloses nothing about the person's occupation and could simply denote one or more finite acts of fishing. It is hard to deny, therefore, that Tryphena and Tryphosa held positions of authority in the church at Rome.

Perhaps most significantly, this passage reveals that there was at least one female apostle, Junia, who along with her husband and fellow apostle Andronicus had been in prison with their relative Paul. Not only is Junia an apostle, a holder of the highest ecclesiastical office foundational to the early church, but she is ranked as "outstanding among the apostles." Aída Besançon Spencer spells out several key aspects of the role Junia played as an apostle in Rome.

> Junia (and her male colleague Andronicus) would be Paul's counterpart in Rome. As an apostle, sent by God as an eyewitness to the resurrection of Jesus, Paul would lay the foundation for a church. Certainly authoritative preaching would have to be part of such a testimony. Junia, along with Andronicus, apparently laid the foundation for the churches at Rome.[25]

Since a prerequisite for being an apostle was having objectively seen the risen Jesus (*i.e.* present in space and time such that he could have been perceived by any other person on hand rather than subjectively present in the mind of, and thus only perceptible to, the observer),[26] Paul's description entails that Junia was an eyewitness to the fact of Jesus' resurrection. This fact fits well with the pre-Pauline memorizable oral tradition now preserved in 1 Corinthians 15:3b–6a, 7, which originated in the early Jerusalem church and dates no later than 35 C.E. Listing the eyewitnesses in chronological order, this primitive creed recounts that Jesus was seen "by the Twelve" (v. 5) and later "by all the apostles" (v. 7), which designation illustrates there were more apostles in the Church than the Twelve prior to Paul's conversion. Then to substantiate his own apostolic authority, Paul followed up his quotation of the creed with the autobiographical statement, "But last of all, as to

---

25. Spencer, *Beyond the Curse*, 102.

26. This is why Paul goes to great lengths to emphasize the objective character of his resurrection appearance: unlike most visions, which are subjective in character, Jesus was objectively present on the Damascus Road, causing Paul's companions to see the light and hear Jesus' voice (Acts 22:9). Paul's companions could not understand what Jesus was saying to Paul because Jesus was speaking in Hebrew (τῇ Ἑβραΐδι διαλέκτω, "in the Hebrew dialect"; Acts 26:14), a language known in the first century only to those with rabbinic training like Paul and not understandable to common Jews, who spoke Aramaic as a first language and Greek as a necessary second.

one untimely born, he was seen also by me. For I am the least of the apostles and do not even deserve to be called an apostle, because I persecuted the church of God. But by the grace of God I am what I am" (1 Cor. 15:8–10). That Junia and her husband Andronicus were included in the group of "all the apostles" who saw the risen Jesus before Paul's Damascus Road experience harmonizes perfectly with Paul's explanatory remark that "they were in Christ before I was" (Rom. 16:7).

Amidst his efforts to clear up a disagreement between Euodia and Synctyche, Paul designated these two women as συνεργούς, or fellow–workers of the same trade, and specified the type of work in which they were mutually engaged with him in Philippians 4:2–3.

> I entreat Euodia and Syntyche to live in harmony in the Lord. Indeed I ask you, true companion, to help these women who have contended (συνήθλησάν) at my side in the cause of the gospel, along with Clement and the rest of my fellow–workers (συνεργῶν), whose names are in the book of life.

The verb συναθλέω, of which συνήθλησάν is an aorist form, is an oratorical and legal term meaning "to contend alongside someone else in public defense and debate," which by definition entailed apologetic dialogue on the part of the contenders. Far from the notion that teaching functions were forbidden to women, Euodia and Syntyche were praised for their courage in publicly defending the faith alongside Paul (*cf*. Php. 1:16). Against the possible objection that this case of public declaration and exposition of the Gospel by women outside the worship assembly carries no distributive force for women doing the same inside the worship assembly, Stanley J. Grenz rightly perceives that, historically speaking, such a differentiation would be anachronistic for the first–century Church: "To pass by this incident as '*unofficial* guidance' as distinct from '*official* teaching leadership' is to draw too fine a line between authoritative and so–called nonauthoritative teaching among the people of God."[27] The Prison Epistles, along with the probably concurrently written Acts, describes women who were leaders of house churches, including Apphia (Phm. 2), Nympha (Col. 4:15), Mary the mother of Mark (Acts 12:12), and Lydia (Acts 16:14–15). Further, Acts confirms the testimony of Paul (1 Cor. 11:3–16) that women, such as the four daughters of Philip, served as prophets in the early Church: "Leaving the next day, we reached Caesarea and stayed at the house of Philip the evangelist, one of the

---

27. Stanley J. Grenz, *Women in the Church: A Biblical Theology of Women in Ministry* (Downers Grove, Ill.: InterVarsity Press, 1995), 83.

Seven. He had four virgin daughters who prophesied" (Acts 21:8–9). In her analysis of the pertinent ancient evidence, Karen L. King explains the function these women prophets performed: "As prophets, women's roles would have included not only ecstatic public speech, but preaching, teaching, leading prayer, and perhaps even performing the eucharist meal."[28]

The Pastoral Epistles relate the existence of female elders in the Ephesian and Cretan churches. 1 Timothy 5:1–2 utilizes the standard term for "elder," πρεσβύτερος (from which the English noun "presbyter" is derived), to describe both men and women: "Do not rebuke an male elder (Πρεσβυτέρῳ, masculine dative singular of πρεσβύτερος) but appeal to him as if he were a father, to the younger men as brothers, to the female elders (πρεσβυτέρας, feminine accusative plural of πρεσβύτερος) as mothers, and to the younger women as sisters, in all purity." Some complementarian critics have attempted to avoid this conclusion by arguing that πρεσβύτερος does not take its ecclesiological significance here and simply refers to "an old person," thus taking Πρεσβυτέρῳ and πρεσβυτέρας to respectively mean "old man" and "old women." Support for this view is garnished by the claim that "old man" represents the appropriate contrast to "younger men" (νεωτέρους) and likewise "old women" to "younger women" (νεωτέρας). However, this line of reasoning is a double–edged sword, which it seems here has been wielded the wrong way round. For given the universal Proto–Pauline and Deutero–Pauline usage of πρεσβύτερος as the title of the ecclesiastical office of "elder," one could similarly contend that νεωτέρους and νεωτέρας are here meant metaphorically for younger men and women in the faith rather than literally in age, a supposition that certainly does no injustice to the Proto–Pauline or Deutero–Pauline usage of these latter terms (that it actually does justice to these terms is prominently seen in the Pauline metaphorical use of "the recently born / young / new man" [τὸν νέον, the positive adjective of which νεωτέρους and νεωτέρας are comparative forms] in, e.g., Col. 3:10). Since reasoning from the literal use of terms which could plausibly be taken either literally or metaphorically to overturn the meanings consistently affixed by an author to contextually adjacent terms commits an obvious *non sequitur*, and since reasoning from in reverse from the univocal terms to the equivocal ones is logically sound, the second exercise of our argumentative sword proves superior. Further evidence against the notion that the Pastoral author intended a contrast between the physically young and old comes from the fact that, in any case, the natural converse to νεωτέρους is γένος ("old man") not πρεσβύτερος, and the natural converse to

---

28. Karen L. King, "Women in Ancient Christianity: The New Discoveries," *Southern Cross Review* 42 (September 2005): 644.

νεωτέπας is γένας ("old woman") not πρεσβυτέρας. Finally, that the author was discussing the male and female elders of the Ephesian church is evident from the larger context of 1 Timothy 5, which make clear that the overall theme of this chapter is the treatment of elders in general and the possible administration of church discipline against elders in particular. We thus see from the following verses that this is precisely the same purpose expressed in 5:1–2, which warns against rebuking a πρεσβύτερος and the πρεσβυτέρας in favor of appealing to them as spiritual parents.

> Let the elders (πρεσβύτεροι, plural of πρεσβύτερος) rule well be considered worthy of double honor, especially the hard–workers (οἱ κοπιῶντες) in preaching and teaching. . . . Never accept any accusation against an elder (πρεσβυτέρου, genitive of πρεσβύτερος) except on the evidence of two or three witnesses. As for those who continue in sin, rebuke in the presence of all, so that the rest also will be fearful of sinning. In the presence of God and of Christ Jesus and of the elect angels, I charge you to maintain these principles without bias, doing nothing in a spirit of partiality (5:17, 19–21).

As a fascinating aside, we find in these verses a further reference to the verbal noun "the hard–workers" (οἱ κοπιῶντες, like the aforementioned aorist τάς κοπιώσας, is a substantive participle of κοπιάω), here filling in the desired information gap left by the reference to "the hard–workers" Tryphena and Tryphosa in Romans 16:12. Confirming our previous hypothesis that "the hard–workers" referred to the holders of a specific ecclesiastical office, the Pastoral author defines "the hard–workers" as elders specializing in preaching or teaching. If we allow the Deutero–Pauline Epistles to inform the Proto–Pauline Epistles, which procedure is valid on my Lukan amanuensis theory, then Tryphena and Tryphosa were preaching or teaching elders in the Roman church.

In a passage whose interpretation is ensured by the epistle's literary structure, Titus also illustrates the presence of female elders at the church of Crete. This letter is in simple alternating, or ABABA, form, with the A sections furnishing instructions for church officers and their spiritual charges and the B sections brandishing denunciations against the false teachers, especially the Judaizers, who so plagued the Cretan congregation:

A[1] (1:1–9)—Requirements for elders, including the ability to preach
    sound doctrine to their congregations and to refute false teachers
    who oppose it
B[1] (1:10–16)—Exposure of the errors committed by the false teachers

A² (2:1–3:8)—Elders must set a positive example of holy living for their flocks as well as teaching various groups within their churches how to behave in a righteous manner

B² (3:9–11)—How to identify and deal with heretics

A³ (3:12–15)—Importance of teaching believers to devote their lives to doing good

A¹ enunciates to Titus the preconditions on which he must insist before appointing anyone an elder:

> For this reason I left you in Crete, that you should set in order what was left unfinished and appoint elders (πρεσβυτέρους) in every city, as I commanded you. *A man* must be *blameless* (εἴ τίς ἐστιν ἀνέγκλητος, masculine singular), the husband of one wife, having faithful children not open to the charge of dissipation or insubordination. For the overseer (τόν ἐπίσκοπον, basis for the English words "episcopal" and "bishop") must be blameless, as a steward of God, not arrogant or quick–tempered or a drunkard or violent or greedy for gain, but rather hospitable, a lover of goodness, self–controlled, upright, holy, and disciplined. The overseer must hold firm to the sure word as it has been taught, in order to instruct others in sound doctrine and to refute those who oppose it (1:5–9).

Thus A¹ shifts from elders in general (πρεσβυτέρους) to special requirements for a male elder in particular, including blamelessness, not practicing polygamy, and having children who genuinely follow Christ, to common requirements for an overseer in general (τόν ἐπίσκοπον, a synonym of πρεσβύτερος). Not only are these transitions marked by changes in vocabulary, but they alone account for the otherwise superfluous repetition of the directive to be blameless. That this directive is given first regarding a male elder in particular and then an elder / overseer in general suggests that the position of elder is open to more than simply men. What is implicit in A¹ is explicit in A², which differentiates between male and female elders by chopping the ᵗερος ending off πρεσβύτερος and replacing it with the exclusively gendered endings –ης (masc.) and –ις (fem.), thus respectively yielding the distinctively gendered spellings πρεσβύτης ("male elder") and πρεσβῦτις ("female elder").

> But as for you, teach what is in accord with sound doctrine. Tell the male elders (πρεσβύτας, accusative plural of πρεσβύτης) to be temperate, serious, prudent, and sound in faith, in love, and in endurance. Likewise, tell the female elders (πρεσβύτιδας, accusative plural of

πρεσβῦτις) to be reverent in behavior, not to be slanderers or addicted to alcohol, but to be teachers of the good (καλοδιδασκάλους), in order that they may train the young women (τὰς νέας, the positive adjective of which νεωτέρας is the comparative form) to love their husbands and children, to be self–controlled, chaste, busy at home, kind, and subject to their husbands, that the word of God may not be discredited. Likewise, tell the young men (νεωτέρους) to be self–controlled. . . . Tell slaves to be subject to their masters in everything, to try to please them, not to talk back or steal, but to show them complete and perfect trustworthiness, so that in every way they make attractive the doctrine of God our Savior (2:1–6, 9–10).

All of the same arguments pertinent to 1 Timothy 5 equally apply to this text, lest it be objected that the passage simply refers to "older men" and "older women." Clearly the respective juxtapositions of πρεσβύτης and πρεσβῦτις with νεωτέρους and τὰς νέας, the latter pair indicating that "young men" and "young women" are not to be taken as indicators of age but of maturity in the faith, substantiate the authorial intent toward "male elders" and "female elders." A further argument in favor of the specific allusion to female elders emerges in the further reference to these women as καλοδιδασκάλους, which is simply the term for "scholar/teacher" (διδασκάλους, accusative plural of διδάσκαλος), itself an ecclesiastical office, with the prefix καλός (good) attached to it. That these women held teaching positions within the church, then, harmonizes precisely with the authorial intent to "female elders" but is incompatible with a general reference to "older women," all of whom did not hold teaching positions. Finally, the signification of male and female elders is demanded by the structural logic of the epistle, as this A^2 passage is a recapitulation of A^1 in which the overarching dictates concerning elders, the careful use of vocabulary concerning whom in A^1 is designed to include both men and women, are applied to the particular situation facing the Cretan community. While A^1 demands that elders be blameless, lovers of goodness, self–controlled, upright, holy, disciplined, and instructors in sound doctrine, A^2 shows male and female elders specifically how to put these ideals into practice as well as how to cultivate these virtues in the lives of their spiritual charges, namely, "young women," "young men," and "slaves."

The Johannine Epistles unmistakably prove that at least one woman was the overseer (or elder) of a church, namely, the woman to whom 2 John was addressed. Material concerning the recipient of this letter includes the following:

The elder,

To the chosen lady and her children, whom I love in the truth, and not only I but also all who know the truth, because of the truth that lives in us and will be with us forever:

Grace, mercy, and peace from God the Father and from Jesus Christ, the Son of the Father, will be with us in truth and love.

I was overjoyed to find some of your children walking in the truth, just as the Father commanded us. And now, dear lady, I ask you, not as if I were writing you a new commandment, but reminding you of one we have had from the beginning: let us love one another. . . . Do not receive into the house or welcome anyone who comes to you and does not bring the teaching of Christ; for to welcome is to participate in the evil deeds of such a person. I have much to write to you, but I would rather not use paper and ink; instead I hope to visit you and talk with you face to face, so that our joy may be complete. The children of your chosen sister send you their greetings (vv. 1–5, 10–13).

Grammatico–historical exegesis discloses that the Elder John wrote this epistle to the lady chosen to oversee a particular church (the chosen lady) and to the community of believers she oversees (her children). In an attempt to evade the *prima facie* meaning of this text, some complementarians have purported that "chosen lady" is simply a metaphorical reference to an entire church rather than a particular female leader. However, this claim is a contextual impossibility, for it destroys the authorial distinction between "the chosen lady" and "her children," thus evacuating the latter term of any meaning, and overlooks the fact that the letter is already known to be addressed to a whole church (To the chosen lady and her children), thus exposing the substantive emptiness of the claim itself in not supplying any additional knowledge about 2 John. The claim is quickly undercut, for example, by the Elder John's recollection of joy at finding "some of your children walking in the truth," which children must, in accordance not only with Johannine usage but also usage by the entire New Testament, be believers who are spiritually guided by the antecedent of the pronoun "your." Recalling the stylistic conventions of John's first epistle, the explanatory scope marshaled by the literal identification of "chosen (elect) lady" is encapsulated nicely by Spencer:

If "elect lady" stands for a church, then who are "her children"? John calls the recipients of 1 John "my little children" (*e.g.* 2:1). A church would have to be called *either* elect lady *or* children in John's language scheme, not both. All the data is best understood if John were writing

the letter to a woman who was the person in authority over a congregation.[29]

Verse 10 supplies another clincher in support of understanding "chosen
lady" literally, to whom this command is issued: "Do not receive into the
house or welcome anyone who comes to you and does not bring the teaching
of Christ; for to welcome is to participate in the evil deeds of such a person."
While this command makes perfect sense if issued to a female overseer,
figuratively construing it as posed to the entire church would, if obeyed,
spawn disastrous consequences for the doctrine of evangelism outlined
elsewhere in the Johannine corpus and the remainder of Scripture. On the
one hand, the straightforward rendering of "female overseer" accords beautifully with the historical context of the first–century Way, which possessed
no centralized church buildings where believers could congregate but rather
met in house churches scattered throughout the cities and countrysides of the
Mediterranean basin; the use of specific church buildings did not appear before the close of the second century. Examining the New Testament, the followers of the Jesus movement are seen "breaking bread from house to
house" (Acts 2:46; 5:42), and, as we have already noted, gathering to pray in
the house of Mary (Acts 12:12) and assembling in houses for public worship
(Col. 4:15; Rom. 6:15; 1 Cor. 15:19; Phm. 2). If addressed to a female overseer, the term "house" connotes a "house church," and the Elder John is
warning the overseer both against allowing false teachers into the house
church, hence depriving them a platform from which to propagate their
views, and against ecclesial extension of hospitality to false teachers, which
hospitality would encourage them in their views and insinuate ecclesial acceptance of their doctrines. Thus verse 10 safeguards the doctrinal purity of
the church. On the other hand, if the prohibition were addressed to all believers attending a particular church, then "house" would connote the dwelling places of these believers, thereby forbidding these believers from receiving non–believers into their homes or even greeting them in everyday
affairs. Such an implication would undercut the biblical commands to evangelism (Mt. 28:18–20; Acts 1:8) and invalidate the force of the independently attested dichotomy that believers are to be "in the world" but not "of
the world" (Jn. 16:33, 17:6, 15–16; 1 Cor. 5:9–10), of which dichotomy the
Pauline account takes pains to prevent misunderstanding:

> I have writtten to you in my letter not to associate with sexually im-
> moral people, not at all meaning the people of this world who are im-

---

29. Spencer, *Beyond the Curse*, 110.

moral, or the greedy and robbers, or idolaters; in that case you would need to leave the world. But now I am writing to you not to associate with anyone who bears the name of brother or sister who is sexually immoral or greedy, or is an idolater, reviler, drunkard, or robber.

Hence a consistent application of rendering the "chosen lady," to whom this verse is directed, as the entire church would call for an unbiblical isolationism of believers from non–believers, precisely the sin with which Jesus charged the nation of Israel in failing to live up to its vocation as "the light of the world," namely, as an open–door community whose latent relationship with the one holy God manifested in belief and behavior would attract members of the surrounding pagan nations, who could then become full members of the covenant family of God just as if they were native–born Jews. Perhaps worse yet than preventing Jesus' ἐκκλησία, or "called–out of exile people," from serving as the renewed and enlightened Israel, a false identification of "chosen lady" is incompatible with the example of Jesus and Paul, thereby insinuating that Jesus acted wrongfully in inviting the sick and demon–possessed under his roof at Capernaum to heal and preach to them (Mk. 2:1–2) and that Paul erred by welcoming into "his own rented house" and sharing the Gospel with all interested non–believers for "two whole years" at Rome (Acts 28:30–31). Therefore, both the positive linguistic evidence and our *reductio ad absurdum* establish that the "chosen lady" to which the Elder John dispatched his second epistle was a female church overseer; furthermore, this conclusion makes it probable that "your chosen sister" who also has "children" mentioned in the last verse of the epistle refers to a female overseer of another church and her flock.

Closing Reflections

The Perspective of the Historical Jesus toward Women

All of the independent pre–Gospel and Gospel strata (Q, Mark, John, L, and M) attest to Jesus' unfailingly positive attitude toward women, raising their social status by publicly associating with them, honoring them as examples of eternal truths, and never reprimanding them for infringing upon religious traditions or breaking cultural taboos. In spite of the traditional rabbinic laws which undercut the personal freedom of women, Jesus encouraged women to become his disciples and even to leave prominent families behind. Since these actions are reported within a first-century Jewish context, which placed women on a very low social rung,[30] and would therefore be scandalous for a Messianic claimant, their historicity is further guaranteed by the criterion of embarrassment. Jesus' paradigm endorsement of personal equality for women appears in Luke 10:38–42, where Martha labored in the conventional female serving role while Mary assumed the posture of a male student by sitting at Jesus' feet listening to his word. Everyone present knew that women were forbidden to study under rabbis; as the first-century Sanhedrist Rabbi Eliezar pointed out, the vocation of discipleship was reserved to men only: "Rather should the words of the Torah be burned than entrusted to a woman . . . Whoever teaches his daughter the Torah is like one who teaches her obscenity."[31] When Martha confronted Jesus about Mary's brazenness, Jesus did the unthinkable, praising Mary for her choice to be his disciple and chastising Martha for following the rabbinic gender restriction instead of her sister's countercultural example: "Martha, Martha, you are worried and upset about many things, but only one thing is necessary. Mary has chosen this good thing, which shall not be taken away from her" (vv. 41–42). In so doing Jesus stripped away centuries of religiously sanctioned male elitism, the ramifications of which are portrayed by Charles Trombley:

> [T]he Talmudic traditions, the patriarchal positions, and woman's social stigma were voided once and for all. Mary's choice to study the Word was more important than tradition. [Jesus] recognized her personal worth, her intelligence, and her rational choices to be as valid as a man's. . . . He didn't remind her that the proper role for women was serving the men. Rather, [Jesus] accepted her as an individual fully capable of making her own choices.[32]

---

30. Women were clearly second-class citizens at best, as illustrated by the following memorizable sayings formulated in the first century which were originally transmitted in oral tradition and later enscripturated in the *Babylonian Talmud*: "Blessed is he whose children are male, but woe to him whose children are female" (Niddah 3); and "A woman is a pitcher full of filth with its mouth full of blood, yet all run after her" (Shabbath 152a). The first-century Jewish historian Josephus echoes these sentiments: "The woman, says the law, is in all things inferior to the man" (*Apion*, 2.201). In addition, both Josephus and rabbinic tradition reports that the testimony of women was regarded as so worthless that they were not even permitted to serve as witnesses in a Jewish court of law (*Antiquities of the Jews*, 4.8.15; *Mishnah*, Rosh Ha-Shanah 1.8).

31. *Babylonian Talmud*, Kiddushin 70a.

32. Charles Trombley, *Who Said Women Can't Teach? God's Vision for Women in Ministry* (Gainesville, Fla.: Bridge-Logos, 1985), 254–55.

Thus here and elsewhere (Mk. 5:24–34; 12:38–40; Jn. 4:7–30; 20:10-18; Lk. 7:11-17, 36–50; 13:10–17; Mt. 15:28; 28:5–10), Jesus underscores the priority of the Kingdom of God over socially constructed gender restrictions, thereby opening the gates for women to fully serve as ministers of the Word. But just as surely as Jesus insisted upon the personal equality of women and men, such that both genders have equal rights to religious functions and denouncing as Scripturally contrived the rabbinic arguments for official female inequity, he demanded that the natural gender roles in marriage stipulated in the Genesis creation narrative be upheld (Mk. 10:2–12; Lk. 16:18; Mt. 5:31–32; 19:3–10).

Since Jesus avoids the extremes of the ideologies now dubbed complementarianism and egalitarianism, we would be wise to do the same by adopting the mediating position here forged. This position affirms the strengths of both ideologies while avoiding their weaknesses, which faults are due to selective utilization of grammatico-historical exegesis when befitting each side and ignorance of such exegesis when problematic. Our study reveals that Jesus and the New Testament authors, most notably Paul, stood in complete harmony on the subject of gender roles, which can be summarized as personal equality with natural distinctiveness and mutuality. On the one hand, the evidence indicates that women and men are entitled to equal access to public or non-familial positions and thus equal access to church leadership offices; anything less would represent discrimination militating against gender coequality in the *imago Dei*. On the other hand, the evidence reveals that part of the natural institution of marriage is the submission of wives to their husbands, just as the church is submissive to its divine Bridegroom. These two conclusions stand or fall together, for both constitute the results of precisely the same grammatico-historical methodology. Thus affirming one of these facts and denying the other cannot be done legitimately, but rather places us on the same slippery slope of piecemeal exegesis—a slope which leads not immediately but ultimately to the chasm of heresy—as the Jewish religious authorities that Jesus castigated. Instead, emulating the exegetical brilliance of our Lord, we are bound "to stop judging by mere appearances, but to judge with righteous judgment" (Jn. 7:24) by accepting the results of sound hermeneutical methodology wherever they lead under the sovereign direction of the Spirit, thereby bringing God glory through the church in this and future generations (Eph. 3:21).

Chapter 9

The Historical Jesus' Non–Violent Yet Socially Revolutionary Conception of the Kingdom of God

The Kingdom of God was the central reality proclaimed by Jesus of Nazareth. This reality was about God's great restoration, the return from exile for his entire creation. Such liberation is inextricably bound up with the entity that Jesus founded, ἡ ἐκκλησία or "the called–out–of–exile people" (Mt. 16:18; 18:17). At this juncture one may rightly wonder, What exile? It may surprise us to realize that all first–century Jews for which we have evidence believed that they were living in some type of exile, although the understanding of that exile differed between sects and individuals. To grasp why, we must peer through the lenses of the first–century Jewish worldview, according to which all history (past and current) could be understood as a three–act play. Each act was made up of two contrasting scenes: an exile, featuring slavery and bondage of some sort; and a redemption of what was previously lost, whose positive magnitude was directly proportional to the negative magnitude of the exile. Thus the "badness" of each exile was directly counterbalanced by the "goodness" of its corresponding redemption. In Jewish thought, moreover, these exiles were not historical accidents but were caused by the sins of the nation. To the degree that Israel violated the Mosaic Covenant, God would remove his protective hand, so rendering the nation susceptible to enemy attack. Once the people repented of their sin, however, God could be trusted to accomplish redemption through a human deliverer. We can therefore map out the logic of any given act:

National sin causes Exile – (Repentance) → Return from Exile under a Human Deliverer

In the grand drama of salvation history, the Jewish people believed that the intensity of each component escalated from act to act, such that the sin and captivity of Act 2 would be worse than Act 1 and the calamities of Act 3 worse than Act 2 but that the repentance, return, and deliverance of Act 2 would be better than Act 1 and the glories of Act 3 better than Act 2. Given the course of Jewish history, the components of the first two acts are not hard to find:

1.   While in Egypt, assimilation of surrounding idolatry causes slavery – (Israelites cry out to Yahweh for deliverance and adopt monolatry) → Return to the Promised Land under Moses
2.   Explicit idolatry while in the Promised Land causes deportation into Babylon – (Israelites display deep penitence toward Yahweh and embrace monotheism) → Return to the Promised Land under Cyrus

In Act 1 we perceive that comparatively mild sin, Israel's veneration of pagan deities before Yahweh had entered into covenant with the nation, led to a relatively brief period (no more than 70 years) of slavery to conclude an otherwise prosperous 450–year stay in Egypt (1700–1250 B.C.E.). Following the Jewish people's entreaty of Yahweh and decision to worship him alone, God raised up Moses, a fellow Jew raised in the Egyptian court, to deliver them from captivity and lead them back to Palestine. What made Palestine specifically a Promised Land as opposed to just any land is that it was the one place on earth where the Jewish people could freely live out their religious identity in all of its fullness, *i.e.* under the 623 *mitzvoth* that God had given them through Moses at Mount Sinai. But despite their possession of the Promised Land and complete control over their religious climate, we find in Act 2 that the Jewish people worshiped pagan deities alongside Yahweh, not privately in homes but publicly for all to see, setting them up on the vaunted "high places" of prophetic disrepute. This far greater sin carried proportionate consequences in the form of the Babylonian Exile (586–36 B.C.E.), as King Nebuchadnezzar marched on Palestine, slaying thousands of Jews, burning the Temple to the ground, destroying the city of Jerusalem, and dragging all the survivors eastward across the Fertile Crescent as slaves to Babylon. Israel viewed such dispossession as the ultimate insult being added to injury, since it reversed and symbolically "undid" Father Abraham's original trek from Ur, now Babylonia, to the Promised Land, thus sending the message that Jewish ownership of Palestine and their centuries of history in the Land was meaningless—ultimately it would have made no difference if Abraham had ever migrated to Palestine at all. Faced with that galling consequence, the Israelites accepted the preceding prophetic critique by Isaiah, Jeremiah, Ezekiel, and others who had forewarned them that their idolatry would withdraw divine protection and thereby enable their conquest by the Ancient Near Eastern superpower. Assuming that their idolatry, and not any external political, economic, or social factors, had brought about the Exile, the Jewish people utterly renounced their checkered past, marked by monolatry (worship of only one god while believing in the existence of multiple other gods) at best and polytheism at worst, a repudiation poignantly demonstrated in penitential literature which eventually assumed more than half of the Book of Psalms. Firmly committing themselves to monotheism (worship of and belief in only one God), the Mosaic Covenant, and the general resurrection model of the afterlife, the Israelites experienced restoration when the Persian king Cyrus, having defeated and displaced the Babylonian Empire in 539 B.C.E., released the Jews from their captivity three years later in 536.[1] A rather superstitious king who wanted to procure the good graces of all the gods of the peoples he governed, Cyrus not only allowed the Jews to return to the Promised Land but actually encouraged and financed their rebuilding of the Jerusalem Temple, a project accomplished from 520–516 B.C.E. Since Cyrus, as a pagan king and a literally raving polytheist, was the "least likely candidate" to serve as Jewish liberator, God's providential moving behind the scenes of history to anoint Cyrus for this task was viewed as a far more miraculous feat than his previous anointing of Moses, a Jew whose royal education in the Egyptian courts arguably rendered him a "most likely candidate" for the job of redeemer. In commemoration of God's amazing selection of a man otherwise expected to be an enemy of Israel, Deutero-Isaiah coined a new term to describe Cyrus' divinely appointed vocation— Cyrus was the *mashiach*, or "anointed one," of Yahweh. Hence in Act 2 the

---

1. For those who find the arguments for Daniel as a *vaticinium ex eventu* wanting, as I do, further evidence for the book's historicity stems from the fact that the events of Daniel 6, reportedly occurring between 539 and 536, would have provided strong motivation for Cyrus (the throne name of Darius the Mede) to dramatically intervene on behalf of the Jewish people and its god. While Cyrus' own superstitiousness constitutes reasonable grounds for him to release the Israelites from bondage to resettle the Promised Land, his financing of the construction of Temple II is an extraordinary gesture which seems to require more than merely his selfish desire to curry divine favor. Here the narrative in Daniel fits explanatorily like a hand in a glove, which relates the following edict of Cyrus: "I issue a decree that in all parts of my kingdom people must fear and venerate the God of Daniel. For he is the living God who endures forever; his kingdom will never be destroyed and his dominion will never end. He rescues and he saves; he performs miraculous signs and wonders in the heavens and on earth. He rescued Daniel from the power of the lions" (Dan. 6:26–27).

magnitude of Israel's sin, Jerusalem's destruction, and Israel's captivity was counterbalanced by the physically liberating effects of God's forgiveness and astonishing restoration of the holy city and its Temple by means of the very pagan resources which formerly oppressed them.

During Jesus' lifetime, the prevailing Jewish tendency was to perceive themselves as living in the first half of the third act, awaiting God's most dramatic restoration yet through a *mashiach* (transliterated Messiah) who would surpass even Cyrus. For the Jewish people believed that the Roman annexation of Palestine, which began in 63 B.C.E., was far worse than Palestine's relatively innocuous past annexations by the Persian and Hellenistic Empires, who demanded tribute money from the Jews in exchange for statehood and its accompanying protection without interfering in Jewish religion. Rome, rather, attempted to do gradually what the infamous Seleucid monarch Antiochus Epiphanes IV (167-65 B.C.E.) had attempted to do instantaneously—namely, commit "religiocide" by destroying Judaism root and branch. Not content to merely collect taxes from Palestine but learning from the failure of Antiochus, whom Israel successfully vanquished in the Maccabean Revolt, Rome occupied Palestine and progressively enacted sanctions which robbed the Jewish people of their religious liberties bit by bit. For example, Pontius Pilate, the Roman procurator of Jerusalem, forbade the Sanhedrin (Men of the Great Assembly), or Jewish ruling council, from administering the death penalty, thereby precluding their enforcement of Torah and removing all legal accountability for the people to follow it. Thus the Promised Land, in effect, had appallingly become "unpromised," as the element of full religious freedom that made the Land uniquely promised had been removed. In short, the following horrific prospect emerged: if the Jewish people suffered spiritual disenfranchisement in the one place on earth intended for them to freely and fully actualize their religious identity, where then could they go to regain this liberty? It would seem that, if Rome succeeded in their de-Judaization of Palestine, then there would be no place left where the Jewish people could live out their identity and genuinely be the covenant people of God; they would be forced into permanent bondage. As Josephus put it, the Jewish people found themselves "slaves in their own land."[2]

---

2. Josephus, *War of the Jews*, 8.5; *cf.* the similar statements in Nehemiah 9:36 and Ezra 9:8-9. Reasoning from the lesser to the greater, if the Jews' extensive freedom (including religious liberty) under Cyrus and the Persian Empire was perceived as homeland slavery on the grounds that it was not full national independence, then we get a glimpse of how much more the Jews' progressive reduction of religious liberties by the Roman Empire was so perceived.

But what was the sin that triggered this debacle? Since its identity was not immediately evident, the rabbis undertook an exhaustive investigation of the obligations mandated by the Hebrew Bible and compared their findings with the day–to–day behavior of the nation. Predictably, as all quality-control assessments of this sort unfold, the guardians of the sacred tradition concluded that common Jews, or the *'am ha–aretz* (people of the land), were not keeping Torah strictly enough. Due to this alleged laxity, the Jewish religious leaders demanded that the common people observe the 623 *mitzvoth* not only to the letter but with a severity that disallowed them from coming anywhere close to breaking them. In the *Pirke Avot*, the Men of the Great Assembly (*i.e.* Sanhedrin) officially launched their project of "building a fence around Torah," a graphic metaphor for their formulation of a set of supplementary laws which, while not found among the 623 *mitzvoth*, prevented their spiritual charges from even having the opportunity to violate the *mitzvoth*. Two of the best known supplementary laws were *corban*, a statute ensuring that no male could ultimately break the tithe (even if attempted) by seizing at death any potential offender's inheritance and using it for the upkeep of the religious establishment, and washing one's hands before eating, a requirement not merely content to ensure Jewish consumption of kosher meals but deterring the possible contamination of these meals by any imagined impurity literally "rubbing off" from dealings with pagans in the marketplace. These factors, then, constituted the first half of the third and decisive act of *Heilgeschichte* (salvation history) in which Jesus' contemporaries believed they were living.

As for the resolution of Act 3, the Jewish people expected God to raise up a Messiah superior to Moses and Cyrus who would liberate the people from the Roman yoke. But what kind of a figure would be greater than Moses and Cyrus and so powerful as to counterbalance this greatest of exiles in the Jewish homeland? Our answer to this question will comprise a kind of "Messianic job description" that Jesus' contemporaries were looking for a divinely ordained individual to fulfill. Like Moses, this *mashiach* would be a compelling religious leader, but even greater than Moses, he would successfully enforce the 623 *mitzvoth*, especially the food laws and Sabbath laws which functioned as markers of Jewish identity, for all who dwelt in Palestine. Like Cyrus, he would be king of an empire who conquered his enemies with the sword, but surpassing Cyrus' governance of a pagan empire, the Messiah would, after violently ridding the Holy Land of all Roman and other pagan influences, turn Israel into the superpower of the Ancient Near East, restore Israel's borders to at least their original expanse following Joshua's Conquest of Canaan (if not militarily extending these boundaries), and employ the new Israelite empire's political influence to spread Palestinian justice and the Jewish way of life throughout the Mediterranean world. Thus completed, we may delineate the dominant first-century Jewish conception of the third act:

3. Failure to sufficiently observe Torah causes Israel to experience exile under Rome in the Promised Land – (Jews comply with the rabbinic fence around Torah to secure the absolute maintenance of its 623 *mitzvoth* by great and small alike) → Restoration and exaltation of the Promised Land by Messiah

The Startling Nature of Jesus' Proclamation

Against this backdrop we are poised to understand the significance of Jesus' Kingdom proclamation. As expected from his culture, Jesus embraced the general contours of this three–act play conception of history, including the specific identification of the components making up the first two acts and the belief that Judaism was presently experiencing the third and decisive act. However, the uniqueness of Jesus' historical perception lay in his vehement rejection of his contemporaries' identification of each component comprising the third act. To put it baldly, Jesus believed that the negative side was not negative enough (*i.e.* it misconstrued the ultimate evil befalling Israel), that the proposed repentance was utterly contrary to Israel's divinely given vocation, and that the positive side was not positive enough (*i.e.* it misconstrued the ultimate redemption of God's people). Thus, Jesus' reconceptualization of Act 3 stipulated that the Jewish people found themselves in a far deeper slavery than simply to Rome: they had voluntarily become slaves to the Kingdom of the World (αἰών), the philosophical system of domination and oppression according to which the world operates. In the Kingdom of the World, one person or group attempts to exercise power over others through the "sword," by which I symbolize all ability to inflict pain on those who threaten and defy one's authority, including but not limited to wielding a literal sword. In other words, the sword is the ability to coerce behavior by threats and to carry out those threats when necessary that functions as "muscle" for the Kingdom of the World. Such a "power–over" or "top–down" domination system is ruled by Satan, as Scripture clearly indicates. To illustrate, when Satan tempted Jesus with "all the kingdoms of the world," asserting that "all their authority and glory has been given to me, and I can give it to anyone I please" (Lk. 4:5–6), Jesus does not dispute this claim, thereby giving tacit admission to its accuracy, but refuses to succumb to the temptation. Given its socio–cultural context, we see that "worshiping Satan" does not mean literally bowing down to the devil or paying him religious homage, but Scripture rather defines this supreme abomination as attempting to implement the reign of God through the devices of the αἰών. Jesus reinforces this point by thrice acknowledging Satan as the "ἀρχή of this world" (Jn. 12:31; 14:30; 16:11),[3] where ἀρχή semantically comes from the domain of politics and denotes the highest ruling authority in a given region.[4] For Jesus, Satan was the highest ruling authority in the αἰών, and the Sanhedrin backed by popular opinion were chillingly attempting to become the people of God by capitulating to the αἰών, aiming to employ political zeal and military wrath to usher in God's great and final redemption and perpetuate it throughout the globe. In Jesus' analysis, Israel's greatest sin and worst idolatry constituted its attempt to be the people of God by becoming top nation in the pagan sense, so beating Rome at its own game. But by choosing to play this satanic "game," the Jewish religious aristocracy had unwittingly become "slaves" and even "sons" of the devil, "a murderer from the beginning" whose violent tendencies they longed to accomplish (Jn. 8:34–44). In these ways, Jesus contended that Israel had abandoned its original vocation to be the light of the world which would reach out with open arms to foreign nations and actively display to them God's love.

To support this hypothesis, Jesus appealed to the original rationale of the Torah and its 623 *mitzvoth*: worshiping Yahweh alone, showing maximal love to humanity, imparting social justice to the foreigner and native alike, and performing distinctive rites, all in order to convey a new way of life grounded in a unique God that people from the surrounding nations would find attractive. How far, Jesus lamented, Israel had fallen with its attitudes and actions toward the Romans from its divine *raison d'être*: "When aliens live with you in your land, do not maltreat them. Rather, the alien living with you must be treated as one of your native–born. Love the alien as yourself, for you yourselves were aliens in Egypt. I am Yahweh your God" (Lev. 19:33–34). Consequently, the purpose of the Mosaic Law was literally evangelistic (*i.e.* spreading the "good news" about Yahweh), as Yahweh chartered Israel to be a collective "city on a hill" powered by individual beacons of light, or Jews who lived in such intimate relations with God that they allowed his love to flow through them toward others who had not yet appropriated his love. Therefore, God instructed Israel to maintain an open–door policy to all outsiders, in which anyone wanting to become part of God's chosen people, regardless of birth or ethnic origin, could join by accepting

---

3. The followers of the Way echo the acknowledgment of their Master in 2 Corinthians 4:4, Ephesians 2:2 and 6:12, 1 John 5:19, and Revelation 9:11, 11:15, 13:14, 18:23, 20:3, 8.

4. Boyd, *Myth*, 18, 20–21.

circumcision (only males were circumcised) and partaking of the Passover feast with the community (for both sexes). Once an outsider participated in this first Passover, one became a full–fledged member of the Jewish community, every bit as much as if one were a native–born Jew, and one's children inherited the blessings of the Mosaic Covenant:

> An alien living among you who desires to celebrate Yahweh's Passover must have all the males in his household circumcised; then the alien may take part like one born in the land. No uncircumcised male may partake of it. . . . [then] you and the alien shall be on equal standing before Yahweh. This is a permanent ordinance for future generations" (Ex. 12:48–49; Num. 15:15; *cf* cf.; Lev. 19:33–34; 24:22; Num. 9:14).

Moreover, God commanded the Jewish people not to appoint a king or install any earthly government, for there was to be no king but God, and the people were to trust in the transformative power of God's ways, knowing that they would be vindicated at the general resurrection even if slain or dispossessed by invaders. After less than two centuries punctuated by rebellion against God (1210–1030 B.C.E.), Israel grew tired of this countercultural outlook and appointed Saul as its king, thus explicitly rejecting God as king and trading theocracy for monarchy. Around 950 B.C.E. King Solomon constructed the First Jerusalem Temple, henceforth seen as a talisman guaranteeing divine protection over the nation.

For these reasons, Jesus strenuously opposed Israel's use of governmental power, itself a continuing opposition to the kingship of God, coupled with its even more unholy alliance with the World's "might makes right" methods of oppression, abuse, and discrimination in hopes of effecting God's victory over the World. This amounted, in Jesus' evaluation, to Israel's greatest abomination precisely because of its subtlety and façade of godliness. After all, from the darkened philosophical perspective of the αἰών, what could make more sense than a politically conquering and dominating Messiah? At the very least, such a Messiah's position of power would render the Mediterranean Basin a great deal better than it was. The Messiah could immediately destroy evil in all its nation–states, alleviate virtually all of its suffering, and institute an international government that implemented "biblically based principles" of law and justice. Further, he would free the Jewish people from their Roman tyranny and enable them to practice their religious beliefs and propagate their cultural values without fear of persecution. As spiritual as all this looked, Jesus reasoned, the success of his contemporaries' Messianic expectations would simply spell a "new and improved" Jewish version of the Kingdom of the World every bit as much under the control of Satan as Rome. Via the appearance of godliness, Israel would fool itself and countless future generations into believing that they loved, and were at peace with, God when they in fact were unwittingly loving, and doing the will of, Satan. N. T. Wright summarizes Jesus' charge against his contemporaries:

> They had misread the signs of their own vocation, and were claiming divine backing for a perversion of it. The call to be the light of the world passes easily into a sense of being the children of light, looking with fear and hatred on the children of darkness. Jesus' analysis of the plight of Israel went beyond the specifics of behavior and belief to what he saw as the root of the problem: the Israel of his day had been duped by the accuser, the 'satan'. *That which was wrong with the rest of the world was wrong with Israel, too.* . . . The battle against evil—the correct analysis of the problem, and the correct answer to it—was therefore of a different order from that imagined by his contemporaries.[5]

We now begin to understand Jesus' logic that implicit idolatry proved far more damning than explicit idolatry, since the second is just as easily avoidable as the first is easily alluring. It would be far easier for a professed monotheist to steer clear of creating and falling down to worship idols than it would be to steer clear of involvement in political agendas and ideologies which, given humanity's dominant philosophical system, seem at face value to bring honor and glory to God. But the end result—worshiping Satan—is precisely the same in both cases. Jesus intertextually echoes the verdict of the prophet Isaiah: "Woe to the rebellious children, declares Yahweh, who execute plans, but not mine, and make an alliance but not with my Spirit, thereby heaping sin upon sin" (30:1). Therefore, Jesus prophetically indicted his listeners that, by endeavoring to defeat the World by embracing the presuppositions and methodology of the World, they had already lost the battle and, by definition, could not be the people of God.

The Origins of the State

At this juncture it should be pointed out that civil government or state, while not identical to the Kingdom of the World, is dependent for its existence on the Kingdom of the World. In other words, the state is literally a "necessary evil" which, in view of wide scale human subscription to the αἰών, forcefully prevents self-seeking individuals from undermining the fabric of society by destroying the conditions necessary for larger groups to

---

5. Wright, *Jesus*, 446; emphasis his.

thrive and flourish. But if there were no αἰών (and thus no one coming under its intoxicating spell of power), then there would be no civil government either. Given its existence, nevertheless, God providentially uses civil government as a servant to maintain basic law and order in the world. According to the Apostle Paul, "those governmental authorities that exist have been ordered (τεταγμέναι) by God," such that "if one does what is evil, one should be afraid, for the authorities do not bear the sword in vain; they are the servants of God to execute wrath on the evildoer" (Rom. 13:1, 4). In his fine exegesis of the Greek vocabulary employed by Paul, John Howard Yoder spells out the significance of the verb τεταγμέναι while simultaneously refuting misreadings of Paul's remarks in Romans 13 as teaching the "divine right of rulers" and the derivative obligation of supporting one's civil government through military service:

God is not said to create or institute or ordain the powers that be, but only to order them, to put them in order, sovereignly to tell them where they belong, what is their place. It is not as if there was a time when there was no government and then God made government through a new creative intervention; there has been hierarchy and authority and power since human society existed. Its exercise has involved domination, disrespect for human dignity, and real or potential violence ever since sin has existed. Nor is it that by ordering this realm God specifically, morally approves of what a government does . . . the librarian does not create nor approve of the book she or he catalogs and shelves. Likewise God does not take responsibility for the existence of the rebellious "powers that be" or for their shape or identity; they already are. What the text says is that God orders them, brings them into line, providentially and permissively lines them up with divine purposes. . . . That God orders and uses the powers does not reveal anything new about what government should be or how we should respond to government. A given government is not mandated or saved or made a channel of the will of God; it is simply lined up, used by God in the ordering of the cosmos. It does not mean that what individuals in government do is good human behavior . . . God did not approve morally of the brutality whereby Assyria chastised Israel (Isa. 10). The immediate concrete meaning of this text for the Christian Jews in Rome . . . is to call them away from any notion of revolution or insubordination. The call is to a nonresistant attitude toward a tyrannical government . . .

how strange then to make it the classic proof for the duty of Christians to kill.[6]

As Yoder's comments insightfully reveal, government is not created by God and is outside the perfect will of God; however, the power–hungry Kingdom of the World has created government as a necessary tool for keeping peace throughout its environs with the only mechanism effective for procuring the conformity of its selfish subjects—brute force. It should be here underscored that government, while powerful to coerce external behavior, is impotent to bring about internal change and has no interest in producing such change. Although, for instance, a government can outlaw murder and execute convicted murderers, it cannot change people's desire to murder. It may well be that the only reason a person abstains from murder is to avoid execution; but so long as one does not murder, government cares nothing about the state of the person's heart.

The ἀγαπή–Powered Kingdom of God

Contrary to its enduring eleventh–century B.C.E. nationalistic trust in the violent power of the αἰών, Jesus aimed to call Israel back to its original vision of living as a "kingdom of priests" through whom God's Spirit would emanate, *i.e.* living as the people of God. This discloses the double–sided nature of Jesus' notion of the Kingdom of God. On the one hand, it refers to the reign of God over all earthly affairs, whether social, political, economic, aesthetic, or religious; as Allen Mitsuo Wakabayashi rightly points out, it is *"the dynamic of God's kingship being applied . . .* in a world that is not yet fully under his authority."[7] Wherever God's light–bearing Kingdom comes, the evil of darkness is dispelled. On the other hand, the reign of God does not look anything like the "top–down" leadership or the hierarchical authority endemic to the Kingdom of the World. Instead of trying to exercise power over others, the Kingdom of God functions as a "power–under" or "bottom–up" transformative system which works for the sole purpose of replicating ἀγαπή (the love that uniquely emanates from God) to all people at all times in all places unconditionally, carrying out the will of God at the probable cost of self–interest. Correcting post–Enlightenment misconcep-

---

6. John Howard Yoder, *The Politics of Jesus*, 2nd ed. (Grand Rapids, Mich.: Eerdmans, 1994), 201–03; emphasis his.

7. Allen Mitsuo Wakabayashi, *Kingdom Come* (Downers Grove, Ill.: Inter-Varsity Press, 2003), 30–31; emphasis his.

tions, N. T. Wright delineates the meaning of this concept for Jesus' original disciples:

> They were not thinking about how to secure themselves a place in heaven after they died. The phrase "kingdom of heaven," which we find frequently in Matthew's Gospel where the others have "kingdom of God," does not refer to a place, called "heaven," where God's people will go after death. It refers to the rule of heaven, that is, of God, being brought to bear in the present world. Thy kingdom come, said Jesus, thy will be done, *on earth as in heaven.* Jesus' contemporaries knew that the creator God intended to bring justice and peace to his world here and now.[8]

The Kingdom of God advances when people lovingly place themselves under others, serving others at their own expense. Although such underwriting does not imply that Kingdom people conform to others' desires, it does entail that Kingdom people always interact with others with their best interests in view. This altruistic and self–sacrificial love, Jesus alleged, has the power to do what the World and civil government can never do: transform the heart and mind of the perceived "enemy." Hence Jesus' Kingdom embraces Jews and non–Jews alike. On this score Gregory A. Boyd comments, "Participants in the kingdom of the world trust the power of the sword to control behavior; participants of the kingdom of God trust the power of self–sacrificial love to transform hearts."[9] While the Kingdom of the World is concerned only with coercion, the Kingdom of God is concerned only with conversion, namely, one's voluntarily renouncing the ways of the αἰών and voluntarily opening one's whole being to God as a dwelling place for his Spirit. Upon this free decision, the Spirit radically reorients the person's fundamental inclinations, desires, and motivations toward the will of God rather than, as before, toward the will of self. For this reason, Jesus insisted, God announced through the Prophets in an age of nationalism that his ultimate triumph over evil would come "not by might, nor by power, but by my Spirit" (Zech. 4:6). All this means that when God reigns, it bears no resemblance to the self–aggrandizing rule of the Caesars, Herods, or any other human monarchs; rather, it looks like the cross. Thus God reigns precisely by doing whatever is necessary to redeem those within his guardianship at all costs to himself. Just as the mother hen takes the chicks under her wings during a barnyard fire, thus sacrificing herself to save the brood, so Jesus achieves the victory

---

8. N. T. Wright, *The Challenge of Jesus* (Downers Grove, Ill.: InterVarsity Press, 2001), 36–37.

9. Boyd, *Myth*, 32.

of God over sin and death on behalf of all humanity by means of the cross (Lk. 13:34). In Jesus, God proves the ultimate "servant leader."

For Jesus, the Kingdom of the World was primarily interested in how people behave, but the Kingdom of God was primarily interested in what people become. Just as primal humanity arrogated to themselves the ability to judge between good and evil without reference to God (Gen. 2:17; 3:6), the World is typified by judgment; on the contrary, God's Kingdom is typified by shocking and outlandish grace. Clearly, when wills and desires are redeemed, transformation of behavior is sure to follow, and without domineering "power over" force. In this way, the Kingdom proclaimed by Jesus would obtain what human proponents of the World seek to obtain, plus far more, since it changes people from the inside out, namely, from their wills to their action. Unlike the World, it has no interest in regulating behavior as an end in itself. With this in mind, we are now poised to fully understand Jesus' charges against his contemporaries. For, as Jesus arraigned, instead of taking advantage of the opportunity to compassionately serve the Romans and thereby beginning to change them from the inside out, thereby overcoming the evil of Roman oppression with good and so emulating God (Rom. 8:28; 12:21), the Israelites exhibited lack of trust in God by fearing, in typical pagan style, the loss of their "rights" and fought for their restoration by political and military means.

We may therefore characterize Jesus' revision of Act 3 within Jewish history as follows:

> 3*. Exile of Jews and non–Jews alike in the Kingdom of the World (αἰών) – (individuals turn away from the World and adopt Jesus' new way of life) → Restoration in the Kingdom of God by Messiah Jesus

Given that Jesus rejected nationalistic ideals of Messiah as military conqueror, we must ask at this point what type of Messiah Jesus envisaged himself to be. We know Jesus believed that he was on a divine mission to redeem the people of God and that no one less than God could do so. Thus, while it would have been anachronistic and nonsensical for Jesus to have claimed, "I am God," as the word "God" in first–century Judaism was defined as "the Father in heaven," the evidence indicates that Jesus regarded himself as a divine person alongside of the person called "God" without detracting from his full humanity or denying monotheism. On the basis of his demonstrably authentic sayings (*i.e.* those which historical criticism proves beyond reasonable doubt to be historical), the majority of contemporary

New Testament critics agree that a divine self–understanding belonged to the consciousness of the historical Jesus. As Horst Georg Pöhlmann relates:

> Today there is virtually a consensus . . . that Jesus came on the scene with an unheard of authority, namely, the authority of God, with the claim of the authority to stand in God's place and speak to us and to bring us to salvation. This unheard-of claim to authority . . . is implicit Christology, since it presupposes a unity of Jesus with God that is deeper than that of all men, namely a unity of essence. This . . . claim to authority is explicable only from the side of his deity. This authority only God himself can claim.[10]

On the basis of texts including Daniel 7:13–14 and Psalm 110:1, Jesus formulated his "Messianic job description" as the simultaneously divine and human Son of Man described by the former and the Adonai whom David worshiped and to whom Yahweh spoke described by the latter. Given his conviction that God had affirmed him as Messiah, Jesus accused the Jewish religious leaders of his day of misreading their own Scriptures and thus deceiving the people (Mt. 23:15) concerning the true character of the Messiah (not to mention the larger question of their vocation spelled out in the Mosaic Covenant). This dominical self–understanding quickly led the early church to redefine the term "God" in such a way that it included Jesus. Notwithstanding his divine status from timeless eternity, Paul asserts that Jesus refused to exploit his deity but rather took for himself a human nature and became a humble servant; though he was rich, for our sake he became poor (Php. 2:5–8; 2 Cor. 8:9). Boyd insightfully notes that Jesus "could have remained in the bliss of his perfect loving relationship with the Father and the Spirit, but instead he willingly became a baby born as a social outcast to an unwed mother in a dirty, smelly stable crowded with animals."[11] By becoming a servant of the world, Jesus outwardly exemplified the Kingdom mission which he internally embodied.

Implications for Daily Living

Those who are Christians, by definition, are called to imitate Jesus in every area of their lives; hence Yoder remarks that "to be a disciple is to

---

10. Horst Georg Pöhlmann, *Abriss der Dogmatik*, 3rd rev. ed. (Düsseldorf: Patmos, 1966), 230.
11. Boyd, *Myth*, 35.

share in that lifestyle of which the cross is the culmination."[12] Accordingly Paul instructed the followers of the Way at Ephesus, "As beloved children, then, be imitators of God, and continually walk in love, just as Christ loved us and gave himself up on our behalf" (Eph. 5:1–2). Thus it is imperative for us to analyze not simply in broad contours but also in specific instances how Jesus manifested this "new reality" or "new being" (2 Cor. 5:17) in time and space. Even though the cross most poignantly encapsulates the program of Jesus, the essence of the Kingdom of God is also exhibited throughout Jesus' entire life and ministry, all of which emanated a Calvary quality. In short, by consistently revealing the humble character of a servant, Jesus' whole identity constituted service to others at cost to himself. Although he created and so owned the universe, he chose to "have no place to lay his head" (Mt. 8:20). Although he validly should have been lauded by the world's greatest luminaries, he elected to befriend tax collectors, alcoholics, prostitutes, and other culturally unacceptable sinners (Mk. 2:15; Lk. 5:29–30; 7:31–50; 15:1; Mt. 11:19). Although he validly could have required service and worship from all, he served the lame and diseased by healing them, the possessed by exorcising their demons, and the outcasts by fellowshipping with them. The sheer beauty of the Kingdom lifestyle was stunningly portrayed at the Last Supper. According to the Elder John, Jesus realized that "the Father had put all things under his power, and that he had come from God and was returning to God" (Jn. 13:3). So how did Jesus use this divine power? He "got up from the meal, took off his outer robe, and wrapped a towel around his waist. After that, he poured water into a basin and began to wash his disciples' feet, drying them with the towel tied around him" (Jn. 13:4–5). Despite Jesus' knowledge that he held all authority in heaven and earth at his disposal and that he was about to be betrayed and die the most ignominious possible death in that culture, he assumes the role of a common household servant and washes the filthy and foul–smelling feet of his disciples, whom he realizes will forsake him in a few short hours. This is how power is exerted in the Kingdom of God. Reflecting on this scene, Boyd outlines its immediate ramifications for Christian discipleship:

> If you have all power in heaven and earth, use it to wash the feet of someone you know will betray you! In serving like this, Jesus declares to all who are willing to hear that he "would not rule by a sword, but by a towel. . . . Insofar as we trust *this* kind of power and think and act ac-

---

12. Yoder, *Politics*, 38.

cordingly, we are bearers of the kingdom of God. Insofar as we do not, we are simply participants in the kingdom of the world.[13]

To qualify as belonging to the Kingdom of God, our actions must be characterized by the humility, grace, and service demonstrated in Jesus.

But the supreme manifestation of Jesus' Kingdom agenda, in which he won the decisive cosmic victory over Satan and the αἰών, occurred at the cross.[14] Since Jesus' crucifixion is the sole criterion for what Kingdom activity looks like, the cross proves the ultimate symbol of the Kingdom of God. Here we see that, when facing the greatest possible personal loss of one's own life, Jesus refused to exercise "power over" Pilate and the Roman government to defend himself. In the eyes of the Kingdom of the World, he could have "won" by ordering his disciples to wield the sword and summoning legions of warrior angels, thereby saving his life and controlling the behavior of his enemies. Nevertheless, he would not have redeemed anyone's soul or enabled anyone to love God or love themselves and others as people loved by God. Thus even if brandished by angels, the power of the sword can never convert the conscience. Boyd wisely observes that "[w]hile the use of the sword tends to deepen the resolve of the punished rather than transform it, Jesus' aim was to transform hearts and, by that means, transform the world."[15] Therefore, Jesus chose to "lose" by the standards of the Kingdom of the World in order to "win" by the standards of the Kingdom of God. So on Easter Sunday, God vindicated Jesus' personal claims and Kingdom program by resurrecting him from the dead as the firstfruits of the general resurrection on the Day of Yahweh. Paradoxically, by succumbing to the fate of "failed messiahs" in the World's analysis, Jesus secured victory over death and the forces of wickedness that bound humanity in slavery, thus proving to be the true Messiah who "disarmed," "made a public spectacle of," and "triumphed over" the usurping powers and authorities (Col. 2:15).

The character and reign of God is extended when, rather than crushing his enemies with violence, Jesus redeems his enemies through love. The epitome of ἀγαπή was displayed in Jesus' prayer for the forgiveness of those who were mocking, spitting on, whipping, and crucifying him (Lk. 23:34). In these ways, Jesus embodied the true nature of divine power; as Paul reports the dominical saying, "My strength is made perfect in weakness" (2 Cor. 12:9). Consequently, Calvary unveiled the fact that God loves humanity with the same love eternally expressed among the three Persons of

---

13. Boyd, *Myth*, 37, 39.
14. Wright, *Jesus*, 595.
15. Boyd, *Myth*, 33–34.

the Trinity whom God is. In spite of our wickedness, God places himself under us to save us and remold us into the image of his incarnate Second Person. Nothing could be further from the "power over" mentality that drives the Kingdom of the World. When the apostles, therefore, argued about which of them would be the greatest in the messianic establishment they were expecting, Jesus endeavored to forever banish this mentality from his followers by drawing a sharp contrast between self–serving Worldly might and other–serving Kingdom might:

> You know that those who are regarded as rulers of the pagans lord it over their people, and their high officials exercise authority over them. Not so with you! On the contrary, whoever wishes to be great among you must be your servant, and whoever wishes to be first must be slave of all. For even the Son of Man did not come to be served, but to serve, and to give his life as a ransom in place of many (Mk. 10:42–45).

For this reason, the Kingdom of God is not a "Christian version" of the Kingdom of the World, as the disciples seemed (in modern terminology) to have expected. Rather, it is a sacred alternative to all renditions of the αἰών, such that our success as Kingdom people depends on recognizing and maintaining this uniqueness. Believers are ordered, both individually and collectively, to imitate Jesus within a violent and defiant world.

Our Charter: The Sermon on the Mount

In his Sermon on the Mount, Jesus challenged his hearers to be the light of the world, thereby fulfilling Israel's true vocation. We must here stress that the teachings within this sermon are only validly interpreted in their first–century context of struggle between the Jewish people and the Roman Empire. If these teachings are pulled out of their context, they are prone to be misinterpreted as moral platitudes at best or as a list of requirements for admission into a permanent immaterial "heaven" at worst. (While the first fallacy commits simple anachronism, the second couples anachronism with absurdity, as neither the Hebrew Bible nor the New Testament teach a permanent immaterial afterlife but rather a new heaven–earth or new universe.) But in their context, the purpose of the Sermon was to promote a countercultural program of non–violent Jewish resistance against their Roman oppressors—*i.e.* to teach the Jewish people how to respond to the Romans in such a way that they would not overcome evil with evil but conquer evil with good. In other words, any appropriate response to evil must refuse to let the evil define the sufferer (so that the sufferer does not stoop to its level) and must poignantly expose the evil for precisely what it is to the one committing the evil. Jesus knew full well that such confrontation of oppressors, which forced them to come to grips with the severity of their crimes, was precisely the logic behind the Jewish sacrificial system. In that system, when people committed a social injustice of a particular gravity, they were obligated to find their most prized of whatever animal was proportionate in value to that gravity and carry out the quite unpleasant task of bringing it to Jerusalem, getting their hands dirty by violently slaying it in the immediate presence of God, and sprinkling its blood on various items. The rationale behind this system was making sinners realize that what they knowingly did to the animal is precisely the same thing they unwittingly did to their fellow human beings by committing social injustice. In short, oppressors would be graphically shown that by their injustices, they have contributed to the cycle of oppression and domination which ultimately ends with other humans suffering the same fate as the animal. Sacrificing the animal in the definitive divine presence reminds one that one's crime against humanity was no less enacted before the presence of God. In this way, one was brought firmly to grips with the ramifications of one's sin so that one would never commit it again.

Of course, to respond to the Romans via the logic of the Jewish sacrificial system instead of getting involved with the military resistance movement would entail thinking "outside the box." At this juncture we must emphasize that by denouncing violent resistance, Jesus in no way commanded (or even sanctioned) doing nothing at all against evil; to the contrary, Jesus continually resisted evil with every fiber of his being, such that the Gospels do not record a single instance when Jesus does not resist evil when confronted by it. Thus when Jesus said, "Do not resist (ἀντιστῆναι) an evil person" (Mt. 5:39), he did not mean, "Let an evil person run all over you without regard for your dignity"; rather, he used the technical term ἀντιστῆναι, which specifically meant "to get involved in the violent resistance movement against Rome," to say, "Take a stand against evil without resisting violently." As Walter Wink points out, Jesus indicates that one must not resist evil on its own terms, for doing so allows one's opponent to dictate the terms of one's resistance; instead, one must resist in a non–violent way that brings the opponent face to face with its severity.[16] Hence when Christ commanded, "If someone strikes you on the right cheek, turn to him the left cheek also" (Mt. 5:39), he was not telling people to be "doormats for Jesus," in the colorful words of Wright, or forbidding them from

---

16. Walter Wink, *Jesus and Nonviolence: A Third Way* (Minneapolis: Fortress, 2003), 10–15.

exercising self–defense in a fight. Rather, this saying only makes sense within its historical context. For Roman custom stipulated that when a Roman citizen got into an argument with an enslaved or oppressed person which became so heated that it resorted to blows, the Roman would give the non–Roman the backhand slap (*i.e.* slapping on "the right cheek"), a gesture indicating that the one being slapped was subhuman, unworthy of basic human rights or respect, and vastly inferior in dignity to the fully human one doing the slapping. But when a Roman citizen got into a similar argument with another Roman citizen, one would give the other a forehand slap (*i.e.* slapping on "the left cheek"), a gesture indicating that the one being slapped was just as human as, and equal in every respect to, the one doing the slapping; in short, although the two disagreed, they recognized each other as equals in dignity and worth and entitled to the same rights. So Jesus instructs his Jewish audience that if a Roman gives one of them a backhand slap, degrading the Jew as subhuman and inferior in worth to the Roman, "turn to him the left cheek also," entailing that if the Roman slaps again, the Roman will be forced to give the Jew the forehand slap, thereby acknowledging that the Jew is just as much of a human being as he is and equal to him in dignity, worth, and every other respect.

Or again, when Jesus instructed, "If someone wants to sue you and take your cloak, give him your undergarment as well" (Mt. 5:40), he was dealing with Jews exploited by Roman moneylenders charging exorbitant interest rates. Since the Romans ruled Palestine, they possessed an economic stability that their poor Jewish subjects lacked, forcing the latter to borrow money from the former. Knowing that the legal system was on their side, Roman moneylenders were not content to merely recollect the original amount or to collect the original amount plus reasonable interest but typically desired around four times the original amount. Since the impoverished Jews barely had enough to make ends meet as it was, they could rarely pay their creditors' fees; in response, the creditors dragged their Jewish debtors into court and tried to take these debtors for everything they had, thereby creating a system of "judicial robbery." Since Roman courts would always find in favor of Romans, Jesus' audience knew they could never win a case. So Jesus proposes, "Alright, you will lose the case. But take the unjust law and, with ingenious skill, throw it into a point of absurdity. When your creditor sues you for your outer garment, give him your undergarment as well." This would mean taking off the only stitch of clothing one was still wearing and thus standing naked in court. While public nakedness was taboo in Roman culture, the shame of nakedness fell not on the person who was naked, but primarily on the person who caused the nakedness and secondarily on all others who observed it. Jesus thus empowers the debtor with a means of redress whereby he can non–violently put his creditor to shame. Imagine the debtor leaving the courtroom, walking into the street and everyone seeing him nude. When they ask, "What happened to you?" he replies, "That creditor took all my clothes." At this, the creditor's own family, friends, and townspeople upbraid him, "What kind of a person are you that you would bring this shame upon yourself, upon all of us, and upon this whole city? How ruthless and greedy are you to take even that man's undergarment?" One could surmise that no Roman would ever exploitatively sue a Jewish debtor in that city again. For by extorting the Jewish debtor, the Roman creditor is putting himself in the position of being shamed by that debtor.

Finally, when Jesus exhorted, "If someone compels you to go with him one mile, go with him two miles" (Mt. 5:41), he was making direct reference to Roman martial law. It is important to highlight that the Roman Empire was not only the most oppressive empire the Ancient Near East had ever seen but also understood the philosophy of oppression quite well. In that philosophy, there is one "trade secret" that any oppressor never wants the oppressed to learn: the oppressor has no power in and of himself, but all his so–called power actually comes from those being oppressed. In other words, the oppressor can only accomplish things powered by the oppressed; without the oppressed to build the oppressor's cities, pay the oppressor taxes, and the like, the oppressor would be nothing. The actually impotent oppressor only stays in power because he perpetuates the façade that he has power in and of himself and that the oppressed is weak, which masks the reality that the oppressed is the storehouse of power and fools the oppressed into surrendering this power to the parasitic oppressor. Knowing this, the Romans wanted to make absolutely sure that the people they oppressed never uncovered their "trade secret"—that Roman power lay exclusively in their ability to trick others into doing their bidding with the ruse that they were more intrinsically powerful than others. Hence martial law was formulated in such a way that soldiers would never do anything to make oppressed peoples aware of this secret. So concerning forced labor, martial law stipulated that a soldier could compel an oppressed person to carry his baggage for a maximum of one mile, since one mile was considered a trivial distance. In other words, a distance of one mile or less would preserve the guise that the soldier could have carried his baggage himself, but that he simply chose not to do it and, in light of his superior position, found it beneath him to carry his own baggage when a lesser individual could do it for him. But if a soldier compelled an oppressed person to carry his baggage for more than one mile, the Roman jurists feared, then the oppressed person would start thinking, "Would this Roman soldier have any power at all if it were not for people like me to carry his baggage for him? Could the Romans have constructed their metropoli without us to perform the manual labor? The Romans can't even carry their baggage minus our power, much less dominate the Mediterranean world!" At this point, the proverbial "jig would be up." For this reason, Jesus advised each of his fellow Jews, when pressed into service by a Roman soldier, to freely carry his baggage an extra mile instead of, as the soldier would anticipate, disgustfully throwing down the baggage at the mile marker. Such an ingenious response would convey two messages to the soldier. First, the Jew would indicate to the soldier, "I am fully aware that you have zero power in and of yourself, but that you can only do what I empower you to do." Second, he would communicate, "In spite of this awareness, I will not violently rebel against you, but I will lovingly serve you by carrying your baggage for an extra mile." Afterwards, moreover, the soldier would face punishment for his oppression, but not at Jewish hands; instead, his own Roman overseer would punish him for violating martial law.

In all of this, Jesus admonished his disciples to pray, "May your will be done, as in heaven, so on earth" (Mt. 6:10). This directive reveals that God's will is often thwarted on earth. I have often heard it said that if something is God's will for a person's (or group's) life, it will necessarily happen, an idea which I dub an "illogical selective determinism." By this I mean that its exponent, while denying deterministic forms of predestination where God compels those he gratuitously elects to be saved and renders salvation logically impossible for those he does not elect, applies an identical determinism to all subordinate facets of human life. Having rejected its applicability to the greater, one still holds out hope that it works for the lesser, in spite of the all–encompassing nature of salvation! Hence it is impossible for one to be salvifically free but bound in one's mundane choices, since it is precisely one's freedom in mundane choices that enables one's salvific freedom. A reversal of Luther's classic dictum, those who maintain that God's will must happen commit the logical fallacy of holding that people are free concerning things above but bound concerning the things below which compose the things above. Due to the fact that sinful humans frequently fail to actualize God's desires, Scripture commands us to devote ourselves to the "power–under" of prayer. Not only did Jesus model a life of consistent prayer (Mk. 1:35; Lk. 5:16; 6:12; 9:28; 11:1), but the New Testament writers insist that we follow his example (Lk. 18:1–6; 1 Thess. 5:17; Eph. 6:18; 1 Tim. 2:8; Jas. 5:14). An expressly Kingdom brand of social action, intercessory prayer must be among our principal acts of self–sacrificial service to our fellow human beings. Boyd remarks on this score:

> Both the Old and the New Testaments emphasize the power and urgency of prayer. In fact, dozens of times the Bible depicts the fate of a

nation as hanging in the balance not on what society did or on what politicians did, but on whether or not the people of God *prayed.*[17]

To illustrate this principle, God told Ezekiel at the outset of the Babylonian Exile that if even a single intercessor had prayed in behalf of Judah, then God would have spared the nation from captivity:

> The people of this land extort and rob; they oppress the poor and needy and treat aliens unfairly, withholding justice from them. But I searched for anyone among them who would . . . stand before me in the gap on behalf of the land so that I would not have to destroy it, but I found none. Therefore, I have poured out my wrath on them (Ezek. 22:29–31).

Recall from chapter three that the prayers of several individuals altered God's original reactions to various circumstances throughout biblical history and so changed the world (Ex. 32:10–14; Deut. 9:13–29; 1 Kgs. 21:21–29; Isa. 38:1–6). As Kingdom people, we possess a distinctive power and obligation to affect the course of history by crying out to God, and we must implement this power on behalf of our neighbors.

Drawing together the threads of the Sermon on the Mount, Boyd summarizes:

> Understood in their original context, these teachings do not tell us to allow people to abuse us, as though we are to love our enemies but not ourselves. To the contrary, Jesus is giving us a way by which we can keep from being defined by those who act unjustly toward us. When we respond to violence with violence, whether it be physical, verbal, or attitudinal, we legitimize the violence of our enemy and sink to his level. When we instead respond unexpectedly—offering our other cheek and going a second mile—we reveal, even as we expose the injustice of his actions, that our nemesis doesn't have the power to define us by those actions. In this sense we serve our enemy, for manifesting God's love and exposing evil (the two always go hand in hand) open up the possibility that he will repent and be transformed.[18]

Jesus' reign is displayed and enlarged via the fidelity of his followers, and thus the Kingdom of God is present whenever his followers select peace over violence and forgiveness over revenge, acting in behalf of others' ad-

---

17. Boyd, *Myth*, 116; emphasis his.
18. Ibid., 40.

vantage rather than their own advantage. By contrast, whenever people choose violence, revenge, and their own advantage, they take part in the Kingdom of the World, regardless of how comprehensible or "reasonable" their behavior is by the World's standards. But the "Way" of living under Jesus' rule, while controversial and unfeasible within the prevailing global framework, is the only way that concords with God and his actions in space and time.

Kingdom Vindication at the General Resurrection

It should be emphasized that if the doctrine of the general resurrection is false, then everything in this section (as well as everything in this chapter and book) fails. But Christians are obliged to predicate their beliefs about the future upon the guarantee of Jesus:

> Truly, truly, I say to you that *an hour is coming and now is* when the dead corpses will hear the voice of the Son of God, and the ones having heard will live. For just as the Father has life in himself, so also he gave the Son to have life in himself, and he gave authority to him to make judgment, because he is the Son of Man. Do not marvel at this, for an hour is coming in which all the people in the graves will hear his voice and will come out, the ones having done the good things to a resurrection of life, but the ones have practiced the evil things to a resurrection of judgment (Jn. 5:25–29; emphasis mine).

Note carefully the italicized tension between the simultaneously future and present aspects of the hour. This is because the Kingdom of God comes in two stages. While Jesus inaugurated the Kingdom with his first coming, it came only in part but in such a way that it guaranteed its later coming in full. In other words, through his crucifixion Jesus won the decisive battle upon which the final victory over evil depends, but that final victory has not yet been implemented. Thus we who live between Jesus' first and second comings experience the Kingdom "now but not yet," here in principle but actualized when Jesus gloriously returns. When Jesus returns on the Day of Yahweh, God will transform this universe into all it was originally created to be by actualizing all of its potentialities, redeeming it from the bondage to which sinful humans have subjected it.

> For the creation is anxiously awaiting and eagerly expecting the unveiling of the sons of God. For the creation was subjected to futility, not willingly but because of those having subjected it, in hope that even the creation itself will be freed from slavery to corruption into the freedom

of the glory of the children of God. For we know that the whole creation groans together and travails in pain together until now (Rom. 8:19-
22).

This new universe is described in Scripture as the "new heaven and new
earth," simply the Genesis phrase "heaven and earth" (*i.e.* physical universe)
with the qualifier "new" distributed across the terms, and represents the perfection and fulfillment of all nature. God will explode the distinction between his timeless and nonphysical realm and our temporal and physical
realm, conflating the two realms into a timeless yet physical realm. Note that
the phrase "Day of Yahweh" recalls the Genesis creation narrative and denotes an "eighth day," a paradox meant to explode our temporal categories
and designating that time itself will come to an end. That timelessness is an
attribute of the transformed universe is also the point of the language that
"on that day there will be no light, no cold or frost, since it will be a unique
day, without daytime or nighttime, a day known to Yahweh, such that when
evening should come, there will be light" (Zech. 14:6–7), that "there will be
neither sun nor moon" (Rev. 21:23), and that "there will be no night" (Rev.
21:25; 22:5). Into this new universe Jesus will bring with him all the redeemed souls, who will be reinfused into their transformed resurrection
bodies, numerically identical to and historically continuous with their
previous physical bodies. Just as Jesus' physical body was transformed on
Easter Sunday from a σῶμα ψυχικόν into a σῶμα πνευματικόν, so our
formerly mortal and perishable bodies will be clothed with immortality and
imperishability. God will transform our physical bodies such that they are
honorable, powerful, and free from the effects of sickness, disease, sin, and
death. They will no longer be instinctively steered toward the wills of our
own souls, but will be instinctively steered toward the will of the Holy
Most astonishing of all, God will literally make his home with human
beings in the new universe, such that God will always be definitively present
(not simply repletively present, as he is currently) on earth with his redeemed:

> Behold, the tabernacle of God is with humans, and he will tabernacle
> with them; they will be his peoples, and God–with–them (*i.e.* Jesus)
> himself will be their God, and he will wipe away every tear from their
> eyes. Death will be no longer. Neither grief nor crying nor pain will be
> any longer, because the former things passed away (Rev. 21:3–4).

Until the Day of Yahweh, we try to replicate to others the selfless love and
service that God showed us, thus changing people from the inside out,
changing the way they think, transforming their hearts and minds so that all

their potentialities would be actualized. In other words, we work to carry out the original plan of God for humanity seen in Genesis 2–3 symbolically depicted by the various trees in the Garden of Eden. We then become God's "change agents" in the world who work to progressively transform people and the universe to fulfill all its potentialities, which efforts will ultimately be consummated by God at the new heaven–earth. Wakabayashi portrays the nature of our "in–between" time, during which the Old Age continues and the Age to Come begins, with an illustration from modern history:

> It's like D–Day in World War II. D–Day was the decisive battle that assured ultimate victory for the Allies against the Nazis. But V–Day, the victory day of the war, was still to come when the Nazis finally surrendered and signed the peace treaty. In Jesus, the D–Day of the war against sin, Satan and death has been secured for us at the cross so that the Age to Come has begun. But the ultimate V–Day of victory is still on its way and will take place when Jesus returns and the Age to Come arrives in all its fullness.[19]

Because the general resurrection guarantees that all our labors for the Kingdom will come to fruition, we should heed the admonition of Paul to be steadfast, immovable, always abounding in the work of Jesus, fully assured that our work is not in vain (1 Cor. 15:58).

The Messy Question of Politics

We now come to the thorny question of Christian approaches to politics. One guiding principle which shall be employed throughout our discussion is that a proper perspective on first–century history insures that we act faithfully in the twenty–first century; by contrast, an improper perspective or lack of perspective on first–century history insures that we will act unfaithfully in the twenty–first. On this basis, we assert that, far from conflating any earthly government with the Kingdom of God, Christ's followers must maintain a healthy suspicion toward every government, particularly their own, if they are to avoid nationalistic idolatry. For Scripture indicates that however beneficial a particular state may be by Worldly standards, it is powerfully influenced by satanic powers. Therefore, no member of God's Kingdom should either trust in any political ideology or be surprised when state heads or parties behave in contradiction to Jesus' teachings. Thus Jesus and the New Testament writers exhibited no surprise or concern over the gross immoral-

---

19. Wakabayashi, *Kingdom Come*, 65.

ity frequently practiced by first–century C.E. Roman officials. They simply regarded such debauchery as the *modus operandi* for heads of state.

Accordingly, Christians are not to put undue stock in politics as the method for solving the World's problems, since politics is itself a department of the World. Therefore, politics are impotent to bring about any permanent change, and no political position can lay claim to being "the Christian position" or "the Kingdom position," for all political positions are fraught with ambiguities. In other words, for each good any political position can accomplish, there are multiple evils that it accomplishes alongside of that good. Owing to its Worldly nature, politics is a matter of attempting to determine the lesser of many evils, which prohibits any clear–cut answers. Rather, Christians must realize that the only way to ultimately bring about change is through Calvary–quality acts of service. With that being said, we now have the necessary background to analyze two interrelated issues: whether Christians may serve in government and how Christians should vote amidst governments which allow public participation.

Can Christians serve in government? Yes, as long as they do so counter-culturally, disregarding the government's intrinsic Kingdom of the World standards and instead governing by distinctly Kingdom of God standards. Thus Christians who govern should, contrary to the power–over governmental system, be servant leaders who are not concerned with their own prestige, success, power, money, or reelection, as they trust God for their material needs (Mt. 6:32–33), but care only about lovingly meeting the needs of the people within their constituencies, so relieving them from having to worry about meeting those needs and thereby freeing them up and empowering them to similarly meet the needs of others. (Obviously it is far easier for people to aid others when their own needs have been fulfilled than when they are just scraping by to make ends meet for themselves.) However, Christians in government should realize that the governmental system itself has no more power to produce godly change than any other occupation in the World, thus avoiding the arrogant stance that they "are doing more for God" than Christians in any other vocation. This is because none of the World's occupations have the ability to bring about Kingdom change; only people following the Kingdom of God irrespective of occupation have this ability. Remembering that we are called to be in the World but not of the World, we must serve faithfully, honestly, and compassionately in whatever vocation we find ourselves. The classic example of Kingdom people governmentally serving in these ways is Daniel, Hananiah, Mishael, and Azariah (Shadrach, Meshach, and Abed–Nego), who were pressed into service by the Babylonian Empire, the very government which had taken the Israelites captive and consequently became the paradigm of an anti–God and anti–Christian government throughout the remainder of Scripture (*e.g.* Ps. 137:1, 8; Isa. 43:14; 47:1; 48:14; Jer. 50:13–14, 18, 23–24, 29; 51:7–24; Ezra 5:12; 1 Pet. 5:13; Rev. 14:8; 16:19; 18:2–21). Without trusting in the Babylonian Empire to accomplish God's purposes, Daniel and his friends lovingly and responsibly served as "resident aliens" in this Worldly juggernaut and thereby advanced the salvific plan of God.

> As for these four young men, God gave them learning and skill in all literature and wisdom; and Daniel was specifically given understanding in all visions and dreams. . . . King Nebuchadnezzar talked with them, and he found none equal to Daniel, Hananiah, Mishael, and Azariah; therefore they entered the king's service. In every matter of wisdom and understanding concerning which the king inquired of them, he found them ten times better than all the magicians and enchanters throughout his whole kingdom. . . . [Later] it pleased Darius to set over the kingdom 120 satraps to rule throughout the kingdom, and over them three presidents, of whom Daniel was one, to whom the satraps were made accountable so that the king would not suffer loss. Then this Daniel became distinguished above all the other presidents and satraps because of his exceptional qualities; therefore, the king planned to set him over the whole kingdom. Then the satraps and other presidents sought to find a ground for complaint against Daniel in his governance of the kingdom, but they could not because he was trustworthy, and neither negligence nor corruption was found in him (Dan. 1:17, 19–20; 6:1–4).

Here we see that Daniel's administration was defined by reliability and honesty, two attributes which prove conspicuously absent from the vast majority of politicians and which thus rendered him blameless in sharp contrast to his peers. Despite that Hananiah, Mishael, and Azariah reproduced these characteristics, all four faced severe persecution from jealous colleagues who feared a loss of their power base and exposure of their own corruption. Since the native Babylonian administrators realized that the behavior of the four Jewish young men followed directly from their allegiance to Yahweh, the consequent harassment aimed to dissolve this allegiance. Astonishingly, the cause–and–effect relationship between Yahweh devotion and social justice proved transparent to even the hypocritical old guard, a fact worthy of note disclosing how right belief and right action (orthodoxy and orthopraxy) mesh to form a persuasive evangelistic tapestry.

> Then the interlocutors said, "We shall find no ground for complaint against this Daniel unless we find it in connection with the worship of

his God." So these presidents and satraps came together to the king and said, "O King Darius, live forever! All the presidents of the kingdom, the prefects and the satraps, the counselors and the governors, are agreed that the king should pass an ordinance and establish an interdict, that whoever prays to any god or human besides you, O king, shall be cast into the den of lions. . . . Thus the king commanded, and Daniel was captured and cast into the den of lions. . . . Certain Chaldeans came forward and maliciously accused the Jewish men . . . Shadrach, Meshach, and Abed–Nego: "These men, O king, pay no homage to you; they do not worship your gods or venerate the golden image you have set up". . . . And he ordered the mighty men of his army to bind Shadrach, Meshach, and Abed–Nego, and to throw them into the fiery furnace (Dan. 6:6–7, 16; 3:8, 12, 20).

Even when facing persecution and virtually certain death, neither Daniel nor his friends compromised or even hid their allegiance to Yahweh's kingship; instead, they trusted that Yahweh would vindicate them either miraculously in the present or at the general resurrection in the future. Thus when Daniel learned that the decree forbidding Yahweh–worship had been passed, "he went home to his upper room where the windows opened toward Jerusalem; three times a day he kneeled down and prayed, giving thanks to his God, exactly as he had done before" (Dan. 6:10). Similarly, Shadrach, Meshach, and Abed–Nego refused to make excuses before Nebuchadnezzar for their illegal refusal to worship his gods but proclaimed their hope in the one living God: "We will not defend ourselves before you in this matter. If you throw us into the fiery furnace, the God we serve is able to deliver us from it . . . but even if he does not, we will not serve your gods or kneel before your image" (Dan. 3:18). Such an attitude of not fearing those who can only kill the body, knowing that whatever injuries they inflict will be more than reversed at the general resurrection, is the one that must characterize Kingdom people in all their words and deeds. It is not surprising, as Wright points out, "that Jesus made the book of Daniel thematic for his whole vocation."[20]

Our assessment of Christians in government is reinforced by the reflections of Balthasar Hubmaier, who found himself caught between the two extremes of a total identification of state and church on the one hand and a total identification of state and the Kingdom of the World on the other hand. Rejecting both perspectives as un–Christlike, Hubmaier contended that the first committed the same sin Jesus accused the Jewish religious leaders of committing (trying to win the victory of God with the World's weapons), and the second led to a separatism and isolationism from the World that Je-

---

20. Wright, *Jesus*, 598.

sus overtly warned his disciples against committing. If one regards civil government as the Kingdom of the World rather than as a *tertian quid* whose existence is necessitated by the Kingdom of the World, then one will inevitably erect a wall around one's own community, divorcing it from society at large and so abandoning Jesus' call to be the light of the world in favor of hiding one's light under a bushel (Mt. 5:14–15). Rather, Hubmaier exhorts Christians to uniquely serve in government following Kingdom standards:

> See, dear brothers, that councils, courts, and law are not wrong. Thus also the judge may and should be a Christian. . . . If a Christian therefore may and should, in the power of the divine Word, be a judge with the mouth, he may also be a protector with the hand of the one who wins the suit and punish the unjust. . . . That is why we have the election of the burgomasters, mayors, and judges, all of whom Christ permits to remain, if with God and a good conscience they rule well over temporal and physical matters. . . . A Christian magistrate is bound by his soul's salvation to protect and guard all innocent and peaceful people. . . . The magistrate is also bound to rescue and release all oppressed and persecuted people, widows, orphans, whether natives or strangers, without any respect of persons, according to the will and most earnest command of God (Isa. 1:17; Jer. 21:12; 22:3; Rom. 13:1; and many other passages).[21]

Since Christians, having no regard for their own advantage or privilege but considering others better than themselves, govern not to receive service from their constituents but as servant leaders who love, protect, and thereby earn the respect of their constituents, Hubmaier submits as obvious that Christian

---

21. "Sehent ir lieben Brüeder, das Ratt, gricht vnd recht nit vnrecht ist. Das auch der Richter mag vnd soll ein Christ sein. . . . Mag nun vnd soll ein Christ in krafft des Götlichen worts ein richter sein mit dem munnd, so mag er auch sein ein bschützer mit der hannd des, der recht gewinnt, vnd mag den vngerechten straffen. . . . Daher khummen die waalenn der Burgermayster, Schulthaissen vnd Richtern, die all laßt Christus beleyben, das sy mit Gott vnd güter gwissen wol zeytlich vnd in leiblichen hendlen regieren vnd richten mügent. . . . Derhalb ist die Oberkhait bey jrer seelen seligkhait schuldig zů beschützen vnd beschirmen all vnschuldig vnd fridsam menschen. . . . Also ist schuldig die Oberkait zů handthaben vnd erledigen all vndertruckt vnd gezwungen menschen, witwen, waysen, erkant vnd fremdling on alle ansehung der Personen nach dem willen vnd ernstlichen beuelch Gotes. Esa. am 1., Hiere. 21. 22., Roma. 13 vnd an andern vill ortten." Hubmaier, *Von dem Schwert*, in Westin and Bergsten, *Schriften*, 441, 438–39.

governors and other law–enforcement officers prove far better than self-seeking Worldly authorities. Unlike the oppression, persecution, and bribery practiced by Worldly powers, Kingdom government officials must non-violently fight for social justice in all its forms, ensuring equal treatment of all (citizens and foreigners alike) under the law and providing care for those who cannot care for themselves. While not advocating an exceptionless pacifism, Hubmaier believes that officials should resort to force only as a last resort to protect innocent people from criminal activity. Moreover, Christians filled with the Spirit who inspired the countercultural wisdom behind the Sermon on the Mount are the only ones capable of truly discerning whether all other options have been exhausted and thus whether corporal punishment is necessary.

> You must, must, must all confess that a Christian in government can perform and will do so much better and more earnestly than a non–Christian. . . . Such a person may say, "I pray God that he will give me grace and wisdom that I may bear the sword and rule according to his word and will." So Solomon prayed and was given great wisdom by God to bear the sword well. . . . it is evident that the more pious they are, the better and more orderly they will bear the sword according to the will of God exclusively for the protection of the innocent and for a terror to evildoers.[22]

However, Hubmaier immediately qualifies this remark by reiterating that God has not ordained the use of the sword by the church under any circumstances, even to protect itself. Thus Hubmaier admonishes the church:

> It is not proper for you to carry [the sword]. You are not in authority; it is not your appointed place, nor are you called or elected for it. For, whoever takes the sword will perish by the sword. . . . No one shall take the sword himself, except one who has been elected and appointed for

---

22. "Jr müest, müest, müest ye bekhennen, das ein Christenliche Oberkhait solhs vil baß vnd ernstlicher verbringen müg vnd thon werde, denn ein vnchristenliche. . . . Yetz mag er sagenn . . . bitte ich Got auff das er mir gnad vnnd weyßhayt verleyhe, das nach seinem wort vnnd willen züfieren vnd regieren. . . . ist wissentlich, das ye frommer sy seind, ye baß vnnd ordenlicher sy das schwert nach dem willen Gotes zü beschützung der vnschuldigen vnd zü einer forcht." Hubmaier, *Von dem Schwert*, 437, 447.

that purpose. For he does not take it up of himself, but it has been brought to him and given him.[23]

From this, Hubmaier concludes that church and government are to remain separate due to the fact that their divinely ordained roles are fundamentally distinct; confusion of one with the other inevitably destroys the purpose and structure of both. Certainly Hubmaier correctly captures the insight of the historical Jesus on this score, who preached relentlessly against the blasphemy of conflating Judaism (whose redeemed community he was inaugurating) with government, opposing this tradition from the birth of the United Monarchy to the present day. Further, Hubmaier insists that the Church must never use force to procure doctrinal or moral conformity. The only sword that the Church may implement is the Word of God, which Hubmaier understands broadly to include all self–disclosures of the λογός in both general and special revelation. Hence for Hubmaier, the apologetic task is paramount in the evangelistic program of the Church and must employ (as we have been following throughout this construction) the Bible, philosophical theology (all valid deductions and inferences which may be drawn from general and special revelation), and all other disciplines in the service of God. For those who resist the double–sided coin of Kingdom living paired with sound apologetic reasoning which our lives are called to exemplify, Hubmaier instructs: "If they refuse to yield to statements of authority or gospel evidences, then avoid them and allow them to continue ranting and raging (Tit. 3:10) so that those who are filthy may become more filthy still (Rev. 22:11)."[24] Appealing to the Sermon on the Mount and the Johannine discourses, Hubmaier points out that Jesus explicitly advocated religious tolerance, which directly contradicts the notion of a state religion:

> For Christ did not come to murder, execute, or burn, but for those who live to live even more abundantly. . . . Thus while burning heretics ap-

---

23. "Es khert dir nit zůfieren. Du bist nit im gwalt. Er ist dir nit beuolhen. Bist auch nit darzů berůefft noch erwölet. Dann wer das schwert nimbt, der soll durch dz schwert vmb khummen. . . . Aber nyemandt soll das schwert selbs nemen, sonder wo ainer erwölet vnd darzů eruordert wirdt, denn so nimbt erß nit auß jm selbs, sonnder man tregt jms dar vnnd gibt jmß." Ibid., 436–37.

24. "Ob sy sich mit gwaltsprüchen oder Euangelischen vrsachen nit wöltind weisen lassen, so gang iren müssig vnd laß sy die weil toben vnnd wütten, Tit. 3 [V. 10], damit die so ietz psudlet sind, noch baß psudlet werdind. Apoc. vlt. [V. 11]." Hubmaier, *Der uralten und gar neuen Lehrer Urteil*, Vol. II, in Westin and Bergsten, *Schriften*, 253.

pears to be following Christ, it is rather to deny him indeed and be more abominable than Jehoiakim, the king of Judah.[25]

In his 1524 *Von Ketzern und ihren Verbrennern*, the first early modern treatise championing religious freedom, Hubmaier contends that magistrates who sentence so–called heretics to the fire are far more heretical than the individuals whom they burn, since, even when suppressing real heresy, they prematurely condemn people to hell who might later have repented of sin and become powerful witnesses of God's grace, which makes good out of evil, if they had lived out the full span of their years. Here Hubmaier is proposing a theological basis for religious freedom more profound than is generally recognized: to persecute a person for heresy amounts to an implicit denial of the incarnation, since the God revealed in Christ is the God of the invitation, not of coercion. The accuracy of this inference is verified by Hubmaier's analysis of the relationship between the character of God and libertarian human freedom:

> The heavenly Father, who now views humanity afresh through the merit of Jesus Christ our Lord, blesses and draws each person with his life-giving Word which he speaks into the person's heart. This drawing and call is like an invitation to a marriage or to an evening meal, through which God gives power and authority to all people inasmuch as they themselves want to come; the free choice is left to them. . . . But those who do not want to come, such as Jerusalem and those who purchased oxen and houses and took wives, he excludes as unworthy of this evening meal. He desires to have uncoerced, willing, and joyous guests and givers—these he loves, as God does not force anyone. . . . Similarly, Lot was not coerced by the two angels in Sodom.[26]

---

25. "Dann Christus ist nit kommen, das er metzge, vmbringe, brenne, sonder das die, so da lebend, noch reychlicher lebind. . . . Darumb ketzer verbrennen ist Christum im schein bekennen, aber in der that verlöügnen vnd greülicher sin dann Joachim, der könig Juda." Ibid., 254.

26. "Des himelischen vaters beschehen vnd erlangt werden, der nun den menschen durch das verdienen Jesu Christi vnsers herrens auff ein neües ansehe, begnade vnd in ziehe mit seinem lebend machenden wort, wölhes er dem menschen in das hertz redt, durch welhe ziehung vnd eruordrung einer ladung auff ein hochzeit oder zů einem nachtmal vergleichet, gibt got macht vnd gwalt allen menschen, so ferr vnd sy selbs wöllen (es ist inen freye waal haimgesetzt) zekhummen. . . . Welher mensch aber nit will, wie Hierusalem vnd die, so ochsen vnd dörffer gekaufft vnd weyber genomen, auch nit khummen wolten, die selben lasset er auß bleiben wie die vnwirdigen diß nachtmals. Er will vngezwun-

This passage reveals that from the theological foundation of libertarian free will, Hubmaier deduces that God, who created humans with the faculty to choose either spiritual good or evil, would not himself violate that very faculty. If not even God compels people into his kingdom but offers them an invitation which they can freely accept or deny, then, it follows that humans have no right to compel people into the Kingdom of God either, through law, politics, or any other Worldly means.

Drawing together all the biblical facets of servant leadership we have discussed, the sixteenth–century reformer summarizes the vocation of Christians in government, spelling out both the virtues to embody and the pitfalls to avoid.

> It belongs to no Christian, out of lust for authority, to contend to be a ruler, but much rather to flee it. . . . Christ speaks to this effect: "The kings of this World dominate their subjects and are called Gracious Lord" (Lk. 22:25). But a Christian, if he is in authority, does not dominate. He does not desire to be called Gracious Lord, or Sir; but he considers that he is a servant of God, and is diligent in performing the ordinance of God, according to which he protects the pious and punishes the wicked. He exalts himself above none, but takes well to heart the word of Christ that the foremost shall be as a servant. . . . So, dear sisters and brothers, make no patchwork of the Scripture, but putting all its texts together in one full judgment, you will then come to a complete understanding of the Scriptures, and you will see how the text does not forbid the magistracy to the Christian, but teaches one not to quarrel, war, and fight for it. Moreover, a Christian magistrate must not conquer land and people with the sword and force; that is against God. Also we should not greatly desire to be saluted as Lords, like Worldly people who are kings, princes, and lords. For the magistracy is not lordship and knighthood, but service according to the ordinance of God.[27]

---

gen, willig vnd frölich gest vnd geber haben, die selben hat er lieb. Wann Gott zwingt anders niemant . . . nit annders gezwungen. . . . Deß gleich Loth die zwen Engel in Sodoma." Hubmaier, *Von der Freiheit des Willens*, in Westin and Bergsten, *Schriften*, 394.

27. "Steet auch khainem Christen zů, auß begirde der hörschung der Oberkhait nach zůfechten, sonder als vil ainer mag mer fliehen. . . . Darzů spricht Christus: Die weltlichen künig die hörschend vnd werdent gnedig herren gehayssen. Abe rein Christ, so er schon in der Oberkhait ist so hörscht er nit. Er begeert auch nit, das man jm gnad herr oder Junckher sage. Sonder er betracht, das er ist ein diener Gottes, vnd fleysset sich, das er der ordnung Gottes nach handle, darmit die frommen beschützt vnd die bösen gestrafft werdent. Er erhebt sich auch vber nyemant, sonder behertzigt das wort Christj recht wol, das der

Therefore, Christians in the highest governmental offices, not to mention the lower ones, must refrain from all power–over military, political, or economic conquests for land, resources, or people–groups, as people who do such things in any circumstances are, by definition, not Christian. But notice that Hubmaier leaves unanswered a set of questions which immediately transpire from this discussion. For instance, are Christians allowed to take up arms in self–defense? Is there ever such a thing as a just war? Can Christians ever validly serve in the military? We follow Hubmaier in making no attempt to adjudicate these questions, as all of them are highly ambiguous and open to legitimate disagreement among Christians. Rather, we highlight them to make the point that these are precisely the questions Christians need to continually ask and wrestle with, instead of uncritically swallowing the caricature that each has only one Christian answer and that all other answers fall outside the pale of following Jesus. Those Christians who come from "just war" backgrounds ought to self–critically assess their traditions and embrace that staunch Christian pacifists are certainly no less faithful and possibly more faithful to the historical Jesus than they are, and vice versa. Here is a case where coming up with the right questions is far more important than coming up with the right answers; the first clearly exist while the second do not.

With this being said, how should Christians in representative governments vote? Each should vote according to conscience, recognizing that one's way of voting is not "the Christian way" or "the Kingdom way" to vote. There is no such thing, of course, because the whole governmental structure depends for its existence on the Worldly dominion of Satan and because of the inherent ambiguities at every turn. One must also realize that the only way to ultimately bring about change is through Calvary–quality loving acts of service. Anyone who denies this logic by arguing that Worldly law and order can be used to advance God's work unwittingly falls into one or both of two camps: (1) those who wish to ignore the fact that many within the Church have failed to keep their own house in order as well as to evade

---

fürnemest solle sein wie ein diener. . . . Also, lieben Brüeder, machent nit fleckhwerck in der Schrifft, sonder stellend vorgeende vnd nachuolgeende wort zůsamen in ein gantz vrtail, alß dann vberkhumbt Jr einen volkummenlichen verstand der Schrifften, vnd sehent, wie das wörtlin (Jr aber nit also) den Christen die Oberkhait nit verbeütt, sonder leert vns, das wir nit darumb zanckhen, kriegen vnd fechten sollend, noch lanndt vnd leütt mit dem Schwert vnd mit gwalt erobern. Es ist wider Gott. Auch sollen wir nit begeern Gnad herren vnd Junckherrn zůsein, wie die weltlichen khünig, fürstenn vnd herren. Dann die Oberkhait ist nit ein hörschung vnd Junckherrschafft, sonder ein dienstbarkhait nach der ordnung Gottes." Hubmaier, *Von dem Schwert*, 452–53.

the responsibility and consequences of church discipline; and (2) those who lack faith in the power of the Kingdom of God. People who belong to the second camp, regardless of nominal affiliation, simply do not meet Jesus' definition of following him; such persons would be wise to carefully consider Jesus' warnings to those who did exactly the same thing in the first century. To those Jews who claimed to be his followers but rejected his power–under Kingdom in favor of a power–over agenda, Jesus admonished:

> Not everyone who says to me, "Lord, Lord," will enter the Kingdom of Heaven, but only those who do the will of my Father who is in heaven. Many people will say to me on that day, "Lord, Lord, did we not prophesy in your name and cast out demons and perform many miracles in your name?" Then I will tell them flatly, "I never knew you. Depart from me, you who practice lawlessness" (Mt. 7:21–23).

For the first camp, politics amount to a placebo through which people can be made to "look Christian" irrespective of the status of their souls. In other words, unwilling or unable to preserve the moral purity of their churches, many are satisfied to give up the ship of dominical church discipline, which we have already seen constitutes the necessary sinews for the church's survival. But the fact that most in the West who claim to be Christian are no such thing is, for many, a hard pill to swallow. Sadly, therefore, those unwilling to face the facts resort to fooling themselves that their fellow nominal Christians are the people of God by using politics to enforce laws that make the members of their societies externally look like Christians without internally transforming their hearts. Hubmaier exposes the fallacy of this strategy by placing it against the backdrop of its salvation–historical context:

> Fraternal discipline and punishment with the sword are two very different commands issued by God. The first is promised and given to the church by Christ (Mt. 10:14; 18:18; Jn. 20:23), for the admission of the pious into their fellowship and the exclusion of the unworthy, to use according to its will. . . . The other command relates to the external and temporal authority and government, which originally was given by God after Adam's fall. . . . After that the wickedness of humans increased and became overflowing; indeed, the bulk of it became rampant. The Jewish people then demanded from Samuel a king and thereby abandoned God. The same king, at the command of God, Samuel gave them; and they thereby became bound to endure the royal authority and subjection that the king exercised thereafter, for their sins, since they

had despised and abandoned God and had earnestly demanded from Samuel a king who was not God, like the other nations.[28]

In the language of the Genesis creation narrative, this strategy urges its exponents to first explicitly reject God by eating of the Tree of the Knowledge of Good and Evil and then, in the ultimate sacrilege, to depart from the presence of God while simultaneously claiming that God commanded them to eat of the forbidden tree and trumpeting that God is walking alongside them every step of their path leading further away from him. Having abandoned the only valid means given by Jesus to maintain ethical behavior among churchgoers, astonishingly many Westerners are surprised that their attempts to cultivate the fruit of the Spirit unanimously fail, obviously learning nothing from the creation account. But rather than honestly and outrightly admitting their failure and reimplementing Matthew 18:15–20, which produces right moral behavior through inward spiritual change, Westerners have by and large pridefully overlooked their disciplinary collapse and instead passed the buck of regulating the carnal behavior of their congregations to the state. Thus compounding the problem, they self–contradictorily attempt to seize Satan's power and use it to compel both churchgoers and admitted non–believers to perform actions which Scripture teaches true believers will voluntarily undertake. As a result, a self–congratulatory pseudo–church, *i.e.* a caricature of the true church, emerges which, by virtue of forcing people to live in ways it deems acceptable, applauds its success not only in upholding "family values" and "Christian discipleship" among the flock but also in its "evangelistic" program of "reaching the culture for Christ." Far from lamenting or even acknowledging its failure, the pseudo–church exhausts tre-

---

28. "Bannen vnd mit dem Schwert straffen seind zween vnderschidlich beuelch von Got geben. Der erst ist verhaissn vnd geben der Kirchen von Christo, Mat. 10.18, Joan. 20, den selben in einlassung der frommen in ir heilige gmainschafft vnd in außschliessung der vnndichtigen, nach seinem willen zûbrauchen. . . . Der annder Beuelch betrifft an den eüsserlichen vnd zeytlichen gwalt vnd regierung, wölher anfengklich von Gott ist geben worden dem Adam nach dem fall. . . . Demnach aber die boßhait der menschen sich noch mer erreget vnd vberflüssiger worden, ja gar der massen vber hand genommen, das das volck danntzmal einen Künig von dem Samuele begeert hat vnd Gott verworffen. Den selben Künig hat Samuel auß Götlichem beuelch auch geben, doch jnen darbey die khünigklichen gerechtigkaiten, burden vnd dienstbarkaiten, die sy dem Khünig zûthon furan schuldig werdent, von wegen irer sünden, darumb das sy Gott verachtet, verworffen vnnd einen Khünig, wie den andern Nationen, von dem Samuel vnd nit von Gott begeert haben, ernstlich anzaigen lassen." Hubmaier, *Von dem Schwert*, 442–43.

mendous effort in convincing itself that it is succeeding and succeeding admirably, "doing its job" in carrying out the Great Commission. Against its twenty–first–century practitioners Jesus' words to the first–century "pseudo–people of God" stand in condemnation:

> Woe to you, scribes and Pharisees, hypocrites, for you cleanse the outside of the cup and dish, but inside they are full of greed and self–indulgence. Blind Pharisee, first cleanse the inside of the cup, in order that its outside may also be clean. Woe to you, scribes and Pharisees, hypocrites, for you are like graves having been whitewashed, which on the outside indeed appear beautiful, but on the inside are full of the bones of dead persons and every kind of impurity. Thus also you yourselves on the outside appear righteous to human beings, but on the inside you are full of hypocrisy and lawlessness. . . . How are you able to believe when you receive glory from one another and do not seek the glory that comes from the only God? (Mt. 23:25–28; Jn. 5:44)

Such a pseudo–church enterprise is, ultimately in our judgment, what lies behind American efforts to legislate prayer in schools, to overturn Roe v. Wade, and to outlaw gay marriage. Let it be emphasized that we are not therefore claiming that abortion or gay marriage are ethically viable, as there exist clear biblical and theological grounds demonstrating their sinfulness. Rather, we are insisting that the only valid devices followers of Jesus may (and must) use in responding to these problems are Kingdom devices; we must not commit the idolatry of attempting to fix the sins of the World through the devices of the World. As Jesus' denunciation indicates, no legislation of prayer or outlawing of abortion or gay marriage can change anyone's soul for the better; actually such power–over tactics change people's souls for the worse, as they are misled into thinking they are Christian simply because they follow the religious morality of praying in schools and abstaining from abortion and homosexuality. However, their externally righteous behavior proves a mere façade for their internal spiritual death.

In short, the pseudo–church movement seems to be a clear recipe for spawning two literally Worldly offspring. First, it yields Pelagians who believe they can be good enough people to earn their own salvation and thus sense no need to surrender their lives to Jesus and his Kingdom program for salvation. Any such person is the earthly parallel to the most ethical demon among the fallen angels; just like a demon who oppresses others only once a year, the person lives far more morally than one's peers even though one still ultimately serves Satan and his power–over philosophy. The problem with this scenario is obvious: even the most ethical demon is still a demon! Likewise, any unregenerate person, regardless of how externally upright, is still unregenerate and thus, in the words of Jesus, a child of Satan rather than a child of God (Jn. 8:44). Second, it yields a society with a thin veneer of Christianity overlying a full–blown allegiance to the World. For these two reasons, Jesus branded as the worst possible sin the attempt to fuse the Kingdom of God with the state for the purpose of winning the victory of God; his words are every bit as much true today as when he uttered them to the Jewish religious aristocracy. Wright reminds us of the specific charges Jesus levied against the shepherds of Israel who went the ways of the World:

> The satan had taken up residence in Jerusalem, not merely in Rome, and was seeking to pervert the chosen nation and the holy place into becoming a parody of themselves, a pseudo–chosen people intent on defeating the world with the world's methods, a pseudo–holy place seeking to defend itself against the world rather than to be the city set on a hill, shining its light on the world.[29]

Contemporary Christians must exercise extreme caution against unwittingly turning into the progeny of the first–century Jewish religious leaders and so forsaking the cause of the Lord who bought them (2 Pet. 2:1). It is in precisely this context that Paul warned, "Have nothing to do with those who have a form of godliness but deny its power" (2 Tim. 3:5)—in other words, do not get involved with those who, employing power–over, claim they are doing God's work but deny the effectiveness of God's power–under approach.

We close this section with a challenge which the contemporary Church would do quite well to consider its pressing obligation. Employing its distinctive power–under Kingdom, the Church is called to think "outside the box" in answer to the following questions. How can we sacrifice for and serve the gay, lesbian, and transgender community in ways that illustrate to them their boundless value? How can we underscore issues of social injustice by entering into solidarity with those who suffer injustice? How can we free people from sin by serving them rather than by lording it over them? How can we most compassionately serve the homeless, poor, and racially oppressed, drug addicts, battered women, pregnant women, children in sexual bondage, and confused, needy people without Jesus?[30] Whenever we attempt to answer these questions and implement our answers, we awaken our fellow human beings to the reality of what it actually means to be hu-

---

29. Wright, *Jesus*, 608.
30. I am indebted to Boyd, *Myth*, 146, for the formulation of these questions.

man: to love one another, to nurture God's creation, and to follow Jesus, thereby worshiping the God in whose image they are fashioned.

Stark Contrast between the Two Kingdoms

Summing up the thrust of this chapter, it would be instructive to compare in broad strokes the differences between the Kingdom of the World and the Kingdom of God, unveiling the ugliness of the former but the beauty of the latter. These diametrically opposed kingdoms have different trusts: the Kingdom of the World trusts the sword and "power over," while the Kingdom of God trusts the cross and "power under." Moreover, these kingdoms work toward different goals. The Kingdom of the World aims to control behavior, while the Kingdom of God aims to transform lives from the inside out. The Kingdom of the World aims to preserve and advance self–interest, while the Kingdom of God aims to carry out God's will at the expense of self–interest. These two kingdoms possess different scopes. The Kingdom of the World is tribal, centered upon defending and advancing one's own people–group, and is thus characterized by constant conflict. By contrast, the Kingdom of God is universal, centered upon living for the sole purpose of replicating the love of Jesus to all people at all times in all places unconditionally. In this way, followers of Jesus transcend the tribal and nationalistic parameters of whatever version of the Kingdom of the World in which they live. These two kingdoms yield different responses to opposition. While the Kingdom of the World is marked by a "tit–for–tat" response, which never fosters lasting peace but only adds fuel to the vicious cycle of violence (thus ensuring that future violence will surpass the magnitude of present violence), the Kingdom of God never returns evil for evil or violence for violence but instead returns good for evil. The Kingdom of God responds to evil in a way that protects its citizens from being defined by the evil and that exposes the evil as evil, thereby opening up the possibility that our so–called "enemies" will be transformed. Finally, the Kingdom of the World and the Kingdom of God fight two different battles. Although the Kingdom of the World fights against earthly enemies, the Kingdom of God has no earthly enemies. Hence the Kingdom of God seeks not retaliation against but the well–being of those who regard themselves as its "enemies," magnanimously providing living proof that Christ has already obliterated their "enemy status" through his redemptive work on the cross (Rom. 5:8). Accordingly, it is our duty to be the reconcilers and peacemakers whose lives both bear eloquent testimony to Christ's shattering of all barriers dividing humanity from God (Eph. 2:14; 2 Cor. 5:18–20) and embody the Father's outstretched arms to all we meet, urging them to return home to their creative Source (Lk. 15:20).

Epilogue

We conclude by mapping out the broad contours of our theological construction. Although eclectically drawing on the full spectrum of the Christian tradition, this ecumenical project primarily integrates the Roman Catholic strength in philosophy with the evangelical free–church strength in ecclesiology and social justice. Particularly prominent figures and movements in our project include the brilliant sixteenth–century Catholic philosophical theologian Luis de Molina, contemporary analytic philosophy of religion, sixteenth–century evangelical Anabaptism plus its theological first–cousin Balthasar Hubmaier,[1] and the Third Quest for the historical Jesus. Chapter 1 traces the necessary prolegomena. From there, our construction accordingly divides into two halves—philosophical and ecclesiological—where the former half inclines mostly toward general revelation and the latter half inclines mostly toward special revelation, but with a porous boundary between the two modes of the divine self–disclosure. Therefore, chapters 2–5 provide the theoretical foundations for the communal and individual applications featured in chapters 6–9.

Chapters 2, 3, and 4 are predicated directly upon the entirety of Molina's conception of divine omniscience, as discovered in the full text of his *Concordia*. Thus Chapter 2 illustrated the subtle yet crucial differences between Arminius' view of *scientia media* and the far more sophisticated and versatile conception of Molina and, in turn, to show how the full elaboration of Molina's hallmark doctrine allows Christians to affirm both sovereign individual predestination and libertarian human freedom. Chapter 3

---

1. While this construction brings many *principles* of evangelical Anabaptism to bear on the theological task, a brilliant system focusing on the leading *figures* of Anabaptism along with a detailed examination and application of their writings is Thomas N. Finger, *A Contemporary Anabaptist Theology: Biblical, Historical, Constructive* (Downers Grove, Ill.: InterVarsity Press, 2004); see especially 17–323, 465–561.

furnished a careful philosophical critique of Openness theology and then proposes a Molinist alternative that neither sacrifices foreknowledge of future contingents nor writes off all biblical passages conveying divine cognitive changes as metaphorical. We argue that the key to solving this conundrum lies in the internal structure of *scientia media*, particularly in the logically (but not chronologically) cumulative fashion in which God apprehends knowledge of subjunctive conditionals. On our view, biblical passages depicting God's changes of mind report some of his initial reactions to various situations logically prior to his apprehension of the full scope of truths about the world. Upon such apprehension, God accommodated himself to humanity by leaving in the world the aforementioned reactions while modifying many other of his initial reactions as well as several other variables. In this way, God both accommodates and does not accommodate himself to humanity as much as would be for our good. Chapter 4 demonstrated that gratuitous evil is not an affront to the existence of God; on the contrary, gratuitous evil is the necessary result of the creative process. Since perfection is an incommunicable attribute of the uncreated God, it is logically impossible for any created entity, such as the universe, to be perfect; hence the universe, simply by virtue of its created status, contains gratuitous evil. God is therefore not responsible for gratuitous evil, and no divine purpose lurks behind it; rather, God hates it as much as we do and, wonderfully, can be trusted to bring good out of it. Chapter 5 employs the best in contemporary philosophical reflection to accurately explain and defend the Trinity and Christology, which together comprise the *sine qua non* of the Christian faith.

Grounded upon this philosophical "first story," the "second story" of our construction unfolds the practical implications of citizenship in God's Kingdom for Christian discipleship. Chapter 6 aims to equip believers with the invaluable skill of accurately interpreting the Scriptures, illustrating the centrality of the hermeneutical task for a proper definition of inerrancy. Once such a proper definition is established, then all objections to formerly problematic narratives instantly dissolve, enabling the reader to grasp the priceless divine truths often hidden behind the veil of hermeneutical ignorance. Chapter 7 discloses the significance and power of church discipline as biblically construed and suggest that the optimal model for such practice is an antithetical relationship between discipline and the sacraments. Chapter 8 continues in this ostensibly evangelical Anabaptist trajectory on the subject of gender roles in the church. While rejecting the either-or nature of the debate between egalitarianism and complementarianism, we maintain on exegetical grounds that women should not be restricted from holding any leadership position within the church. Finally, Chapter 9 both delineates and traces the contemporary ramifications of the historical Jesus' conception of the Kingdom of God, namely, the way of self–sacrificial love embodied in the cross. Consequently, we advocate a social ethic which, while not demanding an exceptionless pacifism, compels believers to display extreme reluctance on matters of war and to exercise discernment toward political agendas by measuring them against the Sermon on the Mount.

Obviously, this construction is not (and makes no attempt to be) a complete "systematic" theology in the "biblical theology" or "confessional theology" sense. But in the "integrative theology" sense, our construction is indeed a systematic one which serves not to take the place of, but rather to greatly supplement and illuminate, any full–blown biblical or confessional theological system within the historic Christian faith. Hence Roman Catholics, Eastern Orthodox, Protestants, and Anabaptists alike will benefit from this construction, empowering all confessions adhering to essential Christian doctrine by exposing and cultivating their unique Kingdom potencies. It is our hope that this book will lead its readers on a personal journey to the very essence of ἀγαπή–love itself. As the eleventh–century Cistercian reformer Bernard of Clairvaux explains, one arrives at this love (*homo diligit Deum propter ipsum*, loving God for his own sake) only after conquering *homo diligit se propter se* (loving oneself for one's own sake) and *homo diligit Deum propter se* (loving God for one's own sake, namely, for the good things he gives one). But once a person reaches right love of God, one is spiritually caught up in God and sees oneself as God does, which causes the person to be astonished at the fact that, in full knowledge of one's sinfulness, God infinitely loves her or him. This astonishment immediately transforms its recipient so that one possesses *homo diligit se propter Deum*, where one loves both oneself and others not with one's own φιλία (the highest grade of human love) but with God's unique ἀγαπή.[2] May all our readers quickly attain this highest stage of love and consistently transmit it by acting as Jesus' ambassadors to the whole world who "wash feet" in all forms such divinely driven service may take.

---

2. Bernard, *De diligendo Deo*, VIII.23–XI.30.

Bibliography

Primary Sources

Agricola, Franz. *Against the Terrible Errors of the Anabaptists.* In *Die Wiedertäufer im Herzogtum Jülich*, ed. Karl Rembert. Berlin, 1899.

Anselm. *Cur Deus Homo.* In *The Major Works*, trans. Brian Davies and Gillian Evans. Oxford: Oxford University Press, 1998, 260–356.

———. *Proslogion.* In *Major Works*, 82–104.

Aquinas, Thomas. *Summa contra Gentiles.* 4 vols. London: Burns, Oates & Washbourne, 1923.

———. *Summa Theologica.* 5 vols. Westminster, Md.: Christian Classics, 1981.

Arminius, Jacob. *Analysis of the Ninth Chapter of Romans.* In *Writings*, trans. James Nichols and W. R. Bagnall. Grand Rapids: Baker, 1956, 3:527–65.

———. *Certain Articles To Be Considered and Weighed.* In *Writings*, 2:706–31.

———. *Declaration of Sentiments.* In *Writings*, 1:516–668.

———. *Private Disputations.* In *Writings*, 2:318–469.

———. *Public Disputations.* In *Writings*, 2:72–317.

Augustine. *The City of God.* Trans. Henry Bettenson. New York: Penguin, 1984.

———. *De Genesi ad litteram.* 2 vols. Trans. John Hammond Taylor. New York: Newman Press, 1982.

——. *De Gratia Christi, et de Peccato Originali, contra Pelagium.* In *Nicene and Post-Nicene Fathers*, First Series, ed. Philip Schaff. Christian Literature Publishing Company, 1887; rep. ed., Peabody, Mass.: Hendrickson, 1994, 5:214–55.

——. *De Gratia et Libero Arbitrio.* In *Nicene and Post-Nicene Fathers*, First Series, 5:436–65.

——. *De Peccatorum Meritis et Remissione.* In *Nicene and Post-Nicene Fathers*, First Series, 5:12–78.

——. *On Baptism, Against the Donatists.* In *Nicene and Post-Nicene Fathers*, First Series, 4:411–514.

Babylonian Talmud. 34 vols. Trans. I. Epstein. London: Soncino Press, 1935–48.

Bernard de Clairvaux. *De diligendo Deo.* In *Sämtliche Werke lateinisch/deutsch* I. Innsbruck: Tyrolia–Verlag, 1990, 57–152.

——. *De gratia et libero arbitrio.* In *Sämtliche Werke* I,153–256.

Biblia Hebraica Stuttgartensia. 5th rev. ed. Stuttgart: Deutsche Bibelgesellschaft, 1997.

Calvin, John. *Genesis.* Trans. John King. Grand Rapids, Mich.: Baker, 1984.

——. *Institutes of the Christian Religion.* Trans. Henry Beveridge. Grand Rapids, Mich.: Eerdmans, 1989.

Catechism of the Catholic Church: Libreria Editrice Vaticana. Boston: St. Paul Books and Media, 1994.

Catherine of Siena. *The Dialogue.* Trans. Algar Thorold. Grand Rapids, Mich.: Christian Classics Ethereal Library, 2000.

Chrysostom, John. *Homilies on the Epistle to the Romans.* In *Nicene and Post-Nicene Fathers*, First Series, 13:331–564.

Clement of Alexandria. *Stromata*. In *Ante–Nicene Fathers*, ed. Philip Schaff. Christian Literature Publishing Company, 1887; rep. ed., Peabody, Mass.: Hendrickson, 1994, 2:299–567.

Clement of Rome. *First Epistle to the Corinthians*. In *Ante–Nicene Fathers*, 1:1–21.

Cornelius, C. A. *Geschichte des Münsterschen Aufruhrs*. Leipzig, 1860.

"Evangelicals and Catholics Together: The Christian Mission in the Third Millennium." *First Things* 43 (May 1994): 15–22.

Grebel, Conrad. *Letter to Thomas Müntzer*. In *Spiritual and Anabaptist Writers*, trans. George Huntston Williams and A. M. Mergal. Philadelphia: Westminster, 1957, 76–81.

The Greek New Testament. 4th rev. ed. Stuttgart: Deutsche Bibelgesellschaft, 1998.

Gregory the Great. *Registrum Epistolarum*. In *Nicene and Post–Nicene Fathers*, Second Series, ed. Philip Schaff. Christian Literature Publishing Company, 1887; rep. ed., Peabody, Mass.: Hendrickson, 1994, 12b:73–243.

Hubmaier, Balthasar. *Der uralten und gar neuen Lehrer Urteil*. Vol. II. In *Balthasar Hubmaier Schriften*, eds. Gunnar Westin and Torsten Bergsten. Gütersloh: Gütersloher Verlagshaus Gerd Mohn, 1962, 241–55.

——. *Die zwölf Artikel des christlichen Glaubens*. In *Schriften*, 215–20.

——. *Ein Gespräch auf Zwinglis Taufbüchlein*. In *Schriften*, 164–214.

——. *Eine Form des Nachtmals Christi*. In *Schriften*, 353–65.

——. *Eine Form zu taufen*. In *Schriften*, 347–52.

——. *Von dem christlichen Bann*. In *Schriften*, 366–78.

——. *Von dem Schwert*. In *Schriften*, 432–57.

———. *Von der christlichen Taufe der Gläubigen.* In *Schriften*, 116–33.

———. *Von der Freiheit des Willens.* In *Schriften*, 379–97.

Hut, Hans. *Interrogation of Hans Hut.* In *Anabaptism in Outline*, ed. Walter Klaassen. Scottdale, Pa.: Herald Press, 1981), 233–34.

Joint Declaration on the Doctrine of Justification. The Lutheran World Federation and the Catholic Church, 1999.

John of the Cross. *The Dark Night.* In *Selected Writings*, trans. Kieran Kavanaugh. Paulist: New York, 1987, 155–209.

Josephus. *Against Apion.* In *The Works of Josephus*, trans. William Whiston. Rev. ed. Peabody, Mass.: Hendrickson, 1987, 773–812.

———. *Antiquities of the Jews.* In *Works*, 27–542.

———. *War of the Jews.* In *Works*, 543–772.

Irenaeus. *Against Heresies.* In *Ante-Nicene Fathers*, 1:309–567.

Leibniz, Gottfried Wilhelm von. *Theodicy.* Ed. Austin Farrer and trans. E. M. Huggard. LaSalle, Ill.: Open Court, 1951.

Leo XIII. *Aeterni Patris.* Vatican City: Libreria Editrice Vaticana, 1879.

Luther, Martin. *The Bondage of the Will.* In *Luther and Erasmus: Free Will and Salvation*, eds. E. Gordon Rupp and A. N. Marlow. Philadelphia: Westminster, 1969, 101–334.

———. *Genesisvorlesung.* In *D. Martin Luthers Werke*, eds. J. K. F. Knaake, G. Kawerau, *et al.* Vol. 44. Weimar: Hermann Böhlaus, 1883.

———. *Preface to the New Testament.* In *Martin Luther: Selections from his Writings*, trans. John Dillenberger. New York: Anchor, 1962, 14–19.

Maimonides. *Guide for the Perplexed.* Trans. M. Friedlander. New York: Dover, 1956.

Marpeck, Pilgram. "Confession." In *The Writings of Pilgram Marpeck*, trans. William Klassen and Walter Klaassen. Scottdale, Pa.: Herald Press, 1978, 129–30.

Meiderlin, Peter. *Paraenesis votiva pro Pace Ecclesiae ad Theologos Augustanae Confessionis*. Rottenburg, 1626.

Mishnah. Trans. Herbert Danby. Oxford: Oxford University Press, 1938.

Molina, Ludovici. *Liberi Arbitrii cum Gratiae Donis, Divina Praescientia, Providentia, Praedestinatione et Reprobatione Concordia*. Ed. Johannes Rabeneck. Madrid: Sumptibus Societatis Editorialis "Sapientia," 1953.

———. *On Divine Foreknowledge*. Trans. Alfred J. Freddoso. Ithaca, N.Y.: Cornell University Press, 1988.

Muralt, Leonhard von and Walter Schmid, eds. *Quellen zur Geschichte der Täufer in der Schweiz*. Zürich: S. Hirzel Verlag, 1952.

Origen. *De Principiis*. In *Ante-Nicene Fathers*, 4:239–382.

Pelagius. *Commentary on St. Paul's Epistle to the Romans*. Trans. Theodore de Bruyn. Oxford: Oxford University Press, 1995.

Philips, Dirk. *Enchiridion*. Trans. A. B. Kolb and Dietrich Philips. Alymer, Ont.: Pathway, 1966.

———. *The Sending of Preachers or Teachers*. In *The Writings of Dirk Philips*, 1504–68, trans. Cornelius J. Dyck, William E. Keeney, and Alvin J. Beachy. Scottdale, Pa.: Herald Press, 1992, 1:1–17.

Philo of Alexandria. *The Contemplative Life, The Giants, and Selections*. Trans. David Winston. New York: Paulist, 1981.

———. *De Opificio Mundi*. Trans. plus introduction and commentary by David T. Runia. Williston, Vt.: Society of Biblical Literature Publications, 2005.

Pius IX. *Ineffabilis Deus*. Vatican City: Libreria Editrice Vaticana, 1854.

Plato. *The Republic*. Trans. Allan Bloom. 2nd ed. San Francisco: Basic Books, 1991.

Pliny the Younger. *Letters*. Vol. 2. Trans. Betty Radice. New York: Penguin, 1963.

Sattler, Michael. *Congregational Order*. In *The Legacy of Michael Sattler*, trans. John H. Yoder. Scottdale, Pa.: Herald Press, 1973, 44–45.

——. *Schleitheim Confession*. In *Legacy*, 36–43.

Simons, Menno. *The Complete Writings of Menno Simons*. Trans. J. C. Wenger. Scottdale, Pa.: Herald Press, 1956.

Schleiermacher, Freidrich. *Der Christliche Glaube*. Edinburgh: T & T Clark, 1976.

Tacitus. *Annals of Imperial Rome*. Trans. Michael Grant. New York: Penguin, 1959.

Tertullian. *Against Praxeas: In Which He Defends, In All Essential Points, the Doctrine of the Holy Trinity*. In *Ante–Nicene Fathers*, 3:597–627.

——. *De baptismo*. In *Ante–Nicene Fathers*, 3:669–79.

Theophilus of Antioch. *To Autolycus*. In *Ante–Nicene Fathers*, 2:85–121.

Tillich, Paul. *Systematic Theology*. 3 vols. Chicago: University of Chicago Press, 1967.

Transcript of the Second Zurich Disputation. In *Huldreich Zwingli Sämtliche Werke*, eds. Emil Egil and Georg Finsler. Leipzig: M. Heinius Nachfolger, 1908, 2:664–803.

Zieglschmid, A. J. F. *Die älteste Chronik der Hutterischen Brüder*. New York: Carl Schurz Memorial Foundation, 1943.

Zwingli, Huldrych. *Of the Clarity and Certainty or Power of the Word of God*. In *Zwingli and Bullinger*, trans. G. W. Bromiley. Philadelphia: Westminster, 1953, 49–95.

Secondary Sources

Abraham, William J. *The Logic of Evangelism*. Grand Rapids, Mich.: Eerdmans, 1989.

Achtemeier, Paul J., Joel B. Green, and Marianne Meye Thompson. *Introducing the New Testament: Its Literature and Theology*. Grand Rapids, Mich.: Eerdmans, 2001.

Adams, Robert Merrihew. "Middle Knowledge and the Problem of Evil." *American Philosophical Quarterly* 14 (1977): 109–17.

Ahlstrom, Sydney. *A Religious History of the American People*. 2 vols. Garden City, N.Y.: Image, 1975.

Aland, Kurt. *Did the Early Church Baptize Infants?* London: SCM Press, 1961.

Alonso–Schökel, Luis. "Wisdom and Covenant Motifs in Genesis." *Biblica* 43 (1962): 295–315.

Anderson, Bernhard W. *Understanding the Old Testament*. 4th ed. Upper Saddle River, N.J.: Prentice Hall, 1998.

Archer, Gleason L. *Encyclopedia of Bible Difficulties*. Grand Rapids, Mich.: Zondervan, 1982.

Audisio, Gabriel. *The Waldensian Dissent: Persecution and Survival, c. 1170–c. 1570*. Trans. Claire Davison. Cambridge: Cambridge University Press, 1999.

Augsburger, Myron S. *The Peacemaker*. Nashville: Abingdon, 1987.

Avram, Wes, ed. *Anxious About Empire: Theological Essays on the New Global Realities*. Grand Rapids, Mich.: Brazos, 2004.

Barrow, John and Frank Tipler. *The Anthropic Cosmological Principle*. Oxford: Clarendon Press, 1986.

Beauchamp, Paul. *Création et séparation: étude exégétique du premier chapître de la Genèse*. Paris: Aubier–Montaigne, 1969.

Beegle, Dewey M. *Scripture, Tradition and Infallibility.* Ann Arbor, Mich.: Pryor Pettengill, 1988.

Beek, Huibert van, ed. *A Handbook of Churches and Councils: Profiles of Ecumenical Relationships.* Geneva: WCC Publications, 2006.

Belleville, Linda L. *Women Leaders and the Church.* Grand Rapids, Mich.: Baker, 2000.

Bender, Harold. *Conrad Grebel.* Goshen, Ind.: Mennonite Historical Society, 1950.

Ben–Sasson, H. H., ed. *A History of the Jewish People.* Cambridge, Mass.: Harvard University Press, 1976.

Bilezikian, Gilbert. *Beyond Sex Roles: What the Bible Says about a Woman's Place in Church and Family.* 2nd ed. Grand Rapids, Mich.: Baker, 1985.

Blanke, Fritz. *Brothers in Christ.* Trans. Joseph Norden Haug. Scottdale, Pa.: Herald Press, 1961.

Blocher, Henri. *In the Beginning: The Opening Chapters of Genesis.* Trans. David G. Preston. Downers Grove, Ill.: InterVarsity Press, 1984.

Boadt, Lawrence. *Reading the Old Testament.* New York: Paulist, 1984.

Boyd, Gregory A. *God of the Possible: A Biblical Introduction to the Open View of God.* Grand Rapids, Mich.: Baker, 2000.

——. "The Open–Theism View." In *Divine Foreknowledge,* 13–47.

——. *Satan and the Problem of Evil: Constructing a Trinitarian Warfare Theodicy.* Downers Grove, Ill.: InterVarsity Press, 2001.

——. *Trinity and Process: A Critical Evaluation and Reconstruction of Hartshorne's Di–Polar Theism Towards a Trinitarian Metaphysics.* New York: Peter Lang, 1992.

Brown, Colin, ed. *The New International Dictionary of New Testament Theology.* 3 vols. Grand Rapids, Mich.: Zondervan, 1975.

Brown, Raymond E. *An Introduction to the New Testament.* New York: Doubleday, 1997.

Byrum, R. R. *Christian Theology: A Systematic Statement of Christian Doctrine for the Use of Theological Students.* Rev. ed. Anderson, Ind.: Warner Press, 1982.

Cairns, Earle E. *Christianity Through the Centuries.* 3rd rev. ed. Grand Rapids, Mich.: Zondervan, 1996.

Campbell, Ken. *Marriage and Family in the Biblical World.* Downers Grove, Ill.: InterVarsity Press, 2003.

Carson, D. A. *The Gagging of God.* Grand Rapids, Mich.: Zondervan, 1996.

———. *Matthew.* In *The Expositor's Bible Commentary*, gen. ed. Frank E. Gæbelein. Grand Rapids, Mich.: Zondervan, 1984.

Cassuto, Umberto. *A Commentary on the Book of Genesis.* 2 vols. Jerusalem: Magnes Press, 1992.

Ceuppens, By. *Genèse I–III.* Paris: Desclée de Brouwer, 1946.

Copan, Paul. *"That's Just Your Interpretation."* Grand Rapids, Mich.: Baker, 2001.

Curtis, Olin A. *The Christian Faith.* Grand Rapids, Mich.: Kregel, 1971.

Craig, William Lane. *Assessing the New Testament Evidence for the Historicity of the Resurrection of Jesus.* Lewiston, N.Y.: Edwin Mellen, 1989.

———. "The Craig–Curley Debate: The Existence of the Christian God." «http://www.leaderu.com/offices/ billcraig/docs/craig-curley00.html».

———. *The Kalām Cosmological Argument.* New York: Macmillan, 1979.

———. "'Men Moved By the Holy Spirit Spoke From God' (2 Peter 1.21): A Middle Knowledge Perspective on Biblical Inspiration." *Philosophia Christi* 1 (1999): 45–82.

———. "Middle Knowledge: A Calvinist–Arminian Rapprochement?" In *The Grace of God, The Will of Man*, ed. Clark H. Pinnock. Grand Rapids, Mich.: Zondervan, 1989, 141–64.

———. "Middle Knowledge, Truth–Makers, and the 'Grounding Objection.'" *Faith and Philosophy* 18 (2001): 337–52.

———. "The Middle–Knowledge View." In *Divine Foreknowledge: Four Views*, eds. James K. Beilby and Paul R. Eddy. Downers Grove, Ill.: InterVarsity Press, 2001, 119–43.

———. "'No Other Name': A Middle Knowledge Perspective on the Exclusivity of Faith in Christ." *Faith and Philosophy* 6 (1989): 172–88.

———. *The Only Wise God*. Grand Rapids, Mich.: Baker, 1987.

———, ed. *Philosophy of Religion*. New Brunswick, N.J.: Rutgers University Press, 2002.

———. "Politically Incorrect Salvation." In *Christian Apologetics in the Postmodern World*, ed. Timothy R. Phillips and Dennis Okholm. Downers Grove, Ill.: InterVarsity Press, 1995, 75–97.

———. *The Problem of Divine Foreknowledge and Future Contingents from Aristotle to Suarez*. Leiden: Brill, 1988.

———. *Reasonable Faith*. Rev. ed. Downers Grove, Ill.: Crossway, 1994.

Craig, William Lane and Walter Sinnott–Armstrong. *God? A Debate Between a Christian and an Atheist*. Oxford: Oxford University Press, 2004.

Crossan, John Dominic, ed. *Semeia* 2 (1974).

———. *Who Killed Jesus?* San Francisco: HarperSanFrancisco, 1995.

Danker, F. W. "Romans V.12: Sin Under Law." *New Testament Studies* 14 (April 1968): 424–39.

Davis, Kenneth R. "Anabaptism as a Charismatic Movement." *Mennonite Quarterly Review* 53 (July 1979): 219–34.

Davis, Stephen T. "The Cosmological Argument and the Epistemic Status of Belief in God." *Philosophia Christi* 2 (1999): 5–15.

Dawn, Marva J. *Keeping the Sabbath Wholly: Ceasing, Resting, Embracing, Feasting.* Grand Rapids, Mich.: Eerdmans, 1989.

Dekker, Eef. "Was Arminius a Molinist?" *Sixteenth Century Journal* XXVII:2 (1996): 337–52.

Delitzsch, Franz. *Biblical Commentary on the Psalms.* Grand Rapids, Mich.: Eerdmans, 1955.

Ellingworth, Paul. *The Epistle to the Hebrews: A Commentary on the Greek Text.* Grand Rapids, Mich.: Eerdmans, 1993.

Erickson, Millard J. *What Does God Know and When Does He Know It? The Current Controversy over Divine Foreknowledge.* Grand Rapids, Mich.: Zondervan, 2003.

Estep, William R. *The Anabaptist Story: An Introduction to Sixteenth–Century Anabaptism.* 3rd rev. ed. Grand Rapids, Mich.: Eerdmans, 1996.

Fee, Gordon D. and Douglas Stuart. *How to Read the Bible for All Its Worth.* 2nd ed. Grand Rapids, Mich.: Zondervan, 1993.

Finger, Thomas N. *A Contemporary Anabaptist Theology: Biblical, Historical, Constructive.* Downers Grove, Ill.: InterVarsity Press, 2004.

Flint, Thomas P. *Divine Providence.* Ithaca: N.Y.: Cornell University Press, 1988.

Foster, John. *The Immaterial Self.* London: Routledge, 1991.

Freddoso, Alfred J. "Accidental Necessity and Logical Determinism." *Journal of Philosophy* 80 (1983): 257–78.

——. "On Divine Middle Knowledge." In *Philosophy of Religion*, ed. William Lane Craig. New Brunswick, N.J.: Rutgers University Press, 2002, 257–64.

Friedman, R. Z. "Evil and Moral Agency." *Philosophy of Religion* 24 (1988): 3–20.

Friedmann, Robert. *The Theology of Anabaptism.* Scottdale, Pa.: Herald Press, 1973.

Funk, Robert W. "The Old Testament in Parable. A Study of Luke 10:25–37." *Encounter* 26 (1965): 251–67.

Gadamer, Hans–Georg. *Truth and Method.* Trans. Garrett Barden and John Cumming. New York: Crossroad, 1986.

Geisler, Norman L. *Baker Encyclopedia of Christian Apologetics.* Grand Rapids, Mich.: Baker, 1999.

———. *Creating God in the Image of Man? NeoTheism's Dangerous Drift.* Minneapolis: Bethany House, 1997.

———, ed. *Inerrancy.* Grand Rapids, Mich.: Zondervan, 1980.

———. *Thomas Aquinas: An Evangelical Appraisal.* Grand Rapids, Mich.: Baker, 1991.

Geisler, Norman L. and William E. Nix. *A General Introduction to the Bible.* Rev. ed. Chicago: Moody Press, 1986.

Gerhardsson, Birger. *Memory & Manuscript.* Lund, Sweden: C. W. K. Gleerup, 1961.

Gerrish, Brian Albert. *Grace and Gratitude: The Eucharistic Theology of John Calvin.* Minneapolis: Fortress, 1993.

———. *Grace and Reason.* Oxford: Clarendon Press, 1962.

Giles, Kevin. *Jesus and the Father: Modern Evangelicals Reinvent the Doctrine of the Trinity.* Grand Rapids, Mich.: Zondervan, 2006.

"God vs. God." *Christianity Today* 44.2 (7 February 2000): 34–35.

Goertz, Hans–Jürgen. *The Anabaptists.* New York: Routledge, 1996.

González, Justo L. *A History of Christian Thought: From Augustine to the Eve of the Reformation*. Rev. ed. Nashville: Abingdon, 1971.

———. *The Story of Christianity*. 2 vols. San Francisco: HarperCollins, 1985.

Gorman, Michael J. *Cruciformity: Paul's Narrative Spirituality of the Cross*. Grand Rapids, Mich.: Eerdmans, 2001.

Grenz, Stanley J. *Women in the Church: A Biblical Theology of Women in Ministry*. Downers Grove, Ill.: InterVarsity Press, 1995.

Gritz, Sharon Hodgin. *Paul, Women Teachers, and the Mother Goddess at Ephesus: A Study of 1 Timothy 2:9–15 in Light of the Religious and Cultural Milieu of the First Century*. Lanham, Md.: University Press of America, 1991.

Grudem, Wayne. *Systematic Theology*. Grand Rapids, Mich.: Zondervan, 1994.

Gundry, Robert H. *Matthew: A Commentary on His Handbook for a Mixed Church under Persecution*. 2nd ed. Grand Rapids, Mich.: Eerdmans, 1994.

———. *A Survey of the New Testament*. 3rd ed. Grand Rapids, Mich.: Zondervan, 1994.

Guthrie, Donald. *New Testament Introduction*. 4th rev. ed. Leicester: Apollos, 1990.

Hardenbrook, Weldon M. *Missing from Action: Vanishing Manhood in America*. Nashville: Nelson, 1987.

Hasker, William. *God, Time and Knowledge*. Ithaca, N.Y.: Cornell University Press, 1989.

Heidegger, Martin. *Being and Time*. New York: Harper & Row, 1962.

Hershberger, Guy F., ed. *The Recovery of the Anabaptist Vision*. Scottdale, Pa.: Herald Press, 1957.

Hick, John. *Evil and the God of Love*. Rev. ed. San Francisco: Harper & Row, 1978.

Holstein, Jay A. *The Jewish Experience*. 3rd ed. Minneapolis: Burgess, 1990.

House, Paul R. *Old Testament Theology*. Downers Grove, Ill.: InterVarsity Press, 1998.

Hugenburger, G. P. "Women in Church Leadership." In *The International Standard Bible Encyclopedia*, rev. ed., ed. Geoffrey W. Bromiley. Grand Rapids, Mich.: Eerdmans, 1988, 4:1099–1100.

Hughes, Barbara. *Disciplines of a Godly Woman*. Wheaton, Ill.: Crossway, 2001.

Hughes, R. Kent. *Disciplines of a Godly Man*. Wheaton, Ill.: Crossway, 1991.

Hunt, Susan. *By Design*. Wheaton, Ill.: Crossway, 1994.

Jackson, Samuel Macauley. *Huldreich Zwingli*. New York: G. P. Putnam's Sons, 1900.

Jewett, Paul K. *The Lord's Day*. Grand Rapids, Mich.: Eerdmans, 1971.

Johnson, Luke Timothy. *The Anchor Bible: The First and Second Letters to Timothy*. New York: Doubleday, 2001.

Kaiser, Walter C., Jr. "Legitimate Hermeneutics." In *Inerrancy*, ed. Norman L. Geisler, 115–47.

Keen, Ralph. *The Christian Tradition*. Upper Saddle River, N.J.: Prentice Hall, 2004.

Kidner, Derek. *Genesis*. In Tyndale Old Testament Commentary. Downers Grove, Ill.: InterVarsity Press, 1967.

King, Karen L. "Women in Ancient Christianity: The New Discoveries." *Southern Cross Review* 42 (September 2005): 633–51.

Kitchen, Kenneth A. *Ancient Orient and the Old Testament.* Downers Grove, Ill.: InterVarsity Press, 1966.

Klaassen, Walter. *Anabaptism: Neither Catholic nor Protestant.* Waterloo: Conrad Press, 1973.

Klein, William W., Craig L. Blomberg, and Robert L. Hubbard, Jr. *Introduction to Biblical Interpretation.* Dallas: Word, 1993.

Kline, Meredith G. "Because It Had Not Rained." *Westminster Theological Journal* 20 (May 1958): 146–57.

———. "Space and Time in the Genesis Cosmogony." *Perspectives on Science and the Christian Faith* 48 (1996): 2–15.

Krahn, Cornelius. *Dutch Anabaptism: Origin, Spread, Life and Thought (1450–1600).* The Hague: Martinus Nijhoff, 1968.

Kraus, C. Norman. *God Our Savior: Theology in a Christological Mode.* Scottdale, Pa.: Herald, 1991.

Kreeft, Peter J. *Catholic Christianity.* San Francisco: Ignatius, 2001.

Lagrange, M. J. "L'innocence et le péché." *Revue Biblique* 6 (1897): 341–79.

Leslie, John. "The Prerequisites of Life in Our Universe." In G. V. Coyne, ed., *Newton and the New Direction in Science.* Vatican City: Speculo Vaticana, 1988, 97–119.

Lewis, David. *Counterfactuals.* Cambridge, Mass.: Harvard University Press, 1973.

Lewis, Gordon and Bruce Demarest. *Integrative Theology.* 3 vols. Grand Rapids, Mich.: Zondervan, 1994.

Lewis, H. D. *The Elusive Self.* Philadelphia: Westminster, 1982.

Lindsay, Thomas M. *A History of the Reformation.* 2 vols. Rep.ed. Whitefish, Mont.: Kessinger, 2003.

Littell, Franklin Hamlin. *The Anabaptist View of the Church*. Boston: Starr King Press, 1958.

Little, Bruce A. *A Creation–Order Theodicy: God and Gratuitous Evil*. Lanham, Md.: University Press of America, 2005.

Longenecker, Richard. "Ancient Amanuenses and the Pauline Epistles." In *New Dimensions in New Testament Study*, eds. Longenecker and Merrill Tenney. Grand Rapids, Mich.: Zondervan, 1974, 281–97.

Louw, Johannes P. and Eugene A. Nida. *Greek–English Lexicon of the New Testament Based on Semantic Domains*. 2 vols. New York: United Bible Societies, 1989.

MacCulloch, Diarmaid. *The Reformation*. New York: Penguin, 2003.

MacGregor, Kirk R. *A Central European Synthesis of Radical and Magisterial Reform: The Sacramental Theology of Balthasar Hubmaier*. Lanham, Md.: University Press of America, 2006.

———. "1 Corinthians 15:3b–6a, 7 and the Bodily Resurrection of Jesus." *Journal of the Evangelical Theological Society* 49.2 (2006): 225–34.

———. "Hubmaier's Concord of Predestination with Free Will." *Direction: A Mennonite Brethren Forum* 35.2 (2006): 279–99.

Madell, Geoffrey. *Identity of the Self*. Edinburgh: Edinburgh University Press, 1981.

Marsden, George. *Religion and American Culture*. San Diego: Harcourt Brace Jovanovich, 1990.

McIntyre, Luther B., Jr. "Baptism and Forgiveness in Acts 2:38." *Bibliotheca Sacra* 153 (1996): 53–62.

McLelland, J. C. *God the Anonymous: A Study in Alexandrian Philosophical Theology*. Cambridge, Mass.: The Philadelphia Patristic Foundation, 1976.

McRay, John. *Archaeology and the New Testament*. Grand Rapids, Mich.: Baker, 1991.

McTaggart, John M. E. *The Nature of Existence.* Ed. C. D. Broad. Cambridge: Cambridge University Press, 1927; rep. ed.: 1968.

Metzger, Bruce M. *The Text of the New Testament: Its Transmission, Corruption, and Restoration.* Oxford: Oxford University Press, 1964.

Miller, Ed L. *Questions that Matter.* 3rd ed. New York: McGraw–Hill, 1992.

Moo, Douglas. "What Does It Mean Not to Teach or Have Authority Over Men? 1 Timothy 2:11–15." (Louisville: Council on Biblical Manhood and Womanhood, 1997), 1–14.

Moreland, J. P. and William Lane Craig. *Philosophical Foundations for a Christian Worldview.* Downers Grove, Ill.: InterVarsity Press, 2003.

Morris, Leon. *The Gospel According to St. John.* Rev. ed. In *New International Commentary on the New Testament.* Grand Rapids, Mich.: Eerdmans, 1995.

Muller, Richard A. *Dictionary of Latin and Greek Theological Terms.* Grand Rapids, Mich.: Baker, 1985.

——. *God, Creation, and Providence in the Thought of Jacob Arminius.* Grand Rapids, Mich.: Baker, 1991.

Murray, Stuart. "Anabaptists." In *The Dictionary of Historical Theology,* gen. ed. Trevor A. Hart. Grand Rapids, Mich.: Eerdmans, 2000, 13–16.

——. *Biblical Interpretation in the Anabaptist Tradition.* Kitchener, Ont.: Pandora Press, 2000.

Nañez, Rick M. *Full Gospel, Fractured Minds?* Grand Rapids, Mich.: Zondervan, 2005.

Neusner, Jacob. *Judaism.* New York: Penguin, 2003.

Neve, J. L. *A History of Christian Thought.* 2 vols. Philadelphia: Muhlenberg Press, 1946.

Newman, Albert Henry. *A History of Anti–Pedobaptism.* Rep. ed. Eugene, Ore.: Wipf & Stock, 2004.

Nikiprowetzky, Valentin. *Le commentaire de l'écriture chez Philon d'Alexandrien: Son caractère et sa portée, observations philologiques.* Leiden: Brill, 1977.

Oswalt, John N. *The Book of Isaiah: Chapters 40–66.* In *New International Commentary on the Old Testament* Grand Rapids: Eerdmans, 1998.

Otto, Rudolf. *The Idea of the Holy.* Trans. John W. Harvey. Oxford: Oxford University Press, 1923.

Palanque, Jean–Rémy. *Church in the Christian Roman Empire.* 4 vols. Trans. Ernest C. Messinger. New York: Macmillan, 1953.

Pelikan, Jaroslav. *The Emergence of the Catholic Tradition (100–600).* Vol. 1 of *The Christian Tradition: A History of the Development of Doctrine.* Chicago: University of Chicago Press, 1971.

———. *Reformation of Church and Dogma (1300–1700).* Vol. 4 of *The Christian Tradition: A History of the Development of Doctrine.* Chicago: University of Chicago Press, 1971.

Pentecost, J. Dwight. *The Parables of Jesus.* Grand Rapids, Mich.: Kregel, 1982.

Plantinga, Alvin. *God, Freedom, and Evil.* Grand Rapids, Mich.: Eerdmans, 1977.

———. "Methodological Naturalism?" In *Philosophical Analysis, Origins and Design* (1997): 18.1.

———. *The Nature of Necessity.* Oxford: Oxford University Press, 1974.

———. "On Ockham's Way Out." *Faith and Philosophy* 3 (1986): 235–69.

Pinnock, Clark H. "God Limits His Knowledge." In *Predestination and Free Will: Four Views of Divine Sovereignty and Human Freedom*, eds. David Basinger and Randall Basinger. Downers Grove, Ill.: InterVarsity Press, 1986, 141–62.

———. *Most Moved Mover: A Theology of God's Openness.* Grand Rapids, Mich.: Baker, 2001.

Pinnock, Clark H., Richard Rice, John Sanders, William Hasker, and David Basinger. *The Openness of God: A Biblical Challenge to the Traditional Understanding of God*. Downers Grove, Ill.: InterVarsity Press, 1994.

Pöhlmann, Horst Georg. *Abriss der Dogmatik*. 3rd rev. ed. Düsseldorf: Patmos, 1966.

Powell, Charles. "Paul's Concept of Teaching and 1 Timothy 2:12." Presented at the 49th annual meeting of the Evangelical Theological Society, November 1988.

Rabeneck, Johann. "De Vita et Scriptis Ludovici Molina." *Archivum Historicum Societatis Iesu* 19 (1950): 122–40.

Ratzsch, Del. "Design, Chance, and Theistic Evolution." In *Mere Creation*, ed. William Dembski. Downers Grove, Ill.: InterVarsity Press, 1998, 289–312.

Reasoning from the Scriptures. Brooklyn, N.Y.: Watch Tower Bible and Tract Society, 1989.

Reymond, Robert L. *Jesus, Divine Messiah: The New Testament Witness*. Phillipsburg, N.J.: Presbyterian and Reformed Publishing, 1990.

Rice, Richard. "In Response to Nancy Howell." In *Searching for an Adequate God: A Dialogue Between Process and Free Will Theists*, eds. John B. Cobb, Jr. and Clark H. Pinnock, 86–95.

Robertson, A. T. *A Grammar of the Greek New Testament in the Light of Historical Research*. Nashville: Broadman, 1934.

Rogers, Jack B., ed. *Biblical Authority*. Waco, Tex.: Word, 1977.

Rogers, Jack B. and Donald K. McKim. *Authority and Interpretation of the Bible: An Historical Approach*. San Francisco: HarperCollins, 1980.

Sanders, John. *The God Who Risks: A Theology of Providence*. Downers Grove, Ill.: InterVarsity Press, 1998.

——., ed. *What About Those Who Have Never Heard?* Downers Grove, Ill.: InterVarsity Press, 1995.

Schwartz, Jeffrey M. and Sharon Begley. *The Mind & The Brain*. New York: ReganBooks, 2002.

Seeberg, Reinhold. *Text-book of the History of Doctrine*. 4 vols. Trans. Charles E. Kay. Grand Rapids, Mich.: Baker, 1956.

Smith, Joseph. *History of the Church of Jesus Christ of Latter-day Saints*. Salt Lake City: Deseret Book Company, 1973.

Snyder, C. Arnold. *Anabaptist History and Theology*. Kitchener, Ont.: Pandora Press, 1995.

Spencer, Aída Besançon. *Beyond the Curse: Women Called to Ministry*. Nashville: Nelson, 1985.

Stayer, James M., Werner O. Packull, and Klaus Deppermann. "From Monogenesis to Polygenesis: The Historical Discussion of Anabaptist Origins." *Mennonite Quarterly Review* 49 (April 1975): 83–121.

Swinburne, Richard. *The Christian God*. Oxford: Oxford University Press, 1994.

Swindoll, Charles R. and Roy B. Zuck, gen. eds. *Understanding Christian Theology*. Nashville: Nelson, 2003.

Tenney, Merrill C. *John*. Vol. 9 of *The Expositor's Bible Commentary*, gen. ed. Frank E. Gæbelein. Grand Rapids, Mich.: Zondervan, 1984.

_____, ed. *The Zondervan Pictorial Encyclopedia of the Bible*. Grand Rapids, Mich.: Zondervan, 1978.

Thompson, Mark D. *A Sure Ground on Which to Stand: The Relation of Authority and Interpretive Method in Luther's Approach to Scripture*. Carlisle: Paternoster, 2004.

Tracy, James D. *Europe's Reformations*. Lanham, Md.: Rowman & Littlefield, 1999.

Trombley, Charles. *Who Said Women Can't Teach? God's Vision for Women in Ministry*. Gainesville, Fla.: Bridge-Logos, 1985.

Vansteenberghe, Edmond. "Molinisme." In *Dictionnaire de théologie catholique*, ed. Bernard Loth. Paris: French and European Publications, 1970, 10.2., cols. 1028–29.

Van Till, Howard J. "Basil, Augustine, and the Doctrine of Creation's Functional Integrity." *Science & Christian Belief* 8.1 (1996): 21-38.

———. "The Fully Gifted Creation." In *Three Views on Creation and Evolution*, gen. eds. J. P. Moreland and John Mark Reynolds. Grand Rapids, Mich.: Zondervan, 1999, 161–218.

Vos, Arvin. *Aquinas, Calvin, and Contemporary Protestant Thought*. Grand Rapids, Mich.: Eerdmans, 1985.

Wakabayashi, Allen Mitsuo. *Kingdom Come*. Downers Grove, Ill.: InterVarsity Press, 2003.

Waltke, Bruce. "The Literary Genre of Genesis, Chapter One." *Crux* 27 (December 1991): 2–10.

Ware, Bruce. "An Evangelical Reformulation of the Doctrine of the Immutability of God." *Journal of the Evangelical Theological Society* 29 (1986): 431–46.

Waterworth, J., trans. and ed. *The Canons and Decrees of the Sacred and Oecumenical Council of Trent*. London: C. Dolman, 1848.

Watts, John D. W. *Word Biblical Commentary Vol. 25: Isaiah 34–66*. Nashville: Word, 1987.

Wenham, David. *Paul: Follower of Jesus or Founder of Christianity?* Grand Rapids, Mich.: Eerdmans, 1995.

Wenham, Gordon J. "Genesis." In *New Bible Commentary*, ed. Gordon Wenham *et al.* Downers Grove, Ill.: InterVarsity Press, 1994.

Westermann, Claus. *Isaiah 40–66*. Trans. David M. G. Stalker. London: SCM Press, 1969.

Williams, George Huntston. *The Radical Reformation*. 3rd ed. Kirksville, Mo.: Sixteenth Century Essays and Studies, 2000.

Wink, Walter. *Jesus and Nonviolence: A Third Way.* Minneapolis: Fortress, 2003.

Witherington, Ben III. *The Christology of Jesus.* Minneapolis: Fortress, 1990.

——. *Women and the Genesis of Christianity.* Cambridge: Cambridge University Press, 1990.

Wright, N. T. *The Challenge of Jesus.* Downers Grove, Ill.: InterVarsity Press, 2001.

——. *Jesus and the Victory of God.* Vol. 2 of *Christian Origins and the Question of God.* Minneapolis: Fortress, 1997.

——. *The Original Jesus: The Life and Vision of a Revolutionary.* Grand Rapids, Mich.: Eerdmans, 1996.

——. *Paul: In Fresh Perspective.* Minneapolis: Fortress, 2006.

Yoder, John Howard. *The Politics of Jesus.* 2nd ed. Grand Rapids, Mich.: Eerdmans, 1994.

——. "The Turning Point in the Zwinglian Reformation." *Mennonite Quarterly Review* 32 (April 1958): 128–140.

Young, Brigham. *Journal of Discourses.* London: Latter–day Saints' Book Depot, 1854–56.

Index of Scripture References

OLD TESTAMENT

Subject Index

A

Z

Zurich, 48, 49, 50, 52
Zwingli, Huldrych, 25, 48, 49, 50,
    140, 195, 196

About the Author

Kirk R. MacGregor (Ph.D., University of Iowa) is a social and theological historian of Christianity specializing in Reformation studies and New Testament. In 2006 he published the monograph *A Central European Synthesis of Radical and Magisterial Reform: The Sacramental Theology of Balthasar Hubmaier*. His articles have contributed to leading academic forums, including the *Journal of the American Academy of Religion*, *Journal of the Evangelical Theological Society*, and *Westminster Theological Journal*. A Charter Member of the International Society of Christian Apologetics, Dr. MacGregor also holds membership in the Sixteenth Century Society, Mennonite Historical Society, American Academy of Religion, American Society of Church History, Society of Biblical Literature, Society for Pentecostal Studies, Evangelical Theological Society, and Evangelical Philosophical Society.

25335699R00204

Made in the USA
Middletown, DE
29 October 2015